Library of
Davidson College

Britain, Rhodesia and South Africa
1900–45

For my parents
and to the memory of Professor J. S. Marais

MARTIN CHANOCK

Britain, Rhodesia and South Africa 1900–45
The Unconsummated Union

Frank Cass and Company

First published 1977 in the United States of America by
FRANK CASS AND COMPANY LIMITED
c/o Biblio Distribution Center
81 Adams Drive, Totowa, N.J. 07512

Copyright © 1977 Martin Chanock

ISBN 0 7146 6001 9

All rights reserved. No part of this publication may be reproduced in any form or by any means, electronic, mechanical, photocopying, recording or otherwise, without the prior permission of Frank Cass and Company Limited in writing.

301.29
C458t

Printed in Great Britain   79-227

CONTENTS

ACKNOWLEDGEMENTS	*page* vii
ABBREVIATIONS	viii
SOUTH AFRICAN EXPECTATIONS AND PLANS FOR RE-PARTITION AND A BRITISH COUNTERPOISE	ix
ORIENTATION	1

PART ONE **British southern Africa divided** 1905–14

CHAPTER ONE *Themes*
1 Britain and southern Africa: the elements of the imperial situation   11
2 The white man's country   13
3 Defending the white man's country   18
4 Governing black men   25
5 Decolonising South Africa   34

CHAPTER TWO *The incomplete Dominion, 1905–14*
1 Britain and Chartered Company government in Rhodesia   43
2 Britain, the settlers and the charter   46
3 Rhodesia and the formation of the Union of South Africa   48
4 English South Africa *v.* the liberal solution   52

CHAPTER THREE *British supremacy and the charter review, 1910–14*
1 Britain and Southern Rhodesia   59
2 The Union and Northern Rhodesia   62
3 The company, the settlers and the Union   64

CHAPTER FOUR *Separation in South Africa, 1910–14*
1 The Bechuanaland Protectorate   75
2 Britain and the South African 'native problem'   81

CHAPTER FIVE *Separation in Rhodesia: the imperial initiative, 1911–14*
1 Governing Africans in Rhodesia   88
2 Towards the Reserves Commission   90
3 The Anti-slavery Society *v.* the Chartered Company   96

PART TWO **The birth of two Rhodesias** 1914–25

CHAPTER SIX *The war and the future of White Africa, 1914–18*
1 The Zambesi line   108
2 Planning re-partition   112
3 The Caprivi Strip   117

CHAPTER SEVEN *Separation: the southward turn, 1918–21*
1 The Reserves Commission reports 121
2 South African policies 124
3 The society and the Reserves Commission 125
4 African reaction and British policies 131
5 Harmonising southern policies 136

CHAPTER EIGHT *The counterpoise suspended, 1918–22*
1 Britain and the charter 141
2 Towards responsible government in Southern Rhodesia 149
3 Responsible government and African interests 153
4 The settler referendum 158

CHAPTER NINE *New patterns in central Africa, 1919–25*
1 Northern Rhodesia, the company and the Union 165
2 The end of the charter 168
3 Dividing Southern Rhodesia 172
4 The Bechuanaland Protectorate 177
5 Making Northern Rhodesia 179

PART THREE **The origins of the Central African Federation**

CHAPTER TEN *Britain and white Africa, 1925–39*
1 East and central Africa 190
2 Britain and South Africa 194
3 Defending white Africa 204

CHAPTER ELEVEN *Towards a second failure, 1930–39*
1 Closer union of the Rhodesias 214
2 Britain and South African segregation 220

CHAPTER TWELVE *The counterpoise outside, 1939–45*
1 The Bledisloe commission and closer union 229
2 Britain, South Africa and the war 234
3 Britain and closer union 243

ARGUMENT 249
APPENDIX I *Personae* 265
APPENDIX II *Documents* 273
BIBLIOGRAPHY 277

INDEX 285

ACKNOWLEDGEMENTS

This book is based on my doctoral dissertation, and I would like to express my appreciation to those who made it possible. At the University of the Witwatersrand, Ronald Ballinger and Noel Garson gave encouragement and assistance. At Cambridge my supervisor, Professor P. N. S. Mansergh, sustained me with both criticism and interest.

Among those who read the manuscript at various stages along the way Ronald Hyam, Robin Palmer and Kate Neale helped me to make it more accurate if not more sensible. Financial support as a graduate student was given to me by the Ernest Oppenheimer Memorial Trust Fund, and I was helped later by a research grant from the University of Malawi. My thanks are due too to the custodians of the Buxton, Gell and Harcourt collections for permission to use them, and to Martin Chanock for typing the manuscript.

ABBREVIATIONS

Cab	Cabinet Records	APS	Anti-slavery and Aborigines Protection Society records
CO	Colonial Office	*SR*	Gann, L., *A History of Southern Rhodeisa*
DO	Dominions Office	*NR*	Gann, L., *A History of Northern Rhodesia*
BP	Buxton papers	HC	High Commissioner
GP	Gladstone papers	RC	Resident Commissioner
MP	Milner papers	SoS	Secretary of State
SP	Smuts papers	BSAC	British South Africa Company
Ch	Chaplin papers		

South African expectations and plans for re-partition and a British counterpoise

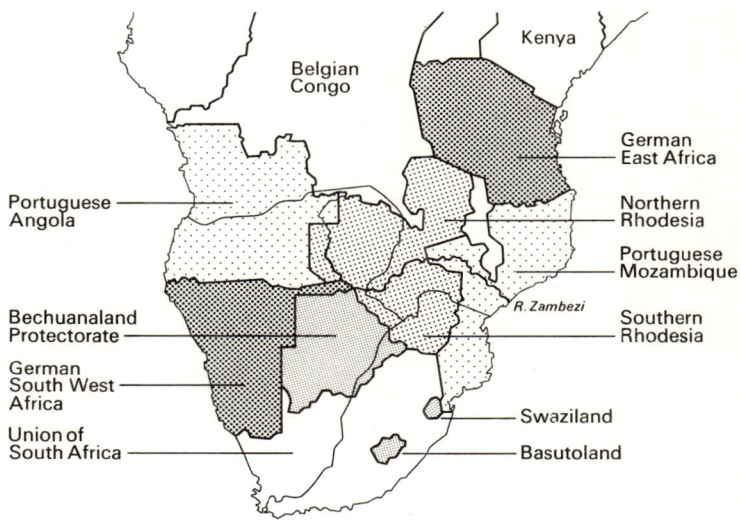

1910: South African expectations and rival imperial presences

- BSAC's territories to be incorporated
- High Commission territories to be administered under the schedule
- Railways serving BSAC's territories

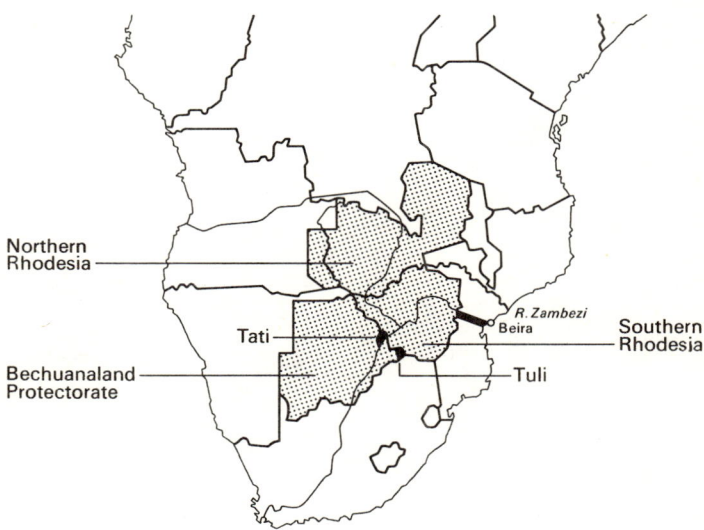

The BSAC's plans for a Greater Rhodesia

- To be incorporated into Southern Rhodesia

x *South African expectations and plans for re-partition*

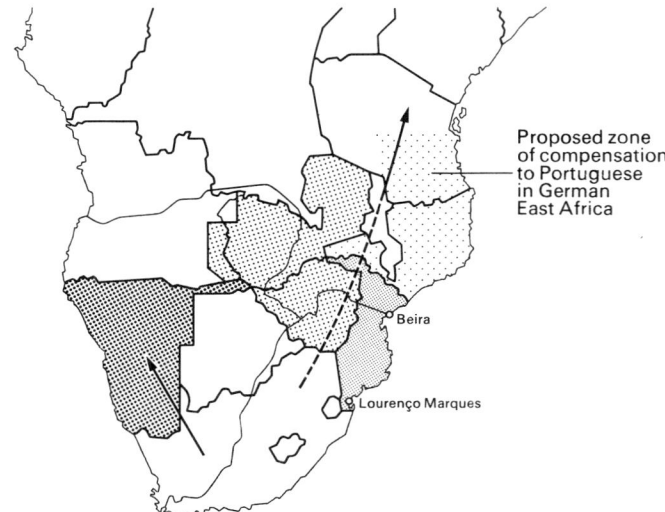

South Africa and the 1914-18 war

⬅— South African military expeditions

▨ Territory coming under Union rule

☐ Proposed additions to South Africa from Portuguese East Africa

▦ Proposed incorporation of the Rhodesias, 1922

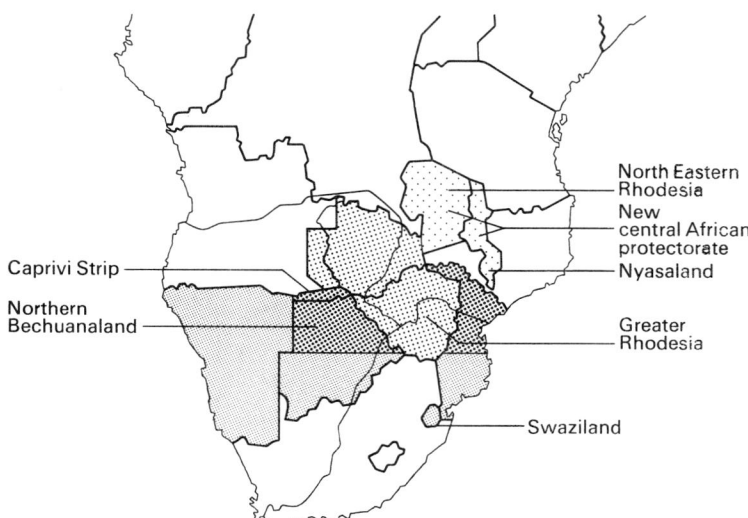

Lord Buxton's proposals for post-war re-partition

☐ To Union

▨ To Rhodesia

South African expectations and plans for re-partition

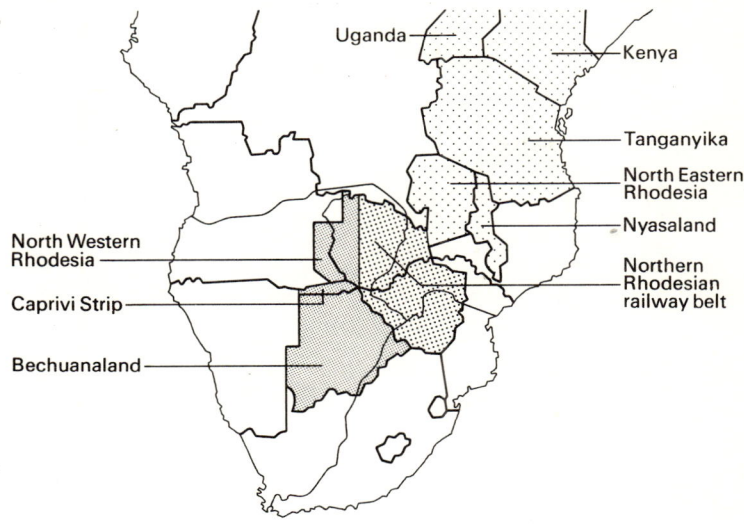

Inter-war planning
- Suggested Greater British East African Territory
- Proposed new protectorate
- Proposed 'Rhodesia'

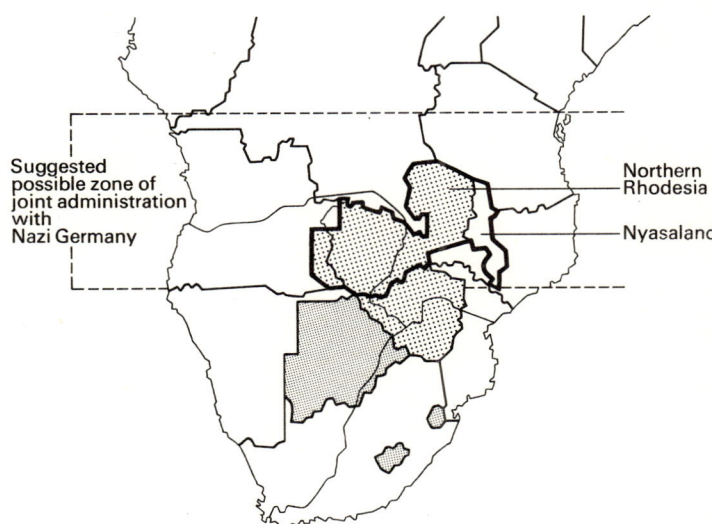

Proposals for central Africa in the 1930s
- Bledisloe and Hailey proposal for amalgamation of Northern Rhodesia and Nyasaland
- Southern Rhodesian proposal for amalgamation of the Rhodesias
- South African proposals for incorporation

ORIENTATION

I set out initially to study British policy for the Rhodesias in the period between the decision to postpone their inclusion in the new southern Union in South Africa and the end of Chartered Company rule.[1] It soon became clear that one could not write about a 'Rhodesian' policy. For the creation of the settler-run State of Southern Rhodesia, the inchoate colony to the north, and their eventual federation can only be properly understood in the context of British policy in southern Africa as a whole and of British involvement in the internal politics of the Union of South Africa. There exists a discrete Rhodesian historiography. In it, customarily, the 'southern factor' appears at the time of the birth of Rhodes's State; again briefly as an option rejected by the settlers in 1922; hovers in the wings as a threat countered by federation in the 1950s; and is on stage again after UDI in 1965. This is a misleading perspective.

I differ also from certain other premises which underpin studies of the Rhodesian and South African situations. First, it is, as was recently written, a 'truism' that Britain won the war in South Africa in 1902 only to lose the peace.[2] The bulk of the historical studies of the Anglo-South African relationship are built upon this premise and around the story of the surrender of imperial power in the face of local white assertion. This study focuses upon the survival of the imperial factor in all its ramifications, including those forces in southern Africa sympathetic towards it, rather than upon its progressive elimination. Secondly, as a corollary I seek a shift in the emphasis on British powerlessness in central Africa: the notion that Britain had 'responsibility without power.'[3] What we must try to understand are the reasons for the abstinence from the exercise of power at certain times. Thirdly I think that discussions of British policy in south and central Africa should not be within the parameters of an argument about 'trusteeship'. Ronald Hyam writes that 'South African expansion was self-interested. Imperial Britain was concerned about trusteeship.' Britain's frustration of South Africa's expansionist aims were, he says, a '. . . notable tribute to twentieth-century imperial trusteeship exercised at the expense of imperial political advantage . . . [Britain] could so easily have bought the favour of the South African government, which economic and strategic interests seriously required . . .'[4] In other areas of the study of a nation's external policy (even Britain's) it is not a customary premise that a power pursues less its own good than the benefit of others. The 'national interest' is the aim, and unremarkably so. It is time that British imperialism in Africa should be so seen. Studies of imperial policy in south and central Africa should be liberated from the form of argument which claims benevolence for Britain on the one hand and is answered by the indignant *exposé* on the other.

My aim has been to put the southern perspective back into Rhodesian history and to correct the picture of a British imperialism on the retreat which tries, with less and less effect, to protect its former wards. Because of South Africa's strong position after the ending of formal colonialism in Africa attention has recently been paid to her relationships with her neighbours, and the underlying emphasis has been on South African strength. Recent historical writing on Africa has stressed the elements of local initiative in African history and minimised the measure of outside influence on historical events. Eric Stokes has criticised that school of English–speaking South African historians who have written as if historical initiative lay with Britain and has called on them 'to enter the African historiographical revolution, and redirect . . . attention to . . . permanent and endogenous rather than the transitory and exogenous, historical forces'.[5] Yet in 1910 when the South African Union attained (qualified) independence it was defenceless in a world of predatory imperialist powers; it was believed by many (and with good reason) to be inherently unstable; and apart from having within its borders valuable mineral resources which were foreign-owned it was poor—a small-time exporter of agricultural raw materials, not self-sufficient in food. It was a new African country which was weak, divided, poor and owned overseas, with the majority of its population effectively excluded from its political processes and distrusted by their rulers. We are familiar nowadays with how to write about the external relationships of such countries and we have the words 'neo-colonialist' and 'neo-imperialist' to describe the relationships between them and their former rulers. Analogies are untrustworthy foundations on which to build arguments but they can be useful for illustration. White-ruled South Africa is not normally cast in the role of neo-colonial victim; more familiarly it is itself seen as a variant of colonial power. The perspective from which this study views the Anglo-South African relationship, however, is as an example of neo-imperialism in action.

In 1910 Britain ruled the southern African hinterland and held a strong sway over the allegiances of many in South Africa, both black and white. She also aimed to build her influence internally with the co-operation of a section of the former Afrikaner enemy. Her main political interest was 'stability' (the perennial concern of neo-colonialism) in the broadest sense. She wished to keep the mines working because they were seen as the basis of the entire structure of the new State—indeed, its *raison d'être*. To do this she would intervene militarily when asked against white labour and provide a guarantee against black disturbance. But, more important, on a long-term basis she would support in power the government which it believed would support stability best—both the existing political relationship with Britain (for disruption would have repercussions on a world-wide empire) and a prosperous internal industry with a secured and willing labour force. Britain had considerable experience already in governing black men to this end and believed her way worked better than the Afrikaner way. (This belief is sometimes called trusteeship.) She sought to persuade South African governments of this (i.e. to adopt a more reasonable 'native policy') and for this had important counters—the High Commission territories and the Rhodesias, rewards for good behaviour, which to some extent South African governments tried to earn. Yet the Rhodesias were more important in the context of maintaining a co-operative government in power in South Africa. The making of the self-governing colony of Southern Rhodesia was the by-product of a failed exercise in neo-imperialism. For as the internal base of the collaborative government waned in South Africa so the addition of Rhodesia was prepared to add to the weight of the imperial factor inside the Union. The failure of this effort to protect the compromise of 1910 meant that a settler State was allowed to come into existence and was later given a larger role in the building of an external counterpoise to an Afrikaner nationalist Union. (There is no need, after all, for the manager to enter the ring: only to arrange the terms of the next fight.)

A lot that is obvious is sometimes forgotten when writing about the weakness of the imperial factor in southern and central Africa. Officials in Whitehall often emphasised their powerlessness but the limitations which the civil servants proclaimed were not the real limits of imperial power. They were only expressing a civil servants' truth: that officials did not provoke trouble where no national interest was involved and where there existed neither political backing nor will. It is correct that Britain was hesitant about even being suspected of intervening in day-to-day administration in southern Africa, but we should not forget that the period covered here opens with an imperial intervention to snuff out the independent existence of white States of which she disapproved. After 1918 she assumed huge new direct territorial and military responsibilities over communities in the Middle East far more difficult to govern and subdue than the Rhodesian settlers (similarly after 1945). Clearly the reason for not intervening was not the lack of capacity to make her will felt but the judgement that the interests involved did not need such pursuit. Clearly also, during this period, it was seen that the greater imperial interest, the favour of the whites, would be endangered if a lesser one, that of Africans, was too openly sought. There existed a reputable British tradition about how to govern others in the nicest possible way and a fastidious dislike of the doings of local whites, but their importance pales not only in the light of the hand-overs of 1910, 1922 and 1953 but also with consideration of the plans to appease Nazi Germany by the recreation of a German African empire. Gradually African protests, both inside and outside southern Africa, against the regime in the Union began to influence imperial policies. By 1945 it was beginning to dawn that Britain would have much to lose by being an open patron of even a securely pro-British South Africa. African opinion, no longer merely the trigger of embarrassing activities by crankier members of Parliament, became a force to be weighed in its own right.

During the 1930s and 1940s British governments moved towards a schizoid analysis of the South African situation. Previously they had been most anxious about the prospect of an Afrikaner nationalist government in power. They feared economic nationalism, a policy of industrial protectionism, the milking of the mines for the benefit of agriculture, the building of a local steel industry, an anti-imperial trade policy, the possible repercussions of a new 'native policy', the embarrassment caused by the renewed harassment of Asian South Africans, and the challenge to the structure of the Commonwealth. But Afrikaner nationalism in power was able eventually to proceed towards the solution of the 'poor white problem' without radical measures to upset existing relationships because of the boom brought about by the higher gold price in the 1930s. The mines rendered forth jobs, State revenue and redistributive subsidies, but the structure of their ownership, and of the general economic relationship with the imperial power, was not broken. Botha and Smuts, then Hertzog and Pirow, then Malan, all realised that Britain was not only the major supplier of capital and the largest market but the guarantor of their independent political existence and the structure of their State. It was in the logic of South African foreign policy, therefore, that it should seek a close British alliance. (Only during the second world war was an alternative put forward by the Nationalists—to shelter under the wing of German power if it replaced British.) British governments came to realise that there was no need for them to have influence over South Africa for this end, or to protect economic interests. A close economic partnership seemed possible, and the rationalisation was evolved that the economic development of South Africa would sap both Afrikaner nationalism and racism. (A policy of optimism plus 15 per cent.) Yet it had become clear that the Union of South Africa was undeniably an Afrikaner and not a British State. The creation of a loyal British State seemed to be the way to hedge bets in southern Africa: but African views could no longer be blithely disregarded. The answer was to move towards the 'multi-policy' Central African Federation, which was to create a counterpoise outside the Union while at the same time purporting to avoid a 'sell-out' on the lines of 1910 and 1922.

In his recent succinct work Ronald Hyam makes the basic and overlooked points that the South African State has suffered severe defeats considering its expectations since independence. He has a particular perspective: that the impetus to expand was South African, that the failure to do so was a defeat for South Africa, and that this defeat was inflicted upon South Africa by Britain. But the South African State did not confront Britain in this way. The absorption of Rhodesia—indeed, northward expansion in general—was always opposed by Afrikaner nationalist politicians. Specifically, they wanted no more imperialist voters, but neither were they especially concerned at this time with the control of the labour supply or the vagaries of future markets which made the north of interest to the mining and industrial establishments. The range of nationalist speculations, greeds and needs was narrower. The failure in Rhodesia in 1922 was a failure for some South African politicians, and for Britain, not for 'South Africa'. The High Commission territories, however, were another matter entirely. Outside the Union they seemed to be a threat to a white Afrikaner South Africa, just as Rhodesia inside it would have been. They represented a diminution from Afrikaner independence—in their black separateness and relative 'liberalism' a possible threat to the South African way of life. Above all, they could have provided the land for the so-called 'solution of the native problem' which white South Africa would not find. That they remained politically outside South Africa underlies its lack of real leverage.

In emphasising the imperial factor I do not mean to suggest that British policy makers created the real world of southern Africa, or controlled the dynamic of its class forces. But this is not really a book about that world. It is about the unreal world of the policy makers, British, South African and Rhodesian. I have made an effort to present the issues in the terms in which the actors understood and defined them. This is only one level of understanding, though at least it cannot be an anachronistic one. But then, the actors themselves did not really have a firm grasp on reality. They were prisoners of their own conceptions: remote in Britain; obsessive in southern Africa. There are no 'great men' coming to grips with vital issues: rather, a series of inconclusive incompetences. In this world the major political facts in southern Africa were 'English' and 'Afrikaner' and 'the native problem'. Chiefly, then, this is an 'official mind' study of the period and, Hyams's pioneering work apart, no other covering the period exists. The major source has been the British government's official papers, those of the Colonial Office, Dominions Office, and the Cabinet. These have been supplemented by the private papers of South African Prime Minister Smuts, of Company officials Drummond Chaplin and Lyttelton Gell, of Colonial Secretaries Harcourt and Milner, of British High Commissioners Gladstone and Buxton, and those of the Aborigines Protection and Anti-slavery Society.

The first chapter outlines basic themes which both introduce the study and run through it. These are, first, the British interest in the creation and maintenance of a white-ruled southern Africa of which it was accepted that Southern Rhodesia (at least) was a part; secondly the involvement of British military power in defending this structure; thirdly the lineaments of British thinking on the 'native problem', and finally the British interest in keeping in power in South Africa those elements sympathetic to the imperial connection. Part One discusses the crucial years during which, first, the decision was taken to exclude temporarily the British South Africa Company's territories from the southern Union and, secondly, these arrangements began to harden into permanence. During these years the decision was taken to extend the charter, due to expire in 1914, to expand settler political power and to define Southern Rhodesian 'native policy' more formally in a southern African mold. Attention is paid to the technicalities of the Rhodesian constitution in order to show the arguments which led the British government to forego the chance of establishing representative government in 1914. Chapter three deals in detail with the Colonial Office's analysis of the constitutional issues and with the developing clash between the Chartered Company and the Union government in which the company, which had determined for economic reasons to remain the administering power in the Rhodesias, exploited the political situation to gain the support of the settlers for an extension of the charter. Chapter four outlines the general British and South African approaches to the 'native problem', while chapter five describes the British government's views about 'native policy' in the company's territories and the steps which it initiated to fit Southern Rhodesia into an idealised southern pattern.

Part Two deals with the period in which the two 'Rhodesian' colonies were born from the Chartered Company's domain. Chapter six discusses the broader issues raised by the war of 1914–18, during which many far-reaching suggestions for a repartition of south and central Africa were made. But the inertia of existing facts prevailed and the territorial framework of southern Africa emerged from the war unchanged, itself surprising in a situation which most parties regarded as provisional. After 1918 London, under Milner's guidance and Smuts's prodding, pursued a policy designed to lay the basis of a 'native policy' for Rhodesia and to hold the Company administration in place until the settlers would opt to join the Union. The failure of this policy is described in chapters seven and eight. Chapter nine describes the effects of the end of the company's regime. In Part Three I move on to the next round. Chapter ten describes inter-war planning for 'white Africa' in which the Rhodesias were seen in the context of the debate about the future of Britain's east and central African colonies and who to federate with whom. British relations with South Africa and defence planning are also discussed. Chapter eleven returns to the major themes of British and South African approaches to the 'native problem' and the use of British Central Africa as a counterpoise, while chapter twelve outlines the development of South African policy during the second world war and the British response. This was the beginning of the multi-purpose counterpoise plan, later to be adaptable as a brake on African nationalism. As over the whole period, because British planning was for southern Africa as a whole, the Southern Rhodesian settlers were allowed a role their own strength did not warrant.

Notes

1 This resulted in my dissertation, 'British policy in central Africa, 1908–26', unpublished Ph.D. thesis, Cambridge University, 1968.
2 D.Denoon, *A Grand Illusion*, London, 1973, p. viii.
3 E. Windrich, *The Rhodesian Problem*, London, 1975, p. xv.
4 See R. Hyam, *The Failure of South African Expansion 1908–48*, London, 1972, pp. 22 and 183.
5 See 'The British moment in South Africa', *Journal of African History*, 1966.

PART ONE

British southern Africa divided
1905–14

CHAPTER 1
Themes

The Union of South Africa came into being in 1910. It was an incomplete Dominion. Britain had only partially relinquished her direct administrative responsibilities in southern Africa, retaining responsibility for three High Commission territories as well as a tenuous control over the territories to the north of the Union which were administered by the British South Africa Company. In order to maintain her supremacy in the area Britain had fought, between 1899 and 1902, the hardest and most expensive of her imperial wars. The war had been won and its purpose achieved. The fact of British victory over the two Afrikaner republics needs underlining, because the classical story of winning the war but losing the peace has been the dominant historical approach to the post-war period.[1] The peace was only lost, however, if one loses sight of Britain's war aims. She fought not to defend or establish African political rights, nor even to hand over power to English South Africans, and the post-war rise of Afrikaner power and racist politics does not detract from the long-term securing of South Africa as a part of the British political and economic world. The imperial factor did not fade away even after 1910. It continued to exert considerable influence on the policies of the new Union, including its policies towards Indians and Africans. The constitution of the new State envisaged not only that it would succeed to British responsibilities over the High Commission territories, but that it would expand and absorb the territories in its northern hinterland. The probable addition of the Rhodesias to the Union was of importance to the British government in two respects. First, Rhodesia was a tool which might be used to strengthen the political forces inside the Union upon which continued British influence rested. Secondly there was a continuing interaction between the policies of the Union government towards Africans and the policies which the British government sought to promote in the territories which it expected to hand over. While the Union would have to show that it 'qualified' for the right of inheritance by demonstrating its good intentions, so the Rhodesias would have to be prepared so far as was possible for entry into the Union. The three governments involved, the British South Africa Company's administration, the Union government and the British government, shaped policies for the political futures of both white and black in Rhodesia in terms of the anticipated expansion of the Union.

1 Britain and southern Africa: the elements of the imperial situation

For the century preceding the South African war of 1899 British governments had struggled with the problem of political control of the hinterland of the strategically valuable Cape of Good Hope. That British paramountcy should be maintained was rarely at issue; how to exert it was the usual question. Early on, the Cape of Good Hope Punishment Act had provided a shadow of authority; the annexation of Natal the substance of sovereignty.[2] Between these two poles wavered policies towards the Afrikaners who had revolted against British authority and fled from the Cape to create States according to their own version of the 'laws of God and the natural distinctions of race and religion'.[3] Annexation was one answer; recognition of a type of independence hemmed in by treaties was another. By the middle of the nineteenth century a third solution began to emerge—the policy of federating the white States. This was the expression of the dominant strand of policy—which was that the entire region was a British sphere of influence. As Carnarvon, the Secretary of State for the Colonies, put it in 1876,

We cannot admit rivals in the East, or even in the Central parts of Africa: I do not see why looking to the experience of English life within the tropics—the Zambesi should be considered to be without the range of our colonisation. To a considerable extent . . . we must be prepared to apply a sort of Munro [sic] doctrine to much of Africa.[4]

British relations with African States proceeded along similar lines. The treaty system alternated with wars of conquest, protectorates with reserves, how, and not whether, to control was the basic problem. But the whites in southern Africa also had ambitions with regard to Africans, not only to control but to govern and to use. Thus was born the 'native problem', with its triangle of forces—imperial, settler and African. In the interests of paramountcy the imperial power would assist the settlers in subjugating the Africans, a task that white South Africa could not do for itself. 'Native policy' became a domain shared by the British government and the local whites with imperial influence diminishing as the potential revival of African power receded and as local economic interests established themselves. The themes of 'native policy' and federation became linked. Unite yourselves, white South Africa was told, and you will be able, by means of a common approach, to 'solve the native problem'. By the end of the nineteenth century the 'native problem' was acute. White conquest was recent and not yet secure; the diamond fields and then the gold mines were demanding regular supplies of labour on a scale hitherto unknown in South Africa; while two farming populations, white and African, contended for the land.

The discovery of gold in the Transvaal in the 1880s meant that one Afrikaner State was able to stand outside the British system. The South African Republic was becoming rich enough to think of escaping British paramountcy, and confident enough to apply its own singular solutions to the 'native problem'. The growing power of the republic, which had its own ambitions of expansion eastward and northward, posed a threat not only to a larger British Monroe doctrine but also to the paramountcy already achieved. To the west and north of the republic Britain had already proclaimed a sphere of influence, but how was it to be made effective? From Cecil Rhodes came a strategy to which the British government gave its blessing. A royal charter was granted to his British South Africa Company in 1889. Rhodes's money would provide the means of conquering, settling and rendering effective the British presence to the north of the Transvaal. Not only would the republic be hemmed in, but the anticipated discovery of a goldfield richer than that of the Rand was expected to provide the basis for the building up of a strong, rich and loyal counterweight to the Afrikaner threat.[5] It soon became clear, however, that the hopes of a Rhodesia wealthy enough to be a rival to the South African Republic would not be fulfilled. Fears of the political weight of the Transvaal and its pretensions towards independence became obsessive among British policy makers for southern Africa. If British supremacy was not asserted a United States of Southern Africa under Afrikaner domination seemed the likely outcome. As an imperialist world power the implications for Britain were even greater. As Joseph Chamberlain put it in 1899, 'What is now at stake is the position of Great Britain in South Africa—and with it the estimate formed of our power and influence in our colonies and throughout the world . . .'[6]

In the South African political equation Afrikaner republicans and outright imperialists were not the only factors. Africans in the High Commission territories looked to the British government for protection, while those in the Cape identified the imperial factor with the defence of the Cape policy of equal rights for all civilised men. But no British government envisaged basing support for its influence on African groups. It was among the divided white population that allies for imperial influence were sought. The English and Afrikaner populations in the Transvaal itself were divided; both had sections which were prepared to compromise, while the co-operation of the Cape Dutch with Rhodes had shown that it was possible to reconcile a sense of Afrikanerdom with loyalty to the empire. Though the war polarised forces and extinguished many fine distinctions, some reappeared in postwar southern Africa. In 1899 the imperial government had taken its stand with the English extremists and had drawn in the English moderates: in 1910 it was to bank upon the Afrikaner and English moderates in the hope of neutralising Afrikaner extremists. The section which was excluded from the 1910 strategy—the English imperialists who had been so gloriously dominant in 1902—still controlled the British South Africa Company and had their territorial base in Rhodesia.

Though Rhodesia in the 1890s failed in its essential role as counterweight, it had been firmly established as a settler colony by military conquest. During the Jameson era before 1896[7] the basis of modern Rhodesia was laid. This involved a war against the Ndebele in 1893 which was followed by the white expropriation of the central highlands and the proposed relegation of the Ndebele to 'cemeteries, not homes'.[8] In 1896 the proceedings of the company and its settlers provoked a rebellion amongst the Shona and Ndebele peoples which could be crushed only with imperial assistance. By this time the British authorities had begun to feel that a presence to restrain the company was necessary, and an imperial shadow interposed itself between company and settlers, and Africans. But the White Man's Country in Southern Rhodesia had been firmly established and the fundamentals of the first division of land were never upset.

2 The white man's country

It was basic to the political rhetoric of southern Africa that it was a 'white man's country'. To Afrikaner South Africa this needed little rationalising. The South African republic's constitution had openly established a State which prohibited even the tendency towards equality between white and black. After 1902 the theme became important to English South Africa, as the promotion of British immigration was one of the prime objects of Milner's post-war policy. He envisaged a wave of British settlers flowing into the Transvaal which, during the period of direct British rule, would grow into a majority of the voting population, after which responsible government could be granted upon an unshakable base of imperial loyalty. This was not the only factor which might have favoured a flow of British immigration into southern Africa, as from the imperial point of view there was considerable interest in emigration from the British Isles. Rhodes had reflected a pervasive current of thinking when he had justified the acquisition of Rhodesia as a space for 'homes' and thus a siphoning off of the pressures which might lead to industrial and political unrest in Britain.[9] Henry Lambert of the Colonial Office, who directed its work on information for emigrants, expressed a similar view in 1906 when he saw emigration as '. . . the best possible remedy, perhaps the only safe remedy, for the temporary distress which arises from time to time in large industrial centres'. In addition to being a danger an unemployed man was a liability: settled within the empire, he could be an asset. In 1907 the imperial conference resolved that British migrants should be encouraged to proceed to British rather than foreign countries.[10]

Immigration into Rhodesia was dominated by these two themes—that the justification for conquest and colonisation was that the territory was a white man's country which would be '. . . the home in time to come of numberless sons and daughters of our race'; and the need to build loyal constituencies on the southern African political map.[11] But the outgoing wave of British migrants passed southern Africa by. Post-war depression reduced South Africa's English-speaking population; limited land settlement schemes crumbled, and official optimism turned sour. By 1905 Milner had come to the view that large-scale imperial-assisted colonisation of South Africa was 'impracticable . . . perfectly wild' and he thought that Rhodesia would never carry 'a very thick population'.[12]

Thus the notion of the White Man's Country had to be refined. To Milner the idea had only one logical meaning—'that the white man must rule'—for dependence on African labour allowed no other interpretation.[13] In his discussion of the White Man's Country claim in east Africa Winston Churchill took the analysis of the phrase a step further. 'Truly a respectable and impressive policy,' he wrote, but impossible to achieve on the basis of a white working class. Yet was there, he asked, also no room for a white middle class in Africa, or would

a vast army of African labourers, directed by cosmopolitan capital—
'the nightmare which haunts the white population of South Africa'—be
the only possibility for the unsettled portions of British Africa? The
answer which the Selborne memorandum gave for Southern Rhodesia
seemed clear; that it was '... a white man's country... and is adapted to
the settlement and upbringing of white families ... its greatest need is
additional white population'.[14] The Rhodesian settlers saw the problem
in similar terms; their existence seemed to depend on increased
immigration and they clamoured for the company to adopt an active
immigration policy.

Capitalist circles had always been anxious about the political
consequences of white working class immigration into southern Africa.
As C. D. Rudd put it in 1903, such immigrants would, when
enfranchised '... simply hold the government in the hollow of their
hands'.[15] Though it had dallied with the idea of small-scale white
yeoman settlement at times between 1891 and 1907, the company later
came round to the view that incoming settlers should possess capital of
at least £750. As Lambert remarked, Rhodesia wanted only the best type
of settler, who could go anywhere, and South African farming, with its
'locusts, drought and cattle disease', was not likely to attract such
settlers to Rhodesia in preference to Canada, Australia or New
Zealand.[16] Consequently, though in proportion to the existing white
population the intake of white immigrants into Rhodesia was high, in
proportion to empire migration as a whole it was a very tiny trickle.
British government agencies which were concerned to see that emigrants
did not go in ignorance of the conditions were not optimistic. In the light
of the evidence of Milner and of Milton, the Administrator of Southern
Rhodesia, who summed up prevailing policy as the hope 'that the
gentleman farmer would settle on the land', the Committee on
Agricultural Settlement in British Colonies reported that although good
land existed in Rhodesia, prospects for settlement were poor.[17] Between
1907 and 1910 the company's selective policy had some success and the
white farming population increased at the rate of over 20 per cent per
year. An effort had been made to attract the sort of settler who went to
east Africa, and as a former company official wrote

... the class of settler already established is distinctly of the right stamp. A very
large proportion are from the old country, and the rest are chiefly of British
descent from the Cape and Orange River Colony ... Rhodesia looks [for] ...
especially those who have retired from the service of the Crown ...

—namely retired officers with capital to invest.[18] Wilson Fox, the company's manager, while he thought that the sons of English tenant farmers would be the most likely source of immigrants, preferred to concentrate on the sons of gentlemen of means.[19] Instead the company was getting in some numbers a class that it greatly disliked. Many of the settlers entering Rhodesia in the new wave of immigration after 1907 were South Africans, among them a growing minority of Afrikaners. These were, it was believed, the vanguard of a dreaded horde—the poor whites. Lord Gladstone, the Governor General and High Commissioner, summed up in 1913 the Rhodesian settlers' constant fear of the 'poor Dutch' and of Rhodesia being 'made a midden heap for the human wreckage of the Union'. This aversion to Afrikaner settlement did not go unnoticed in South Africa, and led to complaints in the Afrikaner press that 'the settlement of Afrikaners in Rhodesia is being emphatically worked against'.[20]

It was in Northern Rhodesia, the border region of the white man's country, that the influx of Afrikaner settlers was least welcomed. Early in 1909 Selborne, the British High Commissioner in South Africa, strongly denounced a proposed Afrikaner 'trek' to the north, informing the Secretary of State that its members could have 'no object whatsoever except to exterminate the game and exploit the natives'.[21] Both Milner and Selborne had been against throwing Northern Rhodesia open to white settlement, and the company's policy had been to try to attract only 'the larger capitalist' in order to promote ranching and the growing of tropical products.[22] When Sir Henry Birchenough, one of the company's directors, visited the north he noted with some surprise the number of white settlers and advised the exclusion of 'speculators, amateurs, wastrels and low Dutch'. The Association of Northern Rhodesian Landowners and other settler groups added to the complaints against the incoming Afrikaners.[23] In 1913 the Chartered Company itself complained to the Northern Rhodesia Copper Company, on whose lands Afrikaners were settling, that

> Their appearance, condition and manner of living are having the worst effect on the local natives, who until recently were accustomed to treat and regard Europeans with respect. They now see that the largest proportion of whites in the district consist of people whose habits of life and morals are as degraded as their own.[24]

The company proposed legislative action, and even though the imperial authorities were alarmed at the obvious offence that this would give to the Union, in the Colonial Office Lambert sympathised with the company's fear. 'The difficulties created by the *bijwoner* class are very great throughout South Africa,' he wrote, referring to the fear that rural depression would eliminate the distinction between landless whites and Africans, 'but of course in a native territory like Northern Rhodesia they are especially serious.'[25]

By 1913 both British government agencies and the company had become pessimistic about large-scale white migration to Rhodesia. White female domestics and farmers appeared to be the only required categories, and the latter were warned of labour difficulties.[26] In any case the company was beginning to have second thoughts about the wisdom of promoting immigration. Wilson Fox argued that the company had been selling its land too rapidly, at too low a price, and in pursuit of a false objective. The period during which the company had depended on an expanding white population to make the territory viable was over, and with regard to land the company was free to act as an estate owner. The company, said Fox, should promote land settlement, not immigration, and settlement was only a means 'to make as much money for the shareholders as possible out of the Company's land'. He outlined a scheme to raise land prices and curtail immigration. He recommended also that the company should increase development on its own account and restrict sales of land to third parties. There was also a political motive. Development of the land was a long-term process during which the company would need to stay as administrator and, as Fox put it, 'The comparatively backward position of the territory makes political changes of any magnitude an impossibility at the present time, and it may well be that it may suit the Company to promote a similar condition of affairs in 1924.'[27]

The main themes in Rhodesian immigration policy survived the war years and reappeared after 1918. An increased flow of settlers to Rhodesia was expected and though there was considerable imperial interest in the promotion of empire settlement, again Rhodesia did not absorb enough even to make it as much of a 'white man's country' as the Union. Not only was there the aim of rewarding ex-servicemen, which was an object given priority in the various settlement schemes, but the view that migration could solve internal problems and strengthen the power of the empire remained influential. As Milner put it, immigration would relieve unemployment and would guard against the risk of it in the future by increasing primary production overseas; it was '... in effect the problem of distributing the white population of the Empire in the manner most conducive to the development, stability and strength of the whole'.[28] The Union government did not co-operate in the various empire settlement schemes, but Rhodesia was anxious for migrants—

though once again of a certain type. Lyttelton Gell told a commission that Rhodesia wanted 'hard workers of the officer class'; that there were opportunities for land settlement for '. . . the sons of substantial British farmers who seek a larger career than is open to them at home and for adaptable and intelligent men of the middle classes who have won commissions in the new armies, men who are accustomed not only to work hard themselves, but to direct the work of others'.[29] After the author Rider Haggard had visited Rhodesia on behalf of the Royal Colonial Institute the company announced that it would make half a million acres available to ex-servicemen who were British subjects of European descent who were not domiciled in southern Africa and who had at least a thousand pounds to invest. The company was still not casting its net very wide, and the Colonial Office was unsympathetic even to this limited offer; prospects for settlers with capital, it was thought, were far greater in Australia.[30]

After the end of company rule the British government continued to identify itself with the theory of an active white immigration policy for Rhodesia. Ormsby-Gore, the Under-Secretary of State for the Colonies, felt that only the immigration of unskilled whites was precluded. He told the imperial conference in 1923 that the new Rhodesian government should have as its first object the settlement of the 50 million acres of Crown lands it had at its disposal. In the Colonial Office support was expressed for the established policy of looking for Rhodesian settlers '. . . of the selected type (. . . superior settlers, public school boys and ex-officers . . .)'.[31] But these men never came. In 1908 Selborne had written that what South Africa needed above all else was 'occupiers of the soil . . . to provide occupants for the unoccupied land', unconsciously accepting the fundamental southern African premise that while on the one hand there was a shortage of land for Africans, the countryside remained underpopulated. Rhodesian settler politics continued to be based upon this premise with regard to land and settlement matters. Rhodes's vision of the white man's country, however, remained a myth, though a powerful one. Milner's—that the white man must rule—and Lyttelton Gell's—that the white man was a director of labour—were the realities achieved by the policies of the company and the British government.

3 Defending the white man's country

The guiding principle governing the provision of military assistance by the imperial government to 'white' colonies had been laid down in 1862 by the House of Commons. It was '... the duty of the Colonial Government, where resources were adequate, to provide for their own internal safety'.[32] At the end of the war in 1902 it was recognised that this principle did not apply in southern Africa. Imperial garrisons remained in the country, the aim of their presence being twofold. They were there to guard against the possibility of both Afrikaner and African rebellion. When responsible government was granted to the two defeated republics the likelihood of an anti-British rising was thought to have been pre-empted, and in making its plans to rearrange the disposition of imperial forces throughout the world the Committee of Imperial Defence proposed considerable withdrawals from South Africa. The new Transvaal Prime Minister, General Botha, protested vigorously, asking for extra troops and offering to contribute towards the cost. He warned the British High Commissioner of the conspiracies of 'Hollanders, Krugerites and a large section of the predikants'. 'Does he,' asked Lambert in the Colonial Office in a pointed minute, 'rely on the troops to keep the backvelders quiet?'[33] Clearly, in the years immediately following the war British troops had to be retained to forestall a revival of Afrikaner military ambitions, but to the surprise of the British authorities the leader of Afrikanerdom in the Transvaal requested that they be kept for the same purpose.

British forces were called on by the government of Natal during the Zulu rebellion of 1906, and in 1908 the British government felt that 'a general rising among the native population of South Africa is a contingency which must be taken into account; and so long as Imperial troops are stationed in South Africa, their services will of course be available, if required, to assist in dealing with such a rising.'[34] This posture was set in a larger context than that of southern Africa alone. As Brigadier General G. G. Aston put it in 1908, only 54 million of the 400 million people in the British empire were white, and, of those, 42 million were in the United Kingdom. If 54 million were to govern 346 million they would need to support each other in times of difficulty. 'Before the Empire can take on an external foe we must be sure that internal troubles can be immediately stamped out ... from the military point of view the South African problem is so like the bigger problem of Empire ...'[35]

After the formation of the Union, Smuts, as Minister of Defence, embarked on the sensitive task of organising a South African defence force based on a civilian population whose loyalty to the empire was still suspect. The British garrison remained, while he was so engaged, to guard against the 'potentially hostile coloured population'. The possibility of a 'concerted general rising' was thought to be remote, but the troops were held ready to deal with sporadic risings, and special stress was put on the need to ensure that the Union government could have no conceivable occasion to reproach the British government for failing to maintain law and order in the High Commission territories. The Union government too conceived its defence force very much as an internal security force sharing the functions of the police. It was a means of putting arms back into the hands of white South Africans to guard against 'trouble', and, as Smuts put it, it was not necessary to specify what 'trouble' the force would guard against, '... as every South African is acquainted with the problems which may have to be faced by the White South Africans from whatever European race they may originally have descended'.[36]

The question of imperial military control over Rhodesia had first been raised in acute form by the Jameson raid and the subsequent African rebellion in Rhodesia. By the provisions of the 1898 order in council the company's forces, the paramilitary British South Africa Police, were placed for the first time under direct imperial command. This force, together with settler volunteers, took part in the war between 1899 and 1902. After the war, because Milner wanted to keep centralised defence control in South Africa, the force had been kept under the High Commissioner's command. When it became clear that Rhodesia would not be included in the coming Union defence unity in southern Africa was broken and consideration of a reorganisation of Rhodesian defence arrangements began. In 1911 Sir Ian Hamilton, the Inspector General of Overseas Forces, submitted a full report. The imperial commander-in-chief in South Africa, Brigadier General Hart, had already reported his concern at the relative lack of military protection for the rapidly growing Rhodesian colony, and with this Hamilton agreed. The country's war strength, he found,

... has not kept pace with the inflowing tide of defenceless humanity and unprotected wealth ... The native peril is and must remain for many years an ever present source of danger ... many families and individuals in outlying stations paid with their lives the penalty of relying too implicitly upon the assumed timidity or forebearance of barbarians. Not only the veterans of 1896, but also the tablets on the walls of the churches and monuments in the public streets ... furnish a constant warning to the present generation.[37]

Rhodesia's defence problem, he wrote, was 'Home Defence', and her service to the empire could best be carried out by ensuring that in no circumstances would she need imperial help against 'domestic foes'. He made two recommendations: that white Rhodesians should be liable to compulsory military service in both North and South and that the system of command, by which the Resident Commissioner took command of Rhodesian forces in cases of emergency—which he ascribed to 'chimeras; nightmares bred from the memories of the Raid'—be changed, and that an imperial professional officer be placed in command. The settlers must ask themselves, Hamilton warned, '. . . on what, in the last resource, their very existence depends . . . for years to come it is by the sword and rifle alone that the white man must retain his hold on the country . . .'

Lord Gladstone, the High Commissioner, was most critical of the report. He pointed soberly to the existing peace and the absence of any organised Ndebele leadership. Hamilton had also, he felt, failed to consider the question as part of the problem of retaining imperial forces in South Africa. Gladstone rejected compulsory service on the grounds that it would lessen the inflow of settlers, and in the north, in any case, he felt that the security of the government had to rest upon African loyalty and not settler guns. Instead he suggested, as he had done before, that a thousand British troops be based on Bulawayo, which could be used as the centre of a scheme for High Commission defence, though to this there was the obvious criticism, founded on former colonial experience, that the presence of imperial troops '. . . might possibly lead to a forward or even an aggressive native policy'.[38]

There is an apparently natural contrast between Gladstone's civilian rationalism and Hamilton's military 'realism', yet Gladstone himself, in common with other white South African and imperial politicians, accepted the essence of Hamilton's analysis. To Lord Emmott, the Parliamentary Under-Secretary for the Colonies, 'the common interests of the white races' were a prime factor for which the empire existed. Smuts was reported to hold the view ('so commonly expressed here') that 'a native rising and war on a scale hitherto unprecedented' would one day come, but that 'the white race would ultimately assert its supremacy once and for all, though perhaps not without assistance from other parts of the Empire'.[39] The Zulu, whom white South Africa regarded with fascinated dread, had rebelled as recently as 1906. The conquest of Rhodesia had been completed only ten years before. White insecurity was real and was made up of a complex combination of fears—of African religious separatism, of Ethiopianism, of a Pan-African movement, and of the revival of traditional resistance. This fear was perfectly mirrored in the novel *Prester John*, which was published by John Buchan, who had served with Milner in South Africa, in 1910. The book portrays an African conspiracy to revolt, led by the Reverend John Laputa. In England '... he was merely the educated Kaffir, a great pet of missionary societies ... You will find evidence given by him in Blue Books on native affairs ...' In Africa 'At full moon when the black cock was blooded, the Reverend John forgot his Christianity ... He told them that he was there to lead the African race to conquest and Empire ... I found a mighty organisation at work from the Zambesi to the Cape ...'[40] It is against this background that Hamilton's report, as well as Gladstone's willingness to call out imperial troops to assist the Union government in 1913 and 1914, must be seen. When the Botha government called for military assistance against a white internal enemy, the largely English-speaking Reef strikers of 1913, Gladstone explained his readiness to assist:

The Government has to give the whole population not only security as regards the natives, but an adequate sense of security. Every day of disorder in South Africa disturbs the native mind, and adds to danger ... the effect of martial law was to relieve the whole country from acute peril, and a state of tension which in itself was a peril.[41]

The possibility envisaged by Gladstone, that British troops would withdraw from the Union to Rhodesia, never materialised. On the outbreak of war in 1914 the troops were withdrawn from the Union and their departure was followed by what Botha had feared in 1907—an armed revolt by Afrikaner irreconcilables. Britain's involvement in war with Germany seemed to be the moment to strike to regain republican freedom. Most of the Union's new army remained loyal, and the revolt was defeated.[42] The Botha government snatched at the only available form of imperial assistance in the shape of the new First Rhodesian Regiment, which had originally been intended for European service but which was placed under South African command to serve first in the Union and then in South West Africa. Much to the disgust of Afrikaner nationalist opinion, the Botha government had undertaken a positive 'imperialist' task at the beginning of the war—the conquest of German South West Africa.[43] Their 'loyalty' in so doing and their action in crushing the Afrikaner revolt had a polarising effect on South African politics. It confirmed Nationalist suspicions that Smuts and Botha were imperialists first and Afrikaners second and it rallied English-speaking South Africans and the British government to a fervent support of the Union government. Finally it provided the ultimate justification for the Liberal government's policy of 'reconciliation'. As Lloyd George had predicted when defending the policy to Lord Riddle in 1913, '... if we had a war tomorrow Botha and 50,000 Boers would march with us side by side. He would, if necessary, drive the Germans out of South Africa.'⁴⁴

When the war began the South African Native National Congress broke off its political activities and pledged itself to assist the British war effort, but the Union government was determined that the war in southern Africa should remain, as the South African War had been, a white man's war. Botha feared the intervention of the African population in South West Africa in his campaign. He found them 'very bitter against the Germans' and reported to Smuts that he was '... using all my influence to prevent natives taking part against enemy in this war'.⁴⁵ Congress, on behalf of Union Africans, offered to raise a force of 5,000 men for the South West African campaign, but was told by the Union government that '... this war was waged between white people only'.⁴⁶ What use ought to be made of southern African Africans to assist in the war effort was a far more delicate question than in other parts of the empire, where 'native' troops were rapidly gathered to arms. A British Cabinet memorandum reported that although there were large numbers of 'warlike natives' south of the Zambesi

> No proposal for training natives on a large scale is likely to be acceptable to [the Union] Government or to the British or Dutch inhabitants of the Union, as the return, after peace, of a large body of trained and disciplined black men would create obvious difficulties and might seriously menace the supremacy of the white.⁴⁷

The early years of the war did bring two anti-white revolts in southern Africa—in Nyasaland and in Mozambique—and there was some fear, for example in Rhodesia, from where it was reported that Africans were disaffected over the land question and their loyalty might not stand any strain, that a German invasion could touch off a larger rising.⁴⁸ In fact African enthusiasm created a problem of a different kind, and in Salisbury a deputation of chiefs asked for conscription of all young men of pass-bearing age;⁴⁹ in the south the Union government, on the advice of the High Commissioner that an outlet be found for African enthusiasm, recruited an African labour corps for service in France. In Northern Rhodesia, despite the heavy demands made on the population for service as carriers during the East African campaign, there was no resistance. Thus fear of African revolt against war service was quickly dissipated, while fear of the consequences of African participation remained. Smuts's own experience in the East African campaign, as well as the widespread belief in the German plan for a vast *mittel Afrika* State whose inhabitants would be trained into a great black army at the service of Germany's goal of world domination, stiffened the Union's opposition to the arming of Africans. 'We were not aware of the great military value of the natives until this war,' Smuts told a London audience in 1917. 'I hope that one of the results of this war will be some arrangement . . . by which the military training of natives [in central Africa] will be prevented, as we have prevented it in South Africa.'[50]

After the war the Union government made it plain that it expected to take over all the southern African defence functions of the British government, excluding the naval defence of the base at Simonstown, but including its land defence, the defence of the High Commission territories and of Rhodesia.[51] The British government conceded that a garrison need not return to Simonstown but some thought was given as to whether or not it should be placed in Rhodesia instead. The wartime Afrikaner rebellion in the Union had greatly alarmed the Rhodesian authorities, and its implications remained one of their dominant concerns. The majority of the Afrikaners in Rhodesia, it was felt, could not be relied upon against the Germans, and they were in close touch with Hertzogite republicanism in the Union.[52] Company officials after the war welcomed the idea of a British garrison which could serve as 'protection of the high road to India'—a guard against renewed disloyalty in the Union's forces and a means of keeping open the port of Beira for imperial reinforcements.[53] These grandiose plans never materialised, as such a policy would have given gratuitous insult to Botha and Smuts, it being clear that British forces were not needed in Rhodesia for any other purpose. 'Native trouble', wrote the Administrator, Sir Drummond Chaplin, could be taken care of by the police and settlers. After the granting of responsible government to Southern Rhodesia the rationale for the colony's defence remained the same. As the new Governor reported, there was no need to make provision against outside attack and what was needed were forces which could speedily crush 'sporadic risings'. There was, he reported, '. . . no difference of opinion that in newly settled countries with a sparse white population . . . living alongside a large native population police and defence duties so merge into one another that they cannot be separately defined'.[54]

Since 1902 the functions of British garrisons in South Africa had been to deal with either African or Afrikaner revolt. The creation of the Union Defence Force, which took over both these roles, made the imperial garrison redundant.[55] The Union took over as defender of the white man's position in the south.[56] Rhodesia never had an imperial garrison. The adventurism which the company's troops had shown against both Africans and Afrikaners in the 1890s was felt to have been guarded against adequately once that force had been placed under the control of imperial officers. The need for a British military presence to control the settlers themselves never entered the calculations of the military planners.

4 Governing black men

The period 1902–10 has been depicted as one during which the British government, as guardian of the liberal 'Cape policy' towards Africans, squandered its liberal estate in an attempt to reconcile a racist Afrikaner element to the principle of self-government within the British empire. The Cape policy of equal rights for all civilised men has been seen as fighting a losing battle with the colour bar of the north: white reconciliation as being bought by the abandonment of Africans. Yet it is misleading to underestimate the interest in and the influence over the development of 'native policy', and of policies towards other non-whites, which the British government had and exercised.[57] Precisely what the Cape policy was and how it differed from that of the north needs to be outlined, as does the way in which the British government interpreted its role in the advancement of African interests, which were not an ascertainable lump but a matter of policy; and finally the place of African interests in the hierarchy of calculations needs to be weighed. Stress has been put on the promise made in the 'treaty' of Vereeninging in 1902 that the question of a franchise for 'natives' would not be dealt with until the grant of self-government to the two defeated republics. The British acceptance of a political colour bar in the Transvaal and the Orange Free State when they became self-governing, and later in the Act of Union, is seen as following from this mistaken undertaking.[58] But while the non-racial franchise was an essential part of the 'Cape policy' it was not the only part, and certainly not the only part which was considered to be important by the British government. The Cape franchise was a limited device: by the end of the nineteenth century it was seen, cynically or otherwise, as a way of giving an outlet to a vocal minority. Whatever moral significance it might have been invested with, politically it was only a partial answer. There remained still the problem of providing for the government of the vast majority of Africans who were denied participation in the white-dominated central political system. In the eyes of British officials, both inside South Africa and out, the Cape had an ideal solution here too—Rhodes's Glen Gray Act.[59] The principles of the Act have been succinctly described as 'Work, segregation in the reserves, individual property in land and local self-government'.[60] In the sense that the Glen Gray policy was aimed at squeezing labour out of segregated reserves it had the makings of a meeting ground with the northern school of policy. In the sense that it provided a protected individual tenure for Africans 'emerging from tribalism' and the introduction of tribal councils as an instrument of local government, it was in the eyes of imperial administrators a more significant Cape contribution to the 'solution of the native problem' than the minority franchise.

The problem of reconciling white interests with the protection of Africans was an old imperial one, and it had a traditional answer. This placed the emphasis on adapting the functions of the executive, rather than on a limited *evolué* policy which provided rights in the legislature.[61] In considering southern Africa, moreover, British policy makers were faced with a variety of situations and attempted to evolve a pattern which would cater for all the territories that were to lie within the dominant South African system. In Southern Rhodesia, with its considerable settler population, there existed a problem similar to that of the Union. First, how to combine devolution of control to the settlers with a trusteeship aimed at the prevention of misuse of settler power, and secondly how to develop a means of governing dispossessed and conquered peoples to whom the legitimacy of their previous institutions had to be denied. These two complicated tasks had to be undertaken in a territory which was governed not by British officials but by a chartered company that was hostile both to settler power and to the imperial factor and whose main purpose in the government of Africans was to drive them as quickly as possible in large numbers on to the labour market. In the three High Commission territories and in Northern Rhodesia, particularly in the Lozi kingdom, African hierarchies had survived, African lands had been guaranteed and the powers of local white authorities had been limited. There existed, therefore, the trappings of an 'indirect rule' situation, where administrative separation, combined with the use and development of African institutions, was the professed aim of policy. In areas of white conquest and appropriation where this could not be done the policy the British government sought to promote had two interconnected aspects. Administration was, as far as possible, to be by experts free from white electoral pressure, and the central direction of 'native policy' was to be taken out of the political arena. A reserves policy to render secure the remnant of African land holding was to be combined with the development in the reserves of councils as instruments of providing for African participation on a local level. Whether or not *evolués* continued to be represented in a white legislature, the British government appeared to pin its hopes on the development of a viable political separation.

In 1903 Milner appointed a commission to provide a comprehensive study of the 'native problem' with a view to working out a common policy for the coming South African federation. The whole of southern Africa, including Southern Rhodesia and Bechuanaland, fell within its terms of reference. The members of the commission were nominated by the colonial governments and were predominantly English-speaking administrators of Africans. Its chairman was Sir Godfrey Lagden, the Commissioner for Native Affairs in the Transvaal. Lagden was one of the two African experts who was to gain a favourable mention in Ramsay MacDonald's *Labour and the Empire* and he was firmly against any further development of an *evolué* policy. Educated Africans were a small number with sufficient privileges, he felt; the real duty of the government was to '... further the development of the whole mass. That is our duty to the inferior race.'[62] The commission addressed itself to the twin problems of African land ownership and the African franchise.[63] On the first it noted that in the Cape, Natal and Rhodesia there were as yet no restrictions on African rights to buy land. 'We may ... approach ... the question of natives purchasing land within spheres of European occupation,' the commissioners wrote, 'with a consciousness of the special protection afforded them in respect of the lands reserved or set aside for their use.' The commission found that there was a noticeable increase in African land purchase and warned that

If this process goes on while at the same time restrictions exclude Europeans from purchasing within native areas, it is inevitable that at no very distant date, the amount of land in native occupation will be undesirably extended ... It will be far more difficult to preserve the absolutely necessary political and social distinctions if the growth of a mixed rural population of landowners is not discouraged.

It recommended that African purchase areas should be defined by law and African land purchase in areas outside of them abolished.[64]

On the franchise too the commissioners anxiously prophesied doom: '... the present number of native voters is ... the merest fringe of an impending mass'. Strife was inevitable if European members were returned to parliament relying heavily on the votes of African constituents. While Cape politicians like John X. Merriman had faith in the workings of a flexibly restrictive qualified franchise, the commission, as General Hertzog was to do, viewed it in terms of an irresistible increase in African political power. The African common roll franchise, where it existed, should go and instead, it recommended, there should be separate parliamentary representation for Africans only, '. . . provided that this can be done without conferring on them political power in any aggressive sense, or weakening in any way the unchallenged supremacy and authority of the ruling race'.[65] The commission thus rejected the basic elements of the Cape policy of equal rights for all civilised men regardless of colour, but over the next twenty years the report which it produced became a touchstone for judgement and the authority for action by the imperial and South African authorities.

The 1905 commission stood for separation, both political and territorial. Political separation meant more than the mere exclusion of Africans from political power in the 'aggressive sense', as arrangements for their government still had to be made. To begin with, there was a belief in men, not measures—as Milner wrote when advising on the reconstruction of Rhodesian government after 1897, the most important aspect of African government was '. . . to secure the appointment of honourable and capable men . . . the successful government of natives is rather a question of men than of regulations'.[66] This explains the stress which the British government put on the retention of ultimate control over appointments and dismissals of personnel in the Rhodesian Native Affairs Department, a power which survived to be written into the responsible government constitution of 1923. In the Natal Native Affairs Commission report of 1906 which followed the rebellion another emphasis was added. 'Personal rule,' wrote the Commissioners, 'supplies the keynote of successful native control, to the exclusion of a mere bureaucratic system of administration, or the frigid and rigid operation of positive law.'[67] As the High Commissioner, Lord Selborne, summed up, the real problem facing South Africa with regard to framing measures for African administration was 'How is the Government to combine with that parliamentary government which is necessary for the whites, that personal, consistent, and continuous, government which is necessary for Natives?'[68]

Administrative separation seemed to be the answer, and in the Colonial Office the idea took hold that Britain should aim not at political rights for Africans in southern Africa but at a permanent civil administration free from ministerial and parliamentary interference.[69] Lord Elgin, when leaving office as Secretary of State for the Colonies, gave his successor Lord Crewe his thoughts upon southern African problems. He distinguished between two approaches to African rights: the first was to make the individual African politically equal to the individual white; the second was to make special legislative provision for the protection of African interests. To the first there were objections that it would lead to white insecurity and the possibility of the subjection of whites to African rule, though Elgin doubted 'whether nature itself so permits'. The second, which he preferred, entailed '... a strong preference for the development of native institutions on native lines, which is urged by those on the spot'.[70] The conventional wisdom of the southern African administrators, with their stress on paternal, personal government and the utilisation of African customs, seemed to coincide with radical wisdom on the 'native problem'. As Ramsay MacDonald wrote, 'In a word the democratic principle of native administration is to develop native civilisation on its own lines ... the imperialist method is to impose upon it an alien civilisation', and to MacDonald and other radicals who interested themselves in South African affairs the exploitationist capitalism represented by the Rand and the Chartered Company appeared to be more dangerous than the segregatory policies of governments.[71]

In southern Africa after 1906 the British government subscribed to the view that the creation of a larger and more secure white political unit would in itself encourage a more enlightened policy towards Africans. Formal controls over the doings of white colonists were believed to be futile; '... it is impossible to devise effectual means of controlling the native policy of a self-governing colony' was the conclusion reached in the Colonial Office.[72] Both in the self-governing colonies which were to make up the Union in 1910 and in the Rhodesias the British government refrained from hostile intervention in African matters with an eye to the unpopularity which the imperial factor courted when it did so intervene. Policy was directed towards 'good faith' and the building of a liberal climate of opinion. In 1910 Britain's withdrawal was to be partial, leaving five territories behind which were destined for incorporation into a larger South African State. The task which faced the British government, therefore, was both to prepare these territories to fit into a larger South African pattern and to influence the Union government towards a policy which would be acceptable to British opinion. The schedule to the South Africa Act represented a statement of imperial policy on African affairs, with its emphasis on the governing of the protectorates by a permanent non-political commission, the fostering of 'tribal' institutions and the protection of African land holding.

The latter question, the ownership and occupation of land, appeared on all sides in southern Africa to be the central issue of 'native policy'. The Natal Commission reported that '. . . the struggle for land, which is present in their minds, is simply the struggle for life'.[73] In 1904 General Botha put forward the unrepentant Afrikaner view—that the reserves which were a centre of African life should be dissolved and reduced. There are, he told the Transvaal Labour Commission, '. . . large portions of South Africa where the Kaffirs have the say . . . these should be broken up.'[74]

In contrast the British government in 1906 laid down the elements of its 'native policy' for southern Africa. The Under Secretary of State for the Colonies, Winston Churchill, told the House of Commons that 'as far as we can' Britain would promote the principle of equal rights for all civilised men, regardless of colour, and in doing so would encourage '. . . the discrimination between different classes of coloured men'. And, he concluded, above all, '. . . we will labour to preserve those large reservations of good, well watered land where the African aboriginal, for whom civilisation has no chances, may dwell secluded and at peace'.[75] The qualifications which the new Liberal government imposed on the extent of its influence are obvious, as is its more positive commitment on the question of reserves. Gradually the imperial view did prevail to some extent over the Afrikaner one. A lot was conceded by the British government at Vereeninging in 1902, and again in 1909 when it accepted the political 'colour bar' in the South Africa Act, but even the 1913 Land Act can be seen as a compromise between the British and Afrikaner views of segregation. The schedule to the Act of Union,[76] which laid down the conditions under which the High Commission territories were to be transferred to the rule of the Union, was in essence a statement of policy, not only for these territories but of imperial 'native policy' for southern Africa as a whole. Merriman greeted the eventual compromise embodied in the schedule with relief, feeling that it contained '. . . provisions which mark an advance in Native policy, and contain the germs of the possible solution of a problem which weighs heavily in the mind of all who consider the future of South Africa'.[77] Though the Cape politicians insisted on the retention of the minority franchise in the Cape, and the British government was to protect it in Rhodesia, this was not the core of the solution. In aiming at the protection of African land holding the British government was to some extent successful. Botha abandoned his desire to break up the reserves and the protectorates; Rhodesia was divided before the possibility of a poor-white influx made it impossible; harmful as it was to African interests, the 1913 Land Act was nevertheless a retreat from the 'pure' Afrikaner position, as had been the acceptance of the schedule and the continuation of the Cape franchise.

Nevertheless the entire course of what was seen as imperial appeasement was vocally opposed by the African leadership, who saw the franchise as a crucial issue. They complained in general about the imperial government's abdicating its influence in the internal government of southern Africa and the consequent worsening of the African position.[78] In 1903 and in 1906 African groups protested against the granting of self-government to the former republics before the settlement of the franchise question. In 1906 the Cape African voters, led by J. Tengo-Jabavu, petitioned the House of Commons against the granting of constitutions to the new colonies 'by which a portion of their inhabitants should be excluded from electoral franchise of the ground of colour alone', which would 'establish a new departure in South African British colonies . . .' In 1909 a South African Native Convention met in Bloemfontein to consider the draft South Africa Act. While they accepted union they told the British government that 'good or just government' was impossible 'where one class is left at the mercy of another class by being absolutely deprived of the right of equal representation . . .' They made an emphatic protest against the colour bar in the constitution and the failure to apply the Cape franchise to the northern colonies, and demanded the amendment of the Act.

A certain consensus existed among the experts on the southern African 'native problem', both white South African and in Britain. It was well summed up by Maurice Evans, who identified four principles:

From the Transvaal policy, the great principle that the white man must rule.
   From Natal, that our rule of the Abantu should be personal, fatherly, sympathetic, and not rigid and impersonal . . .
   From the Administration of the Cape Colony we learn that we must adopt the principle that the Abantu should be encouraged, under white guidance, to manage their own affairs. And we may also learn, that whilst they should be helped to take an intelligent interest in and manage their own matters affecting themselves, they should not be allowed a direct and equal voice in State Policy
   From Basutoland that it is possible to have a people contented, prospering and advancing in material matters under the old customs and tribal rule.[79]

The line of descent was from Shepstonism in Natal and the Cape's Glen Gray Act to the schedule to the Act of Union, and it was to be carried on in the policies of successive Union governments. Absent is the clear clash between 'Transvaal' and 'Cape' methods. Just as a rough consensus was reached on depoliticising the 'native question' and on administrative and political segregation, so too a consensus was reached upon segregated land holding, which involved more or less, in both the Union and Southern Rhodesia, a freezing of the *status quo*. 'Native questions' were to be non-controversial. Yet the policy urged for southern Africa was more aggressive and less squeamish than the 'indirect rule' model which later represented the ideal of British colonial policies. Selborne thought necessary '. . . the gradual destruction of the tribal system'.[80] The need to provide for the administration of the mass of Africans without running the danger of allowing the development of separate centres of power was well described by Sir Percy Fitzpatrick in a memorandum on 'native policy'. He quoted Rhodes to the effect that what was necessary was '. . . for 1 per cent equal rights for 99 per cent an Indian despotism', and went on to argue that political segregation could be achieved with justice as long as 'advanced' Africans were treated differently from the mass. As for the mass, anything on the lines of the Transkeian Native Council or a modification of indigenous systems would suffice, provided that '... the main points [were] that there should be many areas and many councils; that none should be too important or too powerful; that the native representation on these councils should be appointed and not elected ...'[81]

There was tension, but not conflict, between British and Afrikaner ideas on the southern African 'native problem': the British government's influence remained considerable after union, and because it had the High Commission territories and Rhodesia to hold out as a reward for good behaviour British and South African policies developed together. Both were colonial powers and both were seeking the answer to the problem of maintaining white minority control over an African majority, in a region of the empire in which even Lewis Harcourt, the most liberal of Secretaries of State for the Colonies, acknowledged the Union's dominant interests. He wrote:

It seems almost certain that in a future not very remote the Dominions in temperate zones will desire to acquire for themselves 'hothouses' for consumable luxuries and other purposes. It is not unreasonable to contemplate the ultimate absorption of the West Indies by Canada; of the Pacific islands by Australia and New Zealand; of Rhodesia and the Native Protectorates (even of Nyasaland) by South Africa.[82]

But as always in southern African political debate on the 'native question', policy discussions were a mask for reality, not attempts to explain it.

The basis of the system, the pass laws and the labour contract enforceable by the sanctions of the criminal law, remained and were little discussed by the experts on the native question. The attitude which animated imperial policy was set out in Milner's despatch to Chamberlain of December 1901.[83] The government, Milner wrote, would not obtain labour compulsorily for the mines nor fix wages, but

... if by combination among themselves, they [the mine owners] can prevent those wages being forced up to a preposterous pitch, cramping not only industry but agriculture, it may well be doubted whether their action would not be beneficial rather than otherwise to the whole community, not excepting the natives themselves.

But it was no business of the government's to interfere in this field, Milner wrote, and the mine owners had not asked them to do so.

What they *do* ask is, that the Government should do what it can to prevent the natives, whom they have obtained at a great cost, and whose interests are safeguarded by the law in so many ways, from breaking away from their contracts in a mere access of childish levity ... And this is surely a reasonable demand ...

Even the 1905 commission report felt obliged to explain the difference between its fine words and the conditions to which they related, remarking that

The final outcome of a righteous war is not to be judged by the devastations of opposing armies or by the scenes of slaughter and bloodshed on the scenes of battle. No less fallacious would be the attempt to gauge the eventual issue of civilisation of the natives by the many unfortunate features of the struggle which still prevail.[84]

By 1910 most of the leading Afrikaner politicians were learning how to debate the 'native question' as the British did—in terms of what was in the best interests of Africans. Rhetoric masked reality. Merriman succinctly went to the heart of the matter when he wrote in his diary of the Parliamentary debate on the Union's Land Act of 1913; 'Nauseous hypocrisy of caring for Native interests masking desire to get cheap servants.'[85]

5 Decolonising South Africa

The process of the unification of four of the southern African colonies into a 'Dominion' was a matter of intense political (and later historical) controversy. Yet the rhetoric of the reconciliation policy and the magnanimous extension and clasping of the hands of friendship by sections of both the British and South African policies has tended to some extent to obscure the elements of calculation and interest involved on both sides. There was political animosity in the United Kingdom between imperialists and pro-Boers, and in South Africa both English and Afrikaans white South Africans were divided—to put it at its simplest—into 'haves' and 'have nots' as well as into apparently irreconcilable nationalists on both sides and pragmatists who were prepared to take what advantages a developing situation offered to them. As they had done in the years before the war, the Conservative and Liberal parties in Britain differed upon means more than ends. While the former would have preferred to consolidate military victory, building if they could upon an enlarged and unified British population in southern Africa, and upon Rhodes's counterpoise, the Liberals hoped that loyal co-operation could be achieved by successfully detaching a collaborationist group from the leadership of the defeated enemy. Milner's re-establishment of government in the defeated republics had aimed to a very large extent at the restoration, under different political direction, of the *status quo ante bellum*, which meant a continued and more efficient operation of the mines and the system of 'native administration' which procured their labour. That a substantial proportion of the old Transvaal elite found this congenial, once a large degree of political direction had been handed back to them, is not surprising. Though this policy was bitterly resented, coming as it did so soon after the war, both by the Afrikaner *mittereinders* and by the bulk of English-speaking southern Africans and their spokesmen, among the Rand mining interests, the Chartered Company and the Conservative Party in Britain, all of whom feared its consequences, it created the logical framework of white politics in the Union for years to come, and led to the eventual alignment of Afrikaner poor and English-speaking labour against the imperialist-backed alliance of Randlords and landlords.

J. A. Hobson's view that the South African War was a classical example of an imperialist war fought in the interests of capitalism has been mauled by historians[86] but it is relevant and significant that a substantial strand of Afrikaner thinking about the war was to the effect that it was a war against international capitalism. Even Smuts, in 1900, wrote of the Afrikaner struggle, 'If it is ordained that we, insignificant as we are, should be the first among all peoples to begin the struggle against the new world tyranny of Capitalism, then we are ready to do so . . .'[87] Anti-capitalism, based upon hatred of Rhodes and the Chartered Company, had already been a part of Cape politics before the war, and after the war the intense jingoism of the Milnerite ascendency, followed by the Chinese labour crisis, ensured that it became a permanent part of Afrikaner nationalist ideology. Steyn, the former Free State president, Hertzog, Malan and other nationalist leaders all shared and expressed suspicion of the Rand establishment. They were equally distrustful of the machinations of the Chartered Company, and this, more often than any other reason, formed the basis of their objection to the inclusion of Rhodesia into the Union: that it would '. . . mean a new and powerful strengthening of the capitalist forces that already dominate the Union and suck it dry'.[88]

In the English constituency in South Africa too there was a deepening division between 'capital' and 'labour', and even before 1910 the seeds of the alliance between the Afrikaner poor white and the white English-speaking working class were germinating. Once the Transvaal government was taken over in 1907 by Botha and Smuts it proved eager (sometimes, in the eyes of the British government, over-eager) to take militant action against the white working class, and the new rulers consistently proved themselves second only to the mine owners themselves in their exagerrated fear of syndicalist conspiracy and red revolution. The new government of the Transvaal, and later of the Union, shared with the Randlords an interest in a revived mining industry based upon cheap labour, and carried on, therefore, what had been the urgent basis of British policy with regard to the mining industry ever since the conquest of the Rand. Thus the post-war reconstruction and political realignment of South Africa was based essentially upon an alliance of English and Afrikaner 'haves' with the imperial government, against the 'have nots'—African, Afrikaner and English-speaking. Political rhetoric at the time, so soon after the end of a war which had in the public mind been fought between two nationalisms, did not reflect this alliance, though conciousness of it did begin to mature in the years after union.

The end of the Milnerite ascendency and the change of government in the United Kingdom were an enormous blow to those English people in southern Africa who had felt that the military victory had been won to place them in a politically dominant position. The new circumstances in which they found themselves after the Liberal victory entailed the formulation of a new political strategy. As it emerged it was '. . . to go on with full Responsible Government and take our chance of being able to control the policy'.[89] Jameson, according to Chaplin, had already by 1903 decided that the only way to avoid a resurgence of Krugerite dominance '. . . was to play up the more progressive Boers and put them in power'.[90] By 1910 most South African English-speaking politicians felt that 'In the end there must be a split in the Boer ranks' and although there was general recognition that there could never be a distinctively English government in the new Union it was at least hoped that a split would exclude from power what were seen as 'the reactionary section of the Boers'.[91] As Fitzpatrick put it, the aim was '. . . to capture Botha and the best of the Dutch for a progressive British policy . . . the thing is perfectly possible'.[92]

While South African English eagerness to court men like Botha and Smuts waxed so strong, so too did the suspicion it aroused. Ex-president Steyn expressed his distaste for Botha's response to the overtures and his '. . . laying on the loyalty butter so very thick'.[93] Botha's affair with imperialism proceeded well. As Mrs Merriman described its culmination, the occasion of the House of Lords debate of the South Africa Bill, 'Botha is always "the sugared bun" and Lords and Bishops in their robes thronged about him to shake him by the hand . . .'[94] Botha, like Smuts, accepted (as indeed Hertzog fundamentally did when he became Prime Minister of the Union) that the Union was to be a part of the British empire and that its continued existence as it was depended upon its imperial association. 'The true interests of South Africa are not,' said Botha when dismissing Hertzog, '. . . in conflict with those of the Empire from which we derive our free constitution.'[95] He and Smuts opposed the pretensions of the imperial reformers clustered around Milner and the Round Table movement who saw the future development of the empire in terms of a British-dominated world-wide super-State, but the South African leaders were certainly not alone in their opposition to a movement which in any case hardly represented the mainstream of British political thinking on the matter. But this was not enough for Hertzog so soon after the war, for whom reconciliation meant reconciliation with defeat. In 1912 came the long-awaited split in the Afrikaner ranks—what Milner called 'the glorious incident' of the Hertzog–Botha break.[96]

The political atmosphere of the post-independence situation was a tense one. Though independence had been achieved, the frustrating way in which life seemed to go on as before created disappointment and then anger, and personal animosities boiled over into an overall accusation of political conspiracy between the old rulers and the new. In a confrontation in the Cabinet Hertzog challenged Botha to deny that he was being dropped for his anti-imperialist views, shouting, 'He dare not. He dare not ...'[97] Walter Long summed up the general reaction of British conservative and English-speaking South African politicians, which was that Botha's action '... indicates that he is really anxious to adopt an Imperialistic policy'.[98] Botha was nevertheless acutely aware of the dangers of appearing too pro-imperialist: he outmanoeuvred Jameson's bid for a 'best man' government to start off the Union and throughout the war years carefully avoided coalition with the Unionist Party. Even Smuts, of whom Fitzpatrick so enthusiastically exclaimed, '... he will always be with us as long as we have to deal with him'.[99] made, after Botha's death, an attempt at reconciliation with Hertzog's Nationalists before merging the South African Party with the Unionists.

The Afrikaner collaborators were caught in the middle; their only enthusiastic supporter was the British government, while they were reviled by Hertzog and, until the suppression of the Afrikaner rebellion during the war, were deeply distrusted by South African English politicians. After the Liberal government came to power in England and made clear its determination to hand over power to a section of the old Afrikaner leadership, the politics of the South African English leadership came to be dominated by the intense hatred which those who had been a part of the Milnerite ascendency in the Transvaal had for both Afrikaner nationalism and British liberalism, which in collusion had apparently cheated imperialism of its most dearly bought victory. From this antipathy sprang constant plotting to unseat and divide what the Unionists saw as the Afrikaner government of the Union. Fitzpatrick clearly defined the role of the Unionist Party when he wrote, 'We are trustees for the British cause.'[100] There followed the development of a strategy that was not only internal to the Union's politics but external. As long as Botha and Smuts were distrusted as the stalking horses of Afrikaner nationalism South African English politicians clung to Rhodesia as a British power base. Once the Afrikaner collaborators had earned the delighted devotion of British imperialists Rhodesia became important in an internal context.

Notes

1   See, for example, C. de Kiewiet, *A History of South Africa*, Oxford, 1941, and D. Denoon, *A Grand Illusion*, London, 1973.

2   E. A. Walker, *A History of Southern Africa*, London, 1957, chapter 8.
3   The formulation is from the celebrated diaries of trekker Anna Steenkamp.
4   C. F. Goodfellow, *Great Britain and the South African Confederation, 1870–81*, Oxford, 1966.
5   See R. Robinson and J. Gallagher, *Africa and the Victorians*, London, 1963, chapter 7. In Milner's words the creation of a viable Rhodesia would mean 'that we win the South African game all round'. (Quoted in R. Hyam, *The Failure of South African Expansion*, London, 1972, at p. 20.)
6   Quoted in Robinson and Gallagher, *Africa*, at p. 454.
7   See R. Palmer, 'Johnston and Jameson: a comparative study in the imposition of colonial rule', in *An Early History of Malawi*, ed. B. Pachai, London, 1972.
8   An Ndebele description of the reserves created by the first of Rhodesia's land commissions. See C. 8130, *Report of the Matabeleland Land Commission*, 1896.
9   See 'Vindex', *The Political Life and Speeches of Cecil John Rhodes*, London, 1900.
10   See W. Carrothers, *Emigration from the British Isles*, London, 1929, chapter 13. In 1891 25 per cent of emigrants settled within the empire; by 1913, 78 per cent. See also Cd. 2978, *Report of the Departmental Committee on Agricultural Settlement in British Colonies*, 1906, at p. 25, and the evidence given to the committee published in Cd. 2979.
11   Lord Abercorn, speaking to the annual general meeting of the British South Africa Company in 1901. See *The Times*, 24 February 1901.
12   Cd. 2979, paras. 3552–4.
13   G. Bennett, *The Concept of Empire*, London, 1953, quoting from Milner's address to the Municipal Congress in Johannesburg, 18 May 1903.
14   See the Selborne memorandum and W. S. Churchill, *My African Journey*, London, 1908, chapter 3. East African and southern African white settlers also feared that the directing middle class might turn out to be Asian. Lyttleton Gell, on the company's board, had even more far-reaching ideas. Neither whites nor Africans, he felt, could provide a basis for tropical production. On African labour he wrote, 'Surely the idea of making an industrial labourer out of African natives . . . is a Will of the Wisp. Why delude ourselves and ignore the facts of 2,000 years . . . Sooner or later we have got to plant the Zambesi basin with Indian or Kanaka cultivators.' (Gell to Brodie, undated [*c*. 1907–08], Gell papers, B.S.A. 4.)
15   Quoted in B. Sacks, *South Africa: an Imperial Dilemma*, Albuquerque, N.M., 1967, at p. 57.
16   C.O. 417/454, 12 October 1908.
17   Cd. 2978, para. 57.
18   See E. Ross Townsend, 'The Duke of Connaught and Rhodesia', *United Services Magazine*, XLII, 1910–11.
19   W. Fox, Memorandum on land policy (written for the British South Africa Company), chapter 5.
20   *Die Volkstem*, 5 March 1913, and C.O. 417/526, Gladstone to Harcourt, 13 November 1913.
21   C.O. 417/465, Selborne to Crewe, telegram, 23 January 1909.

22 See Gann, *Northern Rhodesia*, pp. 122ff; C.O. 879, No. 899, 7 February 1908, and C.O. 879, No. 932, 3 May 1909; 'Become a Rhodesian farmer', published by Rhodesia and South African Railways, 1912; and H. Birchenough, Memorandum on Northern Rhodesian land policy and settlement, 1912.
23 Lord Winterton, a member of the House of Commons, and the Duke of Westminster and Lord Wolverton, members of the Lords, formed the Association.
24 C.O. 417/538, B.S.A.C. to Northern Copper Co., 16 October 1913.
25 C.O. 417/532, December 1913.
26 *Emigration Information Office Reports*, 1913.
27 W. F. Fox, 'Memorandum on land settlement'. 1924 would have been the time for the next charter review.
28 See Cd. 8672 1917, *Report re Empire Settlement of ex-Servicemen*, and the Overseas Settlement Committee report, 1921, where Milner is quoted.
29 Cd. 8672, paras. 65–7, and appendix III.
30 C.O. 417/617, 3 April 1920, and C.O. 417/689, 25 August 1922.
31 C.O. 767/1, October 1923, containing an extract from the *Times* report of Ormsby–Gore's remarks to the imperial conference on 8 October 1923.
32 Quoted in Cab. 38/13, 2 May 1907.
33 Cab. 11/35, telegram, secret, Selborne to Crewe, 10 August 1908, and C.O. 417/459, 10 August 1908, and Cab. 38/13, Military survey of the Transvaal, 2 May 1907.
34 Cab. 38/13, South Africa internal defence, 6 April 1908.
35 G. G. Aston, *The Defence of United South Africa as Part of the British Empire*, preface by General Lord Methuen, imperial commander-in-chief in South Africa, London, 1910.
36 Sketch of proposed defence Bill and explanatory pamphlet of first draft 6 October 1911, Smuts archive, CXI, No. 3, and Cab. 38/13, 3 May 1911.
37 War Office, 32/1357, No. 34/1657, Inspector General's report on Northern and Southern Rhodesia defence, 1911.
38 C.O. 417/510, 6 March 1912. Compare, however, Elgin's feeling with regard to the Transvaal and Natal that the presence of an imperial garrison preserved some of the influence of the imperial government over native policy. (R. Hyam, 'The African policy of the Liberal government, 1905–09', unpublished Ph.D. thesis, Cambridge University, 1963, p. 124.)
39 A. Fitzroy, *Memoirs*, London, 1925, p. 527, and G.P. Add. MSS, 46,004, Stanley to Gladstone, 7 October 1910.
40 *Prester John*, chapters 5 and 7. See also S. Marks, *Reluctant Rebellion*, London, 1969.
41 G. P. Add. MSS, 46,001, f. 247, January 1914. At Smuts's request British troops had been used in strike breaking on the Rand in 1907. See E. A. Walker, *History*, p. 518.
42 On the rebellion see T. R. H. Davenport, 'The South African rebellion, 1914', *English Historical Review*, 1963, and N. G. Garson, 'The Boer rebellion of 1914', *History Today*, 1962.
43 There was strong Afrikaner opposition within the Union's Cabinet in 1914 to Botha's proposal that the Union should invade South West Africa. See B.

Spies, 'The outbreak of the first world war and the British government', *South African Historical Journal*, 1969.
44 Quoted in B. Sacks, *South Africa*, p. 199.
45 Smuts Archive, CXII, No. 18, Botha to Smuts, telegram, 3 April 1915.
46 Smuts Archive, CXV, No. 4, 'A.N.C. memorial to the King'.
47 C.O. 537/604, secret, 8 October 1915, Recruiting of South African native troops.
48 C.O. 879/1033, 31 December 1914. For Nyasaland see G. Shepperson and T. Price, *Independent African*, Edinburgh, 1958, and on Mozambique see T. O. Ranger, 'Revolt in Portuguese East Africa: the Makombe rising of 1917', in *African Affairs*, ed. K. Kirkwood, No. 2, St Antony's Papers, No. 15, London, 1963.
49 In the Colonial Office Fiddes minuted anxiously, 'I hope it won't get published in South Africa . . . It would be grist to Hertzog's mill.' (C.O. 417/590, 21 September 1915.) In Southern Rhodesia, where an African contingent was raised for service in east Africa, 'The less well affected of the Matabele Chiefs began to put it about that the British must be in a bad way'. (C.O. 879/1033, 31 December 1914.)
50 On *Mittel Afrika* see W. R. Louis, *Great Britain and Germany's Lost Colonies*, Oxford, 1967, pp. 2–3. For Smuts see 'The future of South and central Africa, May 22nd 1917', *Wartime Speeches*, London, 1917.
51 Ch. 8/2/2/11, 2 September 1920 and 3 March 1921.
52 Ch. 8/2/2/11, Malcolm to Chaplin, 24 January 1919. During the war it was felt in Rhodesia that 'The majority of the Dutch . . . could not be relied upon with any degree of confidence to assist us against the Germans, or even rebels from the Union' and the Resident Commissioner reported, 'The backwash of Union politics makes itself felt among them . . . in Southern Rhodesia the Dutch in the main . . . are kept in close touch with the Herzogite movement.' (C.O. 417/558, 1915, and C.O. 417/579, 9 November 1916.)
53 Ch. 8/2/2/11, Malcolm to Chaplin, 2 September 1920.
54 C.O. 767/4, 14 September 1925.
55 Before the creation of an effective Union force, imperial forces were used against the white workers on the Rand. In 1922 these workers, another potentially anti-imperialist threat, were effectively crushed by the Union's forces.
56 Though while the War Office felt that it relied upon the Union to deal with unrest in the High Commission territories, the Colonial Office felt otherwise. (C.O. 417/699, 30 April 1923.)
57 See R. Hyam, 'African interests and the South Africa Act', *Historical Journal*, 1970, and R. A. Huttenback, *Ghandi in South Africa: British Imperialism and the Indian Question, 1860–1914*, Ithaca, N.Y., 1971.
58 E.g. P. N. S. Mansergh, *South Africa, 1906–61: the Price of Magnanimity*, London, 1962, pp. 90–3.
59 As late as 1928 Lord Buxton, commenting on a biography of Cecil Rhodes, and looking back on his period as High Commissioner, wrote, 'It was greatly borne upon me, when I was Governor-General, that the Glen Gray Act constituted a very far-sighted and beneficent policy in the interests of the Whites as well as of the Natives.' (B.P., Rhodes file, Buxton to Macdonald, 21 June 1928.)

Themes 41

60 F. Lugard, *The Dual Mandate*, reprinted London, 1965, p. 327.
61 The Aborigines Protection Committee recommended in 1837 that 'The Protection of Aborigines should be considered as a duty peculiarly belonging to and appropriate to the Executive Government, as administered either in this country or by the Governors of the respective Colonies. This is not a trust which could be conveniently confided to the local legislatures . . . Whatever may be the legislative system of any Colony, we . . . advise that, as far as possible, the Aborigines be withdrawn from its control.' (Report, p. 77.)
62 Lagden papers, Rhodes House, MSS Afr. s. 212, box 1v, Memo on Selborne's draft despatch on native and coloured questions, March 1906. R. MacDonald, *Labour and the Empire*, London, 1907, chapter 6.
63 For a discussion of the work and conclusions of the commission see C. M. Tatz, *Shadow and Substance in South Africa*, Pietermaritzberg, 1969.
64 Cd. 2399, 1905, *Report of the South African Native Affairs Commission, 1903–05*, paras. 188–93.
65 *Ibid.*, paras. 432–441.
66 Quoted in C. Palley, *The Constitutional History and Law of Southern Rhodesia*, Oxford, 1966, pp. 140–1.
67 Cd. 3889, 1908, Natal, *Report of the Native Affairs Commission, 1908*, para. 32.
68 Selborne memorandum on 'native affairs', S.P., XI, p. 390.
69 See minutes, C.O. 417/458, 13 January 1908.
70 Elgin to Crewe, 1908, quoted in R. Hyam, *The African Policy of the Liberal Government, 1905–09*.
71 *Labour and the Empire*, p. 18.
72 Quoted in Hyam, *The African Policy of the Liberal Government*, p. 74.
73 Cd. 3889.
74 Quoted in *Selections from the Correspondence of John X. Merriman, 1899–1905*, ed. P. Lewsen, p. 392. He considered the High Commission territories to be just 'the native reserves'. See S.P., II, p. 37.
75 Quoted in R. F. E. Churchill, *W. S. Churchill*, II, London, 1967, p. 164.
76 See appendix II for the schedule.
77 *Merriman*, ed. Lewsen, IV, p. 135. Merriman to Hely-Hutchinson, June 1909.
78 See T. Karis and G. Carter, *From Protest to Challenge*, I, Stanford, Cal., 1972, pp. 18–28, 45–50 and 50–2.
79 M. S. Evans, *Black and White in South Africa*, 1916 edition, p. 277.
80 See Selborne's memorandum on native affairs, S.P., II.
81 Ch. 8/2/1, Fitzpatrick to Chaplin, 7 October 1908.
82 Quoted in M. Beloff, *Imperial Sunset*, I, London, 1969, pp. 145–6.
83 *The Milner Papers*, ed. C. Headlam, II, London, 1933, p. 313.
84 Cd. 2399, paras. 432–41.
85 *Merriman*, ed. Lewsen, IV, 15 May 1913, p. 232.
86 See *Imperialism: a Study*, London, 1902, and (for example) J. S. Marais, *The Fall of Kruger's Republic*, Oxford, 1961.
87 J. Smuts, in 'A century of wrong', p. 98; quoted in G. Le May, *British Supremacy in South Africa*, Oxford, 1965.
88 *Die Burger*, 1922; quoted by P. Warhurst, 'Rhodesia and her neighbours, 1900–23', unpublished D.Phil. thesis, Oxford University, 1970, p. 377.

89 Ch. 8/2/1, 12 November 1905, Chaplin to Mrs Goodman. He added, 'It is a terrible "come down" since Milner left.'
90 Ch. 8/2/1, 28 February 1909, Chaplin to Gwynne.
91 Ch. 8/2/1, 8 July 1910, Memo on the political situation in the Transvaal.
92 Quoted in J. P. R. Wallis, *Fitz: the Story of Sir Percy Fitzpatrick*, London, 1955, p. 147.
93 *Merriman*, ed. Lewsen, IV, Steyn to Merriman, 16 April 1907, p. 36.
94 *Op. cit.*, Mrs A. Merriman to Mrs J. Merriman, 22 July 1909, p. 141.
95 Ch. 8/2/2/13, Milner to Chaplin, 25 January 1913.
96 Quoted in J. Meintjies, *General Louis Botha*, London, 1970, p. 193.
97 *Merriman*, ed. Lewsen, IV, p. 231, n. 58.
98 Ch. 8/2/2/8, Long to Chaplin, 13 January 1913.
99 Ch. 8/2/1, Fitzpatrick to Chaplin, 10 December 1915.
100 Ch. 8/2/1, F 1722.

CHAPTER 2

The incomplete Dominion
1905–14

1 Britain and Chartered Company government in Rhodesia

In the very delicate negotiations which preceded the making of the Union of South Africa two contentious issues were postponed: not only was the future of the protectorates left undecided, so was the future of the territories administered by the Chartered Company. While section 150 of the South Africa Act provided for the future admission of the Rhodesias into the Union, the administrative framework within which the Rhodesias were ruled was left unchanged in 1910. The order in council of 1898 had given Southern Rhodesia a constitution similar in form to that of a Crown colony with representative government.[1] The difference between Southern Rhodesia and a Crown colony was that the permanent executive was formed not by the British government but by the company, which appointed the Administrator, Executive Council and civil service. A Legislative Council was created in which the elected members, who were chosen on a Cape-model colour-blind franchise, by an electorate made up almost entirely of white settlers, were in a minority. Control over finance remained wholly in the company's hands. To supervise the workings of this system the British government appointed a Resident Commissioner in Salisbury, who was to be an *ex officio* member of both the Executive and Legislative Councils and was to report generally to the High Commissioner in South Africa on Rhodesian affairs. The High Commissioner for South Africa, whose responsibility for Rhodesia was extended by the 1898 order in council, was given control of the company's police force. He had concurrent powers of legislation by proclamation, and appointments to the Native Affairs Department and decisions with regard to the removal and settlement of Africans required his approval. Other provisions were for an imperial veto on Rhodesian legislation; a procedure whereby legislation discriminating between different racial groups had to be submitted to the imperial authorities for approval, and the placing of an obligation on the company's administration to provide 'from time to time' reserve lands required for Africans. The 'Rhodes clause' gave special protection to British goods imported into Rhodesia by providing that duties should not exceed those levied by the South African customs union in 1898. North of the Zambesi the company's administration was likewise put into a new legal framework. The territory was divided into two. The Barotseland–North Western Rhodesia order in council of 1899 reflected in theory the treaty status of the Lozi and gave limited powers to the company while reserving extensive areas both to the Lozi and to the High Commissioner in South Africa. The North Eastern Rhodesia order in council of 1899 reflected a conquest situation and was modelled along the lines of the Southern Rhodesian order, differing from it in that the local imperial supervisory authority was the British commissioner in Nyasaland and not the High Commissioner in South Africa.[2] Finally provision was made in the Southern Rhodesian order that the Colonial Office should receive reports of meetings of the company's board in London which, with the eclipse of Rhodes, and temporarily of Jameson, had firmly taken over control from the South African office, which had until then been the company's mainspring.

Rhodesia, thus satisfactorily reconstructed after the rebellions and devoutly attached to the imperial connection, receded into the background after the outbreak of war in South Africa in 1899. By 1910 the bare bones of imperial control fashioned in the 1898 order in council had gained little flesh. If an active imperial presence was to make its weight felt the post of Resident Commissioner would seem to have required considerable political acumen. But the persons first chosen as holders of the post reflect the overriding concern of the British authorities in South Africa, which was to use their man on the spot in Salisbury to supervise the maintenance of military security. His function was not so much to protect Africans as to protect the British government by ensuring that the company did not provoke another expensive rebellion. In any case, the first holders of the post were not weighty men. As one of the company's officials wrote, 'Fair was a nonentity and Burns-Begg a cock-sparrow'.[3] It was suggested, by Milner first, in 1904, that the post be abolished, and later, by Rodwell, the imperial Secretary in South Africa, that it be amalgamated with that of Resident Commissioner for Bechuanaland because there was so little for the Rhodesian Resident Commissioner to do. When Gladstone took up his office he found that Colonel Burns Begg, his man in Salisbury, did not appear to be a very effective channel of information or control. The Resident Commissioner complained of the extreme sensitivity of the Rhodesian administration to any activity by him, and even with regard to 'native questions' wrote that he had to '. . . work very delicately in order not to appear in any way to undermine the authority of the native department'. The result was the waning of control over this department which the order in council had been specifically designed to give. When the office of Taberer, the Chief Native Commissioner for Mashonaland, was abolished the matter was not mentioned even privately to any of the British authorities, an omission which was actually in breach of the order in council. Similarly, on one occasion during 1913 a police mobilisation against possible African unrest was not only not mentioned to the Resident Commissioner but denied on enquiry.[4] Even when memory of the rebellion receded the degree of effectiveness of control over the Native Department was not the major British preoccupation. By 1914 the Resident Commissioner's function as a watchdog over African affairs was ignored by Lambert when he described the Colonial Office's requirements of the man in Salisbury as '. . . someone who will keep in touch with white opinion without intruding himself . . .''[5]

Likewise imperial control over Northern Rhodesia, in spite of the orders in council, was not effective, though this caused slightly more concern than the relative lack of official information about the south, which was less remote and more open. The Colonial Office had taken a limited view of its responsibilities in the north, and when in 1908 Selborne had protested against the independence of the company regime Sir Hartman Just minuted that Selborne showed '. . . a strange lack of appreciation of the true perspective' and that as long as the company paid the bill it was entitled to govern without substantial interference.[6] But by 1914, as instances of their ignorance mounted, officials in London protested against '. . . the imperfect way in which arrangements for keeping the Secretary of State informed as to events and policy in the B.S.A.C.'s territories works. . . . there is no doubt that we are kept unduly in the dark.'[7] A suggested remedy, the appointment of a Resident Commissioner for Northern Rhodesia, still hung fire when the war began, and never materialised. The provision in the order in council which laid down that reports of the company's London board meetings should be supplied to the Colonial Office was likewise not an effective means of providing information, as only sketchy minutes and heavily edited reports were sent by the company. But by and large the Colonial Office was not over-concerned with the fitful workings of the provisions of the order in council. For it placed more stress in having a political channel to the settlers than on administrative control over native affairs: it was influence, and not control, which the British government sought to exercise, and the preservation of the former seemed in its judgement always to rest on abstention from the latter.

2 Britain, the settlers and the charter

Between 1904 and 1910 the political structure of southern Africa had been almost entirely refashioned. In the unravelling of the many tangled political knots one of the hardest was left tied. The precise position of the Chartered Company was not defined and the charter was not interfered with. The British South Africa Company was the administering authority in the Rhodesias. Precisely what this meant in financial terms was a bone of political contention between the company and the settlers. One of the *raisons d'être* of the charter had been that the territories to which it related should become British without expense to the imperial treasury. Occupation of the Rhodesias did indeed prove to be an expensive undertaking, and by 1903 the company had accumulated an administrative deficit of over £7 million. The point at issue was what assets the company had acquired in return for its financial outlay. How could the assets of the company be separated from the assets of the country? The company claimed commercial ownership of the unalienated lands of Southern Rhodesia. The settlers rejected the claim, while the British government remained equivocal and reluctant to define the company's rights. In 1903 the company made the first of a series of attempts to settle the political differences between it and the settlers. Above all it wanted the settlers to acknowledge the territory's liability for the accumulated deficit and proposed the creation of a public debt. The settlers refused and appealed to the British government to buy Rhodesia from the company. The British government rebuffed a settler delegation in terms which set out clearly the political issues which the company's affairs involved. The legitimacy of the charter was still politically sensitive, and this added a dimension to conventional Treasury reluctance. For if the British government were to accept the principle of compensating the company for its deficit, then the question of how much of its expenditure had been incurred legitimately would become an issue of potential political conflict. The Secretary of State, Lyttelton, expressed the government's position to the settlers as follows:

One of your colleagues expressed the view that the Imperial Government was under an obligation to the British South Africa Company for the part it had taken in the addition of Rhodesia to the Empire. That is, of course, a view which may not be shared by all classes and parties in this country, but in any case the money value of such an obligation would be a matter of great controversy, and the estimation of its amount would be complicated by the fact that the Company's enterprise has naturally been of a more speculative nature than are the actions of a Government in the development of a new territory.[8]

These reasons underlay the British government's reluctance to get to grips with the company for the next twenty years.

In 1907 the company made a second attempt to reach an agreement with the settlers. Rhodesia had been far less profitable than had been anticipated; the second Rand had not materialised and the huge investments had thus far yielded small returns. As mineral wealth had fallen short of expectations an alternative source had to be found to recoup the company's investment. In a prosperous territory well settled by white men land could be an invaluable asset. The company therefore began to take a longer-term view of its position as a government: it embarked on an energetic policy of land sales to promote settelement, and because it now required greater settler co-operation it reduced its heavy claims to mining royalties and conceded a settler majority in the Legislative Council.[9] The settlers appealed again to the British government to impose a financial settlement on the company, and once again London refused to act. Rumours that the government might assist the company provoked hostile questions in the Commons from time to time. In August 1908 a Colonial Office minute pointed out that

When the time comes somebody will have to pay heavily to the shareholders, unless the Government of Southern Rhodesia is to be crippled by the loss of most of the assets on which a colonial Government relies. There is always a chance that in the event of federation that part of this payment may be shifted onto the South African taxpayer.[10]

If the burden of buying out the company could be placed, even only in part, on the South African taxpayer, then the political difficulties which the British government anticipated over a settlement with the company would be reduced. Thus another element of future British strategy became clear; it was to be a holding operation until such time as a South African government would be able and willing to shoulder its share of the payments.

It was the impending debt to the company which stood in the way of Rhodesian entry into the coming Union; neither the British government nor the nascent Union was ready to meet the bill for a transfer of the company's assets. In any case it was not known what the company's assets consisted of, and the British government, as Lord Crewe put it, would 'prefer to avoid' investigating the questions raised by the settlers regarding the division of revenues and the ownership of land.[11] In any case by 1909 the company was no longer counting upon being bailed out of an unprofitable Rhodesia. Fortified by a new issue of capital, it was devoting itself to long-term development.[12]

3 Rhodesia and the formation of the Union of South Africa

The time was hardly ripe, moreover, during the delicate negotiations of 1908–09 which preceded the formation of the Union, for the intrusion of the imperial factor with crude counterpoise tactics. A reluctant company and a jingoistic settler body would have threatened acute embarrassment to the grand reconciliation of English and Afrikaner in South Africa which all were pretending was accompanying the birth of the new State. Both in order to ensure South African willingness and to reduce the influence which the House of Commons would have over a South Africa Bill, the British Cabinet had come to the conclusion that the Union constitution 'should be exclusively the work of a South African Convention . . .'[13] The men who negotiated the South African union were not unanimously in favour of the immediate inclusion of Rhodesia. The Cape Prime Minister, Merriman, a lifelong and bitter opponent of Rhodes, Jameson and the Chartered circle, was acutely suspicious and objected, on the grounds of the company's commercial character, to giving it a voting voice at the Union convention. The company itself was not eager to attend as a voting member lest it be bound by majority decisions which had not been considered by its board and which had financial implications.[14] Yet the question of the future of the Rhodesias could not be ignored. Lord Selborne had been instructed in 1907 that Southern Rhodesia should be looked upon as a constituent part of a federal South Africa, and the Selborne memorandum, which had been published in 1907 as part of the pro-federal campaign in South Africa, argued very persuasively for the incorporation of Rhodesia. It suggested that Canadian history and the absorption of the territories of the Hudson's Bay Company were analogous to the position of Rhodesia *vis-à-vis* South Africa. South Africans, it enjoined, should look north to the Zambesi and ask themselves who was to control the settlement of Rhodesia. Their history, it said, plainly warned of the

... unwisdom of allowing the political organisation of the Northern countries to take place in utter independence of the community established in the South ... Whatever criticisms may be made of the Chartered Company it must never be forgotten that it saved the hinterland to South Africa ...

The company, though it was temporarily bearing the burden which the small white population was unable to bear, must eventually be separated from the functions of government, and 'The longer this problem is postponed the more difficult and the more expensive will its solution become ...' The memorandum directed no appeal to the Rhodesian settlers, as not only was it not then contemplated that they would have the final say but they were expected to be eager to free themselves from the charter and enter a federation in which British interests were well secured. It was to Afrikaner South Africa that the prospect was made attractive. Reference to control of settlement and the small white population was a bait to politicians aware of the increasing white rural poverty and land hunger which had followed the end of the war. Finally the memorandum held out an even wider prospect. The imperial factor would no longer hamper, limit and control Afrikaner expansion as it had done for the last century. Once within the empire Afrikaners would find it the patron of their northward movement. British territory, the memorandum said, stretched far away north to Lake Tanganyika, and '... in whatever degree this great region is a country where white men can work and thrive and multiply by so much will the opportunity of expansion inherited by South Africans through the British Empire be increased.'[15]

Afrikaner opinion was divided roughly into two. There were considerable Afrikaner misgivings over the possible inclusion of Rhodesia. White South Africa was a country with a small heterogeneous electorate that voted along group lines, and psephological prediction played a large part in political planning. Hofmeyr, the Cape Afrikaner leader, for example, expressed his doubts to Steyn, the former President of the Orange Free State, during the convention that '... if one ... adds Rhodesia ... with a nice representation and a pretty debt, our Union population will acquire an entirely one-sided complexion'. Even after the Union had been formed without Rhodesia, Hofmeyr remained gloomy because of the general belief that the incorporation of Rhodesia would take place in the near future; '... we can now at best expect a small majority over the jingo party in the first Union Parliament—a majority which will vanish altogether when Rhodesia is incorporated'.[16] But Steyn, and more particularly Botha and Smuts, showed considerable interest in the acquisition of Rhodesia.

A price of £20 million was mooted and turned down by the company; and Botha also discussed the matter with the other colonial premiers.[17] To the Transvaal, in particular, Rhodesia was not a distant part of black Africa but the immediate hinterland with which it had had much frustrated historical connection. Moreover to Botha and Smuts it presented the most immediate and least disruptive way of solving the 'poor white' problem. Thus Botha not only supported the attendance of a Rhodesian government delegation as observers at the Union Convention but, anxious to win the trust of the settlers, secured their presence as well.

No one was sure what the settlers felt, or how far their feelings should be allowed to influence events. There was general agreement that even if the company were willing to sell out to the Union, the consent of the settlers was desirable, and the British government gave a public assurance that settler opinion would be taken into account before incorporation. But a promise that the consent of the settlers would be secured was not given to the House of Commons, and the Secretary of State for the Colonies, Lord Crewe, told both the company and Selborne that '. . . it would be premature to determine what will be the most convenient method of consulting them'.[18] By 1909 the rapid resurrection of Afrikaner political power in the south had made the settlers more wary. C. V. Boyd, who visited Rhodesia, submitted a private report on the situation to J. E. B. Seely, then Parliamentary Under-Secretary of State for the Colonies. Rhodesia, Boyd wrote, seemed to have turned the corner economically, *'Only the scale is so small . . .'*[19] The gap between Rhodes's rhetoric and reality was still enormous. A white population of 100,000 was still, Boyd wrote,

. . . remote and hypothetical . . . What Rhodesia meant to its founder was 'more homes' and larger opportunities for Englishmen . . . That is an objective which must, I am sure, appeal to you and to the Colonial Secretary. If it is not realised then Rhodesia is comparatively a failure, and Englishmen, the democracy of England especially, may lose what, if the resources of the country were in the least understood, would be recognised to be an estate of vast potential value.

It was on the preservation of the English character of Rhodesia that Boyd laid most stress. He felt, and in his judgement the settlers in Rhodesia felt, that 'opportunities for Englishmen' would be lost if incorporation with the south were to take place. 'It was seen that this meant the coming of the *bywoner* . . . when goodbye to the Rhodesia of development and of large-scale British immigration. General Botha was said to be "obsessed" with the idea of Rhodesia . . .' The *bywoner*—the landless Afrikaner poor white—so called because he remained living on the land of his more fortunate brethren, neither a labourer nor an employer of labour, and thus, like the African sharecroppers, rapidly becoming out of place in rural southern Africa, was a bogey to the Rhodesian settlers. Both national and social prejudices combined to make the vision of hordes of illiterate Afrikaners anathema in Rhodesia. Boyd reported that both the two main political parties in the Transvaal believed that the incorporation of Rhodesia was bound to take place within the next four years. Reflecting English-speaking anxiety, he lent his support to a bizarre proposal for a British reserve in Rhodesia which would give to British settlers—as to tribal Africans—needed protection against Afrikaner land hunger, and would be a means of preserving Rhodesia for British settlement even if its present government should change.

The Rhodesian settlers were not only anti-Afrikaner but also anti-Randlord. They were petit-bourgeois nationalists[21] devoutly attached to nationalist symbols and hostile to both capital and labour—to the twin threats of Randlord domination and possible African advance. The settlers perceived Afrikaner advance as inimical as well (though while the two groups espoused opposing nationalisms there was a good deal that was similar in their political positions.) In August 1910 Coghlan put the settler dilemma: were they to be swamped by Afrikaners from the south or by Africans from the north? He realised that incorporation with the Union was inevitable, he said, though he was not as eager as once he had been. 'Rhodes had never regarded Rhodesia as a country outside South Africa or as a black protectorate like Uganda or Nigeria.' It was therefore in line with the tradition of the founder (always a potent argument in settler politics) that Rhodesia should go in with the south. But in South Africa Rhodes's heirs, the Randlord interest, in the soured atmosphere of 1910, had broken with this tradition. As Coghlan put it, the jingos in South Africa advised Rhodesia to have nothing to do with the Union '. . . and urged them to found a new Empire of Monomotapa and link their destinies with the North. If they did the latter they knew it was impossible ever to make this a white man's country'.[21] This indeed was where the Randlords and the settlers parted company: the former were interested not in a white man's country but in a fief where their interests would not be affected by Afrikaner voters with potentially radical demands in the fields of taxation and labour use.

Thus although the future of Rhodesia was discussed at the Union Convention and figures for buying out the company were named, the matter stood over. Hopwood in the Colonial Office recorded that 'Both Botha and Smuts have told me that they intend to stand in the shoes of the Company as soon as they can get them'.[22] There were good reasons for the British government's not forcing the issue in 1909. It was one South African issue which could be left well alone; it would also have been an expensive one to settle. The formation of the Union, which was the coming to fruition of Campbell-Bannerman's conciliation policy, had provoked not only Conservative opposition but also a fringe of Labour and Liberal disquiet. As Walter Long remarked, the government was 'strangely nervous and afraid of opposition on their own side'.[23] Compensation on a large scale for the Chartered Company could well have provoked opposition amongst a wider section of the Liberal party than the small group disturbed at the colour-bar constitution at a time when the government was concerned to palm off the Act of Union with as little political fuss as possible. Moreover shrill settler protest from Rhodesia, fanned by an anti-Union press both inside and outside South Africa, would have disturbed the delicate political truce that had been reached in South Africa during the last stage of negotiations.

4 English South Africa *v.* the liberal solution

Three distinct yet intricately connected administrations existed in southern Africa after May 1910: the British government, the Union government and the British South Africa Company. The latter was active on three political planes and on each was hostile to the Liberal government in Britain. It had connections with the Conservative opposition in Britain; it was a part of the opposition to Botha's new government in South Africa, the existence of which both Conservative and South African English circles blamed upon the Liberal government; and confronted the Liberal government a third time in its role as the governing authority in Rhodesia. To political English South Africa, the men described by Merriman as having '. . . one eye on South Africa and one eye on the English stock exchange',[24] in particular to those closely grouped around the Randlord interest which inspired the English-language press, the Liberal government was closely identified with the squandering of the fruits of the victory of 1902. Gladstone, whose appointment as the first High Commissioner and Governor General of the new Union had been bitterly criticised in England, found on his arrival in South Africa that his position *vis-à-vis* the English-speaking community was a most uneasy one. Milner and Selborne, Conservative appointees with sound imperialist pedigrees, both of whom had found favour with English South Africa, were gone and much regretted. Furthermore the atmosphere of political bonhomie which had followed the Union Convention and the passing of the South Africa Act had soon waned. The preference of the Randlord interest for General Botha as first Union Prime Minister over John X. Merriman, a lifelong opponent of the political influence of Rand and Chartered finance, led to a flirtation between Jameson and Botha in which raider and Boer general contemplated the formation of a 'best man' government, the impossibility of which soon became apparent. The political honeymoon was short and its aftermath bitter: once the wheeling and dealing of Botha and Jameson had failed, their more principled followers took up their natural positions. Hertzog and the High Mining School began to do battle, and the imperial factor found itself caught in the firing line along with the Union government. This meant that the British government had lost its natural political constituency in South Africa. Many of the influential members of the Unionist opposition were bitterly hostile to the conciliation policy, which in their view had left Afrikaners in control of the Union and had abandoned the Rand to the mercy of a growing *backveld* power, and they were concerned to see that the Liberals did not condemn Rhodesia to a similar fate.

As a British observer put it in 1911, 'The "crux" now is . . . Will the Dutch win? If so, goodbye to the dream of South Africa as a prosperous, progressive portion of the Empire.'[25] The first years of union were anxious ones for South African English politicians. Excluded from power, fearing a bitter reaction and yet determined to use their financial power, their chief hope was for a split in the Afrikaner ranks. But, it was pointed out, Afrikanerdom might not split, in which case there must be '. . . help from outside. Opposing pressure must be chiefly from "Home" and from Rhodesia . . .'[26] Botha's interest in Rhodesia was seen as a danger to 'the only British community left' and, as Chaplin put it before Union, Rhodesia could not '. . . sacrifice its individuality and its possibilities as a British makeweight until we know how Unification is going to work, and how far the policy of a Unified Boer Government is consistent with Imperial interests . . .'[27]

The expulsion of Hertzog from the South African Cabinet was an occasion for great relief in imperialist circles. The way to co-operation with a tame Afrikaner leadership now seemed open. Geoffrey Robinson exulted—'. . . we are bound to pat Botha on the back'—and felt that he would be bound to be wide open to pressure from the Unionist opposition.[28] This outburst of enthusiasm in London was matched by a grudging and suspicious acknowledgement by the Unionists in South Africa that their political position had improved, and they applauded both the break with Hertzog and the government's military action against striking miners on the Reef. But it took the crushing of the Afrikaner revolt in 1915 fully to convince them of the reliability of Botha and Smuts. And while the split may have pleased the politicians, to the ordinary English voter in South Africa and Rhodesia it was the occasion of an alarming growth of Afrikaner republicanism, and the consequent exacerbation of English–Afrikaner political relations made them even less willing to trust Afrikaners in power.

English politics in South Africa were a constant source of embarrassment to the High Commissioner. Gladstone wrote to Harcourt that '. . . there are a host of people here who hate the Liberal Government at home, the Botha Government here, and Mr Gladstone's son as Governor General . . .' Of Rhodesians he found that they were 'bitterly hostile to we Liberals . . .' and that Drummond Chaplin was 'about the bitterest Tory partisan anywhere'. Gladstone felt that the policy of the Unionist Party, which he called 'a weak futile British opposition', was 'almost wholly wrong'. In his view it was they, and not Hertzog, who had been responsible for the rapid relapse in English–Afrikaans hostility which had followed union. When advising the king on South African affairs Gladstone's most urgent recommendation was that he should '. . . realise that Hertzog has been made by the Unionist party'.[29] Gladstone also found a 'standing jealousy of *any* interference by the High Commissioner in Rhodesian affairs', a state of affairs which was exacerbated by his action over the so-called 'black peril' cases, concerning assaults by Africans upon white women. Gladstone sparked off hysteria by commuting a death sentence passed by a Rhodesian court, and for the first two years of his High Commissionership virtually all the attention that he gave to Rhodesia concerned the 'black peril' and the administration of justice. This focus of interest was duplicated in both the British and South African parliaments, and in the Union the matter was one of intense public controversy which did nothing to add to Gladstone's popularity. On his first visit to Rhodesia the administration anxiously provided him with an armed guard to protect him from possible settler vengeance in Bulawayo. Gladstone dismissed the guard but felt the sensitivity of his position sufficiently to call his enthusiastic reception from Africans 'most embarrassing'.[30] When the *contretemps* caused by the 'black peril' had passed Gladstone diagnosed that it was the company, and not the settlers, that was determined to minimise imperial influence in Rhodesia. The settlers wanted the High Commissioner to be a Governor, he felt, while the company was determined to prevent this and was not above manoeuvring to create conflict between the settlers and the imperial authorities.[31]

The company, the Rhodesian settlers and the English in South Africa seemed to combine to embarrass the British government. Not only was there the hostile attitude towards the settlement of Afrikaners in Rhodesia but in 1912 the Rhodesian administration produced an ordinance amending the franchise qualifications which underlined the growing gap between Rhodesia and the Union. The intention to amend the franchise qualification dated from 1907, when an ordinance had been proposed to limit the growth of the number of Africans on the voters' roll, an aim which had been connived at by the High Commissioner and not objected to by the Colonial Office, which had subscribed to the view that 'the best way of preserving the native vote in South Africa is to raise the monetary qualifications'.[32] While the franchise question hung in the balance during the making of the Union the Rhodesian ordinance was shelved, though in 1909, when the Rhodesian Legislative Council debated entry into the Union, one of the benefits anticipated by many members was the abolition of the African franchise.[33] In 1911 it was noted that, unlike the Cape members of the Union Convention, who had so vigorously defended the common voters' roll, Rhodesian settlers were hostile to the non-racial franchise, and that the British government would probably have to insist on its retention as one of the terms of Rhodesian entry into the Union.[34] This history of settler hostility to the African franchise had prepared the British government to respond to attacks upon African rights, but when the Rhodesian franchise ordinance reappeared in 1912 it was a form new even in southern Africa's long history of franchise manipulation. The rise in financial qualification was less than it had been in 1907: the target of the ordinance was no longer the African voter but the Afrikaner immigrant from the south. In terms of the new law the ability to read and write in Dutch would no longer enable an aspirant voter to pass the literacy test, as a reading and dictation test in English alone was specified. Afrikaner opinion in the south was outraged: D. F. Malan presented a petition calling for disallowance to Gladstone, taking '. . . a rather extreme line'. Botha denounced the measure, and the Afrikaans press fulminated against the creation of an Afrikaner *'uitlander'* population in Rhodesia.[35]

Gladstone reported to London that there had been considerable hostility in Rhodesia to the principle of bilingualism that had been written into the Act of Union and that, in effect, the ordinance was an assertion against bilingualism.[36] When visiting England Gladstone attempted to persuade the company's board to replace the exclusively English test with a test of proficiency in any European language, a device which would have enabled Afrikaner voters to register without giving Dutch a special status. The company refused: the board, Gladstone reported, '. . . fear Russian Jews and other foreign undesirables'.[37] The company's position was a strong one. It had aligned itself with settler prejudices, and if the ordinance were to be refused assent it could arouse anti-Afrikaans agitation in Rhodesia and paint the imperial factor, not as the protector of settler interests against Chartered capitalism, but as the power which would abandon British interests to placate Afrikaner nationalism. Thus the Colonial Office accepted the proposal and the company had widened the gap between Rhodesia and the Union, its tactics being dictated by its longer-term strategy— which was to prevent the incorporation of Southern Rhodesia into the Union when the charter came up for review in 1914.

Notes

1 I.e. a local assembly but with a permanent executive which was not responsible to it.
2 Gann, *Northern Rhodesia*, chapter 2, especially pp. 78 ff.
3 Wallace to Malcolm, 13 March 1918, Gell papers, B.S.A. 10. The posts of Resident Commissioner and Commander in Chief were amalgamated between 1905 and 1909. The role of the Resident Commissioner is very fully described in C. Palley, *The Constitutional History and Law of Southern Rhodesia, 1888–1965*, Oxford, 1966, chapter 9. Because of an overemphasis on the formal provisions of the order in council and on formal reports and communications, there is an exaggeration in this chapter of the effectiveness of this channel of imperial control in Rhodesia.
4 C. Palley, *Constitutional History*, p. 174, and G.P. Add. MSS, 46005, 6 February 1912; and G.P., 46011, 2 February 1912, 19 February 1912, 2 May 1913 and 14 October 1913.
5 C.O. 537/531, 9 February 1914, secret, minute; thus Stanley, in spite of Harcourt's feeling that his known intimacy with Union Ministers might be a drawback in Rhodesia, was preferred to Sloley, the Resident Commissioner of Basutoland, who was an acknowledged 'native expert'.
6 C.O. 417/451, Selborne to Hopwood, 27 February 1908, and minute by Just.
7 C.O. 417/535, 20 September 1913.

The incomplete Dominion   57

8   C.O. 879/833, Lyttelton to Forbes, 16 August 1904.
9   See Gann, *Southern Rhodesia*, chapter 6; J. D. Fage, 'The achievement of self-government in Rhodesia, 1898–1923', unpublished Ph.D. thesis, Cambridge University, 1949, chapter 4; and R. McGregor, 'Native segregation in Rhodesia', unpublished Ph.D. thesis, London University, 1940, p. 24.
10 C.O. 417/542, 10 August 1908.
11 C.O. 879/932, Crewe to Selborne, 25 February 1909.
12 The company's capital was initially £1 million. In 1898 it was increased to £5 million, and in 1904 to £6 million. Between 1908 and 1912 the directors raised it to £12 million. See Fage, *Achievement*, chapter 5, and Memorandum in C.O. 879/833, July 1907.
13 Winston Churchill, Cab. 39/97, No. 6, 16 January 1909.
14 C.O. 417/462, 10 September 1909.
15 Palley, *Constitutional History*, p. 194, and Selborne Memorandum, pp. 40 ff.
16 L. M. Thompson, *The Unification of South Africa*, Oxford, 1960, pp. 366, 386–7.
17 P. R. Warhurst, 'Rhodesian–South African relations, 1900–23', unpublished paper presented at the third biennial conference of the South African Historical Society, Johannesburg, South Africa, February 1971.
18 C.O. 879/106, 19 January, Crewe to Selborne, telegram, and C.O. 417/465, 29 January 1909, Selborne to Crewe, telegram.
19 Emphasis in original. C.O. 537/522, 3 June 1909.
20 In spite of the 'myth' of the white Rhodesian farmer, the settler population was not rural in the sense that it was identified with the countryside—which was African. White farms were the outposts of, and oriented towards, white towns.
21 Quoted in *African World*, August 1910.
22 Minute in C.O. 417/466, 23 July 1909.
23 Ch. 8/2/2/8, 11 August 1909, Long to Chaplin.
24 Quoted in *African World*, 12 February 1910.
25 H. H. Fyfe, *South Africa Today*, London, 1911, p. 22.
26 Ch. 8/2/1, C. D. Leslie (general manager of Simmer & Jack) to Chaplin, 5 July 1912.
27 Ch. 8/2/1, Chaplin to Gwynne, 21 March 1909.
28 Ch. 8/2/1, 8 January 1913.
29 On the general atmosphere see V. Markham, *The South African Scene*, London, 1913, and Gann, *Southern Rhodesia*, p. 214. For Gladstone's views see G.P. Add. MSS, 45,997, Gladstone to Harcourt, 31 March 1911 and 14 May 1911, and G.P. Add. MSS, 45,999, Gladstone to Harcourt, 30 December 1912 and 6 January 1913.
30 See C. Mallet, *Herbert Gladstone: a Memoir*, London, 1932; P. Mason, *Birth of a Dilemma*, London, 1958, part 3, chapter 2; and J. P. R. Wallis, *One Man's Hand*, London, 1950.
31 G.P. Add. MSS, 45,998, 8 May 1912, and G.P. Add. MSS, 46,011, 14 November 1913.
32 Palley, *Constitutional History*, pp. 170–1.
33 C.O. 417/466, 23 July 1909.

34 C.O. 417/499, 9 October 1911.
35 G.P. Add. MSS, 45,999, Gladstone to Harcourt, and G.P. Add. MSS, 46,006, Botha to Gladstone, 6 July 1912.
36 C.O. 879/989, Gladstone to Harcourt, 15 July 1912.
37 G.P. Add. MSS, 45,999, Gladstone to Harcourt, 19 October 1912.

CHAPTER 3

British supremacy and the charter review

1910–14

According to article 33 of the company's charter of 1889, the British government retained the right to alter or repeal any of the administrative provisions of the charter after an initial period of twenty-five years, or after succeeding periods of ten years. The most natural time, therefore, for the settlement of the outstanding Rhodesian problems was 1914, and it was widely and confidently anticipated by all sections of southern African political opinion after 1910 that when the charter came up for review in 1914 the anomalous position of a territory remaining under company rule would be resolved and that the Union would come into a part of its inheritance. But 1914 came and went, without this consummation; and the result was that the company remained in place and the position of the settlers improved. By default and postponement alone the claims of the Union weakened, and by conscious decision the British government declined to commit the Crown to a greater measure of control over the settlers. Three strategies interplayed—those of the Union, of the company and of the British government—and from the emerging compromise the settlers were strengthened, if only because their pretensions were taken least seriously by all concerned. 1914, in any case, was not a year for great strokes of empire building, or even for tidying up the wearisome details left over from 1910. Both British and South African attention was focused on more dramatic problems.

1 Britain and Southern Rhodesia

The views of the British government, or rather of the Colonial Office, as to the question of the constitutional advance of the settlers deserve close investigation because they illustrate why by 1915 the way seemed to have been prepared for an inevitable advance towards responsible government. Since 1907 the company had refrained from nominating the full quota of official members to the Legislative Council, thereby leaving the settlers with a *de facto* majority. But the company was unwilling to ensconce a settler majority *de jure* without additional financial protection. After a protracted wrangle the company accepted an order in council which gave a settler majority but which prevented it from considering any appropriation of public revenues not first put to it by the Administrator, and from proceeding without the Administrator's consent with any ordinance interfering with the land or other rights of the company.[1] Thus a settler majority had been created while the substance of financial control and the company's interests remained unaffected. The British government had put pressure on the company in 1911 to concede this majority. What were its motives? It is certain that it was not seen as a step towards responsible government for the settlers. As one minute put it, the settlers were unlikely to use their majority to challenge the company seriously because

... if the elected members mean to make Chartered government impossible ... the only possible result would be absorption in the Union ... for none would seriously propose to rule S. Rhodesia as a Crown Colony under the Colonial Office, or to erect it into a responsibly governed colony outside the Union.[2]

If union for the time being was impossible, the only alternative was the charter. The concession of the settler majority was not a step to anywhere but a means of ensuring smoother running of the extant system: a majority conceded to forestall the demand for an end to company rule.

In early 1912, when considering anti-charter agitation among the settlers, Lambert and Anderson, the Permanent Under-Secretary for the Colonies set down the arguments on which they based British government strategy. Lambert thought of two immediate precedents— both in South Africa: the Natal constitution of 1893 and the Lyttelton constitution.[3] He wrote:

It is a form of constitution which is difficult to work for very long because the Executive instead of being as it is under responsible government, which means historically speaking and in fact, responsible to a parliamentary majority— responsible to the legislature, tends always to get out of touch with it, or ... the legislature, not being responsible for the leaders, falls naturally into a critical attitude ...

If the Crown substituted itself for the company the critical turbulence of the settlers would be vented on it, and there was no political advantage in that. As Lambert pointed out, an executive nominated by the Crown '... would almost certainly sooner or later have to resist the wishes of the

Legislature on some colour question'. There was no reason for the Crown to assume such onerous responsibilities, especially as it could not hasten through this stage towards responsible government because '. . . the experience of Natal does not encourage the setting up of small responsible governments with big native populations'.[4] In any case, as Anderson pointed out, a move towards representative government for the settlers would not be an advance for them, as they already had representative government, 'except that the British South Africa Company stands in the position of the Crown'.[5]

The discussion was in terms of an orthodox and mechanistic view of imperial constitutional development—in terms of the proud progress from Crown colony to Dominion status. Illustrations and examples were drawn almost entirely from South African experience, where no adaptation had previously been made from the white empire model to fit it to the southern African situation.[6] Within the limited range of alternatives considered, representative government offered a way of reconciling the settlers' demands for participation with the responsibility of the British government for Africans. Yet, precisely because of the possibility that these responsibilities might have to be exercised, representative government was shunned. The British government was unwilling to eliminate the company, thereby leaving open the possibility of a naked confrontation between itself and the settlers. 'We are,' Anderson wrote, 'between hammer and anvil often enough already . . . and have no cause to multiply opportunities for occupying that position.'[7] Both responsible government and admission into the Union would, it was admitted, vitiate British control over African affairs, but both were preferable to any form of Crown colony which would '. . . impose on the Colonial Office the task of governing what is now a comparatively large white community. This course may be dismissed as impracticable.'[8] Thus a Crown colony could be 'dismissed as impracticable' and 'no one would seriously propose' responsible government. Furthermore a settlement with the company in order to achieve either of these devoutly unwished ends would be very expensive. Lambert pointed out that the company had spent over £8 million in Rhodesia and it claimed that public works and deficit expenditure which could be refundable accounted for half this. In addition the company's claims to the lands would be hard to defeat. He concluded that

> . . . with a population of 24,000 whites, it is difficult to see how Southern Rhodesia could possibly afford to expropriate the Company, whose claims are likely to be such, and their position so strong, that they can at present only be got rid of if a third party—which must be either His Majesty's Government or the

Union—intervenes ... Southern Rhodesia is geographically and socially contiguous with the Union, and it is impossible to doubt that ultimately it must be admitted to the Union.[9]

If settler opinion precluded this for the time being what more convenient course was there than for the company to hold the ring until the Union government could settle the financial issue, so sparing the imperial exchequer and serving the long-term ends of British policies in South Africa?

2 The Union and Northern Rhodesia

The British government also had to formulate its attitude towards the future of Northern Rhodesia. A Colonial Office memorandum of 1911 mulled rather gloomily over the possibilities inherent in section 150 of the South Africa Act, pointing out that Northern Rhodesia '... will have to be governed for years as a tropical dependency—a task for which the Union Government will be ill adapted except in the improbable event of the Cape ideals of native administration obtaining a permanent mastery in its administration.'[10] The best way for the North to go into the Union, it was suggested, would be under the terms of the schedule to the Act of Union, but if the schedule were to be applied here it would be difficult to resist a demand from the Union that it be applied at the same time to Basutoland and Bechuanaland. Little further thought was given to the matter until April 1913, when Gladstone pointed out that if the British government meant the following year to exercise its powers under article 33 of the charter it would have to deal with the north as well. Gladstone repeated, in effect, Milner's analysis of 1899 in which he had drawn the boundary of self-governing Africa at the Zambesi and had predicted that Northern Rhodesia would evolve along the lines of Uganda or Nigeria.[11] Gladstone wrote that, apart from regions in the area of the Zambesi and the Kafue, the north was 'not a white man's country ... Why not buy out the Company north of the Zambesi while we have only a few thousand whites to deal with and join it administratively with Nyasaland?'[12] His suggestion was greeted coolly by Harcourt, who saw no reason for interfering with the north if it could be avoided and who was acutely aware of the political claims of the Union. The British government could not, he wrote, 'treat the Union Government as not having the ultimate reversion of the territory, for they can claim that the terms of the South Africa Act led them to expect this, though they cannot expect to enter upon their heritage in Northern Rhodesia until Southern Rhodesia has joined the Union.'[13] While section 150 of the South Africa Act was permissive it did give the Union a political expectancy to which the Colonial Secretary gave more importance than the Zambesi-line analysis. Harcourt's letter drew from Gladstone a reply of sharp disagreement. It was, he wrote,

... a view which I did not know had taken much hold ... even as regards the natives in the present area of the Union, matters are in a most embryonic state. We are short of administrators, brains, experience, character and of all that goes to sound administration. Time will no doubt alter this but I should look with consternation on the rule of Pretoria and Cape Town in Northern Rhodesia.

While he accepted that the south should go into the Union, Gladstone belittled the administrative authority that the company had acquired from the northern concessions, which was, he said, 'of a limited and provisional kind'. He ended by pleading that the chance presented by the coming review of the charter should be taken to retrieve Northern Rhodesia from its entanglement with the south.[14] Harcourt played briefly with the idea of sending an enquiring commissioner to Rhodesia, but it was abandoned for fear of fostering the impression that the British government would appear as a *deus ex machina* in 1914, when in fact it had no solution to offer. Anderson summed up the permanent officials' attitude to the south, which was that the settlers and the company were to be left to work out their own solution. 'Do not let us meddle if we can keep out.'[15] But in the case of the north there was no white representative body to provide a cover for imperial inaction. Hartman Just remembered Parliament and pointed out that members might feel that the time had come to normalise the position of Northern Rhodesia and to place it under the Colonial Office like other British possessions in black Africa. The company, Just pointed out, was meeting the deficit and Parliament would realise that it would not be doing so without expecting to profit from the territory eventually. Furthermore the company at present could exercise a free hand with the labour supply from north to south, which would not be as easy if Northern Rhodesia were in other hands. 'The question is whether we are doing our duty by the natives ...'[16] He recalled Selborne's suggestion that Barotseland be administered directly, like the other black protectorates, and though he anticipated that the Union might object to an extension of imperial authority in Northern Rhodesia the nub of his argument was that though Southern Rhodesia might be left alone some justification would be required if the position in the north was to be left undisturbed.

We have to view the matter from the standpoint of 'locking up' a large portion of South Africa in the hands of a commercial association ... In 1889 the Government was not prepared to go to the House of Commons for money for administering Rhodesia, but times have greatly changed since then. We are now prepared to face the white man's burden.[17]

Whether or not Just overestimated parliamentary sensitivity to the anomoly of the Chartered Company (one must take into account that the attention of the Congo reformers would in all likelihood have been turned more fully on Rhodesia) cannot be decided, as the issue was eventually wholly obscured when the charter review coincided with the European crisis in mid-1914. What radical attention was paid to the company's affairs in Parliament was channelled by the Aborigines Protection Society into land questions in Southern Rhodesia. When Northern Rhodesia did specifically raise interest at Westminster it was not through the agency of radicals in the Commons activated by concern for African interests but through Northern Rhodesian landowners in the Lords, Wolverton and the Duke of Westminster. Thus prior to charter review in 1914 the Union's right of reversion and the possibility of buying out the company in the north and establishing a more 'tropical' colony were both canvassed but the only reason for seriously considering action was possible parliamentary pressure, which never came.

3 The company, the settlers and the Union

So went the nice calculations of the Colonial Office officials, which in the absence of the necessity for a political initiative came to serve as policy. In the world outside the Colonial Office other forces were jockeying for position. The company, aware of Liberal political hostility but underestimating official tentativeness, began to campaign tenaciously both in Rhodesia and in Britain against any disturbance of its position. Lurid hints of a Liberal desire to force the loyal settlers into a Union dominated by republican Hertzogism began to appear in Conservative newspapers.[18] It was to the settlers, however, that the company directed its main political offensive. In Salisbury, Rochfort Maguire, one of the senior directors, produced a carefully considered company statement on future financial policy which was part of a two-pronged approach to make company rule more acceptable to the settlers. He proposed writing off Rhodesian liability for the deficit of over £7 million (the company's estimate) if no further doubt were to be cast by the settlers on the company's title in 'all the assets' of the country.[19] Maguire also outlined the company's vision of the past and future of Rhodesia in a way which was calculated to appeal to the settlers and which ignored the country's ties with the south. The 'two outstanding features' in Rhodesia were the company and the white population. The aim of the company's inititative and self-sacrifice was '... to place in this country a white population, to build it up in strength and numbers to fit it to take its place among the people of the Empire ... Your institutions should broaden slowly down until your self government is obtained ...'[20] In return, in short, for settler recognition of the legitimacy of the company's efforts and its right to profit therefrom the company would recognise and become patrons of the settler aspirations to self-government and would protect them from the imperial stepmother who sought to force them into the Union.

The company's efforts in this regard were to prove self-defeating. They were unable to overcome settler suspicion, though they did help to bolster the anti-Union political climate. In addition they alarmed the British government and provoked it into taking action which had not been seriously contemplated. For it was felt in Whitehall that if the settlers did agree to do a deal with the company recognition of the company's claim to own the lands of Rhodesia could create a position in which ultimate union with the south would be made very much more difficult. If there was to be a settlement of the land and revenue controversies Whitehall would have to ensure that it was one which did not prejudice the British position over ultimate union with the south and one which would not be at the expense of its political influence with the settlers. The British government had also to ensure that the political aftermath of the failure of the company and the settlers to come to terms would not be a bitter campaign over unresolved issues which would lead to a settler demand for Crown colony government. Finally, Britain's political obligations to the Union precluded a strengthening of the company at the Union's expense. Thus the British government was flushed from the wings and moved towards a conflict with the company over its land rights.

The second part of the company's initiative was its Land Settlement Scheme, which was its response both to a Legislative Council resolution calling for a plan to encourage immigration and to its own long-term needs in regard to land. The company proposed to promote settlement within a twenty-five mile radius from the railway line. It recommended the creation of a Land Settlement Board which would buy land and prepare it for settlement and proposed that the company should lend to the Board the necessary capital of £250,000.[21] Gladstone urged

Whitehall to reject the proposals. He pointed out that with the bait of increased immigration the company was proposing to lend money to the settlers to buy land that it claimed as its own. The scheme assumed the company's title, and if this were accepted by the settlers it would detrimentally affect the position of both the Union and the British government when the time came to wind up the company's administration.[22] Significantly at this stage neither the openly self-interested nature of the company's scheme nor Gladstone's objections to it moved the Colonial Office from the position it had taken up earlier in the year. Harcourt put the issue to Gladstone:

. . . on the one hand we have the British South Africa Company, whose shareholders have spent millions on the country, for which they have never had a penny of dividend, and who naturally . . . regard themselves as the legal owners of the land. On the other hand we have a white population of 20,000 which pays taxes enough to keep the ordinary administration going and no more, and which, equally naturally, thinks it should control the waste land. The Colonial Office and the Union are necessarily somewhat outside these matters, and I do not think it would be wise for us to stop any settlement to which the two interested parties may voluntarily come.[23]

Harcourt saw no reason for changing what had been the policy of both Lyttelton and Crewe, which had been to regard an agreement between the settlers and the company as the proper solution. This was a far-reaching acknowledgement of the claims of capital in Rhodesia; it was against Lord Durham's cardinal principle that the imperial factor should control 'the disposal of public lands'; and it showed a surprising willingness on the part of a Secretary of State supposedly hostile to the Chartered Company to recognise it as the owner of all Rhodesia as long as the British government could keep clear of a local involvement.

It was at this stage that General Botha indicated that the Union was more than merely an interested spectator of the events in Rhodesia leading to the charter review. In a speech at Nylstroom in the Transvaal he told the audience of '. . . this greatest object of ours—to get a united South Africa as far north as possible'.[24] The speech took Gladstone by surprise, and he protested to Botha that if the Union was going to ask for the inclusion of Rhodesia in 1914 this would represent a new policy. He warned that without the consent of the settlers inclusion was not practicable and that Botha's speech would probably have the effect of making the question of union the dominant one at the coming Rhodesian elections. Indeed, as Gladstone told Harcourt, '. . . it has raised the whole of the Rhodesian and Unionist press'.[25] While Gladstone had thought initially that the speech was 'an unconsidered *obiter dictum* meant to tickle the ears of the North East Transvaalers' (who were a group with a direct interest in expansion into their immediate hinterland) Botha's reply showed that he had considered the matter in the full context of relations between Rhodesia and the Union since 1910. He wrote:

> You will remember even when the time when our Union was being established I stated repeatedly that in my opinion the Union would never be complete until Rhodesia and all the Protectorates had been included. In regard to the Protectorates... special arrangements were entered into. In regard to Rhodesia, however, no such agreement exists. What I have been feeling very keenly of late, however, is that instead of a movement towards union between the two countries being perceptible, there is undoubtedly a decided current in the contrary direction... This to my mind is a most unfortunate and unsatisfactory state of affairs. If something cannot be done to convince the public mind in both countries that a union between them must come eventually and that the way to that consummation should gradually be paved, union may become impossible for ever... I am sure that future generations in South Africa would have to pay the penalty dearly for our short-sightedness.[26]

The Union had no concrete proposals to make at present, he told Gladstone, but public opinion in England and South Africa could be drawn in the right direction.

If the intervention was not made to herald a definite request for the transfer of Rhodesia to the Union, what was Botha's motive? There were good political reasons for his pronouncement. The position of the South African Party in the centre of Union politics was being eroded from both sides, and the clash over the Bechuanaland Protectorate[27] earlier in the year and the continuing polarisation of Union politics underlined Botha's need to weaken the political position of the British South Africa Company. Just as Hertzog was able to make political capital out of the existence of the company, so the company was in a position to exploit Hertzogism in order to maintain its political position. The long-term aim of union could not be achieved as long as this was so, and Botha therefore did not want 1914 to pass without a loosening of the company's hold. Although his intervention did push the British government into action designed to pave the ultimate way to union, he also succeeded in giving political ammunition to the company. As Malcolm wrote, Botha's speech ended toleration of the idea of entry into the Union. 'To have Rhodesia dangled before the eyes of a gathering of backveld "bijwoners" as a happy hunting ground in which to shoot game and propogate malaria is not an attractive proceeding from the point of view of the settlers here.'[28] This political damage proved more lasting than the practical achievement, and it was the responsible government cause that was the ultimate beneficiary.

As a result of Botha's initiative Gladstone urged London again to come to grips with the land question. He warned that the company was not in a compromising mood and that it had been advised that only the Crown could question its title and, believing that the Crown would not do so, asserted its ownership with confidence. Gladstone pointed out that the company was building its policy on its assumption of title. The Maguire proposals meant that development not met by ordinary revenue would now have to be paid for by company loans, and by the land scheme the company would be providing further loans to buy vacant lands: all the loans would have to be paid back when the Chartered administration was wound up. If the company's title were to go unchallenged now the company could '... in ten or twenty years' time hold a political position in relation to admission, prejudicial to Imperial policy in South Africa, with the possibility of immense profits at the expense of the Union of South Africa and of the Southern Rhodesian people.' The arrangements for admission into the Union would then be an enormous financial operation, with the benefits going to the company.[29] Moved partly by the picture of rampant Chartered capitalism, and partly by the reminder that the company's land scheme involved the creation of a public debt which the British government had hitherto always refused to allow in Rhodesia, Anderson spelled out a change of mind in the Colonial Office. The land scheme, which he had been prepared to accept if the settlers would, he now called '. . . a specious proposal for developing what the Company claims as its private property at the expense of the community'. A public debt could not be created until the company's administrative and private assets had been clearly separated. It was essential, he concluded, that this should be determined before the review of the charter.[30] Eighteen months earlier Anderson had made the tentative suggestion, which he now resurrected, that the question of the company's assets should be submitted to the Privy Council.[31] Harcourt was persuaded that the matter could not remain undetermined indefinitely. Thus the earlier decision was reversed: the company's scheme, which had not initially provoked the British government, had been re-examined only after Botha's protest, and as a result had been rejected.

The prospect of a settlement at law was not entirely welcome to the Colonial Office. Doubts as to the validity of any Crown claim had been one of the reasons for the refusal over the past six years to bring matters to a head. The legal position of the Crown *vis-à-vis* Rhodesia was uncertain. It exercised a protectorate under the Foreign Jurisdiction Act,[32] but the implications of this in regard to ownership of land was unknown. The company faced the proposed Privy Council reference more happily, and continued until deliverance of the judgement to believe in the likelihood of its victory. As there was no set procedure for a special reference of the type that had been agreed upon, the Colonial Office also had to consider what part the Crown would play in the proceedings. It felt that the Crown should not be a disputant, that the Legislative Council of Rhodesia should constitute itself as plaintiff, while a watching brief would be held for the High Commissioner on behalf of the Africans.[33] Once entangled in the case, Harcourt was anxious to get it over with. 'Time is of the essence in this matter,' he wrote. 'We *must* get the reference *through* the Privy Council before the Long Vacation.'[34] Early in March the company was told that the Crown anticipated intervening only if necessary on behalf of the Africans, and the Law Officers were told that 'His Majesty's Government have at no time advanced any claim to the lands on behalf of the Crown'.[35]

Harcourt's new strategy, which was to cut through the title tangle before arriving at a decision on the question of charter review, failed hopelessly. For once the case had been removed from the speculation of Colonial Office officials into the professional hands of the Law Officers the advice which they gave upset the officials' plans to keep the Crown uninvolved. The Law Officers, after a long delay, gave the Crown the advice which the company's lawyers had already given the company. They warned that in cases where a question of title was at issue the party with a better title succeeded, and it was therefore vital that if the company's claim was to be tested effectively it should not be challenged by a claimant who had no title at all. In other words, if the settlers brought the company to court the court would have to decide for the company. It could not declare that the land was Crown land unless the Crown itself contested the company's claim.[36] A second cause of delay was that the representation of an African case was taken up by the Aborigines Protection Society. Disturbed by the Liebig scandal of the previous year, and informed that as the Crown was the normal representative of African interests, no special steps were being taken to claim the land on behalf of Africans, the society began to consider ways of intervention.[37]

While the land case languished an election was held for the Rhodesian Legislative Council. The campaign was fought between those who wanted a change to a form of Crown colony government and those who, for varying reasons, wanted a continuation of the charter. These latter were made up of an alliance between the company and those who had formerly been its most outspoken enemies—the advocates of responsible government. The coldness of the imperial stepmother was an initial handicap to the Crown colony candidates, and in addition Botha's initiative was a political gift to the supporters of the charter. Coglan, the settler spokesman, expressed the attitude of the 'pro-charter' candidates when he told a meeting that '. . . it made one almost shudder when one looked back on the hopes which he shared in common with all statesmen in South Africa, to find how far from realisation they were . . . the reason for that was Hertzogism, racialism, and, above all, bilingualism.'[38] Jameson, to the great indignation of Harcourt, quoted to the electors a confidential letter written to the company by the Colonial Office in 1911 in which entry to the Union was envisaged as the natural result of the ending of Chartered rule, and he conjured up the spectre of Rhodesia being pushed unwillingly into the 'vortex' of the Union's strife, racial and otherwise.[39] The Union card was the ace of trumps, unbeatable no matter who played it. 'God forbid . . . that we should have to say, "Rhodesia will fight and Rhodesia will be right", but if there is any attempt made to put this country under the heel of the Union of South Africa you will know what to do . . .' proclaimed Hawksley, the company's solicitor, in Salisbury, echoing the militant rebelliousness of the Ulsterite circles in which the company's directors moved.[40] The result of the election was a clean sweep for the 'pro-charter' candidates, though most of them claimed openly that they were primarily against the Union, or against Crown colony government, and only *faute de mieux* for the charter.[41]

The result was a considerable relief to the Colonial Office, which had silently hoped that the campaign for Crown colony government would fail. But the settlers did not want an unconditional continuance of Chartered rule, and the British government was beginning to be anxious about the fact that the charter gave no further opportunity for review for another ten years, which would limit its freedom of action to make changes without the consent of the company until 1924.[42] Once the election had passed, old settler grievances with the charter re-emerged, and the Legislative Council in May 1914 passed a resolution requesting greater control over expenditure and the right to raise loans for public works.[43] The company jibbed at giving the council control over the allocation of revenue, protesting that financial responsibility and the power to spend could not be separated, and in this it had the support of the Colonial Office.[44] But the company did indicate that it had no objection to 'the form of government known as responsible government' being established in Rhodesia during the next ten-year period. Anderson proposed agreement to this but wanted an arrangement whereby the initiative would lie with the Crown so that it would not be dependent solely on the company's permission to cancel the administrative provisions of the charter. Harcourt hesitated, fearing that to do this would offend the Union, and he picked upon an obvious omission in the plan of Anderson and the company. 'It will postpone any less responsible form of self-government for ten years,' he wrote, and also seemed to preclude inclusion in the Union for a similar period. But Anderson urged that union should be left entirely to the Rhodesian electors, and that under the charter Rhodesia already had 'a very liberal constitution' which could easily be altered, if desired, by order in council. The only point in the constitution which was secured by the charter, he wrote,

... is that the Executive is appointed by the Company ... whereas if the Charter was terminated the Secretary of State would become directly responsible for the appointment and doings of the Executive. It was agreed that we did not desire this, and that from our point of view it was infinitely better that the Charter should remain till Rhodesia was ripe either for responsible government or entry into the Union[45]

In other words, to all intents and purposes the settlers already had representative government, and the only substantial change not involving entry into the Union was, as Lambert put it, that 'the offices now held by the British South Africa Company's officials must be held by the elected members'—responsible government.[46]

Anderson therefore proposed that a supplemental charter be issued, allowing the British government to repeal the administrative provisions of the charter when the Legislative Council asked for this to be done by an absolute majority, in order to '... establish the form of government known as Responsible Government'. The company had no objection to this, Lambert reported, but would like to 'let in a Crown Colony or a Lyttelton constitution'. But Anderson remained firm, both Harcourt and the company acquiesced, and the Permanent Under-Secretary's single-minded logic prevailed to keep the door to increased imperial responsibility over the settlers closed.[47] The supplemental charter was not intended as a promise of responsible government; it was to give to the British government and to the Legislative Council a means of overriding possible obstruction by the company should it be desired in the next ten years to change the administrative provisions of the charter. The aim of the British government in working for the supplemental charter had been to increase its freedom of action; the result was to limit it. The discussions which had already taken place in the Colonial Office had come to the conclusion that representative government was out of the question, and the British government could hardly have made further provision for union (already provided for in the South Africa Act) after an election which had so recently and so firmly rejected this. The result was that, as Anderson put it, 'the only contingency we have to provide for is "responsible government".' The severe limitations which this could have politically were forgotten by officials who concentrated their energies on getting the company to concede the initiative with regard to the winding up of its administrative power. The company was prepared to make this concession: during the recent elections it had presented itself as the guardian of settler self-government against the Union, and it looked forward to winning the land case, in which case control over the administration would not be vital to the protection of its interests. Thus the supplemental charter was issued. In it no step was taken to sever the north from the south. Harcourt suggested the inclusion of a provision enabling the British government to relieve the company of the administration of Northern Rhodesia, but Lambert and Anderson poured cold water on the proposal and Harcourt let it drop,[48] so leaving the company to carry on in the north as before.

Notes

1 The correspondence is printed in Cd. 7264; see also Palley, *Constitutional History*, chapter 10, and Gann, *Southern Rhodesia*, pp. 212 ff. The 1911 order, says Gann, '. . . gave the Company all the protection shareholders could possibly desire against white backveld radicals.'
2 C.O. 417/495, 30 November 1911.
3 The Lyttelton constitution was the proposed representative government constitution for the Transvaal abandoned by the Liberal government when it decided to advance the colony straight to responsible government.
4 C.O. 417/512, 22 May 1912, Minutes.
5 C.O. 417/513, 26 August 1912, Minutes.
6 Comparison with the very different attitude towards some other colonies underlines the way in which Rhodesian development was discussed purely in terms of the white empire model. This was not the only model, and progress through the stages towards responsible government was by no means automatic. H. A. Will points out that in the cases of Jamaica and Mauritius there was a complete absence of mention in the Colonial Office records of responsible government and that the Office '. . . favoured constitutional change on the grounds of administrative expediency rather than as a stage in a long-term process of constitutional development'. ('Problems of

constitutional reform in Jamaica, Mauritius and Trinidad', *English Historical Review*, October 1966.)
7   Harcourt papers, C.O., No. 2, Memorandum, 6 August 1913.
8   C.O. 879/110, No. 989; see also Palley, *Constitutional History*, p. 194.
9   C.O. 879, No. 989, Memorandum.
10 C.O. 417/499, 9 October 1911.
11 Gann, *Northern Rhodesia*, p. 129.
12 G.P. Add. MSS, 45,999, Gladstone to Harcourt, 29 April 1913.
13 G.P. Add. MSS, 46,000, Harcourt to Gladstone, 20 August 1913.
14 G.P. Add. MSS, 46,000, Gladstone to Harcourt, 11 September 1913.
15 C.O. 417/524, 25 June 1913, Minutes.
16 The British government controlled the southward flow of labour from the Nyasaland Protectorate.
17 C.O. 417/537, 28 July 1913, Minute.
18 E.g. the *Morning Post*, 21 April 1913.
19 *Rhodesia Herald*, 24, March 1913, and G.P. 46, 005, f. 217, memorandum by Rodwell. The company also suggested new arrangements for the financing of public works for which, under the charter, it was responsible.
20 *Rhodesia Herald*, 24 March 1913.
21 *Proposals for the Encouragement of Land Settlement and Immigration*, B.S.A.C., 1913.
22 C.O., 417/525, 12 October 1913.
23 C.O. 417/525, 12 October 1913.
24 G.P. Add. MSS, 46,000, 1 November 1913.
25 G.P. Add. MSS, 46,000, Gladstone to Harcourt, 6 November 1913, and G.P. Add. MSS, 46,007, Gladstone to Botha, 2 November 1913.
26 G.P. Add. MSS, 46,000, Gladstone to Harcourt, 6 November 1913, and 46,007, Gladstone to Botha, 7 November 1913.
27 See below, chapter 4.
28 Ch. 8/2/2/11, Malcolm to Chaplin, 5 November 1913.
29 C.O., 417/526, 13 November 1913.
30 C.O. 417/526, 13 November 1913.
31 C.O. 417/512, 22 May 1912.
32 For an explanation of the different legal varieties of protectorate see Palley, *Constitutional History*, chapter 4. In the cases of *R.* v. *Staples* (1899, Privy Council, unreported) and *R.* v. *Crewe* (1910), 2 K.B. 576 (see Palley, p. 68), the Privy Council had indicated that protectorates of the type exercised in Rhodesia made the latter foreign and not British territory in as much as the Crown had power and jurisdiction but not 'that absolute ownership which was signified by the word *dominium* in Roman law'. In so far as the Bechuanaland Protectorate was concerned the Crown had told the company that the Crown did not consider itself to be the owner of the land. Palley, p. 81.
33 C.O. 417/550, 2 February 1914.
34 *Ibid.;* italics in original.
35 C.O., 417/550, 2 March 1914, encl. C.O. to Law Officers, 21 March 1914.
36 C.O. 885/16, Law Officers to C.O., 15 May 1914.
37 The information was given in answer to a question asked in the Commons by Macneill; see Parliamentary Debates, Commons, 11 March 1914.

38 *Bulawayo Chronicle*, 25 February 1914; 'racialism' meant English–Afrikaner strife.
39 See Cd. 7264, where the correspondence is printed.
40 C.O. 417/523, 4 December 1914. Hawksley's Ulsterism reflects the company's close connections with those circles in which there was a militant willingness to defy the Liberal government, and it is to here, rather than to settler determination, that any early advocation of settler resistance can be traced.
41 See J. D. Fage, *Achievement,* chapter 7, and Cd. 7708, where the results are analysed. Radicals in the House of Commons had been hoping for a resounding rejection of the company, and Macneill asked for an enquiry into the strength of its electoral patronage. He was told that there was no question of 'dissecting the quality and quantity of a mandate', but the Colonial Office officials who were doing precisely this noted that the new council represented only two thirds of 53 per cent of the electorate. (Parliamentary Debates, Commons, 31 March 1914.)
42 C.O., 417/526, 11 November 1913.
43 Cd. 7708, 1915, No. 2, 16 May 1914, and Palley, *Constitutional History*, pp. 203–6.
44 Cd. 7708, No. 6, and C.O. 417/540, October 1914, Minutes.
45 C.O. 417/540, 14 May 1914, Minutes.
46 C.O. 417/540, October 1914, Minutes.
47 C.O. 417/540, 14 May 1914, Minutes, and Palley, *Constitutional History*, p. 205.
48 C.O., No. 6, Harcourt papers, 6 August 1914.

CHAPTER 4

Separation in southern Africa

1 The Bechuanaland Protectorate

Since the 1880s the area over which the British government had proclaimed the Bechuanaland Protectorate had been of considerable strategic significance. Lying to the north of the Cape Colony, it was its 'natural' sphere of northward expansion and the vital communicating link with the territories to the north of the Transvaal, and imperial control over the area hemmed in Afrikaner westward expansion. The Bechuanaland area had been included within the sphere of the British South Africa Company's charter, but after it had been used as a launching pad for the Jameson raid the decision was finally taken not to hand over to the company the right to administer the territory. By 1909 it was accepted that the nascent Union would be the heir to imperial responsibilities in the protectorate, but the company's ambitions were far from satisfied. Twenty years earlier three forces, imperial trusteeship, white ambitions and the charter, had contended over Bechuanaland[1] and these forces were still in the field. In August 1909, while the South Africa Bill was still in the Westminister pipeline, the company formally applied to the Crown for title and possession of the unalienated areas of the protectorate not already set aside as reserves.[2] This claim ushered in a protracted struggle between the ambitions of the company and those of the Union government, and between these and the imperial government in the role of protector.

The company's claim was based on a series of pledges which sprang from its charter but which had been redefined after the imperial government's decision not to transfer the administration of the territory. These gave the company preferential but not exclusive rights to both land and minerals outside the reserves; while the company was to be given first option, the Crown was under no obligation to make concessions.³ Early in 1899 it had been decided to hand over the railway belt to the company for development. After the war the vacant lands in the protectorate were vested in the Crown by order in council, and in 1905 the company was given title to blocks of land in the Lobatsi, Gaberones and Tuli areas.⁴ Thus before 1909 concessions to the company had been piecemeal, and the Colonial Office's reply to the company's new initiative was consistent with this. It avoided closing with the company on the legal issues, replying that the submission of proposals for the development of the unoccupied portions of the protectorate would be a condition precedent to consideration of an application for title to any part of them, so making it clear that the total cession for which the company was asking was not being entertained.⁵

With the formation of the Union in the offing the British government was not prepared to disturb the *status quo*. Earlier in the year the company had asked that the administration of the Tuli block be handed to it, and Selborne had supported the proposal on the grounds that it would relieve a native territory of a white area. But the High Commissioner was told that 'His Majesty's Government must maintain the assets of the Protectorate unimpaired, since to do otherwise might afford ground for complaint from the Union Government . . .'⁶ The acknowledged position of the Union as *ultima haeres,* however distant the date of succession might be, was to be the major stumbling block in the way of the company's aspirations. The two initiatives made by the company during 1909 when the future of the protectorate was under consideration were both rebuffed, but if the company was not to get a wholesale concession of lands, or even a piecemeal addition to the territory it already had, it was not prepared to acquiesce in the imperial government's interpretation of its duty as protecting power. Mere protection, it told the Colonial Office, was not enough. '. . . the best and quickest means for elevating and educating the native population and of enabling it to derive adequate benefit from the facilities that are now open to it is to bring it into closer touch with European ideas and surroundings . . .'⁷ The company realised that the consequences of a concession made to it by the imperial government would be an uproar in humanitarian circles and that politically the way had to be prepared by airing the case for a version of protection which implied the duty to develop and thus present the government's policy as positively harmful to African interests. This statement of attitude heralded a third and more persistent approach for a large-scale transfer of concrete assets in the protectorate.

The moves of 1909 were largely tactical—to stake out a claim in the protectorate's future. By 1911 the *détente* between English political forces in South Africa and Botha and Smuts was broken. Furthermore the financially lean decade through which the company had passed was over. It told the Colonial Office that it was prepared to add to its investment of £1,350,000 in the protectorate if it was assured of '... the full benefit of its legitimate expectations'.[8] Once again it asked for full title to the 'unoccupied lands' in the protectorate, offering in return an assurance that the resources of the protectorate would not be allowed to lie fallow. It closed with a *caveat* on the political future.

> The Directors do not now advert to the Company's claim to be eventually entrusted with the administration of the Protectorate, but they deem it their duty to place on record their expectation that His Majesty's Government will not place it outside its power to fulfill the pledges given to the Company.[9]

The implication was that transfer to the Union would be incompatible with those pledges.

Official reaction was far from favourable. Possible African objections were not uppermost in officials' minds: though the Tswana chiefs were known to have been deeply disturbed by the formation of the Union, it was considered that 'The pledge to preserve the *status quo* in the Protectorate can scarcely be accepted as a bar now that Union has come'.[10] Clearly the provisions of the schedule to the South Africa Act did envisage change, but it would be change under the aegis of the Union, and it was the probability of objections from the Union government that carried weight. The company was accordingly informed that, in view of the provisions of the South Africa Act, and of the coming review of the charter, it was not possible to modify the decision not to transfer the administration. Nevertheless the fundamental difference between the imperial government and the company remained: the company did not acknowledge that the lapsed administrative transfer and the wholesale land cessions were connected, while the government's view was that the company's hopes of land had dissolved with its administrative prospects.

At the end of 1911 the company's development proposals reached the Colonial Office. They involved building a light railway westward across the protectorate at a proposed overall expenditure of £280,000.[11] The Colonial Office was deeply suspicious: the proposals were related to the company's desire to strengthen itself before charter review, as there were clearly no prospects of mineral discovery. What the directors had done was comply with a request for a concrete development proposal but in such a way as to maximise the attendant advantages. As they explained in their accompanying letter, so large an expenditure could only be contemplated if they were assured in advance of the ownership of the whole of the area rendered valuable by it.

Simultaneously the company returned to the attack on the question of mining concessions and the proposed Mining Proclamation for the protectorate. The imperial government had originally, as a protecting power, made no claim to mineral rights in the protectorate. These rights they had recognised as vesting in the chiefs, and in 1892 Lord Ripon, the then Secretary of State for the Colonies, had undertaken that imperial officials would use their best endeavours to induce the chiefs to grant concessions to the company. By 1911 the company held a number of mineral concessions, none of which had led to profitable workings, while for several years the imperial government had been contemplating a mining proclamation which would once and for all cut away the company's claim to be the residuary holder of all mineral rights in the protectorate. Once again the Colonial Office's attitude was that rights which would have adhered to the company if it had been a government had now no application, and it stressed that the 'preferential but not exclusive formula' applied to the company's mineral as well as to its land rights.[12]

It was in this context that the future of the protectorate was discussed in 1911 and 1912. In the face of the company's pressure the British government had to fall back uneasily on the preferential but not exclusive formula, being aware, as Harcourt put it, that '... meanwhile the South African Union Act has been passed ... [and the Union government] might not unreasonably claim to be consulted as to any sweeping change in the *status quo* during the intervening period'.[13] When the company's development proposals reached the High Commissioner he used the opportunity to suggest a change in policy on the future of the protectorate. Gladstone was the first imperial official to react positively to the company's suggestions, though his enthusiasm for the company's railway failed to budge the Colonial Office and the scheme was rejected in June 1912.[14] Yet Gladstone was unwilling to drop the question. He saw the future of the protectorate as being linked to the Union and thought that the British government should act to prepare the protectorate for this future. 'We hold Bechuanaland in trust,' he wrote, 'and I think that as far as the Crown lands are concerned our policy should have regard to the land settlement schemes of the Union.' The reserves, he argued, were too vast; what would take place on transfer to the Union?

Not only is all the best land assigned to natives. It is also the land with the best access to 400 miles of railway. Further, it isolated almost all the Crown land from the Union frontier. If the Bechuana don't increase in number materially; if they don't develop their country, if they don't justify their position how will it be possible to lock up this vast area?

Khama and the other Tswana chiefs were, in his view, lamentably unprogressive: the only progress that was being made was in 'the Rhodesian blocks along the railway'—i.e. in the company's concessions. To Gladstone the north-west was a potential Canaan: '... it is occupied by 18,000 natives who are doing nothing. It is a country which could perhaps be made to support millions of men.' On the assumption that Britain would be responsible for the protectorate for some years to come '... it may be necessary sooner or later to consider a rearrangement of the native reserves ... In conclusion the central point is this. How after transfer can you guarantee security of tenure of say 150,000 Bechuanas over 130,000 square miles of the best land ... ?'[15]

This was a radical approach: Gladstone did not shrink from the prospect of large-scale segregatory readjustments in the pattern of land settlement, and his aggressive interpretation of the duties of trusteeship was far closer to the company's views than to those of the Colonial Secretary. In the Colonial Office Gladstone's suggestions were not welcomed. The imperial government had not accepted the company's offer of money, it was pointed out, and 'to bring in the Union to develop would merely be to raise the question of transfer of the Protectorates at an early date while putting the Union in a particularly strong position ...'[16]

It was felt that a policy of settlement and development would only tempt the Union to press for annexation, and the suggestion that the reserves be moved was rejected: '... it is the natives' country,' wrote Anderson, 'and our promise to safeguard their rights is of the most solemn character ...'[17]

Gladstone's enthusiasm was temporarily allayed, but the company returned to the attack, bringing the matter out into the open and involving the imperial government in a controversy with the Union over the protectorate, which was what it had sought to avoid. In an address to the company's shareholders in London in February 1913 Jameson told them of the company's offers to open up the protectorate, but, he went on,

What is the answer we have received? A *non possumus*. I would ask you to remember that the Protectorate was originally, is now because it has never been abrogated, under the sphere of influence of the British South Africa Company ...

we are anxious to develop the country we look upon as our inheritance; but we are refused . . .

In conclusion he exposed the company's strategy, which was to continue to put forward its claims with the intention of blocking an early takeover by the Union in the expectation that a change of government in Britain would bring far more backing for the 'English' in South African affairs and consequently support for Rhodesian expansion at South Africa's expense. The company would, he said, '. . . go on knocking, and it is possible that some day we may find new doorkeepers'.[18]

Jameson's speech was an outright political challenge to Botha, for Jameson was primarily a South African politician and he spoke not only for an internal opposition but, as chairman of the company, for a rival political and territorial entity in south Africa. He was attempting to reassert the English factor in South Africa from his Rhodesian base and, in so doing, to capture as well the allegience of the Rhodesian settlers. As Gladstone reported after talking to Jameson,

. . . he is keen to push Rhodesian [i.e. the company's] enterprise to increase the British population as a makeweight in view of the Dutch predominance at present in the Union. If the British in South Rhodesia and the Protectorate are sufficiently strong in numbers they will not fear absorption . . .[19]

It is not surprising, therefore, that Botha took the matter seriously. While the first stages of the land Bill were under discussion in the Union parliament he announced that South Africa would approach the British government to transfer all the protectorates. In the context of debates on the ultimate settlement of the 'native question' in the Union parliament all manner of flights of fancy are customarily aired, and at first the High Commissioner did not take the announcement seriously. But Botha had meant what he had said. The Union government, he told Gladstone, had been 'considerably surprised' to hear of the company's repeated approaches with regard to the protectorate. It could countenance neither economic development nor political incorporation of Bechuanaland by the company, and therefore was obliged to modify previous policy and press for the earliest possible incorporation of both Bechuanaland and Swaziland.[20]

Caught between the Union and the company, the British government was in a difficult position. The company could press not only the claims of 'English' southern Africa, looking forward as it did, in Jameson's words, to a self-governing British State '. . . from Mafeking to the Congo border. A territory as large, if not larger, than the Union itself,'[21] but was also able to capitalise upon the disquiet aroused in Britain by Hertzog's contribution to the debate on the 'native question'. The *Morning Post* ran an article which contrasted the 'Herztogian' and 'British' approaches to 'native policy' and claimed that the company's policy gave it a better claim to administer the protectorate than the Union had.[22] As Jameson put it at the end of 1913, the British would hesitate to hand over 'so large a body of natives to the Union', adding, 'that is where our pull comes in'.[23]

The British government could give assurances of the purity of its future intentions to the Union government in order to induce it to drop its request for the transfer of the protectorate, but both this, and the alternative course of acceding to the request, raised the question of reconciling the company's preferential rights with a Union take-over. Gladstone pointed out that it was not only the ultimate solution of the 'native question' that lay behind Botha's request. There was also Afrikaner land hunger. The Dutch, he told Harcourt,

. . . want to develop land settlement in the Protectorate . . . But any land settlement plan, any concession or sale will be claimed by the British South Africa Company as subject to their option . . . as it is there are enough possibilities of friction between Rhodesia and the Union . . . Ministers here have no idea of the extent of the Company's acquired and preferential rights . . . [and] would be astonished if they knew the Company's mining rights in Khama's country would continue after a transfer.[24]

The only way out which Gladstone could see was to settle the company's claims. In the Colonial Office officials were prepared to exploit the dilemma, using the company's rights to stave off the Union's claims.[25] Early transfer of the protectorate might be difficult to justify to Parliament in view of the pledges given in the Commons during the South Africa Act debate. 'The bare suggestion,' Harcourt wrote, 'would bring the whole missionary world and others upon me at once.'[26] Botha was to be assured that no administrative transfer would be made to the company, and at the same time he was to be told (it was hoped that this would lessen his enthusiasm) that the company had rights, confirmed by the highest legal authority, which would limit the power of a new government to deal with land and minerals.[27]

2 Britain and the South African 'native problem'

The British government's insistence on a *terra clausa* policy for the protectorate must be seen within the wider context of the South African 'native question'. The protectorate was considered to be a 'native territory' within the South African pattern, and the British government, which was anxious to facilitate and develop the Union's 'solution of the native problem', was wary of development in the protectorate because this would make inroads into an African preserve and reduce the amount of African land at the Union government's disposal. There had long been pressure for white settlement in the protectorate. Rhodes's Ghansi settlement in the semi-desert west had not been an encouraging beginning to white farming, but the railway belt in the east was the target of subsequent settlement schemes. The company had always made clear that its plans involved the increase in white settlement, and on the concessions which had been made to it and to the Tati Company white settlers had been introduced. And as white land holding increased it brought in its train the introduction of territorial segregation.

In August 1912 the company introduced into its title deeds for land sale in its concessions a clause forbidding the sale of land to Africans. Anderson minuted:

So long as substantial justice is done to the natives our policy should be to govern them in accordance with South African ideas. There is no parallel to the native question in South Africa to guide us, and the responsibility for the results of South African opinion must rest in the end on South Africa, and the people there are in a much better position than we can be to know where the native question pinches them. In this case, with ample reserves secured for the natives, I think there can be no question that we should follow South African opinion and as far as possible keep native land holding within the limits of the reserves.[28]

Hartman Just, however, warned that the British government, if it committed itself to a policy of preventing Africans acquiring land outside the reserves, would be 'establishing a policy less liberal than that obtaining over the greater part of the Union of South Africa'.[29] He recalled that in 1909 Hely-Hutchinson, then the Governor of the Cape, had proposed issuing a proclamation to prevent such African land purchase in Swaziland, but that the Secretary of State had refused to sanction it.[30] He pointed out that in the 1905 commission report the Cape representatives had dissented from the recommendation on legal territorial segregation and that the British government had always been understood to be in favour of equal African land purchase rights. The question had arisen contemporaneously in Northern Rhodesia and there was the danger that the company would treat imperial compliance in Bechuanaland as a precedent for adopting a racial exclusion clause in the north.Nevertheless Just, like Anderson, did not feel it necessary for the British government to take a stand on the principle. He concluded that while South Africa might gradually be moving 'in the direction of keeping natives within certain fixed areas. General Hertzog and General Botha have recently spoken in that sense . . . it is not for the Imperial Government to lead in that direction'. The company's proposed deeds were nevertheless sanctioned without any definite commitment in law or principle being made.

The following year the protectorate administration put up for sale a number of farms in the Ghansi district, and was unpleasantly surprised to receive an application from an African from Griqualand East. Gladstone telegraphed urgently to Harcourt that he would refuse the application and 'leave it to the applicant to question his legal right to do so', later explaining his fear that this might be the spearhead of a protest against the reservation of the Ghansi settlement to Europeans.[31] Gladstone's action was approved, and the applicant was informed that he had no more reason to complain at his exclusion than a European farmer would have at being excluded from the reserves, though this explanation cannot have been convincing to a non-Tswana with no *locus standi* in the reserves himself.[32]

His Majesty's government, then, was trustee for the Africans of the protectorate, but trustee for their future within the context of the South African settlement pattern. In 1913 the Union government produced its first spectacular step towards a 'solution of the native problem'—the land Bill. The Bill laid down the principle of territorial segregation: Africans were deprived of their right to acquire land outside already existing African areas, putting an end to what Smuts later referred to, in terms which underline white South African feelings, as the 'evil of promiscuous buying of land by natives among whites . . .'[33] though it was provided that after the passing of the Bill a commission would enquire into the purchase of further land for African occupation. In addition squatting on white farms was limited, and sharecropping tenancy, which was a feature of the Orange Free State rural scene, was abolished.[34] A comprehensive native Bill built upon the recommendations of the 1905 commission had initially been drafted by Hertzog before he had been dropped from the Union Cabinet.[35] Hertzog's draft, Gladstone reported, would 'probably have proved to be most dangerous', and he welcomed Sauer's more moderate Bill, reporting to Harcourt that it 'provides for native segregation up to a more or less practical point and is a vast improvement of Hertzog's wild ideas.'[36] Gladstone's reports on the land Bill were consistently favourable, and he advised strongly against its reservation.[37] He reported that the Bill provided for no more than a temporary freezing of

African land holding until the report of the promised commission.

Gladstone then turned his mind to a consideration of how the British government could facilitate the policy behind the Bill. The Bechuanaland Protectorate, he felt, was an obvious asset to be used in the solving of the native problem, and he told Harcourt that 'It is quite clear that in [Botha's] view the Protectorate cannot be removed from the consideration of a general scheme of native settlement in South Africa . . .'[38] He warned that the squatting position in the Union was acute, that the reserves were overcrowded and that Botha dreaded the dotting of small reserves all over the Union. Apart from the northern Transvaal there were no areas of any size which the prospective land commission could allocate to Africans. If the promise the Union government had just made to buy more land for Africans was to be kept, therefore, the protectorate, which was undeveloped and unsettled, should be taken into account. To exclude the protectorate from the Union's land settlement plans, he argued, would increase the very difficulties in the Union which had led the imperial government so far to postpone a handover.

Yet while the Colonial Office did not object to the principle of the Act it was not quite as enthusiastic in its co-operation as Gladstone. The Act was bitterly opposed by African and coloured political organisations in South Africa, and in mid-1914 the South African Native National Congress, in the face of strong opposition from both Botha and Gladstone, sent a delegation to London to appeal to the imperial government. The Act was attacked in the House of Commons, where Harcourt defended the Union government. Both the Secretary of State and his officials deflected hostile criticism with references to the 1905 commission and to the anticipated recommendations of the commission to come. A Blue book was published as an answer to criticism of the Act, containing the Union government's explanation of it, which had made a favourable impression on the Colonial Office.[39] Unwillingness to be seen to interfere in the affairs of the new Dominion was one reason for the imperial government's refusal to consider the use of its powers of reservation. Nevertheless the imperial government had demonstrated that it would intervene where imperial interests were more seriously involved. The Botha government had amended its initial legislative intentions on Indian immigration, as Harcourt pointed out to the Commons, 'not from local desire but from Imperial considerations'.[40] Any imperial pressure to force the appearance of a second defeat on Botha on a major colour issue was out of the question. For with Hertzog having left the government the Afrikaner pillar of Botha's coalition was beginning to crumble. The South African Native National Congress deputation which met the Minister of Native Affairs to protest against the Act analysed correctly the politics behind it. The Minister, they reported,

... seemed to be drawn by a mysterious force in the face of which the native interest did not count ... General Hertzog in office was not able to bring about the enslavement of the blacks, General Hertzog out of office succeeded in getting the Government ... to force the Act through Parliament, in order to retain the support of the 'Free' State malcontents.[41]

The furore aroused by the Act, added to the tangle over the company's rights and the political balance between the company and the Union, confirmed the policy of standstill in the Bechuanaland protectorate. Harcourt told Gladstone that since 'The trend of recent legislation in the Union has ... been such as to increase the feeling of insecurity of the native as regards his position on the land ...'[42] the British government should not diminish the quantity of land available for Africans. Both Harcourt and Gladstone rejected the company's political ambitions in the protectorate, and both accepted that transfer to the Union would come. Yet while the High Commissioner was anxious to plan the future of the protectorate in this light, the Secretary of State and his officials were prepared to wait until pressures from the Union became unanswerable before they began the process of finding a settlement. By the middle of 1913 they felt their hand strengthened. Lambert was able to minute, '... it is not what the Union requires but what Parliament consents to that must be regarded as the determining factor'. The Union could cause trouble, but this was unlikely '... now that the Rand strike has shown dramatically and unexpectedly their reliance upon us'.[43]

Notes

1 R. Robinson and J. Gallagher, *African and the Victorians*, London, 1961, p. 239.
2 C.O. 879/102, No. 922, B.S.A.C. to C.O., 13 August 1909 and 25 August 1909.
3 C.O. 879, No. 847.
4 *Ibid.*
5 C.O. 879, No. 922, C.O. to B.S.A.C., 2 October 1909.
6 C.O. 879, No. 932, Selborne memorandum, 23 July 1909, and Crewe to Selborne, 20 August 1909.

7 C.O. 879, No. 938, B.S.A.C. to C.O., 7 February 1910.
8 C.O. 879, No. 969, B.S.A.C. to C.O., 13 October 1911.
9 C.O. 417/506, 14 February 1911.
10 C.O. 417/506, 14 February 1911.
11 C.O. 417/508, 14 November 1911.
12 C.O. 879, No. 969, B.S.A.C. to C.O., 14 November 1911, and C.O. 417/508, Memorandum, 14 November 1911, and Minutes.
13 C.O. 879, No. 969, Harcourt to Gladstone, 30 December 1911.
14 C.O.879, No. 989, Gladstone to Harcourt, 8 May 1912. Additional objections were raised by Methuen, Imperial commander-in-chief at the Cape, to a railway which could link German South West Africa with the Union across the desert buffer.
15 G.P. Add. MSS, 45,999, f. 45, Gladstone to Harcourt.
16 C.O., 417/514, 23 November 1912, minute by Lambert.
17 C.O. 417/514, 23 November 1912. Neither Gladstone nor Anderson mentioned the safeguards against alienation of the reserves, even after transfer, contained in the schedule to the South Africa Act.
18 British South Africa Company, shareholders' meetings.
19 G.P. Add. mss, 45,998, f. 145, Gladstone to Harcourt, 8 April 1912.
20 Cmd. 8707, Botha to Gladstone, 5 March 1913.
21 C.O. 417/538, 22 December 1913, Report.
22 Issue of 10 April 1913.
23 C.O. 417/538, 22 December 1913. This interpretation of the importance of the company's pressures differs from that of Lord Hailey's in *The Republic of South Africa and the High Commission Territories*, Oxford, 1963, pp. 52–5. He argues that Jameson's remarks were not intended as a serious claim to the protectorate and that Botha took advantage of them as the pretext to stake a claim. But the company was asking for administrative rights because it did not want to abandon its claim in case a Conservative government in England would support it, while its immediate aim was to extract land concessions. Hailey appears also not to give sufficient weight to the history of the company's pressures and to the context of the South African political scene.
24 G.P. Add. MSS, 45,999, Gladstone to Harcourt, 19 March 1913 and 30 March 1913, ff. 146 and 152.
25 C.O. 417/523, 2 April 1913, Lambert minute.
26 Cmd. 8707, Harcourt to Gladstone, 2 May 1913, and G.P. Add. MSS, 46,000, f. 209, Harcourt to Gladstone, 20 August 1913.
27 Cmd. 8707, Harcourt to Gladstone, 2 May 1913.
28 C.O. 417/513, 19 August 1912.
29 *Ibid.*
30 C.O. 417/523, 24 April 1913.
31 C.O. 417/540, 23 May 1914, Gladstone to Harcourt, and C.O. 417/523, Gladstone to Harcourt, telegram, 24 April 1913.
32 Compare the 'Elgin pledge' given to white settlers in Kenya in May 1906: 'It is not consonant with the views of H.M.G. to impose legal restrictions on any particular section of the community, but as a matter of administrative convenience grants in the upland area should not be made to Indians'. (G. H. Mungeam, *British Rule in Kenya, 1895–1912,* Oxford, 1966, pp. 199–200.) It is not so much the acceptance of segregation that deserves notice than the

extra-legal workings of the colonial administration. Knowledge of its own practices was one reason for the insistence of the imperial government on retaining some control over the personnel and administration of African affairs in Rhodesia, regardless of legal forms.

33   S.P., v, Memo. Hertzog's Native Bills, August 1926, p. 306.
34   For a detailed description of the land Act, see C. M. Tatz, *Shadow and Substance in South Africa*, Pietermaritzburg, 1964.
35   Tatz suggests that Hertzog's draft included proposals to abolish the Cape Africlan franchise. (*Shadow and Substance*, p. 16.)
36   G.P. Add. MSS, 45,999, ff. 99 and 130, Gladstone to Harcourt, 5 March 1913 and 13 October 1913.
37   Under the provisions of the South Africa Act the Bill could have been reserved for the approval of the British government.
38   G.P. Add. MSS, 45,999, f. 186, Gladstone to Harcourt, 10 June 1913.
39   Cd. 7508.
40   Quoted by S. Plaatje, *Native Life in South Africa,* London, n.d., p. 201.
41   *Op. cit.,* p. 173.
42   C.O. 417/525, 9 October 1913, Harcourt to Gladstone, 24 November 1913.
43   C.O. 417/524, 6 July 1913.

CHAPTER 5

Separation in Rhodesia: the imperial initiative

1911–14

1 Governing Africans in Rhodesia

The British government in London took little part in the government of Africans in Rhodesia. It was scantily informed: the Colonial Office received from the company's London office sketchy extracts from Native Commissioners' reports at irregular intervals. From Salisbury the Resident Commissioner confined himself mainly to reporting the clashes between the settlers and the company. Yet attention was paid to certain basic issues, in particular those of imperial concern affecting the security of white rule, of which the two most important were the fundamental pattern of political authority over Africans and the division and occupation of land.

The Colonial Office was clear that there should be a different pattern of authority for Southern and Northern Rhodesia. In its analyses the government of the north was a government for Africans, that in the south primarily one for whites.[1] For the south there were two consequences: first that the British were not prepared to countenance any revival of the broken Ndebele paramountcy, and second that they pressed for a separate administration of African affairs by a department that would be, so far as was possible, an *imperium in imperio*. This latter policy, which was in line with that pressed for by the imperial authorities in the south, was successfully resisted by the company, which demurred on the practical grounds that Africans were affected by the work of every government department.[2] But both the British government and the company were at one in their refusal to entertain any revival of the Ndebele monarchy. When the Ndebele indunas requested that Njube, Lobengula's son, be allowed to return as king to Rhodesia from the Cape, where he had been exiled and educated, the High Commissioner refused 'in the most emphatic terms'. He gave his reasons at length, which were formulated from recent South African experience. In essence they were that in the case of a nation, like the Tswana and the Sotho, which had never been conquered, rule through the existing chieftaincies was permissible. But after conquest there was no longer any place for a defeated monarch.

> Obviously he cannot be allowed to resume his old authority, and in my opinion it is equally impossible for him, whatever may be his first intentions to confine himself to a subordinate role as an officer of the Government. Our experience with Dinizulu is to me conclusive proof of the correctness of my opinion.[3]

To Selborne the High Commissioner had replaced the Ndebele king. As he had reported two years earlier of a visit to Rhodesia, '. . . the Matabele did not give me the proper salute—the *Bayete* . . . I insisted and sat still while they argued the matter out and in the end they gave it to me properly. If they had not done so I should be sitting there now.'[4] Njube reproached Selborne bitterly for the ban, significantly placing it in the context of current South African politics. 'I . . . can only assume,' he wrote, '. . . it is a fresh "Colour Bar" on the eve of Union.'[5] But Selborne did not see it in these terms. When the Secretary of State anxiously asked for more information, Selborne's reply reflected the ruling Rhodesian myth of the *ancien régime* and bore a resemblance, not entirely coincidental, to Rider Haggard's novel *King Solomon's Mines*. 'Your Lordship is aware,' he wrote,

> that his [Njube's] father and grandfather were savage autocrats of the Matabele tribe . . . with no limit or check whatever on their power . . . The Matabele . . . deeply regret the destruction of this power; while this power lasted they were lords of all they surveyed, and they hideously tyrannised to an unlimited extent, over every native tribe north, east and west of them for many hundred miles.

He concluded with a warning that the power of witch doctors could yet overcome the fear of whitemen's firearms.[6] For the Ndebele therefore, a form of indirect rule which preserved a centre of legitimate African authority was inadmissable, as it posed a threat to the security of the white man's country.[7]

In Northern Rhodesia both the British government and the company moved towards refashioning the early piecemeal arrangements according to their different southern strategies. Once the company had established control over the north it began to press the Colonial Office for permission to amalgamate the two halves. This meant transferring North Eastern Rhodesia, where the company's administration was supervised by the Commissioner for Nyasaland, to the jurisdiction of the South African High Commission. No objection to this southward shift was raised in Whitehall, where it was simply noted that as North Eastern Rhodesia was likely to be of importance only as a source of labour for the south it would be better dealt with by the High Commissioner than by the Nyasaland government, which was 'out of touch' with South African policy on these matters.[8] But the Colonial Office would not allow the establishment of a Southern Rhodesian type of administration over the whole of Northern Rhodesia. When the company attempted to persuade it to permit the imposition of a southern-pattern order in council over all the north the Colonial Office refused on the grounds that pledges given to Lewanika, the Lozi king, excluded any such change. In 1909 new agreements with the Lozi were negotiated: while London still declined to take on the responsibility of a protectorate for which Lewanika had long petitioned, Selborne was able to remark with approval on the extension of administrative separation to the north. 'It will be seen,' he commented, '. . . that Lewanika practically abandons all North Western Rhodesia outside Barotseland proper to the Company, and that Barotseland proper is, in effect, reserved for the Barotse as strictly as Basutoland is for the Basuto.'[9] Indirect rule in the north, where feasible, and direct rule for the south, tempered by a separate 'Native Department', were the fundamental features of the British government's approach to government of Africans in the Rhodesias. They reflected clearly the approach it had formed to southern problems: the preservation of traditional political authorities in the High Commission territories and pressure for a non-political administration of Africans in the Union.

2 Towards the Reserves Commission

It was the land question in Southern Rhodesia which, during the period before charter review, and because of the pressure of events due to the company's imposition of a South African pattern of legislation, led to an uncharacteristic imperial intervention in the company's administration. The opening years of Company administration of Rhodesia had seen the alienation of the larger part of the high veld to European settlers and land companies. Once this had been done, quite without imperial control, the basic pattern of division of land between white and black remained unaltered. In 1894 a reserves commission[10] set aside remote and sparsely inhabited areas for the Ndebele in exchange for their former high veld domain. The risings of 1896 and the subsequent restructuring of the company's African administration under imperial supervision led to a supplementary readjustment in which provisional African reserves, to be adjusted from time to time as the need arose, were demarcated in 1902. This was a provisional settlement, and it was not until 1914 that the British government appointed a commission, which was expected to arrive at a final apportionment of Southern Rhodesia between tribal and other land. An examination of the process leading to the appointment of this commission illustrates the framework of thought in London and the influence of the policies developing in the Union on those that were framed for Rhodesia.

In 1908 the Rhodesian Legislative Council passed the Private Locations Ordinance, which was modelled on Cape Act No. 30 of 1899. The aim of the new law was to prevent white landowners from allowing the occupation of their land by African tenant farmers, a system known throughout southern Africa as 'kaffir farming' which was the bane of segregationists and development-minded landowners, and which was one of the chief targets of the South African Land Act of 1913. The settlers, the company and the Native Affairs Department were agreed on the desirability of the new law. The latter's motivation was a bureaucratic disquiet at the lack of control over Africans resident on white farms. Both the settlers and the company aimed at the absentee landlords, the large land-holding companies which had been beneficiaries of Jameson's early hand-outs and in whose hands were locked up large portions of land nominally white but occupied on a tenancy basis by what were regarded as lamentably unprogressive and generally undesirable and idle Africans.[11] Both company and settlers could see no place in Rhodesia for a growing group of Africans who were being forced neither into the reserves nor on to the labour market. Though the 1908 ordinance did not go as far as the South African legislation of 1913 was to do and replace sharecropping and rent tenancies by labour tenancy, it made a beginning by limiting the number of tenants permitted to reside on land outside the reserves.

Though the Colonial Office accepted the ordinance on the basis of the High Commissioner's assurance that there would be no large-scale displacement of Africans as a result and that 'farming Kaffirs is . . . of grave danger to South Africa', the Rhodesian administration was clear that it was intended as a step towards the removal from white areas of Africans who were not in white employment.[12] The ordinance was followed by a Legislative Council resolution in May 1909 which set up a committee to review laws relating to Africans 'with a view to deciding what further steps are desirable to promote their advancement and increased usefulness to the State'.[13] The background to the appointment of the committee was not concern over land but a growing impatience with the shortage of labour. Yet it made several recommendations on the subject of land relying overtly on the conclusions reached by the South African commission of 1903–05. It suggested that the time had come to begin the introduction of Glen Gray tenure for Africans, and, having made its obeisance to Cape principles, spelt out the price, which was that Africans should no longer be allowed either to purchase or lease land outside the reserves, nor be permitted to reside outside a reserve unless in European employment for a minimum period in each year. The committee also recommended that the reserves be finally demarcated and fixed by statute.

With regard to the last recommendation the company's board preferred to mark time. A memorandum prepared for the committee by W. J. Atherstone, the Surveyor General in Rhodesia, suggested that the reserves could well be reduced by a million acres and that their disposition could be rearranged so that final demarcation was for the time being undesirable. The company's manager, Wilson Fox, advised the Administrator of Rhodesia that the company's aim was not to agree to any final settlement that might impede European settlement for all time in areas judged suitable for it.[14] There was little reaction from the British authorities: the Resident Commissioner advised that demarcation should be postponed until a settlement of the question of the ownership of the unalienated land had been arrived at, and though the Colonial Office consistently took the view that this was an entirely separate question the matter rested.[15]

The committee's other recommendations with regard to land were also rejected by both the company and the Resident Commissioner, who objected to the requirement that Africans outside the reserves should be in European employment. The committee had cast its net wider than the locations ordinance and aimed at controlling the numbers of Africans resident on the unalienated lands. In London Lambert pointed out that the committee had espoused a Transvaal view which was similar to that which Botha had held in 1897, and that

> It would probably have the support of Mr Merriman, who had little admiration for our native reserves in Bechuanaland, and it has no doubt the support of all those who are honestly convinced that the native, left to himself, must stagnate in barbarism, as well as those whose motive is a desire to get labour easily and cheaply.[16]

It was customary in southern Africa for those moved by the latter motive to express themselves as believers in the former.

Though in 1911 the company had rejected the idea of a commission to arrange an overall adjustment and final demarcation of white and African areas, and Whitehall had seen no reason to press the point, by the end of 1912 changing conditions led both sides to change their attitudes. First, charter review was drawing near, and the possibility that the Union might take over from the company led to an awareness in the Colonial Office that a reserves settlement might advantageously be made beforehand, possibly by a joint South African–Imperial commission, following the precedent set when Zululand was annexed to Natal.[17] Secondly, as the company pursued its forward policy of opening up more land for white enterprise, both of its own and that of new settlers, it became dissatisfied with piecemeal adjustment and turned its eyes towards the million acres locked in the reserves which Atherstone had suggested might be reclaimed. A reserves commission, it seemed, might well serve the company's purposes by reducing the quantity and the quality of land available for African occupation. At the end of 1912 the Colonial Office, prompted partly by the company's land policy and the increase in white settlement, suggested to Gladstone that a final settlement of the reserves might be desirable.[18]

Imperial advisors in southern Africa were enthusiastic. The Resident Commissioner urged the ending of constant readjustments, which gave Africans a feeling of insecurity.[19] Gladstone, on the other hand, felt that the advantage would be that the European public would be less suspicious of the imperial government's intentions, and envisaged the removal of Africans from land which was 'more suitable' for European settlement.[20] On receiving the High Commissioner's despatch, Lambert prepared a comprehensive survey of the position of Africans with regard to land in Southern Rhodesia. He concluded:

... broadly speaking the native has no rights at all to land in Southern Rhodesia, and is dependent on what the British South Africa Company assign to him, or if they fail to provide for him adequately, on what the Imperial Government insists on their providing . . . But in this respect the native is by no means worse off than he is in other parts of South Africa, where whatever rights he has to land are at the mercy of a legislature of white employers . . .

The company, wrote Lambert, had rejected the 1911 committee's proposals for delimitation and at that time the imperial government had seen no reason to act. However, things had since changed both in Rhodesia and in the Union.

Opinion at least in the Union appears now to be settling in favour of a system of Reserves ('segregation') and there is no doubt that in the peculiar circumstances of Rhodesia—a growing white population with the wastelands in the hands of a commercial company—supply a special reason for watching over the reserves.[21]

The anxiety was, then, that the company might dispose of the unalienated lands and thereby make a South African segregatory settlement impossible.

It was the insecurity of Africans on the lands outside the reserves, however, and the questions which this provoked in the House of Commons, that sustained Colonial Office anxiety to move and to be seen to be moving on the matter of African lands. In June 1913 Swift MacNeill[22] raised the question of the concession of a large tract of ranch land in Rhodesia to the Liebig company.[23] Harcourt had to admit that the British government had no control over land sales in Rhodesia, and Wedgwood's[24] remark that Harcourt '... would not allow this sort of thing to go on in any other South Africa colony' was a challenge to his anti-charter sentiments. MacNeill returned to the attack a week later, pressing for full details of the concession.[25] He was told that in 1911 the company had given Liebig's the right to acquire 1,200,000 acres at a quit-rent tenure of a shilling per acre per annum and that the price had been credited to the Chartered Company's commercial account. The parliamentary questions brought out into the open the Colonial Office's ignorance as to the position of Africans on the unalienated land of Rhodesia.[26] Official enquiries revealed that the company paid no attention to the pattern of African settlement when making grants, claiming that its sole obligation was to assign land from 'time to time' according to paragraph 81 of the order in council of 1898. Both in law and in practice the Colonial Office found that it could not control the removal of Africans from land outside the reserves, and this determined it to press for an exhaustive enquiry into the land question before the review of the charter. It could not now insist on stopping the removal of Africans from land when it was granted to white owners because, the Resident Commissioner reported, isolated African holdings would be frozen in districts which in due course would be largely European owned.[27] Hartman Just agreed that the Colonial Office was '... committed to the policy of ordinance No. 14 of 1908', in other words to a South African-type squatters law which was intelligible only if the aim was to reduce African occupation of land outside the reserves.[28] It had become clear that the provisions of the 1898 order in council were not adequate to protect African interests and a more comprehensive reserves policy seemed to be the answer.[29]

At the beginning of October in Pretoria Dougal Malcolm, on behalf of the company, and Gladstone had wide-ranging talks on Rhodesian affairs during the course of which Malcolm put two questions to Gladstone on the reserves issue. First he elicited from Gladstone that in his view there would be no objection to a commission advising a curtailment of the overall area at present assigned as reserves. Malcolm's second enquiry was whether the imperial government would object to the adoption of the principles of the Union's Land Act. Gladstone reported to Harcourt that 'We agreed that it would be desirable to adopt the principles of the Natives Land Act . . .'[30] But the Colonial Office rejected this suggestion, because, as Lambert pointed out, '. . . Southern Rhodesia has the Cape system [and] though there are . . . few native electors in fact His Majesty's Government could hardly apply to Southern Rhodesia provisions of this sort which the Union did not apply in the Cape'.[31] Significantly, though, there was no objection in principle, and Just pointed out that while the British government could not lead towards segregation it could follow South African opinion on it.

The question of how final the demarcation of land was to be was also of some importance. When the commission had first been discussed both the Colonial Office and the company had wanted to retain a degree of flexibility. The Colonial Office envisaged the need for later additions as the African population grew, while the company wanted to be able to make reductions as the level of white settlement rose and as the African population changed its economic habits. But once the company had established that the British government would not object in principle to the reduction of the reserves it decided, relying (correctly, as it turned out) on a commission to reduce the area reserved for Africans, to press for finality, which would free it from the obligation to supply land according to African needs under section 81 of the order in council of 1898.[32] Colonial Office officials too were persuaded that although the existing flexible system gave the British government leverage over the company it was unlikely to continue to work harmoniously. From now on, Lambert wrote, Rhodesia '. . . will be more, not less, under the control of the elected members, and they will have scant sympathy with native reserves'.[33] He envisaged that it would be necessary to add to the land reserved for Africans and feared that the increase in European settlement would make each fresh reservation more difficult. 'This is the reason for aiming at finality now, when we have a comparatively free hand and can . . . work with the Company. If we do not work with the Company we can no doubt compel them . . . but they will have local public opinion with them.'[34]

Once the commission had been agreed upon, the question of personnel arose. Gladstone proposed a three-man commission with an imperial nominee as chairman, a Native Commissioner nominated by the company and a neutral expert on 'native affairs'. As chairman he nominated R. T. Coryndon, then Resident Commissioner in Swaziland, who had formerly been in the service of the company. Lieutenant Colonel E. C. F. Garraway he thought suitable as the neutral member, vouching for his expertise: 'He knows the natives thoroughly and gets on with them. He can talk kaffir.'[35] In the Colonial Office there was doubt as to the wisdom of appointing Coryndon as chairman. 'Our Commissioner should not be a man who has been in the service of the Company,' Anderson wrote, 'We shall have to defend his work in Parliament and must have a man like Caesar's wife ought to have been.'[36] But Gladstone prevailed—a victory which was to prove politically costly after the report was published.

3 The Anti-slavery Society v. the Chartered Company

The *contretemps* over the insecurity of Africans upon the land, coming as it did at the same time as the decision to refer the question of the ownership of land to the Privy Council, led to the involvement of the Aborigines Protection Society in both issues. The Colonial Office strove to keep the issues separate. In its eyes the Privy Council reference was no more than an attempt to get the bases laid down on which a financial settlement with the company could one day be made.[37] The Colonial Office, fearing that to look too deep would be to cast doubt upon every title to land in Rhodesia, had no intention of lifting the veil. It had requested the Law Officers to draft the terms of reference to the Privy Council specifically excluding discussion of the validity of the concessions on the basis of which the company had occupied Rhodesia.[38] To the society, however, the Privy Council reference was '. . . the opportunity of getting the whole question of native title to land in Africa discussed . . . which may never recur'.[39] The society was fighting what it saw only as a single battle in a wider campaign against a philosophy of empire and African government which it conceived to be inextricably connected with the Chartered Company. Having decided to take up the case, the society, in order to give itself *locus standi* in court, turned to J. L. Dube, President General of the South African Native National Congress. Dube and other members of the Congress delegation, who were in England to present a petition against the South African Land Act, signed the initial 'Natives Petition' to the Privy Council in the Rhodesian case. It was suggested too that Dube should visit Rhodesia and obtain powers of attorney from Ndebele chiefs authorising the society to represent them in court.[40] When war broke out the High Commissioner in South Africa obtained a pledge from the Native National Congress that it would refrain from political activity in Rhodesia for the duration of the war.[41] The society then decided to send John Harris to Rhodesia, and the High Commissioner welcomed him, advising the Rhodesian administration to co-operate with Harris so that it would be 'no longer necessary to recognise the native Dube as a protagonist in this affair'.[42]

The Rhodesian administration protested strongly and refused to allow Harris either to hold meetings with African leaders or to collect funds for the case. Newton wrote that Harris's mission would have an unsettling and dangerous effect that would go beyond the land question and would result in a subversion of law and order that would spread beyond Rhodesia.[43] The Colonial Office watched from the sidelines, its chief anxiety being to see that the responsibility for obstructing Harris rested with the company.[44] When Harris suggested that in view of the company's obstruction the High Commissioner, as guardian of the Africans, should give the society a power of attorney, Lambert objected that this was '. . . calculated to bring us into direct opposition to the elected members. To the latter the Aborigines Protection Society is no doubt anathema, and we should do nothing to identify ourselves with them.'[45] Finally when the company refused to concede 'direct communications with the natives by unofficial persons in the matter of the ownership of land . . .' Harcourt decided against insisting that Harris be allowed to carry out his mission. He compromised instead by withdrawing the Crown's objection to counsel appearing on behalf of the Africans, as did the company's lawyers. Thus the way was clear for the society to proceed with the African case, though the attempt by British radicals to get directly in touch with Rhodesian Africans had been foiled.[46]

On his return to Britain Harris continued the political battle against the company, maintaining close contact with anti-charter settlers in Rhodesia and with the Secretary of State, Harcourt, of whom Harris wrote that his '. . . whole attitude was that of a colleague, fighting a battle in which there was mutual interest'.[47] But in May 1915, to the society's despair, Harcourt was replaced by Bonar Law. Harris, following a precedent from the Congo reform campaign, convened a

Rhodesia Reform Committee in July 1915. He was anxious to preserve the respectability of his cause: Morel, the inspirer of the Congo campaign, was a political impossibility, his patriotism compromised by his attitude to the war; similar suspicions attached to Ramsay MacDonald, who had been chairman of the Congo Parliamentary Committee; and a campaign to arouse public support was not possible during the war. Harris played safe: the committee was made up of 'discreet members of Parliament', with 'humanitarian cranks' expressly excluded. Its aim was to direct attention to the Chartered Company, and, by playing on the ignorance of the Commons regarding Rhodesia, '. . . to set the machinery in motion in the House which will permeate the atmosphere with the suggestion that something is wrong'.[48] As a measure of respectability Harris persuaded J. W. Wilson, a Scottish Unionist, who was totally uninterested in Rhodesia, to chair the committee.[49]

Thus the society's Rhodesian campaign began without a groundswell of public humanitarian concern, and even the limited circles which were interested in southern African matters other than the stock exchange were divided by Harris's attitude to the policies of the Union government. Harris's experiences of Rhodesia had led him to believe that Africans were far better off in the Union, where, he thought, '. . . the attitude of the whites towards the natives is undergoing a marked change'.[50] He consistently placed a favourable interpretation upon the policies and motives of the Botha government, and when the Rhodesia Reform Committee was formed one of its objectives was '. . . to obtain as far as possible a uniform and equitable native policy which, whilst permitting unhampered the progress of the native tribes, will be acceptable to the local settlers and conform to the policy of the Native Affairs Department in the Union Territories'.[51] Thus the campaign chose its ground: it was not directed against white Africa but singled out Chartered rule as responsible for the position of Africans in Rhodesia. Harris defined the Union's policy as '. . . definite inalienable Reserves and some form of self-government' and was unpersuaded of his exaggeration even when Lord Buxton pointed out to him that the Union had never admitted an African right to reserves and that self-government was non-existent outside the Transkei.[52] In the first two years the Rhodesia Reform Committee itself met only once in pursuit of its far from radical objectives, and in the interim Harris turned his attention to reversing the society's stand on the South African Land Act. Though the society had initially supported the African delegation to Britain which protested against the 1913 Act, by 1916 it passed a resolution expressing '... general approval of the fundamental principle of the separation of such areas as set forth in Sec. 1 of the "suspensary" Act of 1913, and resolving to do its best to obtain such amendments in its details and methods as may remove the apprehensions of the natives'.[53] Harris informed Evans, a prominent Cape 'liberal', that the society had decided that a campaign to improve the Act's 'details and application' was 'the wiser and most friendly course'. He advised Steel-Maitland, the Under-Secretary of State for the Colonies, that Botha's policy had been '... hopelessly misunderstood and misrepresented by considerable sections of the native community'; in a letter to Sharp, the editor of the *New Statesman*, he asserted that the policy was not a 'Dutch conception' but a triumph for Cape liberalism, and that '... no vicious principle has been set up which is a barrier to the native working out his own salvation'.[54] Harris relied heavily upon Dube's initial acceptance of the principle of segregation and ignored warnings from Solomon Plaatje and Walter Rubusana, two members of the Congress delegation, that the Beaumont commission's recommendations, insufficient as they were, would not be accepted in the Union. In 1917 the society angrily broke off relations with the Congress leaders, and Harris continued a stream of letters to radical and liberal editors and members of Parliament urging support of Botha's policy.[55]

If, in the southern African perspective, the society's aims were limited, with regard to the empire as a whole it saw the Rhodesian land case as one involving vital broader issues. Harris, formerly a missionary in the Congo, had been a star witness at the first Congo commission of enquiry in 1905, and had cut his political teeth on the Congo Reform campaign, coming into prominence in humanitarian circles in 1905 when he addressed a series of public meetings on Leopoldian atrocities.[56] The Congo reformers had two ruling obsessions, 'government commercialism' and the expropriation of African lands. In Rhodesia Harris identified precisely these two enemies, and the astonishing success of the Congo Reform campaign gave the humanitarians both confidence and impetus for an onslaught on the Chartered Company, though the latter proved to have stronger defenders in Britain than King Leopold had had. The views of the Aborigines Protection Society were also influenced by the publication of Henri Rolin's *Les Lois et l'administration de la Rhodésie* in 1913. Rolin's book demonstrated that the English reformers had been throwing stones at the Congo from a glass house. He stressed the absolute lack of proprietary rights in land of Africans in Rhodesia, and a corresponding absence of means of protecting even their possession by ordinary legal processes. It was read as well in the Colonial Office, where Lambert noted that it

> is well worth reading and is a criticism of the whole policy of the Company and the white community towards thé natives—who he considers are being divorced from the land and reduced to a *régime de salariat industriel et agricole*. This view is very far-reaching . . . It might be right or it may be wrong.[57]

Lambert's phlegmatic refusal to allow Rolin's analysis to disturb the even tenor of his bureaucratic way encapsulated the difference between the Colonial Office and the society. To the officials Rhodesia was an administrative problem, the politics of the structure within which they manoeuvred was a matter of theory, and in the absence of a lead from the politicians the administrative approach was the policy of the British government. But the society saw itself in a battle transcending in magnitude the campaigns over Congo reform, the Putnamayo atrocities or Portuguese African slavery. Africans in Rhodesia, as Harris put it, were not cruelly treated, but the '. . . proposal to dispossess them of all their rights in property, to declare them politically and for all practical purposes aliens in their own territory' was something which threatened the very basis of the empire.[58] *Vis-à-vis* the company as well the land case was only a single battle in a wider war, and Harris analysed the two major ambitions of the 'Chartered circle' as being a desire to build '. . . a new British Central African State in opposition to Botha' and 'to persuade the Empire Resources Committee to adopt in tropical and subtropical regions the main feature of the policy of the Chartered Company, which is in turn based upon the Leopoldian conception of colonisation'.[59]

The politics of the company's board did consist of an archetypal conglomeration of views from the British right. Individual directors had supported Milner in South Africa and were associated with his plans for imperial political union; had opposed the Lloyd George budget and the Parliament Act; had aligned themselves with Ulsterism; had early sounded the alarm at German economic competition. It is not surprising, therefore, to find the names of Birchenough, Jameson, Fox and Grey among the thirty-three signatories of the 'Creed' (as they called it) of the Empire Resources Development Committee, which was published in January 1917. Well before the war had crystallised their economic views the company's directors had formulated their approach to the economic future of Africans in southern Africa. They had argued that the Colonial Office claim that an increasing African population would automatically require augmented reserves was erroneous and that the reserves were a temporary sanctuary where Africans had a right of refuge only as long as they were '... living in a state of tribal savagery ... and cannot at once ... be assimilated to European conditions of life'. Contact with Europeans and the gradual breakdown of tribal organisation would mean that indigenous primitive agriculture would cease to be the sole means of livelihood, '... and as the opportunities for labour are multiplied, the natives tend more and more to take their place as an industrial class in a mixed community. All native education tends in the same direction, viz. towards the break-up of the old tribal system which necessitates reserves ...'[60]

The company was eager to be midwife to the new society. The doctrine which it was enunciating was an addition to a chorus; the insistent demands of the Randlords; the echo of Milner's 'feeble forceful voice', with its 'emphasis on plentiful capital and cheap labour'; all were to swell into the 'farrago of cant and greed' of the League for the Development of Empire Resources.[61] The league had been formed to advocate the redemption of debts incurred by Britain during the war by the State-directed development of imperial natural resources, and was part of the body of opinion which looked forward to the continuation of economic warfare with Germany once conventional hostilities were over.[62] Imperial self-sufficiency in minerals and the exclusion of Germany from the trade of south and central Africa were ideas which found eager adherents in southern Africa. Merriman, acutely describing the English-speaking political world, picked out 'the commercial element with their wild talk, "shutting out Germany after the War" ... Mr Wilson Fox and his ridiculous proposals—and his talk of the British Empire being managed ... I suppose like the Chartered Company ...'[63] Indeed, in a vision reminiscent of Chartered Company methods, Grey defined the policy of the Empire Resources Development Committee as '... the development of the resources of the Empire, by the Empire and for the Empire ... looking into the future, we can visualise the State as the owner of vast herds of cattle overseas, raised on lands which are today unutilised; as a proprietor of forests and valuable plantations ...'[64]

Wilson-Fox, who was secretary to the committee, epitomised its outlook in a series of wartime articles. He attacked 'laissez-faire' in the relations between capital and labour, calling for productivity agreements in place of haggling over wages. He demanded 'British vessels for British trade' and restrictions on alien land holding and business activities in Britain. He deplored peacetime pandering to consumer interests, advocating instead greater concentration on production and the long-term organisation of the State economy for possible war. From these premises he drew conclusions about the future of the empire. The African empire, including Rhodesia, was not, he thought, destined to develop as an empire of settlement. The chief value of the tropical possessions was that '. . . they provide the trade which enables an increased number of our people to live at home'. Europeans in the tropics, he wrote '. . . will continue to be primarily overseers of native labourers. In these circumstances there is no reason to suppose that these territories will ever receive any large measure of self-government, and there will be the less difficulty in regarding them mainly from the standpoint of estates of the Crown . . .'[65]

Sharp exchanges took place between the League for the Development of Empire Resources and the Aborigines Protection Society. The society, with the co-operation of the *Manchester Guardian*, attacked the concept of empire as an estate instead of a trust; the proposed creation of State monopolies; the consequent deprivation of Africans of their land rights; and their conversion from free producers into forced labourers.[66] For his part Fox accused the society of using old catchwords: if, he wrote, trusteeship imposed obligations towards Africans, then there must be '. . . corresponding duties owed to the Empire by the native inhabitants . . .', among them the duty to contribute to payment for the war.[67] It is against this background of the debate between the declining and retreating radical wing of the Liberal Party, where attention was turning increasingly away from the humanitarian colonial issues of the pre-war era towards planning for a world without war, and where the trusteeship–development synthesis of the 'dual mandate' had not been fully rationalised, and the advanced spokesmen of an emerging managed imperialism, that the animosity generated between the society and the company over Rhodesia should be seen. In the South African context the company's outlook descended from Chamberlain, the society's from pro-Boerism. Between these two political contestants the Colonial Office steered a bureaucratic path, trying to combine the tradition of non-intervention in South African affairs with a desire to clear the administrative decks as a prelude to replacing Company rule.

Yet in 1913 the Colonial Office had not seen the land question as one entirely of administrative exigency. Anderson had taken issue with the company on policy. The point of view of the British government, he wrote, was entirely different from that of the company.

Education and civilisation of the native appear to them to mean an increasing number of natives working for Europeans as wage earners. Our idea is to develop the native tribal organisation so that they may more and more govern themselves and manage their own affairs. An increasing body of natives divorced from the land is incompatible with this policy.[68]

In 1902 J. A. Hobson had drawn a distinction between the 'policy of Basutoland . . . sane imperialism, devoted to the protection, education and self-government of a "lower race" ' and the 'policy of Johannesburg and Rhodesia', and had seen between these two policies 'the widest and ultimately the most important of the struggles in South Africa'.[69] Characteristically this formulation absolved the Boers of suspicion. But if imperial policy was in fact the policy of Basutoland it had to contend with and make adjustments to two rival concepts in southern Africa, not one. The company's assimilationist 'doctrine' has been contrasted with a settler desire for segregation.[70] What was really at issue between the two groups, however, was different versions of how best to make use of African labour. Both white farmers and white industry were opposed to a 'sane imperialism' if it was to mean allowing an independent economic existence to an African peasantry. Recruiting labour for towns, inevitably meant more assimilation than recruiting for farm work from near-by reserves. The political consequences of the former seemed to be the breaking down of traditional African authorities and the creation of a political class seeking to integrate itself into the white political system. Both Boers and Rhodesian settlers wanted labour without this consequence, and with this desire the British government's policy on Basutoland shared a small common area of interest. How to widen this area without sacrificing the whole of its view was the British problem.

Notes

1 C.O. 879/102, 27 December 1909, Selbourne to Crewe, 6 December 1909.
2 C.O. 417/525, 2 August 1913, Harcourt to Gladstone, and C.O. 417/572, 28 August 1915.
3 C.O. 879/102, No. 932, 15 November 1911.
4 C.O. 879/104, No. 947, Selborne to Fair, 16 November 1909.
5 C.O. 879/104, 12 February 1910, Njube to High Commissioner, 25 November 1909, and T. O. Ranger, *The African Voice in Southern Rhodesia*, London, 1970, pp. 30–6.
6 C.O. 879/104, No. 938, 14 May 1910. *King Solomon's Mines* was published in 1887.
7 The monarchy was also undermined by the integration of *indunas* into the government administrative structure and by the tendency of the Native Commissioners to rule directly, taking over the functions of former chiefs. In

addition the government played on the division between supporters of the old property regime and the new inheritors of the former 'king's cattle'; see P. Duignan, 'The native administration of the British South African Company', unpublished thesis, Stanford University, 1961, and C.O. 879/107, No. 969, 8 February 1911.
8   C.O. 525/21, 22 November 1907 and C.O. 879/98, No. 899, Manning to Secretary of State, 21 January 1908. B. S. Krishnamurthy, 'Land and labour in Nyasaland, 1891–1914' (unpublished Ph.D. thesis, London University, 1964), indicates that the Nyasaland administration was out of sympathy rather than out of touch with South African policy.
9   E. Stokes, 'Barotseland: the survival of an African State', in *The Zambesian Past*, ed. E. Stokes and R. Brown, Manchester, 1965, p. 290; and C.O. 879/102, No. 932, Selborne to Crewe, 27 December 1909.
10 C. 8130, *Report of the Matabele Land Commission*, 1896.
11 R. McGregor, 'Native segregation in Rhodesia' (unpublished Ph.D. thesis, London University, 1940), says that the ordinance was 'one of the early demonstrations of the settlers' newly won supremacy in government' (p. 113). But the company had no reason to oppose it, as Africans squatting on its lands (the 'unalienated lands') who were paying rents to the company's commercial account did not come within the purview of the ordinance.
12 C.O. 879/899, Selborne to Crewe, 12 December 1909, and C.O. 417/466, 22 May 1909, encl., Newton to Resident Commissioner, 4 May 1909.
13 'Report of the Southern Rhodesia Native Affairs Enquiry Committee, 1910–11'; the bulk of the committee's recommendations, with which the British government did not concern itself directly, are discussed in P. Mason, *Birth of a Dilemma*, London, 1958, part 3, chapter 3.
14 Gann, S. R., *Southern Rhodesia*; Fox to Milton, 29 April 1910, p. 187.
15 C.O. 879, No. 970, 9 October 1911, and C.O. 417/534, 25 June 1913.
16 C.O. 417/534, 25 June 1913.
17 C.O. 417/499, 9 October 1911.
18 C.O. 417/514, 4 November 1912.
19 C.O. 417/523, Burns-Begg to Harcourt, 1 April 1913.
20 C.O. 417/523, Gladstone to Harcourt, 28 January 1913.
21 C.O. 417/534, 25 June 1913, Memo by Lambert on position of natives in relation to land in Southern Rhodesia.
22 An Irish Nationalist member of Parliament from 1887 to 1918 and Professor of Constitutional Law at King's Inn and at the National University of Ireland; a consistent campaigner against the influence of commercial companies in government.
23 Parliamentary Debates, Commons, 18 June 1913.
24 Wedgwood served as a magistrate in the Transvaal from 1902 to 1904, and on Smuts's staff in east Africa in 1915; member of Parliament from 1906; vice-chairman of the Parliamentary Labour Party, 1922–24; and Chancellor of the Duchy of Lancaster, 1924; one of the few members to show a consistent interest in Rhodesian questions.
25 Parliamentary Debates, Commons, 26 June 1913.
26 Parliamentary Debates, Commons, 10 July, 13 August and 14 August 1913. Lambert complained plaintively that the Southern Rhodesian Legislative Council itself had taken no notice of the sales. The Liebig deal was acclaimed

prominently in the company's annual reports, but this escaped the Colonial Office's notice. A blue book on the Liebig deal was printed but never issued.
27 C.O. 417/526, 20 November 1913.
28 C.O. 417/526, 30 October 1913.
29 Ibid.
30 G.P. Add. MSS, 46, 099, f. 132, 8 October 1913.
31 The 1913 Land Act in the Union had not been applied to the Cape Colony because a restriction of African right to purchase land would have meant a restriction on the right to qualify for the franchise and such restriction was protected by the 'entrenched clauses' in the Act of Union.
32 C.O. 417/526, 13 November 1913, Gladstone to Harcourt.
33 C.O. 417/538, 3 April 1914.
34 C.O. 417/550, 16 January 1914.
35 Coryndon had been in the company's service for seventeen years. A member of the 'Pioneer Column' in 1890, he had fought in the wars of 1893 and 1896, and had been private secretary to Rhodes during the Raid enquiry from 1896 to 1897. From 1900 to 1907 he was Administrator of North Western Rhodesia.
     Gladstone in fact thought that Sloley, the Resident Commissioner of Basutoland, was a better candidate but said he could not be spared. In any case, Gladstone had stipulated that the chairman should 'carry weight with the European residents as well as with the natives' and Maguire had earlier stigmatised Sloley as a 'negrophilist'.
     From 1910 to 1913 Garraway had been Gladstone's military secretary. Fiddes commented, ' ... even tender-hearted Lord Gladstone found Garraway so useless he had been retired'. (C.O. 417/567, 8 December 1915.)
36 C.O. 417/550, 16 January 1914.
37 C.O. 417/552, 21 May 1914.
38 C.O. 417/539, 30 April 1914, and C.O. 885/16, C.O. to Law Officers, 9 May 1914.
39 A.P.S. papers, G 159, Harris to V. Buxton, 24 August 1914.
40 A.P.S. G 159, and T. O. Ranger, *The African Voice*, pp. 58–9.
41 C.O. 417/542, 4 September 1914.
42 C.O. 417/543, Buxton to Newton, 25 November 1914.
43 C.O. 417/543, 25 November 1914, Newton to Buxton.
44 Minute on C.O. 417/544, 8 December 1914.
45 Minute on C.O. 417/544, 12 December 1914.
46 C.O. 417/569, 19 January 1915.
47 Memo in A.P.S. G 159.
48 A.P.S. G 159, Harris to Raymer, 25 August 1915.
49 A.P.S. G 159, Wilson to Harris, 17 October 1915.
50 A.P.S. G 159, Harris to F. Buxton, undated copy (after August 1914).
51 Memo in A.P.S. G 170.
52 Harcourt papers, C.O. No. 3, Buxton to Harcourt, I, 18 January 1915.
53 A.P.S. G 202.
54 *Ibid.*, Harris to Evans, 11 July 1916; Harris to Steel-Maitland, 6 October 1916, and Harris to Sharp, 7 October 1916.
55 A.P.S. G 202.

56 See S. J. S. Cookey, *Britain and the Congo Question*, London, 1968, pp. 135 ff.
57 Rolin wrote, '. . . la politique indigène de la Compagnie est domineé par la désire d'édifier, sur les ruines du collectivisme des tribus, un régime de salariat industriel et agricole, ou, en d'autres terms, de transformer les masses des noirs, jusqu'ici co-propriétaires collectifs du sols, en un proletariat' (p. 258).
58 A.P.S. G 159, Harris to Johnston, 30 May 1916, and Harris to Horton, 24 March 1916.
59 A.P.S. G 159, Harris to Longden, 19 April 1916, and A.P.S. G 160, Harris to Roberts, 19 February 1917.
60 C.O. 417/534, 30 July 1913, B.S.A.C. to C.O.
61 On the 'official doctrine' of integration see Mason, *Birth of a Dilemma*, pp. 260 ff. The impression of Milner is Beatrice Webb's, quoted in A. M. Gollin, *Milner*, London, 1964, p. 118. On the League see W. K. Hancock, *Survey of Commonwealth Affairs*, London, 1937, xi, part 1, pp. 106 ff.
62 See Birchenough's report, 'British trade in southern Africa' in Cd. 1844, 1903–04, and his article 'The war and trade in Africa', *Journal of the Royal African Society*, 1915.
63 B.P., Letters of interest, 1914–16, Merriman to Buxton, 20 November 1916.
64 *United Empire*, ix, 1918.
65 Articles by H. Wilson Fox, 'A platform for an imperial party', *The Nineteenth Century*, November 1916; 'The empire and the new protection', *Nineteenth Century*, March 1917; in the *Geographical Journal*, October 1916; and the *Journal of the Royal Society of the Arts*, December 1916.
66 E.g. *Manchester Guardian*, 15 May 1917.
67 'The development of empire resources', *Nineteenth Century*, October 1916.
68 C.O. 417/534, Minute, 30 July 1913.
69 J. A. Hobson, *Imperialism: a Study*, 1902 edition, p. 260.
70 Mason, *Birth of a Dilemma*, pp. 260 ff.

PART TWO
The birth of two Rhodesias
1914–25

CHAPTER 6

The war and the future of white Africa

1914–18

1 The Zambezi line

Though the careful manouvering of the years 1910–14 had not resulted in the conjunction of Rhodesia and the Union, during the war plans for the remaking of the world were laid on a far grander scale, and consequently the political patterns of south and central Africa were once again matters for reconsideration. Most of the leading protagonists planned considerable changes for the area for the post-war period. Though an undoubted backwater, southern Africa was shaken during the war years by three revolts and two minor military campaigns. The unsuccessful African risings in Nyasaland and Mozambique made little immediate impact; the revolt which really alarmed Whitehall was the Afrikaner rebellion of 1914. The loyalty of Botha and Smuts to the empire in the face of this revolt, and South Africa's contributions to the imperial war effort in South West Africa and east Africa gave the South African government a considerable claim to imperial gratitude, though it also underlined the dependence of imperial power in the area on continued South African support. And while some Afrikaners had shown reliability in collaborating with the imperial cause, the Afrikaner revolt highlighted again the desirability of securing a trustworthy and loyal British base. How far this would be compatible with South Africa's claims was a matter for calculation: would the imperial position be more secure with an undoubtedly British Rhodesian base, or best helped by rewarding and strengthening a friendly government in the Union? When Lord Buxton, the new High Commissioner, visited Rhodesia in 1914 and submitted a report on the territory to the Cabinet he stressed that 'The most marked feature of Rhodesia, as far as the white inhabitants are concerned, is that they are typically English . . . They are proud of being purely British and that they form part of the Empire; and they crave public recognition of this fact.' Afrikaners were poor and kept to themselves, Afrikaans expressions were taboo, and even 'the ugly colonial accent . . . so pervading and intrusive at the Cape . . .' was absent.[1] This chauvinistic patriotism, which had seemed a liability in peacetime, was now an asset that could no longer be entirely ignored.

When, in 1915, the company first publicised its intention of pressing for the amalgamation of Northern and Southern Rhodesia one of its motives was to add the 'more distinctively English' element in Northern Rhodesia to the South.[2] Furthermore by adding an almost entirely African territory to Southern Rhodesia the company hoped to pre-empt any plans to push Rhodesia into the Union as part of the post-war settlement which Whitehall might evolve. As Malcolm reported the board's views, 'Even the present Imperial Government, which can refuse Botha practically nothing, would hesitate before handing over to the Union Government . . . uncontrolled power over the million or so natives in the North . . .'[3] Company circles had welcomed the coming of the coalition government in Britain; they looked forward to the 'Unionist leaven' having a 'steadying effect on the Colonial Office' and, when Harcourt was replaced by Bonar Law, who was not only a conservative imperialist but a man *au fait* with the politics of big business, to a more sympathetic attitude towards the company itself.[4] Law's attention, however, was on the conduct of the war and far from colonial affairs, and official reaction was markedly hostile to the company's plan. The keynote was struck by Just, who wrote that 'Southern Rhodesia is undoubtedly a "white man's country" . . . Northern Rhodesia is not . . .' Anderson, who was on the point of leaving the Colonial Office, placed the proposal in the context of imperial policy for post-war southern Africa. 'We do not want to force Rhodesia into the Union but we ought not to allow anything really aimed at keeping them out, and there is no doubt that this is the real object of this proposal.' The recent South African rebellion had shaken even those committed to the 'Liberal solution' in South Africa, and Anderson's analysis of the future was strangely Milnerian. 'What will be the position after the War?' he asked.

The conquered territory [i.e. South West Africa] will no doubt for a time be governed as such, but not for very long, and when it is admitted to the privilege of sending members to the Union Parliament, these members will unquestionably join hands with their late allies, the Nationalists, and enrole themselves under the Hertzog banner. If there is no prospect of an addition of strength to the loyal element in South Africa from Rhodesia, our tenure there will be very uncertain.[5]

There were objections too from the point of view of Africans in Northern Rhodesia. 'It is mainly a vast native territory from which a large part of the labour supply for the mines and farms of Southern Rhodesia is drawn.' Anderson noted that with amalgamation of the Rhodesias control of Africans in the north would pass to the Southern Rhodesian Legislative Council, which would inevitably lead to friction between it and the Colonial Office. Though '. . . the natives cannot of course be consulted as to their wishes', the Colonial Office was their protector. He concluded, 'I suspect that the adjustment the Company looks for after the War is the absorption of Nyasaland . . . the proper solution would be the contrary one of absorption of North Eastern, and in fact the greater part of Northern Rhodesia itself in a big Central African Colony which would include Nyasaland . . .' Buxton, however, supported the company's proposals and in July 1916 announced publicly that no imperial interest was affected and that Southern Rhodesian opinion would prevail. This dismayed the Colonial Office, where it was pointed out that the imperial authorities could not be neutral about the adding of three-quarters of a million Africans to the control of a white minority which had so far not been considered fit for responsible government.[6] In fact, as neither the British government nor the company was contemplating the extension of the constitutional powers of the Southern Rhodesian Legislative Council, on the letter of the law African interests would not be affected, as the British government would have retained the same control over African affairs. The point was that the Colonial Office was unwilling to extend the possibility of its having to come into conflict with a Southern African white legislature over African affairs, as officials anticipated the recurrence of the kind of deadlocks which had been experienced in Natal in the 1870s and 1880s.[7]

Both Lambert and the Under-Secretary of State, Steel-Maitland, raised the wider consideration of drawing the line between white and black Africa. At present, wrote Lambert, South Africa ended at the Zambesi.

[It] is essentially a country in which a large black population is ruled by a white oligarchy. This is so everywhere (except our three black protectorates) and must be so wherever there are enough white men—when they reach a certain number they will claim control of the country and the control has always been given to them. Southern Rhodesia could have responsible government tomorrow if she had enough white men—it is only the scantiness of her white population which makes it impossible . . . But Northern Rhodesia has no white population to speak of and may never have . . .

Steel-Maitland wrote in similar terms. 'At some time not far off there must be a line south of which, there is self-government by the white population, North of which, for many years, Crown Colony government.' Precisely where the line would be—the most natural border seemed to be the Zambesi—would '. . . obviously be determined by the percentage of whites to black in the population, by geography, climate, etc, and by native races.'[8]

British official opinion was not the only source of this formulation. Commentators interested in south and central Africa were few and far between, but there was general agreement on this issue. In 1911 Gouldsbury, a Northern Rhodesian Native Commissioner, had written of a body of opinion which was too apt to regard Rhodesia as a single unit and 'to invest it . . . with all the attributes of a South African dependency'. The north-east, he urged, 'belongs far more definitely to Central than to South Africa . . . [that] Europe in Africa' and ought consequently to be developed as a 'native State'.[9] In 1917 Alexander Hetherwick, the head of the Blantyre mission in Nyasaland, declared:

We may put aside at once any idea of incorporating Nyasaland within the South African Union. Nyasaland is a black man's country. There is no scope within it for the settlement of a white population . . . the future problems and lines of development of Nyasaland are altogether different from those of South Africa. The river Zambesi has always been a natural boundary between Central and South Africa . . . the natural future of Nyasaland will be in association with its neighbour on the west—Northern Rhodesia.'[10]

In another article in which South African aspirations were discussed it was pointed out that the former Commissioner of the Nyasaland protectorate, Harry Johnston, had once written that 'The Union of South Africa by all trends of South African history might legitimately aspire to rule Central Africa as far North as Tanganyika'. South Africa in its present state had been compared to the first thirteen states of the American Union, and South Africa's military efforts in east Africa had given her a renewed claim. The author, however, advised the '. . . preservation of the identity of the South Central African dependencies . . .' Amalgamation of the two Rhodesias must be fought, because 'Southern Rhodesia, whether within or without the Union, is part of South Africa . . .' and if it were joined to the north this would mean the extension of South African influence well beyond its natural boundary—the Zambesi.[11]

The American 'official mind' saw the problem in a like manner. G. L. Beer, in a paper prepared early in 1918,[12] divided Africa into three parts.

The first was the Mediterranean littoral; the second white man's Africa, where 'beyond the Kunene and Zambesi rivers ... a distinctly European or Western type of civilisation is developing subject to the adaptations necessitated by local conditions, of which the most fundamental is the presence of a large native population far outnumbering the white settlers.' The third section was middle Africa. Beer's divisions were not hard and fast: the exceptions were the three black protectorates, the potentially white East African highlands and Northern Rhodesia, of which he wrote that though it was '. . . distinctly tropical, her connection with Southern Rhodesia and the growing white population there, the fact that the trade outlet is toward the south-east, and, finally, the political interest in the destiny of this area, link up all of Rhodesia in a measure with white man's Africa'.

While Beer recognised the Zambesi line he felt that it would be breached in the case of Northern Rhodesia. In South Africa Smuts's ambitions were even wider-ranging. Speaking in London in May 1917, he said, 'We have started by creating a new white base in South Africa, and today we are in a position to move forward towards the north. . . . The time will come when it will be almost a misnomer to speak of South Africa, because the northern limits of our civilisation will have gone so far.'[13] The possibilities that he, and other South African politicians, had in mind may be illustrated by a letter to Smuts in which John X. Merriman mused whether east Africa, even if not a white man's country, might become an '. . . African India in which South Africa might play the same part that Scotland has played in British India by supplying soldiers and administrators and in becoming a field for the ambitions of our young men'. Merriman told Smuts in conclusion that he was '. . . Trying to find you a good book on Java. A study of that country is very useful in view of possible contingencies.'[14]

2 Planning re-partition

South Africa's immediate expansionist aims were to her east and west, and Botha and Smuts hoped that the post-war settlement would not only provide incorporation of the conquered German territory in the west but would be the occasion of the fulfilment of their long-standing ambition to take the port of Lourenço Marques into the Union, and even, possibly, to secure Beira under their wing. This ambition pre-dated the formation of the Union: the Transvaal mines drew heavily on

Mozambique for labour, and Southern Rhodesia's attempts to negotiate a share of the Mozambique labour pool had been a serious cause of friction between the Transvaal and its northern neighbour. Of more long-term existence were the desire of the Transvaal to control its main port and the optimistic expectation of both British and Afrikaner in southern Africa that the festering grip of the despised Portuguese on Mozambique must soon come to a justly inglorious end. Counterpoise calculations had been closely related to ambitions in Mozambique. Before union Smuts was suspected of promoting a trek, the purpose of which was to create an Afrikaner presence in Mozambique, and the British government was pressed to act to ensure that any gains in Mozambique should be attached to Natal, or preferably Rhodesia, to counterbalance Afrikaner ascendancy in other parts of the coming South African Union.[15] While the imperial government, which had hitched its wagon to Afrikaner supremacy, did not see the situation in these terms, the company, which had the interests of Rhodesia to look to, certainly did. It feared, as Chaplin wrote in 1909, that if Botha failed to get Rhodesian agreement to entry into the Union he would '... try to isolate it by forcing the hand of the imperial government over the Portuguese question—Lourenco Marques and Beira. The Rhodes policy *mutatis mutandis* . . .'[16]

Consequently the company too had expectant eyes upon Portuguese territory, though the British government had done nothing to encourage company aspirations to take over the port of Beira. In 1911, when unrest threatened at the port, Harcourt sharply warned the company that any independent action to protect Rhodesian interests could result in a cancellation of its charter. When the company pressed its claims to Beira Harcourt favoured instead a partition of Mozambique between Nyasaland and the Union.[17] To Botha's government any increase in the independent pretensions of Rhodesia, which it felt it was destined to absorb, and which in Jameson's hands provided a territorial base for the Unionist opposition, had always been inadmissable. When, for the first time, the Union government was consulted by the imperial government on a matter of foreign policy—the conclusion of the Anglo-German convention regarding the eventuality of Portugal surrendering her African territories, the Union government refused its overt approval. As Gladstone explained, 'There is nothing to show that Beira won't go to Rhodesia. I know the possibility of an independent and powerful Rhodesia is a bugbear to them.'[18] Thus the Union and Rhodesia had rival expansionist aspirations in Mozambique as well as in Bechuanaland. Gladstone pointed out that Jameson's open claim to

Bechuanaland had made the Union government 'all the more fearful about Beira . . .'

In 1915 Smuts turned his attention to the possible post-war partition of Mozambique. While he did not favour exchanging the newly conquered South West Africa for Mozambique, he had '. . . another idea, and that was that if East Africa were conquered and annexed, that the northern part might be added to British East Africa, and the southern and central part be "swopped" with the Portuguese for the southern part of Portuguese East Africa . . .' 'No doubt the scheme he has in mind,' reported Buxton to Harcourt, 'is one considerable reason why he is keen to send a contingent from here to East Africa.'[19] By 1916 the South Africans were confident that Portugal would accede to an arrangement on the lines Smuts suggested, though a change of government in Lisbon dissipated their optimism. The assessment of Walter Long, the British Colonial Secretary, was more realistic. While he agreed with Chaplin's view that it would be 'splendid' if the Portuguese would retire north of the Zambesi and east of the Shire, he warned that they were 'very difficult people to deal with' and that they showed 'no sign of being ready to consider anything involving giving up any territory'. Long suggested to the Chartered Company that an alternative strategy would be to leave the Portuguese with their sovereignty while aiming at control of the great concessionary companies that controlled so large a part of Mozambique.[20] The Union's policy remained more conventional: in 1918, when considering his coming visit to Europe, Botha stressed the need to see '. . . difficulties solved for which we shall perhaps never have another chance—especially the question of Mozambique . . . there is no doubt about it, this is a matter which we must bring up and settle in our favour'.[21]

Those who had supported Liberal policy between 1906 and 1910 had been given anxiously needed vindication by the firmly imperialist course of Botha and Smuts in smashing the 1914 rebellion and in supporting the war effort. Conservatives in England, already warmed by the exclusion of Hertzog, were also eager to please their new allies. The British government's policy, therefore, was one 'of doing everything in our power to support Botha',[22] and it was evolved also in the context of the newly pervasive fear in official circles that followed the Nationalist gains in the 1915 elections in South Africa, as to the possibly stimulating effects of Botha's and Smuts's enthusiasm for empire on the growth of Afrikaner nationalism. With this background the British government began to make its own assessment of possible territorial adjustments. Buxton submitted a memorandum in which he proposed the partitioning of Mozambique south of the Zambesi between Rhodesia and the Union, with the proviso that the company's charter ought not to be extended to cover Rhodesia's new acquisitions. Inclusion of Swaziland in the Union would follow the partition. He suggested that the amalgamation of North Eastern and North Western Rhodesia had been a mistake which could now be rectified by incorporating the northeast with Nyasaland in a new Central African Protectorate. He assumed that South West Africa would go to the Union (it will, he wrote later, '... always be more of a European than a native territory, since thanks to the Germans there are comparatively few natives, and it is a temperate climate . . .') and suggested that Bechuanaland should, like southern Mozambique, be divided into two. The north, he wrote, had more in common with Rhodesia than with South Africa and 'If it ever comes into the Union it should come in as part of Rhodesia if and when Rhodesia joins the Union'. The Caprivi Strip and the unoccupied territory in northern Bechuanaland would go to the company in settlement of its long-standing land claims in the area. The transfer of the southern part of Bechuanaland to the Union would then be 'a convenient and natural step'.[23] Buxton envisaged a compromise between Rhodesian and Union claims and a satisfaction of the Union's ambitions in South West Africa and Swaziland. If Rhodesia was to join it, then the Union would scoop the pool.

In London a Cabinet sub-committee on post-war territorial changes turned its attention to Africa and to the future of the conquered German colonies. It took cogniscance of the Colonial Office's powerfully argued objections to the possible return of South West Africa to Germany, on the grounds that Botha and Smuts, who had staked their political existence on loyalty to the empire, had to be vindicated in South African eyes. The committee therefore recommended the propitiating of South African wishes, because the rapid suppression of the 1914 rebellion '... should not obscure from our view the danger with which the whole fabric of the British position in South Africa was menaced'. Turning its eyes to the north, the committee said that it would be possible

. . . to treat the whole of the great region between the southern frontier of Abyssinia and the Soudan to the future northern frontier of the South African Union (whether fixed at the Zambesi or further north) as a single administrative area. This larger British East Africa has certain general characteristics differentiating it both from the South African Union and from a purely black man's country like the Soudan or West Africa. It is not likely to become a white man's country, even in the sense in which the expression is used in South Africa. But it is a country which is capable of containing, in the more bracing uplands, a considerable settlement of white farmers, owners of plantations, and directors of industry.[24]

This was a slightly different formulation: the line between white Africa and black Africa was not quite as clear, but the committee clearly accepted that there was a white Africa, up to the Zambesi or beyond, and that within this area South Africa's aspirations towards expansion and control were wholly legitimate. To the north of this area was an intermediate Africa which might be fused into a large new colony, or even, perhaps, be set aside for Indian settlement.

The company had different ideas. It sought to retain and enlarge its sphere north of the Union and instead of an Intermediate Africa it urged that the guiding principle in the disposal of German East Africa should be the building of a British community north of the Union in order, as Chaplin wrote, to counterbalance the 'extreme Dutch element ... This should be the function of an enlarged Rhodesia'.[25] The concern of the company and of the political circles represented by it, and of the British government remained fundamentally similar: both were concerned with the Afrikaner threat and both were still following Rhodes's counterpoise policy. The company remained convinced that the counterweight would be more effective outside the Union; London, following the logic of the 'liberal solution' sought to strengthen the imperialist elements inside the gates.

The British government's advisors in South Africa were also prepared to see the southern sphere of influence cross the Zambesi line. The High Commissioner commended the company's plan for the amalgamation of the Rhodesias. He could see no objection to the extension of Southern Rhodesian 'native policy' to the north. He thought furthermore that an amalgamated Rhodesia could without damage to African interests become a part of the Union. He wrote:

Northern Rhodesia could be included in the Union and still remain a native territory. The Union government are only now beginning to shape their native policy, but they are beginning on the right lines, and I should not contemplate the ultimate transfer of the Angonis or the Mashukulumbwe to their charge with any greater misgiving than I should regard the early transfer of the Swazis.[26]

Another possibility, he suggested, was partition of the north, and Buxton now put forward a detailed district-by-district plan drawn up in consultation with Stanley, the Resident Commissioner in Salisbury, and Wallace, the company's Administrator in the north. The railway belt was to go in with the south, and four remaining pieces were to be divided

The war and the future of white Africa 117

between a future east African territory, Nyasaland, and two separate African territories in the Kafue area and Barotseland.

The instincts of the Rhodesian settlers, though they accorded with the company on the question of the counterpoise, were far closer to those of the Colonial Office regarding the Zambesi line. They too saw the Zambesi as the division between white and black Africa. Union with the north would, they felt, delay the achievement of self-government. In addition they looked with aversion at the already different economic structure in the north. African clerks, artisans and traders were pointed to with distinct distaste. Union with the north would mean, as one northern settler pointed out, that a new class of whites would have to be imported into the north to 'enforce . . . the idea of a white man's country'.[27] Settler opposition served as a smokescreen behind which the Colonial Office was able to parry the company's amalgamation plans. Lambert repeated the rule of behaviour that '. . . the confidence of the elected members in the Colonial Office is a valuable asset and the Secretary of State must never take sides with the Company against the elected members in large issues affecting the future of the territory unless he is forced to do so (as he might be in a native question).'[28] Though the Rhodesian Legislative Council approved the amalgamation proposals, the majority of the elected members had voted against them. To the considerable disillusionment of the company, which had expected greater sympathy from Walter Long, an old associate, as Secretary of State, the proposals were turned down. Chaplin complained, '. . . a weak friend at headquarters is worse than an enemy', hostile officials and 'the radical gang in our deplorable House of Commons' were the influences he blamed for the frustration of the Company's ambitions.[29]

3 The Caprivi Strip

The Caprivi Strip, which obtruded between Bechuanaland and Northern Rhodesia, was another bone of contention between the company and the British government. As early as 1897 it had been suggested to Lord Salisbury that the German government be approached with a view to transferring the strip to British jurisdiction, but characteristically 'Lord Salisbury pooh-poohed the whole idea, and said that as no white man would be there for five hundred years it was not worth while raising a thorny question with Germany'.[30] At the end of 1907 Selborne, concerned with problems of control over the borders of Bechuanaland and improved access to Lozi country, suggested that

Britain might acquire the strip, though he made no mention under which South African authority he thought it should fall. During 1908 negotiations were entered into with the Germans, but the single concession the British government would offer—an adjustment of the Orange river boundary between the Cape and German South West Africa—was eventually not put to Germany for fear of offending the Cape government. Negotiations were then dropped pending the formation of the Union and after a German indication that they intended sending a district oficer to control the area.[31]

The North Western Rhodesian administration remained anxious about the area. It pointed out that regardless of the lines on European maps Lewanika still regarded the strip's inhabitants as his subjects, and that the Lozi continued to graze their cattle across the border.[32] Yet when the company approached the Colonial Office, asking whether 'the most unnatural and inconvenient frontier' could not be rectified, it received no sympathy because of the belief that the request stemmed from the company's ambitions in Bechuanaland.[33]

On the outbreak of war in 1914 the strip was occupied by Southern Rhodesian forces and, pending the peace, was administered as part of Northern Rhodesia. The administration and the company gave support to what they reported was a strong and undoubted claim which the Lozi had to the strip.[34] During the war the Lozi were given permission to cultivate in the strip, which permission was extended annually until 1920. In his advice on territorial changes Buxton supported the Rhodesian claim, though he considered that the strip should pass to the company, along with the northern part of Bechuanaland. He noted that Botha and Smuts were strongly opposed to his proposal.

In spite, however, of some grandiose plans, the basic territorial configuration of south and central Africa remained unchanged by the war. The German presence was removed: German South West Africa was handed over intact to the Union, though the latter's hold was not entirely untrammelled. The Caprivi Strip was to be administered by the Bechuanaland authorities for the Union. In 1921 Yeta, the new Lozi king, was finally told that their claim had been refused.[35] Though new lines were drawn on the maps of Europe and the Middle East, no other changes were made in southern Africa. The two Rhodesias remained separate. And South Africa failed to absorb even a part of Mozambique. The Portuguese strategy of joining the allies in order to make it more or less impossible for them to be parties to the partitioning of her colonies succeeded. Smuts remained only with the forlorn hope, when formulating plans for the mandate system, that the Portuguese colonies could also be placed under international control, 'thereby giving Britain a pretext for intervention'.[36] But though territorial gains were few, by 1919 the position of the Union government as heir to the British position in southern Africa, as trustee both for the imperial cause and for the Africans, had been strengthened.

Notes

1 C.O. 417/582, 14 August 1916.
2 Ch. 8/2/2/2, Chaplin to Birchenough, 10 August 1915.
3 Ch. 8/2/2/11, f. 130, Malcolm to Chaplin, 12 October 1915.
4 B. K. Long, *Drummond Chaplin*, p. 206, and R. Blake, *The Unknown Prime Minister*, London, 1955, p. 43.
5 C.O. 417/574, 26 January 1915.
6 C.O. 417/577, 8 August 1916.
7 C.O. 417/579, 22 December 1916.
8 *Ibid.*; he confessed, 'I have been trying to dig into the affinities of the native races but have not yet got far.'
9 Gouldsbury and Sheane, *The Great Plateau of Northern Rhodesia*, London, 1911.
10 'Nyasaland today and tomorrow', *Journal of the Royal African Society*, 1917.
11 'A Central African Confederation', *Journal of the Royal African Society*, 1917
12 G. L. Beer, *African Questions at the Paris Peace Conference*, New York, 1923, pp. 71–4. Beer was chief of the Colonial Section of the American delegation and was later designated head of the League of Nations Mandate Division.
13 J. C. Smuts, 'The future of south and central Africa', *Wartime Speeches*, London, 1917 (delivered 22 May 1917).
14 S.P., III, Merriman to Smuts, 5 June 1916, pp. 374–5.
15 C.O. 879/925, No. 106, secret, Col. A. J. Arnold to Selborne, 11 May 1908.
16 Quoted in B. K. Long, *Drummond Chaplin*, p. 149.
17 G.P. Add MSS, 45, 997, Harcourt to Gladstone, 3 August 1911, and C.O. 417/508, B.S.A.C. to C.O., 20 December 1911, and minutes.
18 G.P. Add. MSS, 45,999, f. 134, Gladstone to Harcourt, 12 March 1913.
19 B.P. 1915, Buxton to Harcourt, 15 May 1915; see also W. R. Louis, *Great Britain and Germany's Lost Colonies*, Oxford, 1967, and S.P., III, Smuts to Merriman, 30 August 1915, p. 318.
20 Ch. 8/2/2/8, Chaplin to Long, 11 February 1917, and October 1917; and Long to Chaplin, 14 April 1917 and 4 September 1917.
21 S.P., III, Botha to Smuts, 26 February 1918, p. 609.
22 B.P., Letters of interest, Fiddes to Buxton, 4 January 1917 and 7 January 1918.
23 B.P. 1919, Memo, n.d., In C.O. 417/589, August 1916, there is a note from

Rodwell to Fiddes referring to a memo on post-war adjustments by Buxton which indicates that it was produced in mid-1916.
24 C.O. 537/990, secret, Interim report of the Territorial Changes Committee re African colonies, 22 March 1917; see also W. R. Louis, 'The south-western origins of the sacred trust, 1914–19', *African Affairs*, LXVI, January 1967.
25 B. K. Long, *Drummond Chaplin*, Chaplin to Long, telegram, 1917, p. 216.
26 C.O. 417/589, Buxton to Secretary of State, 14 August 1917.
27 C.O. 417/591, 22 October 1917, encl., *Buluwayo Chronicle*, 21 July 1917.
28 C.O. 417/589, 13 August 1917, Minutes.
29 B. K. Long, *Drummond Chaplin*, p. 206.
30 C.O. 879/98, No. 899, Gould Adams to Rodwell, 9 August 1907.
31 *Ibid.*, and C.O. 879/102, No. 932.
32 *Ibid.*, Wallace to Selborne, 30 September 1909.
33 C.O. 417/518, 1 February 1912.
34 C.O. 417/559, 27 March 1915; C.O. 417/585, 29 September 1915; and Wilson Fox in *Journal of the Royal African Society*, July 1915.
35 C.O. 417/658, 21 March 1921, Buxton to Milner.
36 W. R. Louis, *Great Britain and Germany's Lost Colonies*, pp. 7–8.

CHAPTER 7

Separation: the southward turn

1918–21

1 The Reserves Commission reports

During the war years, while plans for territorial dispositions were being bandied about, the Southern Rhodesian Native Reserves Commission set about preparing the country for its future as a part of white Africa. At the end of 1915 the commission presented an interim report. Its basic task had been to take into account both the present and future land requirements of the African population of Southern Rhodesia, bearing in mind not only natural population increase but the anticipated spread of white settlement.[1] This led the commission to a sketchy consideration of the basic issues affecting the socio-economic future of the African population: in short, was proletarianisation to continue, or ought the aim to be the establishment of conditions which would allow as many Rhodesian Africans as wished to do so to exist as a peasantry separate from the economic world of white Rhodesia? In setting out the principles which had guided it, the commission, remarking on the phrase 'from time to time', which had defined the company's obligation to set aside more reserve land, said that certain people

... appear to have regarded these words as meaning that as the native population increases every individual is to retain an indefeasible right to land sufficient for his agricultural and pastoral requirements . . . If this interpretation be allowed it is evident . . . that there can be no limit to the expansion of the Native Reserves, and if the argument is pursued to its logical conclusion the whole of Southern Rhodesia will in course of time be required for this purpose. This extreme view is only mentioned to show the absurdity which it might involve.[2]

Though the Colonial Office, when it had drafted the commission's terms of reference, had not pressed the point to its logical conclusion, it had all along been motivated by a preservationist and not an assimilationist view of the reserves system. The current of opinion now ran the other way, and the Colonial Office's acceptance of the commission's approach was a major step in the direction of the creation of a 'white man's country' in Rhodesia, and a step away from the direction which it had appeared to be allowing for when the Reserves Commission was created in 1914.

Like the company, then, the commission espoused eventual assimilation—the policy of Johannesburg and not the policy of Basutoland. When in the Colonial Office Lambert commented on its final report he too argued in favour of assimilation. Fortifying himself with references to the 1905 commission, he wrote:

Reserves are necessary in the early stages of white settlement when the uncivilised tribal native has neither the habit nor the power of work, but the idea that the native has an inalienable right to vegetate in reserves while the white man has to work does not seem to me to be either just or good for the native. It is far better that he should come under gradual economic pressure . . . While therefore there is good reason still . . . to provide for the present needs of the native it is doubtful whether large provision *ought* to be made ahead.[3]

Thus land set aside for Africans was to be 'literally reserve lands' and not for the preservation of a way of life. As Mason put it, 'a temporary shielding of the African until he is ready for assimilation' and the civilising experience of work within the white system.[4]

When therefore the commission proposed an overall reduction in the size of the reserves the pill was not too difficult for officials in London to swallow. The mass of detail in the final report overwhelmed British officials both in South Africa and in London. So multitudinous and detailed were the recommendations that they saw no way between accepting or rejecting them as a whole,[5] and the actual recommendations, which comprised a series of additions to and reductions from existing reserves, were never examined in detail in London. Before the commission began its work 72 million acres were outside the reserves. Of these 14 million were in the hands of white settlers and 10 million in the hands of land companies; the remaining two-thirds, 48 million acres, were as yet unalienated and these were the subject of the reference to the Privy Council. The reserves were approximately 25 million acres in extent.[6] On them, according to the commission's reckoning, lived 400,000 of the country's 713,000 Africans. Though there was evidently no shortage of white land, the commission initially recommended the overall reduction of the reserves by as much as 3 million acres, but at a meeting held in the Resident

Commissioner's Buluwayo home he and Garroway persuaded a very reluctant Coryndon of the political inadvisability of so blatant a reduction, and it was amended to an overall cut-back of one million acres.[7]

The commissioners thought they had erred on the side of generosity to the Africans. They made it clear that they found 'little evidence of conflict' between settler and African interests, and that they considered progressive white development to be as much of an African interest as a settler one.[8] They were insensitive to the link between European land appropriation and African grievances which was so well summed up in 1920 by the Superintendent of Natives, Buluwayo, when he wrote of the Ndebele, 'The word *amaplazi* . . . meaning "farms", stands it may be said for all that is most distasteful in our rule.'[9] In general the commission acted in accordance with the company's policy of excluding Africans from areas within twenty five miles of the railway. It acted too as an agent of the company's plans, and its numerous adjustments removed good farming land from the reserves; it worked closely with the company's land settlement board, relating recommendations to the company's settlement schemes, ranching and forestry projects and railway plans.[10] As Duignan summed up, 'The object was to get all the land that might be usable for future settlement and Company projects.'[11] The commission never considered the appropriation of settler- or Company-owned lands: while it felt itself free to displace Africans, with regard to Europeans it commented only that 'vested interests limit our choice so much . . .'[12]

In spite of the stress which the commission and the assimilationists in the Colonial Office and the company laid on the desirability of Africans living outside the reserves it was clear that it was the intention that they should live outside only as labourers. It was noted complacently that the rent charged on vacant lands held by the company and other absentee landlords, as well as the pressure of the Locations Ordinance, would lead to Africans moving into the reserves. But because the reserves were to be limited in size there would come into existence the landless labourer whom Anderson had been so concerned to avoid. The commissioners wrote:

The relationship between indigenous farm labour and the occupation of the reserves will gradually develop and settle itself along lines which are not as yet sufficiently important to need analysis . . . There appears to be a likelihood that gradually there will grow up a class of farm labourers who will live on farms and not on reserves. This class is already in existence in the Transvaal and in other parts of the Union.[13]

Implicitly the commission rejected administrative segregation in two more ways. It did away, as far as was possible, with reserves bordering on the Union, Bechuanaland or Portuguese territory, and created 'moderately sized reserves distributed evenly throughout the territory', explaining that reserves too large and remote would be 'far from adequate control and from centres of education and progress . . .'[14]

2 South African policies

During the war, too, in the Union of South Africa, a land commission was at work. The Act of 1913 had been an interim measure which froze land holding while a commission under the chairmanship of Sir William Beaumont, a former Administrator of Natal and Supreme Court judge, investigated the bases of a more permanent territorial segregation. It had to work in more difficult circumstances than its sister commission in Rhodesia, where sufficient land could be made to appear available without an attack on white holdings. In the south even an outward show of division could not be made without the purchase of land already in white hands, and this was to be an immediate political stumbling block. Beaumont's commission reported in 1916 and it recommended limited increases in the African areas that had been frozen by the Act of 1913. The report was followed by the introduction into the South African House of Assembly of the Native Administration Bill by General Botha in March 1917. The High Commissioner, Buxton, both co-operated with and guided the development of the policy behind the Bill, which traced its pedigree to two imperial ancestors: the Lagden commission, which had laid down territorial segregation; and the schedule to the Act of Union, with its outline of administrative separation. Buxton recalled in 1924 that he and Botha had frequently discussed 'native questions in which I was hereditarily, and as High Commissioner, greatly interested' and he recorded that 'I was entirely in accord with the main proposals he had in mind'. He claimed too that the step towards institutional separation that the Bill contained—the Native Affairs Commission— was '. . . at my suggestion to General Botha . . . to be on all fours with the Commission contained in the Schedule to the Act of Union.'[15]

Botha admitted that the 1913 Act had borne more heavily on Africans than on Europeans, and he recommended his Bill as a step towards both territorial and political segregation. The Bill would have created a permanent Native Affairs Commission and provided for the gradual introduction of Native Councils and individual tenure schemes, the professed aim being to settle African political aspirations by giving both traditional and new leadership an opportunity to concern themselves with African affairs in African areas.[16] The Bill was shelved by the Union parliament. Botha's attempt to 'solve the native question' came to grief on the rocks of Unionist opposition, which was made up partly of those representing the interests of Transvaal land companies, partly of those who foresaw a threat to the Cape franchise, and of Natal sentiment which opposed the commission's recommendations for extra land purchases in the province. Botha's political position was a sensitive one: his alienation of nationalist Afrikaner sentiment meant that he had to lean on Unionist support for his war policies, while at the same time he could not give way to Unionist pressures for more imperialist policies. What better way was there to propitiate his allies than by sacrificing a mere 'native Bill', especially when the Beaumont commission's investigations had revealed Union-wide hostility to the extension of African land holding? The attempted solution was postponed until after the war.

In Southern Rhodesia the British government, by accepting the Coryndon commission's report, was committing itself to the South African pattern of land settlement—a reduced area of land for African occupation, and acceptance of pressures to clear Africans into a system of reserves deliberately created too small to sustain the African population as peasants. No recommendations were made so far as the 'positive' aspects of the policy were concerned, but it was noted by some that further developments along South African lines would be possible: if there was further demand by Africans to acquire land under individual tenure, Stanley noted, this would lead to a demand for restrictions on their land purchase outside reserves; and secondly, the possibility of initiating 'something in the nature of local self-government by means of Native Councils' was suggested by Chaplin as a step to be taken in the future.[17] The commission had brought Rhodesian policy to a stage at which it was in essence but one step behind South African: the failure of Botha's Bill, which disappointed the imperial authorities,[18] was a lesson to them on the difficulties that further implementation of the policy would face.

3 The society and the Reserves Commission

Though imperial officials were willing to accept the Coryndon commission's recommendations without demur, the Aborigines

Protection Society was not, and the problem which faced it was how to divert the Colonial Office from its course before the report was frozen into law. In mid-1917 a barrage of questions on African land rights was inspired in the Commons, and though the government took its stand on the legal rights of Africans to buy land and the Colonial Office was unconcerned, Harris reported optimistically that a front-bencher had told him that Rhodesia was beginning to ' "grip" the minds of members in the House'.[19] After the Privy Council judgement on the lands case had been handed down, and the Crown was judged to be the owner of the unalienated lands, the Crown became the main target of the society's attacks but it was a stronger adversary than the company had been, and equally hostile. A series of Society delegations visited the Colonial Office. In October 1918 they asked Walter Long to end the displacement of Africans from non-reserve lands and suggested that steps be taken to 'harmonise' Rhodesian land policy with that of the Union and the protectorates, an indication that Botha's tardiness in following up the pledges he had given in 1913 had not diminished the society's faith in his good intentions.[20] They were turned away. In March 1919, supported by a plea from the Archbishop of Canterbury, they met Milner. He succinctly put the official position to them—that the object of the government's reserves policy was the provision of 'sanctuaries' sufficient for Africans' needs and that there could therefore be no objections to rents, or removals of Africans who were outside their 'own territory'.[21]

Having drawn a second blank at the Colonial Office, Harris went ahead with a public campaign, writing letters to the press, organising the missionary societies and Free Church councils and briefing members of Parliament. In 1919 he managed a further outbreak of parliamentary questions, circularised members with a pamphlet on the 'expropriation of the rights of an entire people' and succeeded in inspiring a brief debate on Rhodesia during the Colonial Office vote for the first time since 1914. Harris's allegations were strongly attacked by the Under-Secretary of State, Ormsby–Gore, who claimed personal knowledge of the 'magnificent native reserves' and averred that the treatment of Africans in the Rhodesias was better than in either South or east Africa. Two members raised the possibility that Rhodesia would be handed to the Union before the latter had settled its land problem, and one of these, Wedgwood, said that if Rhodesia were to go in with the south, Africans should be more fully safeguarded than they had been in 1910, and the reserves must be fixed and not left to a South African government to settle.[22] In September the society appealed direct to the Prime Minister, Lloyd George, proposing to send a delegation composed of all principal missionary and philanthropic bodies. In December Harris asked for a public enquiry and reiterated his suggestion of a joint Union/imperial commission on 'native policy' south of the Zambesi.[23] Milner advised the Prime Minister against seeing a deputation and on the request for a commission told him that 'An elaborate Commission sat after the South African War and investigated the whole of the South African Native question'.[24]

At the beginning of February 1920 a Society delegation succeeded in seeing Leopold Amery, the Under-Secretary of State, who attempted to browbeat them from the field with a display of hostility. The society had proposed, in view of the Crown's refusal to contribute to its legal costs incurred in the Privy Council reference, some £7,000, to campaign for money throughout British Africa on the grounds that issues affecting the entire continent had been at stake. Amery reacted violently. '. . . I suppose there is nothing to prevent its being extended to the West Indies, among the black subjects of the Crown who know nothing about the issues . . . against His Majesty's Government as an oppressor of the native races. It seems to me that the proposal is a monstrous and criminal one.' Brushing aside Harris's attempted interruption with a preremptory 'Just please listen to me, Mr Harris,' Amery suggested that the society was attempting to blackmail the Colonial Office. They proposed, he said, going to '. . . savage communities . . . putting it to them on the ground that the British government has treated the natives of Rhodesia unfairly . . .' An appeal to black men, in west Africa or anywhere else, against the justice of a Privy Council decision would be most 'unfortunate'. He concluded by defining the role of the society, which was to see that the British people fulfilled '. . . their duties as trustees for the natives. If you depart from that and go upon the lines that you are to be the organisers in any shape or form of native opinion against British rule, then all I can say is that it is a very doubtful policy.' Amery defined the 'inhabitants' of Rhodesia as '. . . the political community of Rhodesia for the time being', and it was clear that to him the political community of the empire was the British public, and that both Rhodesian and other British-ruled Africans were outside the political constituency in which the Rhodesia issue might legitimately be canvassed.[25]

A bruised and disappointed Harris summed up the difficulties that faced his campaign. First there was Amery, who was '. . . in the saddle and is determined to do nothing which can be regarded as justice for native races'; secondly an apathetic public opinion: 'The Rhodesian tussle is a very hard one, particularly because it makes very little public appeal,' Harris confessed. Thirdly there was the problem of maintaining the interest of sufficient members of Parliament.[26] The Aborigines Protection Society floundered around in the post-war political scene like a fish out of water. The groups which it had represented, typified by Lyttleton Gell's description of the society's president, Charles Roberts, a former Under-Secretary of State for India, as '. . . in the middle of a body of influential sentimental radicals—a fanatical Home Ruler, pro-Boer in the Boer War . . . and a leader of the extreme teetotal organisation . . .',[27] were in eclipse. The influence of the religious lobby had declined and radical sentiment in Parliament was less powerful. The coalition government, with two arch-imperialists at the Colonial Office, was less sensitive to the type of pressure that the society could mobilise, and even Lloyd George, to whom the society appealed, together with the mobilised cohorts of the Free Church councils, was not the man who might have been susceptible to such pressures before the war.

After Amery's rebuff the Labour Party backed another appeal to the Prime Minister, requesting a new formal enquiry. Lloyd George suggested that Milner meet the supplicants together, but the Colonial Office, greatly piqued, refused. An area usually immune from Prime Ministerial interest was being enquired into. Lloyd George was told that the Colonial Office were 'at a loss to understand' the grounds of the request for an enquiry. The society's claim that Africans were being dispossessed of their land was denied: the reserves were said to be large, and rents outside them low. Furthermore stress was laid on the point that article 83 of the order in council of 1898 '. . . expressly provides that the natives may acquire, hold, surrender and dispose of land on the same conditions as a person who is not a native'.[28]

The Labour Party had asked that the proposed reimbursement of the company for its administrative deficits should be held up pending a new enquiry into African conditions in Rhodesia. Both it and the society, applying a suspicious but commonsense view that the records amply justify, insisted that the Land Commission, which had been composed of people acting in the interests of the company, had made its recommendations at a time when the company had a commercial interest in the land, and that this was the ruling feature in its decision as to which land should be assigned to Africans. They felt that if the Crown had owned the land (and the Privy Council had now decided it did) different criteria would have been applied. The official position remained that the question of the ownership of the land had been irrelevant to the commission of 1915, as, whoever owned the land, any government was bound by the order in council and the terms of reference of the commission to make adequate provision for Africans, and that this had been done. The Labour Party regarded all Rhodesian issues as interdependent, and tended to fix its attention on the Cave commission and the reimbursement of the company more than upon land issues.

A further campaign against the commission's proposals was waged by A. S. Cripps, an Anglican missionary in Rhodesia, who met with some success in his objections to the cutting down of the Sabi reserve.[29] In a letter to the *Times* Cripps appealed for the Rhodesian land question to be settled before Rhodesia joined the Union, or a larger Central African Dominion, or became 'what may be called a responsibly governed State, in effect oligarchical and isolated'.[30] The same problem was exercising the mind of the Colonial Office, which was considering how to protect the reserves once they had been established. The likelihood of constitutional changes, either entry into the Union or responsible government, led the Colonial Office to insist on the finality of any settlement as a means of preventing settler pressure on the reserves, 'which it is our main object to forestall'.[31]

The Coryndon commission had made no recommendation on the question of individual land tenure for Africans, but British advisors in South Africa were concerned that if there were to be an increase in African acquisition of land outside the reserves this would lead to settler demands for a restriction on Africans' right to purchase.[32] Even if there were no European demands to abrogate this right it might prove necessary, it was thought, to set aside land for African purchase, as Africans would not be able to compete in a free land market. But, as Buxton pointed out, '. . . any earmarking of a portion of the unalienated lands for the natives might in effect, even though not in law, involve as a corollary their exclusion from the remainder'. He thought that segregation of this sort was not undesirable and could prove inevitable. In London too this sort of approach was taking hold by 1920. At the end of 1920 Davis, considering the question of replying to a Free Church Council resolution on African landlessness in Rhodesia, minuted: 'As it is on the cards that we may have to consider the question of territorial segregation as between natives and Europeans it seems undesirable to lay stress on the existing law, if it can be avoided.'[33]

By the beginning of 1920 the society had sharpened the ideological differences between itself and the government, and it attacked the consensus of satisfaction with regard to the southern African 'native question'. Replying to the Colonial Office contention that the reserves policy had been activated by the British government in the interests of

Africans alone, it said, 'It is not a fact that the policy of segregation of racial settlements in South Africa looks solely to the interests of the natives ... it arose out of the demands of Europeans made in their own interest.' It was true, it continued, that Southern Rhodesia 'having been invaded', it was in African interests 'that some residue at least of the land of which they were prior occupants' should be reserved. But its fundamental complaint was that the Colonial Office did not recognise '... any kind of injustice or hardship to the natives in these operations'.[34] The Labour Party too was outside the southern consensus. In April 1920 two Labour members, Spoor and Wedgwood, raised the Rhodesian issue during the debate on the Colonial Office vote. Neither approached the question on the basis of a Zambesi-line division between white and black Africa. They linked the Rhodesian issue with the contemporaneous controversy regarding the best form of government for black Africa and whether different models were appropriate to east and west Africa. Wedgwood, outlining Labour policy, rejected the commission's philosophy. The party would, he said:

... reserve for the natives their own land for them to cultivate, so that if they prefer to remain cultivating their own land they will not be driven to work for somebody else. They may be tempted to do so if the wages offered are higher ... The natural law of supply and demand has got to regulate labour supply.

He attacked the Colonial Office tendency 'always to hand over control to white settlers', concluding, 'The question before us is really this: is the British empire going to be purely a white commonwealth ... or are you going to follow the wider plan of absorbing all the races who can be absorbed?'[35] The Colonial Office reacted by ranging itself on the opposing side. By 1920 its impatience with the society and the Labour Party had grown to a point when a not untypical minute could read:

... the natives never had any title and never had any right ... titles are derived from a system of law, and rights from merit and labour, and it is precisely because of the absence of these among the natives that only two have been able to repurchase land in the last twenty years.[36]

The society, and the Labour Party, in their campaign against the reserve commission's report and the order in council of 1920 that followed it, succeeded in making the division of Rhodesian land a political rather than an administrative issue. Though, like all Rhodesian matters at the time, it was a minor problem (when compared, for example, to Ireland and the Middle East), the society's campaign had meant that the Colonial Office did not take decisions without full and deliberate consideration, and the issues were thrashed out in public. But the interested audience was small and the society's campaign failed because the emotional roots of the pre-war anti-colonial sentiment had been swamped between 1914 and 1918. New issues now attracted radical sentiment, and tinkering with colonial abuses was subsumed into wider plans for the abolition of war and exploitation by the League of Nations and socialism at home.

4 African reaction and British policies

In Rhodesia the Ndebele leadership was turning towards segregation of a different sort as a solution to their problems, and the desire for separation, both political and territorial, emphasises the depth of Ndebele discontent as well as their own southward political orientation. Nyamanda, the claimant to the Lobengula succession, put it thus to his indunas in 1920: 'Look at Khama! He has his country, and Lewanika, he has his plot . . . and Mosheshe, he has his land. Also the son of Dinizulu has his country.'[37] The Ndebele National Home movement resulted in three petitions to the imperial authorities. The first, which was taken to England by the Rev. H. Ngcayiya, the leader of the Ethiopian Church in South Africa, in June 1919, objected both to the inferior land which the commission had allocated to the Ndebele, describing it as 'unhealthy lands and consist of forests where wild beasts obtain', as well as to the scattering of the Ndebele nation, and it referred, sophistically, to the repudiation of the right of conquest by the civilised world at Versailles in 1919.[38] The third petition, which Nyamanda presented personally to Prince Arthur of Connaught, the new High Commissioner in South Africa, in August 1921 called for '. . . one large composite Reserve or Native Territory' and asked that '. . . the government and control of the . . . territory be under the imperial government',[39] an indication of his preference for protectorate status along the lines of his southern neighbours. But the commission, in rejecting consolidation of African territory, had rejected this type of separation. Separate institutions, if they were to be created, would have to rest upon a territorial patchwork.

All the protagonists, Nyamanda, the company, the British government and the Aborigines Protection Society, had southern patterns in mind when they considered the Rhodesian land problem, and the development of southern policies remained a basic influence upon the settlement of the question in Rhodesia. In 1919 the South African Native National Congress, which had suspended its activities in

1914 in a fervour of misguided loyalty to the Crown, resumed its appeals to the British government to intervene in South Africa. In a memorial to the king the congress recalled its act of loyalty; its offer to fight in South West Africa; its passivity during the Afrikaner revolt, '. . . when difficult circumstances offered dangerous and ill advised temptations to an oppressed people'; and its 'despairing regret' about the limitations placed by the Union government on the contribution to the war effort which could be made by Africans from the Union. The memorial reflected the combination of both 'traditional' and 'modern' elements in the congress. It stressed African land grievances and specifically asked first '. . . that the territory of Zululand shall remain integral for the use and occupation of the original inhabitants' and secondly for '. . . an exhaustive review of the landed rights of the peoples of Mashonaland'. In addition to its concern about land, congress asked for both '. . . provision for the protection of the aboriginal native institutions being respected and developed' and for Union-wide representation of Africans in parliament, making it clear that acceptance of the first did not preclude the second.

Congress also turned its attention to the post-war territorial settlement in Africa. It urged the containment of the Union: in the memorial to the king it argued that German South West Africa, German East Africa and the Belgian Congo should be placed, subject to the people's wishes, under the United States in trust for Africans '. . . until they became sufficiently advanced for their own civilised government'.[40] It was hoped to persuade the peace conference to consider '. . . the dangerous and unpopular land legislation of the Union government' as well as the '. . . non-enfranchisement of the majority of our people without any safeguard with which to check the reactionary or discriminative administration'. Congress felt that these two things should be a bar to South Africa's international acceptability and that neither South West nor East Africa should be handed to the Union government '. . . without alteration of the colour bar franchise'.[41]

In May 1919 the delegation which Congress had sent to Europe met Amery, to whom they emphasised their loyalty to the Crown against the background of growing republicanism in the Union. Black loyalty, though, was no longer at a premium, and Amery followed the established British government line of claiming no power to interfere internally in the Union. He '. . . enlarged upon the nature of responsible government, and urged that the educated native should work patiently within the limits of the constitution of the Union, a constitution which, being British, necessarily contained within itself the power of developments'.⁴² Not satisfied with the advice to have faith in the innately progressive nature of British institutions, the Congress delegation pressed further. They wrote to Milner, then Secretary of State for the Colonies, asking pointedly, 'Are we to understand that South Africa is an independent State?' The aim of Congress was a revision of the Act of Union at a time when the '... world was on the threshold of an era of freedom, justice and peace'. If Britain had fought to liberate the world from Prussian authoritarianism how could it allow 'tyranny and autocracy to flourish in one of her Dominions?'⁴³ Finally the delegation appealed to Lloyd George: '... alas,' they wrote,'

the Victorian days are gone, and with them British Liberty and Justice, so far as the subject races are concerned, have disappeared ... To liberate the natives of [South West Africa] from the cruel claws of the German eagle, and then to place them at the mercy of Boer tyrants, is like taking them out of the frying pan and placing them into the fire.⁴⁴

Having secured Botha's consent, Lloyd George met the congress delegation. The meeting made an impression upon him, and he wrote to Smuts, who had by then succeeded Botha as Prime Minister, that '... it could not fail to impress any audience with the sense that the natives of South Africa believe themselves to be labouring under real grievances, and to be faced with a future which had little hope of progress and property ...' He warned, referring to Labour Party sponsorship of the delegation, that it had aroused '... the sympathy of people of power and influence in this country,' and continued, 'Further, there is no doubt that there are forces in the world actively arousing the negroes and other primitive peoples to revolt ... [they aimed at] upsetting not only the British Commonwealth but the whole existing structure of society.' Daily, Lloyd George wrote, he received telegrams describing Bolshevik training of agitators for Asia and Africa, and he enclosed a cutting from *The Times* in which Marcus Garvey, the black American leader, called upon Africans '... to make Africa a republic for the negro' and which prophesied 'the bloodiest war the world has ever seen'. In urging Smuts to consider the grievances which the congress had put before him Lloyd George closed with the reason for his anxiety: the colour question was a world question. 'What South Africa does is of vital importance to the rest of us, just as what we do is going to be of vital importance to you.'⁴⁵ Two months later Lloyd George followed up the letter with a despatch on the details of his interview with the Congress delegation. It is clear that he had no knowledge of the grievances laid before him. 'They were sure that some recent Land Act ... deprived the native population unjustly of its land,' he wrote; but he urged an enquiry into the complaints, which were against the land Act, the military colour bar, and the 1917 native administration Bill. The Prime Minister concluded:

> There is one general consideration which occurs to me. It is clear that the dark age of Africa is commencing to pass away. The negro population of the world is beginning to stir . . . It has developed many leaders of force and ability, as you will realise if you have followed the recent movements among the negroes of America . . . What is done in South Africa affects us all.[46]

Smuts's reply was no more than a flat denial of the delegation's submissions, and with regard to the question of land he quoted approvingly from the judgement of the Privy Council in the Rhodesian land case that 'The old state of things, whatever its exact nature has passed away and another, and . . . better has been established in lieu of it'.[47]

Like the Aborigines Protection Society, Congress, in basing its appeal on liberal sentiment and on mythological liberal history, was out of date. In its demand that the colour bar should disqualify the Union from further expansion it was anticipating the future. And like Congress, Lloyd George's position was between past and future: an appeal to liberal principles was no longer persuasive, while the possibility of a black revolution was not yet sufficiently threatening. Lloyd George's letters, a random outburst from an isolated and erratic radical, could not alter the fact that in the present Britain shared, by virtue of her colonial position, a common stance with South Africa. As Philip Kerr wrote to Lionel Curtis concerning the difficulties that were to arise in inter-Anglo-Saxon relations during the Versailles negotiations, '. . . the real problem is going to arise from the treatment which must be accorded to politically backward peoples . . . there is fundamentally a different conception in regard to this question between Britain and South Africa on the one hand and the United States and Canada on the other . . .'[48] An uninformed sense of disquiet, even in a Prime Minister, was negligible when weighed against the community of interest between the white rulers in Africa. In southern Africa Britain faced the problem of evolving a system of government in her remaining dependencies that would be acceptable to the Union government, and of guiding the Union government towards a policy that would make it an acceptable heir to British responsibilities. The Prime Minister's letters counted far less than the expertise and continuity of the officials and men on the spot, who had for long shared in the inspiration and elaboration of the policies which the congress had complained against.

In a memorandum prepared in 1920 Buxton described the development of the Union's policy after the war. He and Botha had come to the conclusion after the failure of the comprehensive 1917 Bill that

... it would be better, instead of attempting to deal with segregation at once, to deal with the native question by stages. It was evident that if in some way the opinion of the natives could be ascertained by a commission and by giving them a voice in their own affairs, it would be easier to remove their suspicions, and to make them understand the advantages to them of segregation, and thus to get their assent to that policy later on. The first step was therefore obviously the appointment of a commission and the creation of Local Councils. We thought that if the Bill were relieved of the dead weight of Segregation general assent might be obtained for the other proposals ... as a first instalment.[49]

In other words, it was clear that the white parliament could be expected to accept a Bill which postponed the question of fulfilling the promises of 1913 to add to the African land areas and at the same time moved in the opposite direction from giving Africans an increasing share in the Union's central political institutions. The product of this new approach was the Native Affairs Bill of 1920. The High Commissioner, who travelled the country explaining and commending the Bill to Africans, told the Colonial Office that it '... marks a significant advance in South African public opinion on the Native question ... the idea was that separate institutions should prevail in the respective areas ...' Africans, he wrote, 'might as well cry for the moon' as ask for anything more in the way of political rights or an abolition of the colour bar. He noted the strong feeling in the protectorates against inclusion in the Union and argued that the way to make this more palatable to protectorate Africans was to give full support to the Botha–Smuts policy. Representative institutions of any other kind were as yet out of the question, not only because there was no chance at all that the whites would agree to a further extension of the franchise to Africans but because they were beyond the African conception. 'The more paternal, and the more direct the personal relations between the government and the natives the better, for that is the form of government they appreciate.' Something ought to be done, he felt, to restore the confidence of Africans in the government as 'their father', which had been undermined during the war, though he noted with approval that the war had improved the security situation, as Africans who had participated in it had emerged with a '... wholesome respect for the strength of the white man's armaments'. While Buxton came to the conclusion that full segregation was no longer possible, he felt that a measure could be achieved and that 'the natives would be able to return to their own ways' under local self-government, free from fear of further encroachment of their land'. Significantly he noted that Swaziland and Southern Rhodesia had been fortunate in having an early delimitation of land, '. . . before the question of boundary between White and Black had become very acute. Thus, whatever may be the future of Southern Rhodesia, and however much it might develop, the Natives are secured in the possession of their land.'[50] In the South African context the Southern Rhodesian reserves policy was something of a model.

An air of unreality pervaded the discussion of the 'native problem'. Labour matters were passed over: the subject was generally reserved for experts, and the pronouncements of men who 'knew the native mind' were treated with considerable respect. Yet the quality of the advice given to the British government was low. 'The native mind is an unknown quantity,' confessed Taylor, whose reports on the thoughts and requirements of the Rhodesian Africans carried great weight both in Rhodesia and in the Colonial Office. Panzera, the Resident Commissioner of Bechuanaland, another respected 'native man', told London, when chided with his failure to foretell an outbreak of unrest, that 'Anyone with long experience of natives must easily realise the impossibility of foretelling the working of the native mind'.[51] Buxton's memorandum on the Union's native affairs Bill, which deeply impressed the Colonial Office and which was to be referred to in the future as a guide, contains a curious argument for the form of African self-government that he was recommending:

. . . The Native must not do this, that or the other. All the former interests and excitements of his life are *verboten*. They must not drill: they must not fight: they must not kill or raid their neighbours . . . 'Smelling out' and the practice of witch-doctoring lead to imprisonment or the rope. Their life has become very drab and must be boring. It is an advantage therefore to give them alternative interests in life by allowing them to have a voice in and to manage or mismanage their own affairs.[52]

Few passages could better illustrate the inadequacy of understanding, the stereotyped views and the depoliticisation of discussions of African affairs. Typically Smuts summed up, 'The Native Question is so large. We know so little about it . . .'[53]

5 Harmonising southern policies

The Rhodesian Land Commission's report, and its acceptance in London, were the occasion for a definite step towards making Southern

Rhodesia into a white man's country. The policy of the Colonial Office had been confused throughout. Prior to 1914 it had seen the commission as a way of protecting African possession of land, of defining rights and increasing security. The company and settlers were also eager to define African rights, but by limiting and reducing them, and it was this conception that the commission followed. The Colonial Office then accepted this approach; by 1918 the main problem seemed to it to be how to secure Africans against still further white pressures. It had already lowered its horizons to accept small, scattered reserves and the creation of a farm labourer class by these means. Yet further white pressure was anticipated, especially if Africans increased their land holding by exercising the still protected right to purchase land under individual tenure. It was thus envisaged that further definition would be needed; perhaps by forfeiting this right an end to white demands could be secured and the area of African land holding be rendered permanent.

The anxiety which occasioned this retreat to a minimum position was engendered by the situation in the south, and the expected union between the Union and Rhodesia, which it was anticipated would lead to an influx of whites, particularly Afrikaners, into Rhodesia. The British government, precisely because it accepted the tenets of the Union government's 'native policy' and the sincerity of its attempts to 'solve the native problem', appreciated how difficult the situation that faced the Botha government was. By establishing legal segregation in land holding in 1913 and *then* trying to increase the African areas Botha had inevitably run up against an unscalable wall of white opposition. White South Africa would demand an extra price for conceding an increase in African land—a price that was gladly paid by Hertzog in 1936 when the Cape African common roll franchise was abolished. In Rhodesia, in order to avoid the Union's difficulty, the British government moved towards securing what it regarded as a reasonable minimum of African land before conceding the principle of territorial segregation to settler opinion. Complete political segregation, though pined for by some settlers, was not yet on the Rhodesian agenda. Though aroused by the Rhodesian land issue, opinion in the South African Native National Congress distinguished between Rhodesia and the Union, and from one representative came a letter of praise and support for the company in its squabble with Harris, who had fallen out with Congress over his support for Botha's policies. Outlining the greater job opportunities and rights to land and franchise in Rhodesia for both Africans and coloureds, the letter concluded, '... it will be a sorry day for men ... of colour when our Boer administration incorporates Rhodesia in this Union'.[54] The

138 *Unconsummated union*

society by the 1920s had pushed the Labour Party into a rejection of the British government's policy on land in Rhodesia, but this, and Lloyd George's reaction to the Congress delegation, serve only to underline the basic satisfaction of the British government with the pattern that was emerging. Segregated land holding and a shadow of political separation—African councils for scattered and diminished African reserves in place of African participation in white policies—it was in this direction that in the arcane field of 'native policy' the South African, Southern Rhodesian and British governments were moving by 1920.

Notes

1 Cd. 8674, 1917–18, Papers relating to the Southern Rhodesian Native Reserves Commission Report, 1915.
2 Cd. 8674, Interim report, para. 39.
3 C.O. 417/578, Minute, 27 October 1916; stress in original.
4 R. Macgregor, 'Native segregation in Rhodesia', Ph.D. thesis, London University, 1940, p. 76, and P. Mason, *Birth*, p. 261.
5 See comments on C.O. 417/578, 27 October 1916. It is noteworthy that the imperial authorities at no time thought of undertaking in Southern Rhodesia the detailed examination of varying land claims they had carried out in Swaziland and Nyasaland.
6 The figures are taken from H. Wilson Fox, *Notes and Information Concerning Land Policy, 1912*, B.S.A.C.
7 C.O. 417/578, 27 October 1916, Stanley to Rodwell, 20 August 1916.
8 Cd. 8674, paras. 62–3.
9 Quoted by T. O. Ranger in *The Zambesian Past*, ed. E. Stokes and R. Brown, p. 179.
10 See R. Palmer, 'Aspects of Rhodesian land policy', *Central African Historical Association Local Series*, No. 22, 1968, and P. Duignan, 'The native administration of the British South Africa Company, 1890–1923', unpublished Ph.D. thesis, Stanford University, 1961.
11 Duignan, *Native Administration*, p. 207.
12 Cd. 8674, para. 47.
13 *Ibid.*, paras. 22 and 45.
14 *Ibid.*, paras. 73–4.
15 Earl Buxton, *General Botha*, London, 1924, p. 285, and C.O. 551/127, 26 March 1920, Buxton memorandum on the Union's Native Affairs Bill of 1920.
16 Tatz, *Shadow and Substance*, chapter 3, and P. Walshe, *The Rise of African Nationalism in South Africa*, London, 1970, pp. 56–61.
17 C.O. 417/578, 27 October 1916, and Cd. 8674, No. 10, Chaplin to B.S.A.C., October 1917.
18 Buxton, *General Botha*, chapter 13.
19 The questions were usually drafted by Harris and put by members of his

Rhodesia Reform Committee; see Parliamentary Debates, Commons, 16 and 18 July and 2 August 1917, and A.P.S. G 159, 'Rhodesia Native Lands', Harris to Brade, 20 August 1917.
20 A.P.S. G 161/2, 'Rhodesia native lands', Harris to Mackenna, 8 March 1918, and Harris to Finnemore, 30 June 1918.
21 C.O. 417/633, 9 April 1919.
22 Parliamentary Debates, Commons, 30 July 1919.
23 C.O. 417/633, 18 September 1919, A.P.S., 'Rhodesia native lands', General file No. 4, 5 December 1919 and 13 December 1919.
24 I.e. the 1905 commission; C.O. 417/633, 15 December 1919, Thornton to Kerr.
25 The record of the interview is in C.O. 417/656, 12 January 1920.
26 A.P.S., G 161/2, Harris to Morgan, n.d., and other correspondence. More than once Harris conferred on the running of his campaign with E. D. Morel, who had organised and inspired the pre-war campaign for the reform of the Congo Free State.
27 Ch. 8/2/2/6, Gell to Chaplin, 22 September 1919.
28 C.O. 417/655, 4 March 1920, and Cmd. 547, 1920, *Correspondence with the Anti-slavery and Aborigines Protection Society relating to Native Reserves in Southern Rhodesia*. Publication of this command paper was held up by the Colonial Office, who were reluctant to publicise a colonial controversy while the peace conference was sitting.
29 Cripps published a book on the subject, *The Sabi Reserve: a Southern Rhodesian Native Problem*, Oxford, 1920. While the Archbishop of Canterbury described Cripps to Milner as a 'remarkable man ... an enthusiast and a genius in his own way', Gell told Chaplin that Cripps was a 'fanatical negrophile' and a 'hysterical woman' who had been 'captured and exploited by Harris—a trickster of far lower moral character'. (C.O. 417/656, 13 August 1920, and Ch. 8/2/2/6, Gell to Chaplin, 6 May 1920 and 10 June 1920.)
30 C.O. 417/656, 9 March 1920, Cripps to *The Times*.
31 C.O. 417/656, 1 April 1920, 'Davis minute'.
32 C.O. 417/578, 27 October 1916.
33 C.O. 417/638, Buxton to Milner, 29 June 1920, and C.O. 417/656, 5 November 1920.
34 Cmd. 547, A.P.S. to C.O., 6 January 1920.
35 Parliamentary Debates, Commons, 26 April 1920.
36 C.O. 417/656, 14 May 1920, Minute.
37 Quoted by T. O. Ranger in *The Zambesian Past*, ed. E. Stokes and R. Brown, p. 184.
38 See T. O. Ranger, *The African Voice in Southern Rhodesia*, London, 1970, pp. 73–4.
39 *African Voice*, pp. 83–4.
40 Smuts Archive, cxv, No. 6, 16 January 1919. The African Political Organisation, which represented the 'coloured' people of the Cape, also asked that South West Africa should not be handed to the Union.
41 Smuts Archive, cxv, No. 4; R. W. Msimang to W. Schreiner, 10 January 1919.
42 Report of interview in Smuts Archive, cxv, 8 May 1919.

43 Smuts Archive, cxv, No. 17, R. V. Selope–Thema and L. Mombasa to Milner, 22 May 1919.
44 Smuts Archive, cxv, delegation to Lloyd George, 4 June 1919.
45 C.O. 537/1197, secret, Lloyd George to Smuts, Private and personal, 7 January 1920.
46 C.O. 537/1197, Lloyd George to Smuts, 3 March 1920.
47 C.O. 537/1197, Smuts to Lloyd George, 12 May 1920.
48 Philip Kerr, later Lord Lothian, was Lloyd George's private secretary. Lionel Curtis, who had been with Milner in South Africa, became the guru of the Round Table movement; quoted in J. R. M. Butler, *Lord Lothian*, London, 1960.
49 C.O. 551/127, Buxton memorandum on the Native Affairs Bill, 26 March 1920. Buxton had consultations on similar lines with Smuts at which he assured the new Union Prime Minister that on the 'native question' 'I would give him my wholehearted support'. (Milner papers 80, Buxton to Milner, 4 September 1919.)
50 C.O. 551/127, Buxton memorandum.
51 Taylor, in C.O. 417/571, 10 June 1915, and Panzera in C.O. 417/526, 20 November 1913.
52 C.O. 551/127, Buxton memorandum.
53 Hancock, *Smuts*, II, p. 123.
54 C.O. 417/629, S. Plaatje to Chaplin, 6 April 1919.

CHAPTER 8

The counterpoise suspended

1918–22

1 Britain and the charter

In 1914 Harcourt had instituted the Privy Council reference, hoping for a quick decision to clear the decks before the review of the charter. The Privy Council eventually gave judgement in the land case in July 1918.[1] The company's case had rested on its concessions, on occupation, and on the continued acquiescence of the Crown in its claims and its proceedings. The settlers' case rested basically on the rights of conquest and on their expectations as the inheritors of the company's administrative powers. The case put forward on behalf of the Africans by the Aborigines Protection Society denied that Lobengula had had the power to grant the concessions and claimed that the land had remained the Africans' by virtue of tribal law. The Crown claimed that it had assumed full sovereignty by virtue of its protectorate.[2] In delivering the court's judgement Lord Sumner dismissed the African case on the grounds that the Ndebele kingdom had disappeared with the death of Lobengula and had no legitimate succession. Of any remaining African rights the court took the view that the Ndebele were too low in the scale of social organisation for their legal ideas to be enforceable. The court would entertain no doubt that the holders of land under grant from the Crown held indefeasible title. It thus remained to determine whether the company had been acting on its own behalf or for a principal. The court ruled that any conquest by subjects of the Crown was made on the Crown's behalf. The company (and the settlers), therefore, could have acted only as agents of the Crown. The land thus belonged to the Crown, but the company, as agent, was entitled, when its agency was terminated, to be recompensed for any losses it had incurred.[3]

The Privy Council's decision, though it defeated the most optimistic of the company's expectations, nevertheless put it in a strong position for financial bargaining, as it placed the duty of paying the company's claim for deficits on the British government. The duality of the company's position was also underlined. There had already existed on the board the feeling that the company's administrative and commercial functions were incompatible and that steps should be taken to disentangle it from the government of Rhodesia so that it could devote itself to purely commercial activities. Thus the company had hoped to have its ownership of the land acknowledged and then to sell its assets, which would make it, as Michell put it, 'a very powerful commercial corporation'.[4] The Privy Council decision meant that the company no longer had a financial interest in continuing its administrative functions, and its tactics now were to press the British government for immediate cash payment of its claims for deficits. By ceasing to provide capital freely for Rhodesian development, as it had done in the past, the company hoped to make the settler demand for political change irresistible and thus to hurry the Crown into meeting the obligations laid upon it by the Privy Council.

The company also began to mount a political counter-offensive against the Aborigines Protection Society. Gell defined for his shareholders in an address following the judgement the imperial achievement of the company, which had been to secure permanently for the empire vast territories '. . . for the protection of its position in South Africa, for British trade, as an outlet for British settlement and industrial exploitation . . .' Botha and Smuts, he said, underlining the transformed attitude in Anglo-South African circles towards their former enemies, had ensured that South Africa would remain 'a cornerstone of the British empire for all time'. He denounced those who had '. . . not the faintest conception of the depths of tyranny, bloodshed, torture, terror, poverty, squalor, pestilence, vice and idleness, from which the Chartered Company and its sagacious administrators . . . have raised the natives in a single generation (cheers) and into which . . . they would easily relapse . . .'[5] Gell's view of the pre-colonial period was matched by his analysis of the political forces that were opposed to the company, which he described as being made up of '. . . the Radicals and Labourites—the pro-Boers, pro-Germans and Little Englanders—*Daily News, Manchester Guardian* and *Daily Herald*—the APS and all anti-British sentiment which has been created by German money ever since the Chartered Company arrested German expansion.'[6] The fantasies of the far right and the tone used to perorate to potentially aggrieved shareholders were but an extreme expression of the views of Milner and Amery, who now ruled at the Colonial Office, and they were views far more congenial to the 'hard-faced men' of the parliamentary majority than those of the society. Although, after 1918, the League of Nations had to some extent institutionalised the ideology of trusteeship, Amery and Milner were themselves identified with the other side of the imperial coin—which expressed after the war a renewed determination to make empire pay. Amery told Parliament in 1919 that Britain had been too timid in capitalising the territories under her control, and Milner warned that the government should not be put off its duty to promote development by ignorant humanitarian clamour.[7]

The preservation of the imperial connection in South Africa became after 1918 a major preoccupation of imperialists in Britain, South Africa and Rhodesia. The 1915 election in South Africa showed that Botha and Smuts had broken with Hertzog and suppressed the rebellion at heavy cost to their support amongst Afrikaner rural voters. Hertzog's National Party, which was overtly republican, won twenty-seven out of one hundred and thirty seats in the House of Assembly, and in 1919 it sent a delegation to Versailles to plead for the restoration of South African independence in accordance with the Wilsonian principle of self-determination. The Nationalists accused Botha and Smuts of being dominated by the Unionist Party and of pursuing an imperialist policy of conquest, of sending black troops overseas, and of allowing the Union's natural resources to be siphoned off for Britain's benefit. One pamphlet attacked Botha as a 'fiery imperialist' who had attacked South West Africa 'to expand the empire'. The government, it said, was in the same camp as 'the Unionists, the millionaires, mine magnates and capitalists'. The Nationalists, on the other hand, it was claimed, were anti-capitalist and anti-imperialist: as Hertzog put it, '... national freedom means death to capitalism and imperialism'.[8] Botha felt that the damaged fabric of the Afrikaner nation might yet be mended. With regard to the expansion of South Africa in the immediate post-war period he was content to absorb South West Africa, as the inclusion of Rhodesia, with its extra English voting strength, might stand in the way of a *hereeniging* (a reunion) of the two Afrikaner parties, which was to him a more important objective. After Botha's death an attempt by Smuts to persuade the Nationalists into *hereeniging* foundered on the republican question; an overture which Smuts made to the Labour Party was rejected, and Smuts travelled the full road indicated by the logic of his politics since 1910, embracing the Unionists into the fold of the South African Party.

Smuts had noted after the war that the younger Afrikaners were all becoming 'Nationalists or rebels', and he had not welcomed what he called the 'ugly prospect' of coalition with the Unionists. In an attempt to reduce the damage to his political image among Afrikaners, he tried to pack Sir Thomas Smartt, the Unionist leader, off to London as High Commissioner and permanent representative at the League of Nations, but Smartt would not co-operate. In the end Smuts could only pretend that he had achieved a victory over the old imperialism by having dissolved the 'party of Rhodes and Jameson'.[9] Smuts was more eager to get Rhodesia than Botha had been—He '. . . was perfectly candid—he wants *both* Rhodesias', Gell reported in 1919.[10] But delay there had to be: fusion with the Unionist party came first, Rhodesia second. To have pressed for them both simultaneously might have been too much for the Afrikaner wing of the South African Party, already in shock over the flirtations with Labour and the Unionists. In the elections of 1920, which were held before the merger of the South African and Unionist parties, the nationalists made further advances, emerging as the largest single party, leaving an almost equal parliamentary balance between Smuts's party and the Unionists—the parties of empire and social conservatism—and Nationalists and Labour—which embodied the discontents of the rural poor and of urban labour.

It is in this context that British policies for southern Africa were formulated. Rhodesia itself was a very small part of what Amery called '. . . that southern British world which runs from Cape Town through Cairo, Baghdad and Calcutta to Sydney and Wellington . . .',[11] but the Union was a vital imperial interest, faced by a growing Afrikaner challenge, while Rhodesia was demonstrably loyal. At the same time Ireland, Egypt and India, all vital in the imperialist world view, were challenging Britain's over-extended and straitened strength. Milner confessed to Buxton, as pressure for Colonial Office action on the Privy Council's decision in the Rhodesian land case mounted,

. . . it is simply impossible to give you any idea of the state of overwork in which we are all living here, with the whole world rocking, and every question, which has agitated Europe or been discussed between different parts of the empire, popping up afresh and staring one in the face simultaneously. Besides we were all tired men when this new chapter began . . .

So far as Rhodesia went there was not the slightest chance of being able to give a statement of government policy '. . . for the simple reason that . . . no member of the government except myself has any views on the subject at all, and it would be totally useless to bring a big new question, about which one's colleagues were not informed . . . before the Cabinet just now'.[12]

Milner's own view was that Southern Rhodesia 'definitely' and North Western Rhodesia 'probably' should join the Union. While in the past he had felt that Rhodesia should be filled 'with a good British population' before joining the south, he now realised that this would take too long. Responsible government, he thought, was 'impossible and absurd'.[13] The company could not be removed for nothing, and Britain could not shoulder the cost 'at this time of all others'. Milner did envisage the possibility that if the settlers refused to go into the Union they could have '. . . some sort of intermediate stage of "representative" government, during which time they will be able to look around and muddle for themselves . . .' but he predicted that this would end with a 'tumble' into Union on disadvantageous terms. His conclusion was that the company should hold on until the settlers would join the Union, but he stressed '. . . that it would never do, and it would be absolutely fatal, for us to put the screw, or seem to put the screw, upon them to take that course'. It must be done *'of their own free choice'*. Entry into the Union would be both the best thing for Rhodesia '. . . and for imperial interests in South Africa, as Rhodesian representatives would certainly strengthen the non-republican party in the Union parliament, while Rhodesia herself would fill up more rapidly than is now possible'.[14] Milner, as he told Bonar Law in April 1920, took '. . . a rather bleak view of the future of South Africa . . .' What could Britain do if the two 'Boer parties' combined and voted for a 'declaration of independence'? It would be especially unpalatable, he wrote, because while 'It is true that *of the voters* probably *three fifths* would prefer independence', the whole African population would be against it '. . . and we have obligations to the natives'. Moreover there were the three High Commission territories, and it was inconceivable that they could be retained permanently '. . .within and adjoining to an independent State without sooner or later being involved in another South African war'.[15]

The immediate question that faced Milner was the determination of the amount which would be payable to the company as a consequence of the Privy Council decision and to decide how and by whom the debt would be discharged. Buxton advised that the British government should bear at least part of the debt, because—and he stressed the same point as Milner had—it would be unwise to drive Rhodesia into the Union by threatening to impose the whole burden on her. Buxton felt that the settlers would not look favourably on negotiations between the Union and the company to discharge the debt, because they were '. . . proud of the British atmosphere of Rhodesia and want to keep it British'.[16] The company had been pressing since November 1918 for immediate ascertainment of the sum it was to receive. Milner had initially hoped for a South African offer to the company, but when he found Botha and Smuts otherwise preoccupied he aimed instead at a rapid settlement of the company's claim. In the Commons there was some pressure for a commission with a political bias—in effect a second Raid committee—to enquire into the amount that should be paid. In the Colonial Office Lambert pointed out that the Privy Council had declared the company to have acted as the Crown's agent, and he urged, therefore, an investigation of the management of the agency. But both Amery and Milner were acutely unwilling to get involved in a long-drawn-out tussle with the company of the sort that Harcourt had engaged in, and they laid down the criteria that were to guide the British government. It was essential, Amery wrote, that the enquiring commissioners should '... regard their task as judicial, and not endeavour to reopen old political issues', and Milner insisted that the Colonial Office should not '... be drawn into the case as if it were the antagonist of the company'.[17] The commission which was appointed in July 1919, under the chairmanship of Viscount Cave, who had been Home Secretary from 1916 to 1919, proceeded to Rhodesia, where it examined the company's accounts and heard evidence from settler representatives at public sessions. When it returned to Britain the Colonial Office received bitter complaints from the Treasury solicitor that his instructions had been inadequate, that the nature of the enquiry was uncertain and that there were errors in the company's accounts. The Colonial Office was asked that a delay be granted while the Crown's own accountants carried out investigations.[18] Against the advice of his officials Milner tried to persuade a conference of Ministers not to grant the Treasury solicitor's request, but it was decided, for fear that the Attorney General would claim in the Commons—where Bonar Law had pledged that the matter would be discussed before the company was paid—that if he had been given his way the award might have been halved, to defer the commission's award indefinitely pending further enquiries.

It had been Milner's personal influence, exerted on behalf of his friends in the company, that had secured both the early appointment of the commission and the limitation of the area of its enquiry. He pressed the Cabinet strongly on the company's behalf, telling them that it had 'created Rhodesia', which was now self-supporting, and that the shareholders had received no dividends, but he was unsuccessful. The Chancellor of the Exchequer had already discussed a possible deal with Smuts, and refused to commit himself to an undertaking to pay the Cave award.[19] In company circles the commission's failure to rubber-stamp the company's claim was put down to 'the sulky jealous antagonism' of the Colonial Office and the opposition of the Attorney General, who was described by Gell as a 'Scottish radical who like Lloyd George and his friends was involved in the pro-Boer hostility to the South African loyalists'.[20] But it was not an anti-charter conspiracy that made the government reluctant to face payment: it was the unwillingness to face the political consequences a large award to the company could have had.

With no initiative from the Union, and with his own attempt to hurry payment to the company blocked, Milner had to hold off political pressures from the settlers. In August 1919 he poured a cold douche on their aspirations, advising them that the white population was too small and the finances too weak for responsible government. The British government would place no difficulties in the way of the settlers' joining the Union, but if there was no present desire to do so the charter should continue.[21] Significantly, at this stage, both Amery and the permanent officials were prepared to consider a period of representative government, though it had been ruled out by the Colonial Office in 1914.[22] In January 1920 Milner wrote to Smuts asking for a statement of his views on Rhodesia, adding, '. . . as long as there is any fear . . . of the Nationalist Party getting the upper hand in the Union—it would be out of the question to think of getting Rhodesia into it'.[23] In February Buxton reported that Smuts had no intention for the time being of raising Rhodesian incorporation.[24] In March came the significant republican gains in the South African elections, and in April the Rhodesian electors, in fulfilment of Milner's prediction, responded by giving an overwhelmingly anti-Union and pro-responsible government vote. The Rhodesian Legislative Council then passed a resolution, as provided for by the supplemental charter of 1915, purporting to give the required evidence of fitness for responsible government. Though the Colonial Office was unimpressed by the settlers' claim, it seemed that some adjustment would have to be made in Milner's policy. A memorandum was prepared for the Cabinet (though it was not presented) which expressed the Office's view of the position. The smallness of settler numbers was seen as the first difficulty in the way of responsible government. African interests, it affirmed, had always been a special imperial responsibility. The present system of African administration was excellent, but

Whether those interests can be safely handed over to the Southern Rhodesian settlers in their present state of political development must be a doubtful point. It is well known that the natives in other South African territories that are at present under the direct control of the imperial government are most anxious to retain their present form of government and not to be included in the Union . . . [but] some preparation has been made against the contingency of the grant of Responsible Government by the settlement of the native reserves question . . .

The British government were thus fully aware of African preference for the 'imperial factor' and doubted the capacity of white Rhodesian settlers to act as trustees, but it was beginning to see the reserves policy as its insurance in the case of responsible government as well as entry into the Union.[25]

In reply to the settlers Milner told them that the British government sympathised with their aspirations but that the difficulty was the time for implementing them. Southern African politics were full of uncertainties, and there was an influx of new settlers into Rhodesia '. . . who will naturally desire to be consulted as to the constitution under which they will have to live'.[26] Milner wanted to temporise in the hope of the possible electoral influence of new settlers, unprejudiced against the Union, and to wait for the success of Smuts's manoeuvres to strengthen his position in South Africa by a merger with the Unionists. The postponement was sweetened by two provisos: first, an assurance that responsible government would be reconsidered if it received a favourable mandate at the next elections, and secondly—and more important, as it alone made the continuation of Chartered rule for the time being politically acceptable in Rhodesia—was a promise of a development loan of £150,000 per annum from the British government to fill in the gap left by the tailing off of company investment. In order to avoid having to ask either Parliament or the Treasury for the money for the proposed loan Amery hit on the idea of borrowing it from the Crown Agents' West African surplus, as this would 'keep . . . the matter out of Parliament for two years at least'.[27]

The Cave award was eventually published in January 1921.[28] The company's claim was cut down from £7,866,117 to £4,435,225 (there remained some deductions to be made for land granted to the company by itself), and its claim for accumulated interest on the amount was dismissed. In spite of attempts both in the Rhodesian hearings and in Britain to politicise the basis of the award—for example, by challenging the major defence items, which were the costs of the wars and rebellions of the 1890s[29]—there were no spectacular reasons of principle for cutting down the company's claim, only *ad hoc* differences about accounting and the allocation of revenues. The award was published at the time when the Committee on National Expenditure under the chairmanship of Lord Geddes was in the process of applying the 'Geddes axe' in order to reduce government expenditure, and it must be considered in the light of the drastic all-round reduction in government spending. The target of the Geddes committee was to reduce government expenditure by a total of £175 million in 1922–23. The total Colonial Estimate for 1921–22 was just over £2 million pounds, and the provisional estimate for the next year about £1·75 million. This excluded expenditure on the Middle East, which was estimated at 27·25 million and £13 million respectively for two years. As Churchill told the imperial conference in 1921, 'The great expense of Palestine and Mesopotamia has thrown such burdens on our backs that everything in regard to Crown colonies has been severely pruned.'[30] The award to the company amounted, therefore, to more than double the entire Colonial Estimate outside the Middle East—a large sum of money to pay to a commercial company which was still under a political cloud in radical circles. Similarly the loan of £150,000 was a generous one: excluding Tanganyika, which was receiving nearly £1 million for post-war reconstruction, the total spent on grants in aid in the entire colonial empire was about £1 million. In the light of the Geddes committee's conclusion that assistance to African dependencies must be limited to 'the most urgent requirements' the settlers had done well, as the British government was maintaining a level of capital expenditure that had been set by the company, and the anxiety of the Colonial Office to keep the matter out of the Commons can be easily understood.[31] In August 1921 the government was asked to give parliamentary time for discussion before any definite arrangements affecting Rhodesia were made but replied that it would not be practicable to do so, and similar requests were turned down in May and August 1922.[32]

2 Towards responsible government in Southern Rhodesia

At this stage Milner achieved his long-standing aim of ridding himself of office. In February 1921 he was succeeded by Churchill, a change of personnel which embodied symbolically the conflicting traditions of imperial policy in south Africa. Yet though the old animosities still made the protagonists wary of each other the gap between the approaches had narrowed. From the start company circles feared that Churchill would succumb to the temptation to reverse Milner's policy, and the initial haste of the new Secretary of State made it seem that he was set on doing so. Amery emphasised to Churchill the urgency of arriving at a firm decision,[33] but Churchill needed little urging to get the Rhodesian *contretemps* out of the way. His attitude to Colonial Office questions in general was illustrated by his bickering with Curzon over departmental responsibility when he told the Foreign Secretary that '. . . vital foreign matters, which affect the whole future of the world, and the mere departmental topics with which the Colonial Office is concerned' could not be compared.[34] It was clear that Rhodesia was a mere departmental topic, and a minor one amenable to quick settlement when compared to the problems of Ireland and the Middle East, which came under the Colonial Office. His first proposal was a departmental committee to produce a programme of action 'within two or three weeks'.[35] He was advised by the High Commissioner in South Africa that the principle of responsible government appeared to have been conceded by Milner and that the transition process should be considerably speeded up.[36] Thus Milner's policy, which was to delay while awaiting a change in the southern African political situation, was abandoned, and his concession of the responsible government principle, which had been intended largely to fob the settlers off, had now become the excuse for hurrying its achievement on. Amery suggested that responsible government should be given at the beginning of 1923 without a further election of any sort. Churchill left for Egypt, leaving Rhodesian affairs in Amery's hands. At his suggestion Buxton was appointed chairman of the Colonial Office's Rhodesia Committee, and the terms of reference instructed him to enquire 'When and with what limitations (if any) Responsible Government is to be granted to Southern Rhodesia'.[37]

Churchill's apparent reversal of Milner's procrastinatory policy came as a blow both to the company and to Smuts. Smuts's South African Party, now fused with the Unionists, had just won a resounding electoral victory in South Africa,[38] thus fulfilling the first of the conditions for the success of Milner's plan. Smuts's chief anxiety was that Buxton would make 'some silly suggestions of a radical nature' before the Union government could take advantage of the newly favourable political situation and begin negotiations with the Rhodesian settlers. The company too urged that only Milner's plan would allow the necessary time for Rhodesia to pass into the Union: now that fears of secession from the empire had receded, it argued, the time was ripe for Rhodesia to throw in its 'weight on the loyal side', but 'a period of propaganda and political education is required . . .'[39] But the appointment of the committee and its confining terms of reference had destroyed the basis of Milner's policy. The report advised that a constitution for responsible government be drawn up in London after consultation with a settler delegation and that a referendum be held in Rhodesia to see whether the resultant proposals were acceptable.[40] Smuts was '... deeply disappointed with Buxton's report, which seems to ... prejudice the whole issue'. As he explained a year later to Bonar Law,

A very bad mistake was made last year when Buxton's committee was appointed by Churchill to report on a scheme of responsible government for Rhodesia. The result was in effect to commit a British government to a grant of a constitution after a referendum. It was a sharp reversal of Milner's previous policy, which had laid down that Rhodesia must wait until the charter expires in 1924.[41]

The company reacted in similar vein to the Buxton report, though it felt with some justification that if Churchill had been unduly hasty Smuts had been unnecessarily tardy in coming up with an offer for Rhodesia. Malcolm summed up the company's attitude that the report was 'perfectly hopeless' and that it was 'a thousand pities' that Smuts's intervention had not come earlier.[42]

Once the report was out Smuts did break his silence, though both the Union and the British governments had a weaker hand than before. The South African Prime Minister was to be in London in June 1921 for the imperial conference, and he asked Churchill to arrange the visit of the settler delegation to coincide with his presence. But the plan to arrange an apparently coincidental meeting misfired; the settler delegation would not be hurried into conference with Smuts and Churchill together, and only after weeks of wrangling did they agree to stop off in Cape Town on their way to Britain for a separate meeting with Smuts. Coghlan told Douglas-Jones, the Resident Commissioner in Salisbury, that in any case the business of the deputation was to negotiate the terms of a responsible government constitution and that discussions with the Union government could be only 'academic'. In the face of this Smuts's chances of making any headway with the settler delegation were small.[43]

Smuts now pressed Churchill to remedy the damage the Buxton report had done by seeing that the settlers at their referendum not only had before them the possibility of accepting or rejecting a responsible government constitution but would also be faced with firm terms offered by the Union government. Both Smuts and the company suggested that the British government could cool off the ardour of the settler delegation by warning them that a responsibly governed Rhodesia would get no financial assistance from Britain. As Chaplin put it, Churchill '... has the game in his hands, as if he would not help with the money required to start Resp. Govt. I do not see how they can find it'.[44] The settlers, Smuts told Churchill, were under the impression that the British government would pay the Cave award, but they could be disabused of this expectation and told that a responsible government would start off owning neither land nor railways. He continued:

> That it is advisable from the larger point of view that Rhodesia should join the Union now rather than later seems to me very clear. Today I could carry incorporation . . . Could I carry such a policy later, when I shall have been politically weakened and Rhodesia will most probably have made a great financial mess of the new experiment?

Union with Rhodesia, he concluded, should take place '. . . very especially to help in producing stability in the Union . . .' The 'disruptive forces' (i.e. the Nationalists) would soon be strengthened by the political incorporation of South West Africa (where the majority of whites were German-speaking and assumed to be anti-empire), and a new, loyal community should be added to cancel this out. The policy of incorporation of Rhodesia was one of '. . . very far-reaching imperial significance'.[45]

The Buxton report was also attacked in Parliament, where one member complained that an expensive paraphernalia of government was being established for 'a community less than half the size of an average single-member constituency' and advocated entry into the Union, as did Wilson Fox, who argued that in a time of financial stringency Britain could not afford to give responsible government.[46] But in the Colonial Office Lambert pointed out the dangers which an overtly pro-Union policy held for the British government. The first was that if, by financial threats or otherwise, it enthusiastically espoused a cause which turned out to be an unpopular failure Britain's influence in Rhodesia would be damaged during the vital early period of responsible government. The second was that the counterpoise policy might fail and that imperial interests in southern Africa could be damaged by the disappearance of Rhodesia as a British community, as '. . . once Southern Rhodesia is part of the Union a Dutch influx may upset all calculations'.[47] In June 1921 Churchill told the imperial conference that, although 'ultimately' Rhodesia would join the Union, it should 'join man's estate' first.[48] But finance, the persuasive efforts of Smuts and the company's directors and a closer acquaintance with the facts, including the census figures, combined to change his mind. By September he had come round to being opposed to responsible government, writing on the draft letters patent that the census had 'disclosed a population of only 30,000. It is far too small . . .'[49]

Once the settler delegation was in London, Churchill did his best to chivvy them into the Union. Coghlan found him 'very bellicose and unfavourable'—a Churchillian interpretation of a course of action he had described to the Cabinet as discussing matters '... with bias a little in favour of joining the Union'.[50] The permanent officials leaned in the opposite direction, Coghlan finding in Lambert and Masterton-Smith 'two staunch friends'.[51] The negotiations between the settlers and the officials on the draft letters patent were uneventful, but the tripartite negotiations between the company, the officials and the settlers were far more strained. Masterton-Smith summed up the atmosphere when he commented that Malcolm was 'provocative' and Coghlan 'uncompromising and always suspicious'.[52] The company, which feared depredation by a hostile and insolvent settler government, demanded legislative provisions to protect its railway and mineral rights. The Colonial Office, largely at the insistence of Churchill, who expressed himself strongly on the need to protect the interests of British investors in Rhodesia, overrode the settlers' objections, and constitutional protection was provided for the company's interests. This accession to the company's demands not only emphasised the incomplete powers which the new 'responsible' administration was being given but created the basic conditions under which the company accepted responsible government when it came. The official view of the letters patent, with the restrictive powers given to the prospective Rhodesian government, was expressed succinctly in a letter from the Resident Commissioner in Salisbury to Stanley: it was that Rhodesia was not being given responsible government in the normal sense. 'The scheme in effect is an entirely practical compromise between representative and full responsible government. It should suit the peculiar circumstances of Southern Rhodesia very well until such time as the people decide to go into Union.'[53]

3 Responsible government and African interests

The settler demand for self-government had made it necessary for the British government to think carefully about the constitutional position of the Rhodesian African population. For the smallness of the settler population appeared to make their aspirations to rule themselves and the Africans impossible. Was there not a way in which the whites could be given authority over themselves alone? In 1919 Amery's mind had turned to dyarchy. Would it not be a possible solution, he had suggested,

to have *both* Crown Colony and Responsible Government under a *'dyarchy'* system? Crown Colony, i.e. Imperial Government to be responsible for external and native policy (and possibly minerals) and for the debt, and the elected members responsible for land, railways, fiscal policy, settlement, agriculture, etc. They could then develop the country on British lines, raise loans, etc, and eventually negotiate with the Union on equal terms. Meanwhile they would not be saddled with the debt or responsibility for 750,000 natives.[54]

Amery's idea derived from Lionel Curtis's 'Letter to the People of India' and the dyarchic system which he proposed would have involved a departure from the traditional southern African responsible government constitution, which separated powers by the 'reservation' of some controls over Africans to the imperial government. The essence of dyarchy, as explained by Curtis, was the coexistence of two authorities in the same area—one responsible for certain specialised functions to the local electorate and the other to the British electorate through the Secretary of State. Its rationale was that the local electorate needed a period of political education before it could take over all powers, which was a principle not calculated to appeal to the self-confident white settlers of Africa. But in any case this novel attempt at separation of settler and African government aroused no echo among the permanent officials except a brief and scornful response from Fiddes to the effect that even if a 'paper formula' for separation could be devised 'native policy is so interwoven with the functions of a Responsible Government that it would be unworkable in practice and soon disappear'.[55]

While Amery was musing over the possibilities of administrative separation Buxton, who supported settler aspirations, nevertheless felt obliged to report African apprehensions. In May 1919 he added as a postscript to a letter on the financial feasibility of responsible government the following afterthought.

I am loth to drag in the NATIVES, but I ought, I think, to mention that, unless my judgement is wholly at fault, such native opinion as may be said to exist in Southern Rhodesia would almost certainly, at this stage, regard with grave apprehension the transfer of supreme control over native policy and administration from the High Commissioner and Secretary of State to the Union Government and Parliament.

Thus African opposition to incorporation into the Union was noted, and representative government under the Crown was suggested as the form of government most suited to African interests.[56] It was Buxton, with Stanley and Lambert, all of whom were supporters of responsible government rather than union, who, in framing the report on which the draft letters patent were based in 1921, devised the constitutional strategy to fit the African position. They initially took as their model the Natal constitution of 1893, and though they recognised that the status of the Dominions had since changed they felt that this should not affect the principle on which responsible government was granted. Buxton's aim was that the giving of a responsible government constitution to the settlers should not change the position of Africans, and that to achieve this end the substance of the protective provisions of the 1898 order in council should be preserved.[57] He pointed out that under the proposals contained in this report Africans would be far better off with responsible government than they would be if Rhodesia joined the Union, because in the latter case they would come directly under Union law without any reservations at all. The Buxton report recommended few changes in the existing position. The reserves and African rights to purchase land outside them were both to be protected, and discriminatory legislation was to be reserved for imperial approval. (Though the latter provision, as a Colonial Office minute put it, was '. . . not intended as a prohibition of differential treatment of natives; they are intended as recognition that such differential treatment, within reasonable limits, is in the natural order of things in a country like Southern Rhodesia'.)[58] The stress on the High Commissioner's control over the personnel of the Rhodesian Native Department, which had been a feature of the 1898 order in council, remained. Appointments, salaries and suspensions were all subject to his approval, and he was also entitled to request information on African affairs and to compel reference of matters to a High Court judge.[59]

In addition the letters patent included provisions which originated with Stanley for Native Councils on the lines of those envisaged in the Union's Act of 1920. Stanley advised that the settlers should be committed in principle to the establishment of councils and that the draft constitution should contain '. . . the *policy* of consultation with the natives and of their eventual participation in the management of some of their special concerns'. Section 47 of the letters patent thus specifically adopted the Union's policy, by providing that the High Commissioner could establish, in any reserve, councils representative '. . . of local chiefs and other native residents as may seem to him expedient' for discussion of matters of interest to Africans, and to give them such powers in connection with local affairs '. . . as can in his opinion be safely and satisfactorily undertaken by them'.[60] There were thus two main features of the Buxton constitution's provisions for African affairs: first a minimum of change from the existing provisions, and secondly an updating of them along the lines of Union policies. But the changes that had taken place in the constitutional position of the Dominions over the last twenty years made it implicit that a grant of responsible government meant greater independence from the centre than it had done when the Natal constitution was drawn up in 1893, and this quite undermined Buxton's approach.

In a letter to the *Rhodesia Herald* in March 1922 Abraham Twala, a Zulu living in Rhodesia, commented that those Africans who were 'brooding over the so-called "Imperial Reservations of Native Affairs"' were 'living in a paradise of fools'. South African experience had shown that the imperial government would refuse to intervene in internal affairs after the granting of responsible government: '... whatever constitution will be acceptable to the inhabitants of Southern Rhodesia ... will mean resting powers with the colonists'.[61]

The British government did consider what would happen to the elaborate system of controls it was devising if Rhodesia joined the Union. It realised that it was inconceivable that the Union would agree to the retention of any imperial responsibility for Africans and that it was therefore '... more obligatory on His Majesty's Government to safeguard the Native Reserves to the utmost extent.'[62] Rhodesia would be incorporated into the Union without the safeguards which would apply in the case of the transfer of the government of the protectorates, and the only suggestion Stanley could make was the giving of a public assurance by Union Ministers not to interfere with existing arrangements.

Buxton's proposed controls were heavily criticised by the company. Not only, it claimed, would they be illusory in practice but the entire conception was based on a false view of the separability of African and white administration, as the work of '... practically every department of government consists of the administration of the law as it affects natives ...'[69] Smuts's approach was quite the opposite and aimed at an even more ambitious measure of administrative separation than Buxton's report. Smuts not only undertook to protect the existing reserves in case of incorporation but proposed the very form of administration for Africans for which British officials had not dared to hope. Reporting on the consultations which the settler delegation had with Smuts in Cape Town in 1922, Coghlan described it as follows:

Smuts told us that the Union Native Affairs Commission suggested that the Natives should be governed and legislated for by the Governor General in Council as would be the case with Basutoland and the Bechuanaland Protectorate when the administration of these territories is taken over by the Union Government ... and that only the Europeans should come in as constituting an ordinary province. That would mean of course with regard to Native Affairs Rhodesia would rank as a Black Protectorate and we should have two different sets of legislative and administrative authorities concurrently dealing with the affairs of the territory.

The settlers, alarmed at the Union government's evident intention to relegate Rhodesia from the status of a white territory, found themselves wholly in accord with the assimilationists of the company. 'A more ridiculous and unworkable suggestion I have never heard of,' Coghlan wrote. 'Chaplin, Longden and I with one accord fell upon it and demolished it.'[64]

It was left to the Aborigines Protection Society to initiate an examination of African franchise and representation, a subject which had been passed over in the official discussions. Buxton's reply to the society's first query on the matter was that '. . . the *first* election must be on the existing franchise . . .' but that it could later be altered by the responsible government subject to the constitutional reservations. Harris pressed for something more than this. He pointed out the difficulty that Africans had in qualifying for the franchise: no public education was provided, Africans living in the reserves could not avail themselves of the property qualifications, and wages were low; he suggested an alteration of the qualification by raising the educational but lowering the property qualification.[65] The society was also aware of the main weakness of the qualified franchise system, that even with different qualifications it would leave virtually the whole of the African population unrepresented in the legislature. Harris therefore suggested that there should be a form of mixed representation until more Africans had qualified for the ordinary franchise, that opinions could be expressed through '. . . Advisory Councils set up amongst the Native Tribes, and some non-official person or persons elected by these Councils to set forth their views in the Legislative Assembly.'[66] Harris's suggestion would have entailed the linking of the two separate aspects of the Cape system within a single legislature. It was rejected by the Colonial Office. While it was prepared to envisage a council system along South African lines to sound out opinion, this system was not to provide a means by which tribal Africans could share in political power. It was, the society was told, '. . . out of the question to grant the franchise to natives living under tribal conditions'.[67] To the General Council of the Trades Union Congress and to the Labour Party executive, both of which he was advising on Rhodesian affairs, Harris put forward another suggestion, which was that the legislature should include members nominated to represent African interests. This too the Colonial Office rejected, preferring a Union-style separation of Africans from politics and feeling that the more effective means of using experts in African affairs '... would be to associate them with the Ministry for Native Affairs as a consultative body on the lines of the Union Native Affairs Commission'.[68]

Harris and the society on the whole supported the responsible government solution, though their traditional hostility to the charter did not blind them to the possibilities of a deterioration in the position of Africans under settler rule. 'I do not suppose for a moment,' Harris wrote, '... that when the Rhodesian settler realises all that our programme implies he will agree, and we shall then have to fight him. The main point is that we have at a critical juncture put forth a sound native policy as the price of responsible government.' Harris was suspiciously aware, also, '... that when a change of Government comes about they are quite determined to disenfranchise the native'.[69] Nevertheless it would have been impolitic openly to alienate the heirs to power, and the society greeted the settler delegation to London warmly and ferried them amicably around the radical world. The society was pleasantly surprised by the reservations contained in Buxton's constitution, and considering that the land situation was to remain unchanged for the time being and that the alternative to responsible government was union with the south without any safeguards, it was relatively satisfied. In the Commons there was little radical hostility to responsible government. The Labour Party opposed entry into the Union largely on the grounds that it was being arranged for the benefit of the company, though Wedgwood did attack the franchise provisions in the proposed responsible government constitution and asked for an African vote '... proportionate to the importance of their interests'. Ormsby-Gore, on the other hand, thought that union would be the best protection for a 'liberal solution', and he cited heavy east African taxation of Africans as the probable course that Rhodesia, as a 'little dominion' would follow.[70]

4 The settler referendum

While the responsible government proposals were being framed Smuts went ahead with the framing of his alternative. Two sets of negotiations were involved. First the Union and the company had to reach agreement over the financial terms under which the Union would take over the company's assets. The Union's final offer was one of almost £7 million, for which it would have acquired the company's railways in Northern Rhodesia as well as its assets in the south. In order to clinch the agreement Smuts had to persuade the Colonial Office to abandon the British government's claim on the company for wartime expenditure, a substantial financial concession which the officials were unwilling to make but which was forced upon them by Churchill, who instructed them that 'My policy has always had a distinct bias in favour of Union . . .' and accused them of obstruction.[71] At the end of July 1922 Smuts published his terms of entry to the Rhodesian settlers. The existing Rhodesian franchise law would remain in force. Section 137 of the South Africa Act, which provided for the equal status of the two official languages of the Union, would be applied to Rhodesia. The lien which the company held on the lands pending the payment of its deficits would be immediately discharged and the lands made available for settlement, an attempt being made to assuage Rhodesian fears that this would lead to a *bywoner* influx by an undertaking that land settlement would be under Rhodesian control. In a brief section on Africans Smuts offered protection of the reserves, the setting up of native councils in them, and, in the only point on which he differed from British policy and came closer to the settlers' wishes, the setting apart of African purchase areas adjacent to the reserves. He promised that there would be no labour recruiting in Rhodesia, and an annual development grant to replace the company's investment was promised. Rhodesia would start with ten members of the House of Assembly and five senators, which would have been a more generous representation per head of white population than any other province in the Union.[72]

In August Smuts toured Rhodesia to drum up support, stressing the desirability of a greater South Africa and concentrating on the promise of more rapid development. But he could not conceal the intensity with which the National Party in South Africa campaigned against the inclusion of the black and British north. To the Nationalists not only was Smuts's policy 'imperialist' and 'capitalist'—conceived in the interests of Britain and of Chartered capital (and its allies, the Rand mining interests)—but it was also clearly a manoeuvre to add to Smuts's parliamentary strength. As the Cape Nationalist paper, *Die Burger*, put it, 'It is quite clear that there is on the one side a sacrifice of the Union for imperialistic and especially for capitalistic ends, and on the other an arbitrary exploitation of the Union taxpayer for the purpose of bolstering up Jan Smuts's tottering position.'[73] And tottering Smuts's position was. The strong political position with which he had begun the bid for Rhodesia had been shattered by the Rand revolt, which destroyed the image of the government and lost him the support of the labour voters that had given him his large majority in 1921. The revolt and its aftermath also alarmed the Rhodesian voters, and the bitterness of the atmosphere of Union politics appalled the settler delegation when it visited Cape Town to negotiate terms with Smuts.[74]

In October 1922, as the referendum approached, Smuts persuaded the new South African High Commissioner and Governor General, Prince Arthur of Connaught, to ask Churchill to issue a pro-Union message before the voting, Connaught told Churchill that Smuts

... is playing for a stake big enough to encourage one to risk subsequent criticism, and your intervention from imperial point of view may have decisive result. I am sure that little importance attached by Smuts to prospect of additional support in the House and he is influenced mainly by ambition to achieve united British South Africa, to secure control of Beira and railway transport from Rhodesia to Katanga. He would thus be placed in a strong position *vis-à-vis* Mozambique.[75]

Churchill's reaction was in favour of issuing a statement, and his minute to the effect crossed Masterton-Smith's draft of a proposed statement which told the electors that the British government would welcome it if they decided '... to take advantage of the provision made by the wisdom and foresight of the framers of the South Africa Act ...', and that this would '... accord with the Imperial interests involved ...' On the same night, 15 October, Churchill was taken ill, and three days later was operated on for appendicitis. During this time he could not be approached with official business. On 19 October the meeting at the Carlton Club disposed of the Lloyd George government. Wood and Masterton-Smith decided that no action could be taken until a new Secretary of State took office, especially as the Resident Commissioner had forecast a large majority in favour of responsible government. On 19 October Smuts again pressed for a message to be issued, but it was not until the morning of the 24th that Masterton-Smith saw Churchill in the nursing home. Churchill then felt that a Secretary of State technically in office only for a few hours longer could not make so important a pronouncement. On the same day the incoming Secretary of State, the Duke of Devonshire, decided that it was too late to send the message. Concluding his account of the events, Masterton-Smith excused the Colonial Office from responsibility: '... no pronouncement from Downing Street could conceivably have affected the issue... The simple fact is that the result was a foregone conclusion before Mr Churchill became Secretary of State.'[76]

Yet the settlers' feelings towards the imperial government were complex. 'They know they are thoroughly loyal, they want to remain thoroughly British . . .' wrote Stanley, but they felt that London wanted only to avoid financial liability and to help Smuts: '. . . they imagine that they are now finding a stepmother'.[77] Even so, the tawdry patriotism of the settlers may have been moved by a message from London defining their imperial duty and cast in Churchillian prose, though Churchill was still a suspect radical and not yet a nationalist totem. Certainly this would have appealed more than Smuts's message, which placed its emphasis on the manifest destiny of the Union.

> The Union is going to be for the African continent what the United States has become for the American continent. Rhodesia is but another day's march on the high road of destiny. Rhodesia will not stop the march, rather she will proudly form the vanguard.[78]

The settlers preferred to stay on with their reluctant stepmother, fundamentally to keep the Afrikaners out. While Smuts defended his policy at home by stressing the need for land to solve the *bywoner* problem, Keller, of the Rhodesian Railway Workers' Union, urged that if Rhodesia had responsible government '. . . we can get an English settler on every farm in Rhodesia first . . . we can keep them [Afrikaners] out for good'.[79] In a 78 per cent poll 8,774 votes were cast for responsible government and 5,989 for union. As Chaplin put it, the electors were swayed by '. . . what one may call the "bloody Dutchman" prejudice'.[80]

Notes

1. See *in re Southern Rhodesia*, A.C. 1919.
2. See C.O. 417/556, 2 December 1914, and C.O. 417/568, 26 January 1915.
3. Lord Loreburn dissented from the view that the company was entitled to repayment for its deficits.
4. Ch. 2/2/14, f. 64, D'Erlanger to Chaplin, and Ch. 8/2/2/12, Michell to Chaplin, 9 February 1918.
5. Statement to shareholders contained in C.O. 417/613, 8 September 1918.
6. Ch. 8/2/2/6, Gell to Chaplin, 18 August 1919.
7. *Hansard*, 30 July and 1 August 1919, and 'Africanus', 'Reconstruction in central Africa', *Journal of the Royal African Society*, 1919.
8. See 'Politieke Tweespraak tussen Oom Jan ('n Botha man) en Neef Piet ('n Jonge Nasionaalist)', n.d., and Hertzog, quoted by B. Bunting, *The Rise of the South African Reich*, London, 1969, p. 30.
9. S.P., v, Smuts to I. Smuts, 21 January 1919; Smuts to A. Clark, 8 May 1920; Smuts to T. Smartt, 30 September 1920; and Smuts to J. S. Hofmeyr, 5 November 1920.

162 *Unconsummated union*

10 Ch. 8/2/2/6, Gell to Chaplin, 18 August 1919.
11 Amery, quoted in Paul Guinn, *British Strategy and Politics, 1914–18*, Oxford, 1965.
12 M.P. 80, 8 April 1919.
13 Ch. 8/2/2/11, Malcolm to Chaplin, 16 April 1919.
14 M.P. 80, Milner to Buxton, 8 April 1919; Milner's emphasis.
15 M.P. 81, Milner to Bonar Law, 9 April 1920; Milner's emphasis. Lloyd George also invoked imperial responsibility to Africans in his reply to Hertzog's republican deputation in 1919: the deputation, he said, was not representative of South Africa, as Africans wished to remain within the empire. (C. M. v.d. Heever, *Hertzog*, Johannesburg, English edition, 1946, p. 190.)
16 M.P. 80, Buxton to Milner, 12 May and 19 May 1919.
17 C.O. 417/632, 6 October 1919, and C.O. 417/633, 17 June 1919, Minutes.
18 On the commission's work see J. D. Fage, *Achievement*, pp. 223 ff, and Cmd. 1273. C.O. 417/632, 6 October 1919, and C.O. 417/650, 27 January 1920, Minute, 2 July 1920.
19 C.O. 537/1178, 14 July 1919, Secret War Cab. 592.
20 Ch. 8/2/2/6, Gell to Chaplin, 26 January and 10 June 1920.
21 C.O. 417/620, 31 July 1919, Milner to Buxton, 12 August 1919.
22 C.O. 417/619, 24 June 1919, and C.O. 417/620, 31 July 1919.
23 B.P. 1920, Milner to Smuts, 1 January 1920.
24 B.P. 1920, Buxton to Milner, 18 February 1920.
25 C.O. 417/637, 18 May 1920.
26 Cmd. 1273, appendix I.
27 C.O. 417/621, 25 September 1920.
28 The details of the award are in Cmd. 1129.
29 See Harris's book *The Chartered Millions*, London, 1920, which he had originally entitled *Jameson's New Raid*.
30 Cab. 32/3, 1921. Figures from Cmd. 1589, *Third Report of the Committee on National Expenditure*.
31 The Geddes committee refrained from criticism of the £150,000 loan, as it was given to understand that it was a temporary measure pending the establishment of self-government. A further £13,000 was set aside to pay the interest on wartime expenditure.
32 Parliamentary Debates, Commons, 4 August 1921; 3 May and 4 August 1922.
33 C.O. 417/670, 10 February 1921, Minute.
34 Quoted in Lord Beaverbrook, *The Decline and Fall of Lloyd George*, London, 1963, pp. 44–5.
35 B.P. 1921, Churchill to Buxton, 26 February 1921.
36 C.O. 417/657, Connaught to Churchill, 18 February 1921.
37 Churchill wrote to Buxton, 'I am particularly anxious to get these questions settled without delay.' See R. Hyam, *Failure*, p. 59. Churchill had initially suggested that the chairman of the committee should be Lord Southborough, formerly Francis Hopwood, who had been Permanent Under-Secretary at the Colonial Office from 1907 to 1911. The other members were Lambert, R. M. Greenwood of the Treasury Solicitor's Department, Sir E. Grigg and Major M. Waring, M.P.

38 In the general election of February 1921 the South African Party won seventy-nine seats; the Nationalists, forty-five; and Labour, nine. Smuts's gains had been from the Labour Party and not the Nationalists, and this did not go unnoticed in Rhodesia.
39 Ch. 8/2/1, Smuts to Chaplin, 22 March 1921, and C.O. 417/460, 3 March 1921, B.S.A.C. to C.O.
40 See Cmd. 1273.
41 Ch. 8/2/1, Crewe to Chaplin, 21 March 1921, reporting a conversation with Smuts; Smuts to Chaplin, 11 May 1921, and Smuts to Bonar Law, 20 November 1922.
42 Ch. 8/2/2/11, Malcolm to Chaplin, 28 April 1921.
43 C.O. 417/661, 25 June 1921, and C.O. 417/662, 8 July 1921, containing report of the interview in Salisbury between Coghlan and Douglas Jones, 29 June 1921.
44 Ch. 8/2/1, Chaplin to Smuts, 11 September 1921.
45 C.O. 537/1184, Smuts to Churchill, secret.
46 Parliamentary Debates, Commons, 14 July 1921.
47 B.P. 1921, Lambert to Buxton, 3 April 1921.
48 C.O. 417/622, 15 July 1921, contains a copy of the speech.
49 C.O. 417/674, 27 September 1921.
50 J. P. R. Wallis, *One Man's Hand*, London, 1950, p. 190, and Cab. 78/21, Extract, contained in C.O. 417/674, October 1921.
51 B.P., 'S.R. constitution', Coghlan to Buxton, 20 December 1921.
52 C.O. 417/674, November 1921, Masterton-Smith to Churchill, 14 December 1921.
53 Ch. 8/2/2/1, Birchenough to Chaplin, 10 November 1921, and C.O. 417/660, 3 June 1921, Resident Commissioner to Imperial Secretary. The draft 'letters patent' are printed in Cmd. 1573. Section 28(e) provided for the automatic reservation of legislation on railways until such time as a railway rates tribunal had been established. In his remarks on the 'letters patent' in the 1928 edition of *Responsible Government in the Dominions* A. B. Keith regards only the limitations in favour of the company's property rights, not the control retained over African affairs, as detracting from 'full responsible government'; see pp. 11 and 37.
54 C.O. 417/619, Amery minute, 6 June 1919: emphasis in original.
55 C.O. 417/637, 18 May 1920, Minute. Curtis did not entertain the possibility that an African electorate could be educable through a dyarchy system: '... there is no political opinion in Central Africa. We can scarcely invite their opinion for the reason that they themselves cannot formulate any opinion.' (*Letter to the People of India*, Bombay, Madras and Calcutta, 1917. Curtis to Kerr, 13 November 1916, quoted p. 24.)
56 M.P. 80, Buxton to Milner, 11 and 19 May 1919.
57 Cmd. 1273, paras 59 and 63.
58 B.P. 1921, Memorandum, and C.O. 417/687, 5 December 1922, Minute by Davis.
59 See Palley, *Constitutional History*, chapters 11, 12 and 14 and appendix.
60 C.O. 417/658, 12 March 1921, Memorandum by Stanley, 18 October 1920, emphasis in original; and Cmd. 1573.
61 Quoted in T. O. Ranger, *African Voice*, p. 91.

62 C.O. 417/677, 28 February 1922, Stanley to Masterton-Smith.
63 C.O. 417/671, 18 May 1921, B.S.A.C. to C.O.
64 C.O. 417/679, June 1922, Coghlan to Newton, 17 April 1922.
65 A.P.S. G 165, Buxton to Harris, 28 October 1921, emphasis in original; and A.P.S. G 165, Harris to Churchill, 23 November 1921.
66 *Ibid.*, and A.P.S. G 171, Memorandum.
67 C.O. 417/675, 23 November 1921.
68 A.P.S. G 171, Memorandum, and C.O. 879/120 Afr. No. 1085, Secretary of State to Hyde Commission, 8 April 1922.
69 A minority of the society preferred union with the south, but as Botha had responded to none of the society's suggestions on 'native policy' union had lost favour. Gann, in both *Southern Rhodesia* and *Northern Rhodesia*, stresses the society's support for the settlers without considering their reservations. So does P. Slinn, who writes that '... the Society's hatred of Company rule seems to have left it curiously blind to the shortcomings of "settler democracy" as far as native policy was concerned...' ('The role of the British South Africa Company in Northern Rhodesia, 1890–1964', *African Affairs*, LXX, October 1971.) This judgement seems unfair. See A.P.S. Rhodesia Native Lands general file No. 4, Harris to Olivier, 18 October 1920, and A.P.S. G 165, Harris to Keable, 1 January 1921.
70 Parliamentary Debates, Commons, 25 July 1921 and 4 July 1922.
71 C.O. 551/151, 9 May 1922; C.O. 551/153, 19 June 1922; and C.O. 551/152, 19 June 1922, Minute by Churchill, dated 23 June 1922.
72 *Union Government White Paper, 1923*, correspondence *re* terms on which Union government would recommend to Parliament the inclusion of Southern Rhodesia into the Union of South Africa.
73 Quoted by M. A. G. Davies, *Incorporation in the Union of South Africa or Self-government: Southern Rhodesia's Choice, 1922*, Pretoria, 1965, p. 29. See also P. R. Warhurst, 'Rhodesian–South African relations, 1900–23', paper presented at the third biennial conference of the South African Historical Society, Johannesburg, 3 February 1971.
74 The settler delegation arrived in Cape Town during the acrimonious debates which followed the rebellion. The Resident Commissioner in Salisbury reported, 'One thing which appears to have impressed the delegates more than anything else... is... the bitter party and racial feelings existing.' (C.O. 417/679, Douglas Jones to Stanley, 3 May 1922, and Hancock, *Smuts*, I, p. 151.)
75 C.O. 551/152, 13 October 1922, telegram.
76 C.O. 551/152, Memorandum by Masterton-Smith, 13 October 1922.
77 C.O. 417/679, Stanley to Masterton-Smith, 30 May 1922. The 1921 census showed that some two-thirds of Rhodesia's 33,000 settlers were South African-born. Just under one-fifth of the settler population were Afrikaners.
78 *The Star*, 24 October 1922.
79 See Gann, *Southern Rhodesia*, and Fage, *Achievement*, for a full account of the campaign. The way in which the Union government had quickly parcelled out the unoccupied lands of South West Africa to land-hungry applicants from South Africa seemed to indicate what it would do, despite promises, in Rhodesia.
80 Ch. 8/2/1, Chaplin to Crewe, 8 December 1922.

CHAPTER 9

New patterns in central Africa

1919–25

The settler decision and the pending Company withdrawal broke up the political unity of central Africa. In staking out their own claim to power the settlers not only interdicted the Union's absorption of Southern Rhodesia but also spared the north. New patterns began to emerge in central Africa. While for some time it was not clear for how long the south would remain separated from the Union, and land and 'native policy' in general continued to follow the logic of fashioning an improved Union model, the new colony began to develop its own political ambitions towards the north. The Union, though it continued actively to concern itself with the Rhodesias, now turned its immediate expansionist aims towards the High Commission territories. In Northern Rhodesia partition, which was on the agenda, was not reached by the end of the decade, and the territory continued to hover uncertainly between southern and eastern Africa.

1 Northern Rhodesia, the company and the Union

In 1919 when the company considered its financial future with regard to Northern Rhodesia it made it quite clear that it did not wish to retain administrative authority there after it had relinquished it in the south. The company would not, Malcolm wrote, '. . . part with the baby which had now ceased to be an expense . . . and be left with a baby which was still sucking'.[1] Though the future of the north got little detailed consideration from the British government at this time, Amery told Parliament that there was no question of its incorporation into the Union, and a year later Milner warned the Cabinet that the British government should be ready to take over its administration and firmly told the company that north and south must remain separated.[2]

White settler power in the north was as yet negligible. An Advisory Council, elected by the settlers, had been created during the war, though its existence was not embodied statutorily. Chosen by a tiny all-white electorate, it had been supposed to confine its business to matters affecting the white community only, but in practice the attempt to separate the interests of a white council from 'native affairs' had been a failure. After the war the Northern Rhodesian settlers pressed the British government for greater powers, and in a minor constitutional storm challenged the company's right to taxation without representation. Though the political ambitions of the northern settlers seemed absurd in London, the white agitation triggered off thinking about what the future of the north would be when the company was replaced. Amery seemed to take partition for granted, '. . . presumably North Eastern Rhodesia with Nyasaland to the East African group, Barotseland another Bechuanaland under the High Commissioner, and the rest of Northern Rhodesia with the white settlement area to share Southern Rhodesia's self government—whether separately or in the South African Union.'[3] The company pressed a similar view on the Colonial Office. Northern Rhodesia, it urged, was '. . . ill adapted to be a separate single unit of government'. The east had its natural outlet through Nyasaland, and communication between Livingstone and Fort Jameson, except by telegraph, took over a month. In the west the Lozi reserve, the Kasempa district and part of the Kafue district were purely 'native areas' containing no whites bar Company officials. In the centre was the railway belt.

All its trade runs north to the Congo and south to Southern Rhodesia and the Union . . . All its affinities are with the South whence, except for some direct immigration from Britain, its colonisation so far as it has taken place has proceeded. The area contains practically the whole white population of Northern Rhodesia . . .

It concluded by advising partition: the east to Nyasaland; the west to Bechuanaland, '. . . allowing them for the future to follow the fortunes of that Protectorate' (envisaging, therefore, possible entry into the Union) and the centre to join the south, whether or not the latter entered the Union.[4]

After the Buxton committee had reported on Southern Rhodesia it was instructed by Churchill to prepare a report on the north. It noted both the territory's lack of homogeneity and the suggestions for partition but expressed no opinion on them other than that they must be determined largely by financial considerations.[5] The committee's main recommendation was that the undecided questions and land ownership and liability for the deficit in the north—the two issues which had bedevilled the south—should be referred as soon as possible to the courts. The anticipation of a long-drawn-out, expensive, complex and eventually unsatisfactory repetition of the struggles that had accompanied the company's disengagement from the south thus hung over all the planning of Northern Rhodesia's future, and made the search for any workable compromise that would avoid this an important determinant in the ultimate settlement. At first it seemed to both the company and the British government that the obvious answer was to turn to Smuts and, by getting him to make a bid for the company's assets to which all could agree, so avoid having to resort to legal determination of the tedious questions. Smuts was willing: in October 1921 Malcolm was able to report, 'Now Smuts wants the North as well as the South and wants it soon. . .', and he suggested that if Smuts got the south the company should sell Smuts its concessions and its 'position' generally in the north. 'Once he acquires it HMG will practically have to acquiesce in what that position is.'[6] But the company could not rely alone on what Smuts wanted, and it sought to extract assurances from the British government that it would not be landed with continuing financial responsibilities in the north and that it could entertain a firm offer from Smuts. The British government was not over-interested. When Birchenough wished to discuss the matter with Churchill he found him '. . . so entirely absorbed in Irish problems . . . that we cannot secure his attention, or that of his officials, for Rhodesian business'.[7] It appeared nevertheless that the Permanent Secretary was prepared to countenance the Union taking over the north.[8]

A clear expression of Colonial Office policy was never given. Those officials who supported partition as advised by the company were prepared at least to see the railway belt go into the Union. Churchill's attitude, though it was not made explicit, seemed to be a departure from Milner's insistence that the line be drawn at the Zambesi, and he struck the word 'Southern' from the Colonial Office documents on Rhodesia and the Union which were prepared for the Cabinet, so giving himself authority to negotiate the north as well. All the anticipations came to nothing, as all were agreed that the north should not go in without the south. After the referendum and the change of government in Britain, settlement of the north became inextricably bound up with the achievement of a general bargain which would settle all obligations to the company.

2 The end of the charter

The new British government had to clear up the manifold confusion which the failure of Churchill's Rhodesian policy had left, though again it was far from being a crucial concern. The South African High Commissioner in London accurately depicted its place, writing to Smuts, 'Rhodesia: I don't suppose that Devonshire has thought more about this question than that it is one of those bothering things somebody or other will have to deal with some time.'[9] Smuts was not disposed to accept the settlers' choice, and he tried to persuade the new Prime Minister, Bonar Law, that it was in the power of the British government to apply financial pressure on Southern Rhodesia that would make its separate existence short-lived. It would not be good policy, he wrote, '. . . to extend any financial favours to Rhodesia, as she ought to seek relief from her financial troubles in the Union . . .' To the defeated Union Association in Rhodesia Smuts proposed that it should keep itself in being and should continue to work for union. He envisaged keeping his offer to the company open, and considered attempting an arrangement with the company over Northern Rhodesia. If properly handled, he thought, responsible government might last as little as two years.[10] Neither the company nor the British government was prepared to go along with a policy designed to make responsible government unworkable. The company declined to support a Unionist campaign for the first legislative elections, as the result of almost inevitable failure would be to alienate the settler government, '. . . with consequent increased risk of serious detriment to our big interests in the country'. Still less would the company be willing to combine in a financial squeeze on the new colony which would bring about the collapse of responsible government. In such a collapse, as Malcolm pointed out, the company's financial interests, and other connected capitalist interests, would be bound to suffer heavily.[11] Bound up as it was with the future of Rhodesia, the company would have to work for the continuance of financial confidence. Likewise the British government felt that, the choice having been given and made, there was no alternative but to go ahead with the implementation of the draft letters patent.

At the end of 1922 the company approached the new British government in an attempt to obtain out of court an overall settlement of the matters of issue between them. In particular it wanted to avoid northern questions going to the courts, and it complained bitterly about the proposed method of paying the Cave award. The Buxton report, and the draft letters patent, provided that the company should be reimbursed for its deficits by the new Rhodesian government out of the gradual income received through the sale of land in Rhodesia, a proposal which, the company complained, deprived it in effect of its right to reimbursement.[12] In December the new Parliamentary Under-Secretary, Ormsby-Gore, prepared a memorandum on future policy.[13] It proposed rejection of both the company's main requests. The British government, he wrote, should not propose to Parliament a cash settlement of the Cave award, nor should it do a deal over Northern Rhodesia which would involve having to ask Parliament for money for a financial settlement that had not been legally determined.

While the memorandum envisaged no change in direction with regard to the company and to the south, it presaged a difference in approach to the future of Northern Rhodesia. It ought, Ormsby-Gore wrote, to be considered as a tropical dependency, and he advocated that the suggested partition, and the separation of the railway strip and its incorporation with the south, should be ruled out once and for all. So should the separation of Barotseland, and the territory as a whole should be administered by a Governor who would come directly under the Colonial Office and have no connections with the South African High Commission. The north should be seen as being in the same category as Nyasaland, and it should be stated that it was British government policy to assimilate it with the policies of the east African colonial group.

At the instigation of the Duke of Devonshire, Treasury and Colonial Office officials began to work out an overall approach to a settlement with the company, dealing with both north and south together.[14] The company claimed ownership of all the lands of North Western Rhodesia under its concessions and, in addition, ownership of a concession area in the north-east. Colonial Office officials and Lord Milner had submitted the problem to the Law Officers in 1921 with considerable trepidation lest, in view of the decision of the Privy Council in the Southern Rhodesian case, it turned out that the British government, if it claimed the land, would incur financial responsibility for the administrative deficits in the north.[15] In addition to this legal gamble, if the British government took the company to court over the north it would have been faced with a petition of right from the company claiming cash payment of the Cave award.[16] In April 1923 Devonshire put to the Cabinet the case for a negotiated settlement, which he anticipated would cost around £3¼ million. Although he emphasised that following on their rejection of the policy of Union the new Rhodesian colony should be given a liberal start, he felt that a new government could be made to bear the charges on a loan of £2½ million. A reference to the courts might not only be long-drawn-out but could involve the government in the payment of the northern deficits, and would raise embarrassing questions with regard to land ownership in Nyasaland which the Colonial Office would prefer to leave undisturbed.[17] In addition a negotiated settlement would ease pressure from Coghlan, who was demanding immediate responsible government and threatening anti-British agitation if it were held up, while at the same time making the new colony bear part of the cost. The contemplated bargain with the company would mean on the Crown's part a cash settlement of the Cave award, a waiver by the Crown of its long-standing claim against the company for wartime expenditure for the defence of Southern Rhodesia, and an agreement to take over the administration of the north as soon as possible. In return the company would withdraw its petition of right and would waive its claim for administrative deficits in the north while agreeing to a compromise solution on the question of land ownership. The company was also left with mineral rights in Northern Rhodesia, though this part of the agreement was not considered important enough by the Colonial Office (nor by the Cabinet) to warrant mention as one of its main features.[18]

Thus finally the strict Treasury point of view which had held out against finding money from the British exchequer to pay the company was cast aside, as was the avoidance of asking Parliament to vote money to pay out the Chartered Company. Harris succeeded in raising some flutters of anxiety in the Commons about the negotiated settlement, but no Commons intervention in any way diverted the government's course. Attention was drawn to the fact that the government had chosen to ignore the Lozi challenge to the validity of the company's concessions in North Western Rhodesia. As a Labour member put it, the government was '... preparing to settle the question with one party when, in fact, there is another party'.[19] But this did not alter the policy of countenancing no challenge to the concessions. In July 1923, during the Colonial Office vote, Roberts and Wedgwood, who were Harris's most prominent Liberal and Labour supporters on Rhodesian issues, welcomed the settlement in a debate which was dominated by Kenyan questions.[20] With regard to partition of the north it was Ormsby-Gore's rejection that remained the most important strand in British government policy. To induce the Treasury to agree to the overall agreement Devonshire had held out the hope that a future partition would bring about a cheaper form of administration in the north.[21] At the end of 1923 the Treasury sought to remind the Colonial Office of this, and suggested that in order to save the expense of a separate colony the north should come under the supervision of the Governor of Southern Rhodesia while its future was being investigated, but the Colonial Office refused. And though the Treasury had specifically remarked that it awaited proposals on partition of the north the Colonial Office told Stanley that it was not an urgent matter.[22]

In terms of the settlement finally arrived at the company received £3¾ million in cash, of which £2 million was to be paid by the Southern Rhodesian government, financed by a loan from the Bank of England, and £1¾ million by the British Treasury. Having relinquished the reins of government, the British South Africa Company remained a powerful corporation. Its assets were £5¾ million in liquid securities, mineral rights in both Northern and Southern Rhodesia, 2½ million acres in North Eastern Rhodesia, a half share in the proceeds of land sales in North Western Rhodesia for forty years, and an 86 per cent shareholding in the Rhodesia Railways. The board and the shareholders felt that the terms were neither generous nor just. Birchenough called the deal 'a lame ending to a great enterprise', doubting 'whether any government has ever made a shabbier bargain with a great corporation . . .'[23] A valedictory article written by Malcolm in 1924 captures the mood in Company circles. He complained bitterly about the treatment the company had received at British government hands over the years, in particular at Harcourt's claiming the land on behalf of the Crown in 1914, which deprived the shareholders of legitimate expectations of profit.[24] The company's self-image showed that the political gap between it and its opponents remained as wide as it had been in the 1890s. The sordid stockjobbing image that it had enjoyed in Liberal circles, and the rapacious monopolist exploiter Harris had described in *The Chartered Millions*, contrasted absolutely with the picture that Malcolm drew. It had always been difficult for members of the company's board to look dispassionately at things Rhodesian, for there was more involved than imperial politics or financial speculation. There was an element of irrationality in the reactions to radical criticism of the company's workings because Rhodesia was *au fond*, a mythology, drawing upon the mystique of Rhodes, patriotism, power, youthful dreams of 'wild' Africa, middle-aged dreams of wealth all of which made up the amalgam which Chartered circles felt had been betrayed. Malcolm lauded the '. . . half-*conquistador*, half-commercial spirit of the merchant adventurer' which motivated the company. Most of all, in 'this romantic story', Jameson had been 'possessed by the Elizabethan spirit adventure'.[25] The Rhodesia Pioneer Column was 'as daring a band of adventurers as ever Pizarro or Cortes led'. This, added to nearly forty years without dividends, made up the feeling that the grand imperial venture in central Africa had been quixotic, that the financial interests of the last of the great chartered companies had been sacrificed. But the company had not been a financial failure. In May 1924 it returned over £2 million to its shareholders at 5s per share, thereby reducing its authorised share capital to £6¾ million. In November it paid its first dividend, and between 1924 and 1939 it paid out over £8 million in dividends, giving an average return on capital for these fifteen years of over 8 per cent. Over the entire period of the company's life up to 1939 the average return on capital was 2·68 per cent per annum.[26] Initially there had been enormous over-investment which was highly speculative in nature, banking not only on exaggerated expectations of mineral wealth but primarily influenced by Rhodes's political motivations. To this must be added the expenses of the rebellion provoked by the company in the 1890s. In addition the company opened up to Anglo-South African capital a huge new field of investment in land and mining. The thirty-odd years the first shareholders waited for a return on one particular investment in that area are a minor factor in considering the overall profitability to investors in southern and central African undertakings of the Chartered Company's venture; even taking the British South Africa Company alone, its financial performance is not evidence for the unprofitability of Chartered Company rule.

3 Dividing Southern Rhodesia

Soon after the inauguration of responsible government in Southern Rhodesia a chorus of interested parties began to press for action on the land question. Churchill had promised during the negotiations over the letters patent that although the British government would insist that the right of Africans to buy land on the same conditions as whites be retained in the responsible government constitution, legal territorial segregation would be considered by the British government if further enquiry found it to be desirable. The new Governor of Rhodesia, Sir John Chancellor, was a firm believer in segregation 'by the territorial limitation of ownership of land', and from the time of his arrival in Rhodesia pressed his Ministers to deal with the unresolved land question.[27] Reluctantly, missionary opinion came round to the view that a fair division of Rhodesia between white and black might be the best way of defending African land interests, as now that the reserves had been fixed in size and African agriculture had lost its battle with its State-aided settler competitors there seemed little prospect of Africans being able to increase their land holding by exercising the right of purchase in the open market.[28] A Rhodesian government commission was set up, under the chairmanship of Sir Morris Carter, who was nominated by the Colonial Office.[29] It was to enquire into the desirability of separate purchase areas, though the High Commissioner, the Governor and Colonial Office officials all assumed that it would recommend separation, and all laid stress on the immediate necessity to proceed with a partition which would prevent the situation that had arisen in the Union. In particular the Colonial Office insisted that the actual delimitation was to be carried out at the same time as the decision on principle to avoid reproducing the state of affairs which had existed in the Union after 1913.[30]

British officials had good grounds for their renewed anxiety about the land situation in the Union. In 1924 General Hertzog, its first Nationalist Prime Minister, enunciated his 'solution' to the 'native question'. Lord Athlone, the High Commissioner, greeted the policy proposals with the most outspoken suspicion of South Africa's 'native policy' by an imperial representative since before 1910.[31] Hertzog's policy, he wrote, 'constitutes a fundamental departure from that which has been pursued since Union' and was motivated by '... the Dutchman's insatiable appetite for land ... and his constitutional inability to see why natives should be allowed to occupy more land than is needed to maintain them in labour colonies ... This rather than the system of individual tenure contemplated under the Glen Gray Act is what they understand by segregation.' Athlone appeared to have discovered a difference between the imperial model of segregation and the South African brand. After six months' more experience he arrived at a fuller appreciation of developments in the Union since 1910. He blamed the 'negligence and bad faith' of the previous government for making it impossible for the Union to provide Africans with land according to the recommendations of the Beaumont report. 'Thus today in the Union we are confronted with an *impasse* in the native land question which the people of Rhodesia may be faced with tomorrow.' African rights in Rhodesia to land purchase, even if they would not be exercised for many years to come, should be safeguarded in a manner that would not obstruct the progress of white settlement. This, Athlone urged, could best be done by setting aside a fixed proportion of the land and by protecting Africans against a rise in land prices.[32]

Cripps raised the point whether the new commission was to be allowed to enquire into the adequacy of the existing reserves, but the Governor advised Carter that on no account should this question be reopened. Furthermore Chancellor urged that as a matter of policy (before any evidence had been taken) the commission should assign plateau land to settlers and land adjacent to the reserves to Africans. The Ndebele, Chancellor reported, had 'extravagant hopes' that the new commission would make allotment for them in their old lands.[33] One task of the commission was to make clear that the hopes would not be fulfilled. Rhodesian Ministers also toyed with the idea of asking the commission to report on the establishment of native councils in the reserves, but Chancellor persuaded them to drop the plan on the grounds that it would detract from the main purpose of the enquiry. Thus the opportunity of linking the policies of territorial and institutional segregation was rejected, and, as in the Union, the latter would limp behind as a sop to theorists and critics.[34]

The commissioners reported in April 1926.[35] They had studied not only the Rhodesian but also the South African situation, and in their analysis of the effects of allowing the growth of a mixed population of rural landowners drew heavily on the report of the South African commission of 1905, which they gratefully acknowledged. Missionaries and Native Department officials supported the change to segregation, they reported, on the grounds that it would facilitate development along 'suitable lines'. They stressed that the evidence they had been given left no doubt as to the support of Africans for the change, though it is clear that there was little understanding of African views, and that the report did not represent the Africans' appreciation of their economic situation and their requests for land of better quality to be added to the reserves rather than chimerical purchase areas for which the money could not be accumulated, situated in lands that the settlers had rejected.

Africans in Rhodesia had welcomed the appointment of a commission in the belief that the injustices of the previous settlement would be remedied, and hoped in particular for an increase in reserve lands. Others held out for an unrestricted right of purchase, and some were prepared to accept segregation but on the basis of a different bargain from the one being proposed. But the commission made it clear that there was to be no further land for communal occupation and no equal division. African evidence to the commission complained of the way in which the dice were being loaded against the African farmer. Africans had not the money to purchase land, and the proposed areas were far from railways and markets. It seemed clear that the proposed arrangements had nothing to do with fairness. One witness, Matthew

Zwimba, said:

If we are to be in a position to buy land and to pay for it we should also expect to be paid higher wages . . . When we sell our cattle we should like to get more money for them. We should also like to get more money for the produce of our lands. And as far as our work is concerned we seem to be going backwards, and we do not seem to acquire anything from our work. If we are to live with the white people let the treatment be the same; let us get the same pay as the white people. Then we should be in a position to acquire land when there is any to be obtained.[96]

But neither the Colonial Office nor the commissioners dealt with this kind of reality. The commissioners found their refuge in philosophical justification. 'In the world generally,' they wrote, 'the relationships between white and coloured races tend to become more and more embittered.' Those who had given the subject most thought,[37] they found, feared coming wars of extermination between the races. Segregation of land holding was therefore 'no mere passing phase of local feeling' but was in accordance with what was now regarded in the world at large as the only practicable solution to the problem of relations between black and white.

The commissioners felt that it would be the settlers who would be making the greater sacrifice if separate purchase areas were established, as so far the African right to purchase land anywhere had been more or less worthless, and the settlers had a real and effective right to buy the whole country; should Africans *then* want it they would have to pay 'European' market prices. On the other hand, because there was 'a crying need for increased European settlement', too much could not be given to Africans. Their policy in making the delimitation was to leave settler interests undisturbed, as had been done by the 1915 commission. All the land in existing white areas was to be for white purchase, while African purchase areas would border the reserves. In sum, the commission recommended that 62 per cent of the colony be reserved for whites and 37 per cent for Africans. This meant that, reserves apart, provision was being made for 50,000 African individual holders of land under a Glen Gray-type system, an average holding of 27.1 acres each.[38]

In London the Colonial Office's attitude to the report was delineated by Davis. He wrote:

No one can argue as an abstract proposition that the proposed distribution as between Europeans and Africans is inherently just and reasonable. But the report, having been published, must be regarded generally as representing the maximum which public opinion in Southern Rhodesia would be prepared to concede to the natives, and the question is whether the interests of the natives will be better served by the proposed distribution than by maintaining the *status quo*... in Southern Rhodesia time will undoubtedly run against the natives, as it has proved to run against them in the Union, and if Southern Rhodesia is to be a white man's country (on the contrary assumption the whole question is academic) it must be assumed that the natives will not be able to acquire against European competition anything like the amount of land which the Commission have allotted to the natives ....[39]

In the Commons Wedgwood hailed the report as a model approach to the questions of African land and labour. Though formerly hostile to segregation of land ownership, he accepted the commission's argument as conclusive, Olivier likewise expressed his 'pleasure and satisfaction' in the Lords. But both he and Wedgwood attacked the proportion of lands allotted, while Olivier regretted the preservation of the fragmented pattern of the Rhodesian reserves.[40] Likewise the Aborigines Protection Society and Cripps criticised the proportions and called for more compact areas within which native councils could operate. Athlone, while generally in agreement, drew attention to the absence of African purchase areas in mining centres, towns and near railways.[41]

African leadership condemned the report. There were calls for a new enquiry and for an equal division of the colony between white and black. There was also a blunt recognition that this was the meaning of the European conquest. 'When Lobengula came here,' said one member of the ICU in Bulawayo, 'he did not go to the mountains. He stayed here in this fertile country, where good crops are easily grown. This is your country.' And another, 'The best part of the land is taken by Mr Whiteman, and you are not allowed to plough there, so we have to run away and go to work for the white man.'[42]

Yet in summing up the comment the Colonial Office reiterated that the only real question was whether Africans were getting an equitable bargain in return for a right which had been barely exercised. Wedgwood's suggestion that Southern Rhodesia become a country of settlement for Africans from all over southern Africa was dismissed out of hand.[43] But the British government's acceptance of the Carter commission report and the land apportionment legislation which eventually followed it can best be understood in terms of the British desire to establish a 'model' for white southern Africa in Southern Rhodesia. White power was seen as an established fact and segregation as inevitable. If segregation was not to mean the creation of labour reserves, as had happened in the Union despite British efforts at 'influence', the Rhodesian settlers would have to be pre-empted while they were still amenable to British influence.

4 The Bechuanaland Protectorate

Though the decision to give Southern Rhodesia responsible government, and the election of the Nationalist government under General Hertzog in the Union in 1924, had broken the unity of southern Africa as an area of white settlement and Union–British co-operation, the fag ends of the policy of union still remained smouldering. Hertzog, though for electoral purposes a vocal 'little South African', like Smuts regarded both central and east Africa as a South African sphere of interest. The prospect of substantive changes in east African policy by the British government following on the Devonshire declaration alarmed the new Union Prime Minister, and when Ormsby-Gore passed through Cape Town with the East African Commission in 1924 Hertzog laid particular stress on the 'repercussive effects' which any change in policy towards Africans in the north would have in the Union, urging that there should be consultations before any steps were taken.[44] In November 1925 discussions on Rhodesian 'native policy' were held between Hertzog and Chancellor in Pretoria during which Hertzog enquired as to the likelihood of the colony wanting to join the Union in the near future, and he urged the Governor to '... tell the people of Southern Rhodesia that he regarded them as South Africans'.[45] Hertzog also wanted, as Chancellor reported, '... to establish a body of common doctrine with regard to native policy'.[46] Nevertheless the Unionist cause in Rhodesia was dead: the pro-Union party dissolved itself, and by 1926 the leading members of the disintegrated Unionists were admitting that they had been mistaken.[47]

Thwarted with regard to the north, the Union government continued to seek the rest of the destiny promised by the Act of Union. Likewise the British South Africa Company, armed with cash, reopened its development offensive on the Bechuanaland Protectorate, and the British government had once again to defend the protectorate from the onslaughts of both Union and 'Rhodesian' interests. In 1919 the Bovril company had applied to the Colonial Office for a 2 million acre grant for ranching, but the Office had turned it down by hiding behind the British South Africa Company's preferential rights, in order to preserve Harcourt's policy of keeping 'a little corner for the black man'.[48] In 1920 an informal European Advisory Council for the protectorate was created which demanded the opening up of Crown lands and an end to the policy of arresting the 'legitimate progress and exploitation' of the territory.[49] Whitehall however stood firm on the policy of not opening up the Crown lands to white settlement or enterprise.

In 1923, after the death of Seretse Khama, the company asked whether the British government might now allow it to turn its preferential rights to more practical account, and in 1924 reopened its attack. At the company's annual general meeting Maguire proclaimed that the prosperity of southern Africa had been based upon the exploitation of its mineral resources. 'Mining in Rhodesia had been the great solvent which had brought the two races to minister to each other's wants, to the mutual benefit of each. Without that mining... the native would have remained in his reserves, and the white man outside them, and there would have been that stagnation which was called segregation.' He contrasted African wealth in Rhodesia with the poverty of those in the protectorate, who were '... scarcely distinguishable from the herds of undergrown sheep and cattle among which they passed their monotonous lives'.[50] At the same time, like Yeta of the Lozi, Sekgoma Khama on his accession to the Ngwato chieftainship was attempting to persuade the Colonial Office to cancel the company's mineral concessions, claiming that his father had been ignorant of the fact that he had been dealing not with Crown representatives but with a '... company formed by some rich men on certain basis of exploring the country merely for treasures'.[51] 'We are aware,' wrote Sekgoma, 'that the British South Africa Company might in the future bring us an unexpected disastrous calamity... the object of the British South Africa Company in its confidence and determination is... to secure whatever rights we had possessed.'[52] During the brief Labour period in office the British government supported Segkoma's campaign on the grounds that the carrying on of mining operations by concessionaries in the reserves was inherently undesirable—the protectionist view to which the company and Amery had voiced such scornful opposition.[53] When Amery returned to the Colonial Office he personally intervened to prevent the cancellation of the company's concession.

Matters were complicated by interventions from the Union. The Imperial Cold Storage Company, whose influential chairman, Sir David Graaff, a South African politician and businessman, lobbied both at Westminster and Whitehall, negotiated draft agreements with the High Commissioner in South Africa for the purchase of 10 million acres in the protectorate. This arrangement was turned down in London during Labour's period. In October 1924 Hertzog indicated to Athlone that he intended to ask for the transfer of Bechuanaland to the Union. The High Commissioner was wholly unsympathetic. He emphasised that he thought that the South African government was incapable of carrying out the terms of the schedule to the Act of Union. On the Union's Native

Affairs Commission, he reported, there was '... a divergence of opinion on native policy between its British and Dutch personnel so fundamental in character as to defy reconciliation'. Athlone told London that Hertzog wanted the protectorate for the reserves which he would not create in the Union and that it would be in the interests of Union Africans if the British government refused the request, thereby forcing Hertzog to find land inside the Union.[54] By December Hertzog, discouraged by Athlone's references regarding the schedule and the need for parliamentary approval in Britain, let his request for transfer drop.

Hertzog's unsuccessful skirmish over the protectorate had affected Rhodesian ambitions. From 1918 onwards settlers in the Tati District had been campaigning to be taken out of the protectorate, and in 1921 they were joined by those in the Tuli Block. Both at first asked for transfer to Rhodesia, and the Colonial Office was not unsympathetic, as it regarded Bechuanaland as a 'native reserve' which would be well rid of white areas.[55] In 1921 the Rhodesian Legislative Council asked for the incorporation of the Tati District; the Union had been consulted and had not objected, and the matter was held over pending the negotiation of the Rhodesian constitution.[56] In 1923 the settlers' advisory council asked for the inclusion of all three white blocks in the Union, but after the fall of Smuts the Tati settlers renewed their request to be taken in by Rhodesia.[57] But a concession could not be made to Rhodesia if at the same time London was barring Hertzog's request for the protectorate as a whole, especially as Hertzog requested that the Rhodesian claim should not be considered until the Union's was reopened.[58] There the matter of proposed territorial changes rested. Apart from a limited period grant to the Imperial Cold Storage Company the *status quo* in the protectorate was preserved.[59]

5 Making Northern Rhodesia

In the new colony of Northern Rhodesia, which it had taken over from the company in 1924, the British government could shape its approach free from the close presence of the Union and the power of the settlers. In November 1924 Smuts wrote to Amery, staking out the white claim to the northern territories. The Devonshire declaration, with its apparent proclamation of the paramountcy of African interests in east Africa, had outraged white opinion.[60] With Amery back at the Colonial Office, the time appeared to be ripe to press for a dilution of this policy. As Smuts wrote:

All the highlands of Eastern Africa from the Union to Abyssinia are healthy for Europeans and can be made a great European State or system of States during the next three or four generations . . . the present tendencies seem all in favour of the Native and the Indian, and the danger is that one of the greatest chances in our history shall be missed. The cry should be 'The highlands for the whites' and a resolute white policy should be pursued . . . It is an expansion of the Rhodes policy. Why should it not be your policy?[61]

On the whole Amery was in agreement with these views, the main question being which whites should dominate. For the time being the Union's ambitions were in check; the expanded Rhodes policy would have to build upon the basis of the British settlers in east and central Africa. Thus even if the Union's noose had slipped from Northern Rhodesia's neck the territory was still imprisoned within the framework of the British government's plan for the role of its settlers throughout the region. While Northern Rhodesia might not be shaped into a white man's country in the southern sense, it would still form part of an area in which, in Amery's conception, the settlers would act as co-trustees with the British government.

The first point to consider was whether a southern model reserves policy would be adopted. In 1914 a delimitation had been postponed until after the war, but it had been anticipated on all sides that reserves would be created on Southern Rhodesian lines and squatters legislation of the southern type introduced.[62] Once the war was over the company pressed for a 'final solution' according to southern precedent, but the Colonial Office had persistently deferred action until the Crown took over the territory.[63] By 1923 there appeared to be developing in the Colonial Office an incipient tendency to treat Northern Rhodesia as a 'tropical dependency', and opinion appeared to be hardening against reserves, but this tendency had to struggle against the beginning of the process of African displacement by the copper mining companies, and early in 1924 the Northern Rhodesian administration had come round to the view that at least provisional reserves should be created.[64]

Stanley, the new Governor, was eager to press forward. In the Colonial Office Strachey made a final effort to challenge the assumption that reserves should be instituted at all. In Nyasaland, he pointed out, the reserve concept had been rejected and instead 'European reserves'— the delimitation of a limited area for white settlement—had been adopted.[65] Lambert gave the go-ahead for a compromise. To adopt the

Nyasaland policy, he thought, would be too radical a departure from Rhodesian precedent and would cause controversy, but a limited delimitation should take place only in the north-east, where the North Charterland Company, a subsidiary of the British South Africa Company, had long been pressing for a definition of its rights within its large concession area. The commission reported strongly in favour of maintaining and supporting the tribal system and recommended the creation of principally tribal reserves. To this the North Charterland Company objected: in a memorandum to the commission in 1924 the company had stated its views, which were aligned to those of the hard-line colonial developers and which clashed with the timid gropings towards 'trusteeship' being made by the Colonial Office in Northern Rhodesia. 'The older countries of the world are the industrial centres,' the company proclaimed. 'We must devote ourselves to producing the raw materials to feed the industrial centres. The natives will never do that . . .' The commission, objected the company, had wrongly interpreted its instructions to provide land 'sufficient' for African needs, and its award would encourage Africans to grow 'surplus crops for competition with European settlers'. In its reply the Colonial Office firmly underlined a very different doctrine from that which had guided the Southern Rhodesian Commission eleven years before. The lands provided, it said, were not meant to be 'lands required for sustenance only' but were for '. . . all purposes necessary for the existence and development of native communities, including the growth of economic crops to provide for taxation and for the purchase of goods . . .'[66] In theory, and in London, the labour reserve concept had been rejected for Northern Rhodesia.

In May 1926 Stanley proposed a further commission, this time for the railway belt. His policy was, he explained, to establish reserves only in those parts of the territory where circumstances 'actual or probable' made it desirable, in the interests of Africans or of economic development. In the draft terms of reference which Stanley submitted to London provision was made for the removal of Africans from land assigned to them if it was required for mineral development.[67] The Colonial Office had no comment to make, and the commission proceeded with its work. Nevertheless there was to be no overall partition of the territory on southern lines, and the provision in the order in council which protected African rights to buy freehold land was not tampered with.

Likewise the political arrangements for the territory reflected its ambiguous and equivocal position between north and south. The electoral roll for the new Legislative Council was 'colour-blind' but it was expected that the number of qualified Africans would be very small and that the franchise would not be the main protection for African interests. The Chief Native Commissioner was to be a member of both the Executive and Legislative Councils, but other nominated representation of Africans was rejected, specifically the appointment of a missionary representative, as had been arranged in Kenya.[68] To the settlers, who had five members on the fourteen-member Legislative Council, the arrangements were a logical first step along the well established road toward greater representation and increased local power. But it is clear that the Colonial Office and the Governor strove to avoid both Southern Rhodesian and Kenyan precedents, and regarded the council not as a parliament but as a means of getting advice for the Governor on local problems.[69] When Stanley submitted his second set of estimates the opportunity was taken by the Colonial Office to consider the nature of the new territory's administration. It was felt that expenditure was far too high—Nyasaland, with a larger population, spent less. The promise to the Treasury that a report on partition of the territory would be made was recalled, and it was pointed out that Northern Rhodesia was composed of three distinct areas and that the expensive administrative structure was suitable only to the central railway belt.

Absolutely no account was taken in London of Stanley's reasoning that the need for a British grant in aid would not run for long, as various mining enterprises were expected to be in production by 1928. There could well be, the Governor wrote, in the course of a few years '. . . a large and profitable production of base metals in the Territory' which would change the entire economic balance.[70] The aim of the Colonial Office was still reduction of expenditure, if necessary by partition, whereby it could shed responsibility for the expensive centre belt. The vision of Northern Rhodesia as a quiet, backward, cheap and uncontroversial collection of tropical dependencies which prevailed in the Colonial Office was doomed to be upset by the activities of the mining companies. At the end of 1922 the British South Africa Company initiated a 'forward' prospecting policy. At the highest level the British government was concerned about supplies of copper under imperial control. In 1924 or '25, Lord Geddes recalled, the Prime Minister, Baldwin, approached him regarding the supply of copper, and Northern Rhodesia was the only place within the sterling area with known deposits.[71] Little of this interest or activity is reflected in the concerns of those immediately responsible for the government of the territory. In 1925 Stanley refused a request for help in road building from the prospecting companies, saying that he would '. . . base no part of our programme for the development of Northern Rhodesia on the doubtful possibility of finding mineral deposits of importance'.[72] He showed little interest in what the companies were doing, maintaining that the encouragement or discouragement of prospecting was a matter for the British South Africa Company and not the government.[73] By 1926, when the existence of large-scale deposits was confirmed, slightly greater interest was shown by the administration. Together with the established 'Rhodesian' connections of the white settler community, this was to stand in the way of a radical break with the south. The railway belt, it was recognised, would become 'the home of an increasing white population on the lines of Southern Rhodesia and the Transvaal, which must be expected to advance towards self-government'.[74] And when the East African Commission recommended that Northern Rhodesia adopt the Tanganyikan practice of granting land to prospective settlers on revisable long leases rather than freehold, as had been the company's practice, Stanley came out strongly as a 'Southern African'. He rejected the Tanganyika concept, which, he wrote, 'implies the admission of European settlers on sufferance . . . an interloper in a Native Territory'. On the other hand, he wrote, '. . . the Rhodesian concept . . . envisage[s] the entry of European settlers . . . to make in Rhodesia a permanent home . . . socially superior to the natives, politically dominant . . .'[75] The leasehold proposal was set aside.

Some moves away from a 'southern' orientation were made. There was a fifteenfold increase in the government's subsidy to African education, and an interest was taken in the promotion of African cash crops.[76] In September 1924 taxation in North Eastern Rhodesia was reduced.[77] In August 1924, when Stanley proposed a system of continuing consultation on 'native affairs' between the governments of Southern and Northern Rhodesia and Nyasaland, Lord Arnold, the Parliamentary Under-Secretary, gave him a gentle nudge towards the north, reminding him that the terms of reference of the East Africa Commission, which was intended to further co-ordination between east African territories, covered Northern Rhodesia. Co-operation with the south, Stanley was told, should be limited to the exchange of information to avoid Northern Rhodesia being placed in an '. . . embarrassing position through resolutions being passed on important matters of policy involving common action in Northern and Southern Rhodesia . . .' which might conflict with east African policies.[78] By 1926 the Southern Rhodesian government had become alarmed at the north's drift towards participation in east African matters, and despite

Chancellor's attempt to dissuade them began to press for the incorporation of the north.[79] It was after the first open southern move that Stanley produced his long-awaited report on the plan for northern partition and the amalgamation of the railway belt with the south. He ruled out the inclusion of the whole of the territory in the south, and as the East Africa Commission had for the time being recommended against partition, amalgamation of the railway belt fell away. The south, Stanley argued, only wanted the north because of its prospects of mineral development, and would compete with it in its only export market, Katanga. The north's main need, a westward railway link with Lobito, would, he felt, be resisted by Southern Rhodesia. The attraction of the *status quo*, however, worked both ways. Though Northern Rhodesia was not to go in with the south, it was not to be pushed northwards into the East African group. As Strachey minuted,

As regards the unification of the East African Dependencies it seems to me that the geographical position of Northern Rhodesia, with its central railway binding it to Southern Rhodesia and all its history, sentiment and tradition being essentially South African rather than East African, the arguments for its adhering to any future federation based on Nairobi must be far weaker than those for its adhering to its Southern neighbour, with whom it has so much in common, including a customs union.[80]

Notes

1 Reported by Buxton in M.P. 80, Buxton to Milner, 6 September 1919.
2 Parliamentary Debates, Commons, 4 June 1919, and C.O. 417/637, 18 May 1920. Gell reported that Milner told him of the two Rhodesias that 'It is intended that they should be separated'. (Ch. 8/2/2/6, Gell to Chaplin, 16 June 1920.)
3 C.O. 417/675, 4 February 1921, Minute. The possibility of amalgamation of the 'railway strip' with the south was canvassed in *Round Table*, XI, 1920–21, pp. 702 ff.
4 C.O. 417/670, 3 March 1921, and Gann, *Northern Rhodesia*, p. 187.
5 Cmd. 1471, *Second Report of a Committee appointed to Consider Certain Questions relating to Rhodesia*, 1921.
6 It was in any case anticipated that Smuts would have acquired the Northern Rhodesian railways along with those in Southern Rhodesia. (Ch. 8/2/2/11, Malcolm to Fox, 3 August 1921.) Chaplin reported that Smuts would give Northern Rhodesia one member of the Union parliament but would otherwise treat it as 'a native dependency' and that he had similar plans for Swaziland. (Ch. 8/2/2/6, Chaplin to Gell, 10 September 1922.)
7 Ch. 8/2/2/2, Birchenough to Chaplin, 1 June 1922.

8   Ch. 8/2/2/6, Gell to Chaplin, 7 June 1922.
9   S.P., v, E. H. Walton to Smuts, 12 December 1922, p. 156.
10 Ch. 8/2/1, 20 November 1922, Smuts to Bonar Law, 20 November 1922 (copy); quoted in W. K. Hancock, *The Fields of Force,* p. 154, and Ch. 8/2/2/9, J. G. Macdonald to Charter, London, telegram.
11 Ch. 8/2/2/11, Malcolm to Chaplin, 9 November 1922; *ibid.*, 30 November 1922; and Ch. 8/2/2/9, Malcolm to Macdonald, 20 December 1923.
12 C.O. 417/690, 23 November 1922, Gell to Devonshire.
13 C.O. 417/702, January 1923.
14 C.O. 417/699, 29 March 1923.
15 C.O. 417/669, 9 July 1921, containing C.O. to Law Officers, 6 May 1920.
16 C.O. 417/687, 10 March 1922. The company was claiming that the arrangement with regard to land sales in the draft letters patent whereby the Cave award would be paid for out of revenues derived from selling Crown lands would have frustrated the intention of the Privy Council's judgement. It asked either for cash payment of the Cave award or for control of the authority which was to deal with the land sales. The board offered to withdraw the petition if an overall agreement were to be reached.
17 The company had 'concessions' covering a large area of northern Nyasaland, and the Colonial Office did not want it to have a legal basis to claim land ownership there.
18 When asked for his views by Ormsby-Gore, Smuts warned specifically against leaving the company with such rights. If the company, he wrote, were left '. . . to nurse their assets and wait for the unearned increment they would be on velvet. This, however, is not a policy that could for a moment be agreed to.' (S.P., v, Smuts to Ormsby-Gore, 19 January 1923, pp. 160–1.)
19 Parliamentary Debates, Commons, 18 July 1923.
20 *Ibid.,* 25 July 1923.
21 Cab. 24/160, No. 201, 19 April 1923.
22 The grounds were that this could lead to a Southern Rhodesian Governor having to act against the advice of his Ministers (C.O. 417/699, 26 November 1923.) Strachey was Assistant Under-Secretary of State and had had extensive west African experience. (C.O. 417/699, 26 November 1923.)
23 Ch. 8/2/2/2, Birchenough to Chaplin, 12 July 1923.
24 *Quarterly Review*, xxiv, 1924. The article was reprinted in extended form in 1939 as *The British South Africa Company*.
25 Cf. the remark to W. T. Stead, who had referred to Rhodes as 'the Elizabethan Englishman', by John X. Merriman, that 'a crime is not less a crime because you choose to call it Elizabethan'. (*Selections from the correspondence of John X. Merriman*, CXI, pp. 438–9, Merriman to Stead, 16 March 1904.) The fervour and mystique which the company's directors built around their apparently mundane activities is illustrated by d'Erlanger's introduction to his article on the 'History and finance of the Rhodesian railway system', which begins, 'Imagination is the soul of poetry, and there is poetry in things most material. However, the great initiated, the prophets alone, are able not only themselves to kindle under the divine spark, but to reveal to the world at large the light which shines within them. To these elect of mankind Cecil Rhodes belonged. He was a poet . . .' (*The Story of the Cape to Cairo Railway and River Route, 1887–1922*, ed. L. Weinthal.)

186 *Unconsummated union*

26 D. O. Malcolm, *The British South Africa Company*, gives these figures. By way of comparison, the major area of investment in South Africa, the Rand gold mines, yielded an average return of approximately 4·1 per cent on capital invested between 1886 and 1932. (Figures from Hailey, *African Survey*, p. 323.)
27 Major Sir John Chancellor, formerly Secretary to the Colonial Committee; Governor of Mauritius, 1911; Governor of Trinidad and Tobago from 1915. See Chancellor Papers, Rhodes House, MSS B. Emp. s. 284, box 10, file 3, Chancellor to Oldham, 19 April 1927.
28 See T. Ranger, *African Voice*, chapter 6. Ranger appears to overestimate the effect of Harris's and White's change of mind on the decision to appoint the commission.
29 Carter had been Chief Justice of Uganda, 1919–20, and president of the East African Court of Appeal, 1921–24.
30 C.O. 767/3, 13 November 1924.
31 C.O. 417/705, 26 September 1924.
32 C.O. 417/713, 26 March 1925.
33 C.O. 7674, 13 May 1925, Cripps to Secretary of State, and D.O./1, 6 January 1926, Chancellor to Secretary of State.
34 C.O. 767/3, 17 November 1924.
35 For analyses of the report see MacGregor, *Native Segregation*, and Palmer, *Land Policy*.
36 On African evidence and reaction to the report see Ranger, *African Voice*, chapter 6; Zwimba is quoted on p. 136.
37 The commissioners referred to B. Mathews, *The Clash of Colour*; E. H. Brookes, *History of South African Native Policy;* J. H. Oldham, *Christianity and the Race Problem*; and Lugard, *Dual Mandate*. On the prevalence of segregatory ideology see R. Gray, *The Two Nations*, part 1.
38 The maximum allowed for an African holding was to be a thousand acres. In the Union the maximum allowed Glen Gray holding was eight and a half acres. See W. M. Macmillan, *Africa Emergent*, 1949, pp. 124–5.
39 D.O./2, Minute, 29 July 1926.
40 Parliamentary Debates, Commons, 29 July 1926, and Lords Debates, 23 June 1926.
41 Correspondence in D.O./2, 7 December 1926.
42 Quoted by Ranger, *African Voice*, pp. 181–2. The ICU was the Industrial and Commercial Workers' Union.
43 D.O./2, 7 December 1926.
44 C.O. 532/276, High Commissioner to Secretary of State, 5 September 1924.
45 D.O./1, Chancellor to Secretary of State, Secret, 6 January 1926.
46 Chancellor papers, MSS B. Emp. 284, Chancellor to Oldham, 19 April 1927. Chancellor supported this suggestion. Chancellor to Hilton Young, 7 April 1928.
47 D.O./1, 8 October 1926, Chancellor to Secretary of State.
48 C.O. 417/620, 19 July 1919, and C.O. 417/634, 3 June 1919.
49 C.O. 417/637, 25 May 1920; C.O. 417/661, 8 June 1921; C.O. 417/704, 24 March 1924.
50 D.O. 116/2, 9 April 1923; B.S.A.C. to C.O.; and C.O. 417/712, July 1924, containing *The Times* report of 25 July 1924.

51 C.O. 417/693, 18 May 1923, containing Segkoma Khama to Resident Commissioner, 5 April 1924.
52 D.O. 116/2, Segkoma Khama to Resident Commissioner, 5 April 1923.
53 D.O. 116/2, C.O. to B.S.A.C., 20 June 1924.
54 C.O. 417/709, 29 October 1924.
55 C.O. 417/662, 7 July 1921, Minutes.
56 C.O. 417/660, 3 June 1921; C.O. 417/663, 29 September 1921; C.O. 417/693, 29 June 1923; and C.O. 417/694, 6 September 1924.
57 C.O. 417/705, 31 May 1924.
58 C.O. 417/705, 28 May 1924; and C.O. 417/713, 3 February 1925.
59 C.O. 417/705, 26 September 1924, containing Amery to High Commissioner, 14 January 1925.
60 For the Devonshire declaration see Cmd. 1922 of 1923 and the *Oxford History of East Africa*, xi, chapter 6. Strachey, in the Colonial Office, wrote that he could not forget the 'surprise and disgust' with which Birchenough had greeted the exposition of the policy of African paramountcy. (C.O. 795/10, 12 January 1926.) See the *Oxford History* for the development of Amery's views on an East African Federation in which the settlers would share the white man's burden.
61 Quoted in Hancock, *The Fields of Force*, p. 223.
62 A system of *de facto* reserves was already in operation in the North Charterland concession area, and throughout the territory it was the administration's policy to concentrate the African population into what it was hoped would form the nucleus of future reserves. (C.O. 879/1003, 6 January 1915, and 'Northern Rhodesia: report of the East Luangwa Native Reserves Commission'. See also the appendix to the 'North Charterland concession enquiry. Report to the Governor of Northern Rhodesia', Colonial, No. 73.)
63 Appendix, 'North Charterland Commission enquiry', C.O. 417/688 28 January 1922; C.O. 417/689, 25 July and 24 June 1922. One of the reasons given by the Colonial Office for deferment was that it would make a great difference to a reserves commission whether or not the land was African-owned, and this had not yet been legally determined; cf. its attitude over Southern Rhodesia, when it consistently claimed that the questions of land ownership and the reserves were quite distinct.
64 See notes in C.O. 417/702, August 1923, and C.O. 417/704, 3 January 1924.
65 C.O. 795/2, 10 August 1924, Minutes. On the Nyasaland commission see W. M. Macmillan, *Africa Emergent*, pp. 145–6.
66 Commission report, annexure, Company's memorandum, 15 November 1924. Appendix, 'North Charterland Commission enquiry', 28 June 1926, and C.O. 795/11, 6 August 1926.
67 C.O. 795/11, 16 May 1926.
68 C.O. 417/702, January 1924, Minutes.
69 C.O. 795/1, 8 May 1924, and C.O. 795/3, 31 October 1924, and minutes thereon.
70 C.O. 795/8, 23 November 1925, Stanley to Secretary of State, and Minutes.
71 Geddes, quoted in *Northern Rhodesia Journal*, v, p. 399, by K. M. Hughes, reviewing J. Bancroft, *Mining in Northern Rhodesia*.

72 Quoted by T. Gregory, *Ernest Oppenheimer and the Economic Development of Southern Africa*, Cape Town, 1962, p. 391.
73 C.O. 533/350, 16 May 1926, Stanley to Secretary of State.
74 C.O. 795/3, 14 November 1924, Minutes.
75 C.O. 795/10, 12 January 1926.
76 C.O. 795/3, 25 September 1924, and C.O. 795/3, 3 October 1924.
77 C.O. 795/3, 19 September 1924.
78 C.O. 795/2, 2 August 1924, Arnold to Stanley, 24 September 1924.
79 D.O./1, 6 January 1926 and D.O./2, 4 August 1926, reporting interview between Coghlan and Amery of 30 July 1926. Coghlan, while in London for the imperial conference, told Amery that he wanted the whole of the north and asked for an assurance that the south would have 'at least' the reversionary right to it. This was refused.
80 C.O. 795/10, 18 January 1926, and C.O. 795/11, May 1926. Strachey's minute is on D.O./2, 4 August 1926.

PART THREE

The origins of the Central African Federation

CHAPTER 10

Britain and white Africa
1925–39

1 East and central Africa

The uncertainty of the political future of east Africa, which now included the mandated territory of Tanganyika, continued to hold up decisions as to what the British government should do with the responsibilities it had taken over from the company. Amery had clear opinions as to what might be done, and he was the first Secretary of State with knowledge of and interest in the region, as well as a long, undisturbed term of office. His attitude toward the potential political role of the British settlers was formulated not in the light of the ultimately subordinate position to which the Devonshire declaration had relegated them *vis-à-vis* local African populations, but on a larger scale and in a different context, and was based upon the belief that they had a role to play, independent of the Union of South Africa, which was more important than had hitherto been credited. Throughout the second half of the 1920s he sought to reverse the apparent intention of the Devonshire declaration by a policy of involving the settlers as co-trustees with the British government. As he told the cabinet in 1927, 'It is clear that sooner or later we shall have to share the responsibilities of government in an increasing degree with the communities of our own race who make their homes in these territories.'[1]

There were several reasons for projecting a devolution of local power to the settlers. The difficulties incurred by not doing so had been experienced through centuries of colonial administration from Whitehall, and it was believed in the 1920s that there would be an increasing flow of white colonists into east and central Africa, and that consequently '... the rapid settlement of the white man in the territories to the north of the Union ... is widening immensely the scope of what used to be called the South African problem'.[2] As the *Round Table* pointed out, there were two schools of thought regarding what was taking place in the region. The first was that the white man was 'in essence an intruder', while the second was 'convinced that if left alone the native is incapable of progress'. Smuts was quite sure which school he belonged to. In the Rhodes lectures, delivered at Oxford in 1929, he attacked what he called the quasi-humanitarian policy of Africa for the Africans: on the contrary, he proclaimed, the 'gospel of labour' was 'the most salutary gospel' for Africa, and from this it followed that there should be a definite policy of European settlement in order to establish a white community which would form 'the steel framework of the whole ambitious structure of African civilisation'. He envisaged the two Rhodesias, fortified by developments on the Copperbelt, marching northwards and felt that the establishment of another great European community would be '. . . the next critical step in the evolution of our Commonwealth of Nations'. There should, he declared, be a '. . . free passage to the further North, the open door for a civilisation from the South . . .'[3] Amery too felt that Africans '. . . advance more rapidly . . . when in close contact with a higher civilisation and culture, though excluded from political power and even deliberately held back in the economic field by white trade unionism, than under the most benevolent trusteeship exercised by a handful of officials'.[4] In the 1930s he argued that the economy of the colonial empire had to be developed in a way complementary to that of Britain's and that a positive policy, as in the Sudan or Java, was preferable to a negative one of 'protection' of African interests. He predicted that the dominant influence, for the next century, throughout east and central Africa would be the white civilisation of the south. While he rejected the Union's policy of complete domination as being inconsistent with the British policy of 'trusteeship', the latter, he felt, should not be allowed to continue to mean that 'black vested interests' always outweighed the 'demands of progress'. This advocacy of a more active development policy had implications for the political map of the area. A Greater Rhodesia, he felt, could stand between South and east Africa on the vital questions of 'native policy' and development. By 1935 Amery had lost the battle for east Africa, but settler aspirations in Rhodesia emerged out of his arguments as the embodiment of the 'dual mandate', the happy and profitable middle way between the conflicting policies of southern dominance and Colonial Office-protected 'stagnation'.[5]

Throughout the 1920s there had been an alternative ideological approach to that represented by Amery. Those who had been suspicious of settler aspirations remained so, and their suspicions were increased and made more vocal by the apparent attempts to reverse the policy of the paramountcy of African interests. Coteries of officials, enveloped in the mystique of indirect rule, were infiltrating the colonial administrations of east and central Africa, and they tended to think in terms both more cautious and less brazenly commercial than Amery and his followers. To some extent the argument was about the development of the African territories. Cripps, in his plea for territorial segregation,[6] warned of the threat to African self-development posed by those who hankered after '... a sort of Anglo-Saxon imperial efficiency programme ...' 'Those who care for Africans,' he wrote, 'need to be vigilant in these post-war times, as recognising what an attractive country Africa must appear to the reactionaries of Europe ... who find both land and labour to be scarce and unmanageable nearer home.' Olivier, in *White Capital and Coloured Labour*, summed up most powerfully the arguments against imperialist development, embodying a tradition of thought which drew particular strength from earlier attacks upon the Chartered Company's operations in the Rhodesias. He attacked a colonial policy that aimed at the exploitation of African resources in British interests through the use of African labour—the exploitation of coloured labour by white capital. Of Kenya he remarked that the assumptions of development were being '... approached from the starting point of the European requirements and those of his industrial system, and not those of the native and his agricultural and social economy'. Cutting through the verbiage of indirect rulers, dual mandators and positive developers alike, he concluded with a sour succinctness that 'No European power has ever exercised or is ever likely to exercise dominion in Africa exclusively as a trustee for the natives'.[7]

Apart from the arguments about development, there was a need for the British government to adjust the political constellations which would follow upon the expected growth of white power. The problems involved in creating regional groupings in east and central Africa occupied the minds of the Colonial and Dominions Offices after 1924. And these problems were closely related to questions about policy towards the Union. The political aspirations of the settlers in Kenya and the problem of reconciling these with the paramountcy policy were considered in terms relating to the entirety of the white presence in Africa and the maintenance of British influence over it. Stanley, for example, urged that conditions in the Union, far from proving that white power should be limited as far as possible, provided the strongest argument for the fulfilment of settler aspirations in Kenya. 'The course of events in the Union of South Africa,' he wrote, 'suggests the expediency of encouraging and strengthening British solidarity northward of the Limpopo.' A large regrouping of British territories to the north was desirable, and it was necessary '... to ensure that the policy of the group was so shaped as not to exclude the possibility of Southern Rhodesia coming in later'. Unless this was done—and here Amery agreed with him—both Rhodesias could inevitably be dragged southwards. As Amery put it,

... the tendency would be for first Southern Rhodesia and then Northern Rhodesia to gravitate towards the Union, and Kenya also would become an outpost of South African principles. In the event the South African tradition would extend right up the east coast, with isolated territories in between in a position analogous to the present High Commission Territories ...[8]

From the Kenyan perspective Sir Edward Grigg argued that Kenya was only the most northern outpost of a string of territories which would develop on white self-governing lines, remarking that 'In Kenya ... the policy embodied in the Glen Gray Acts in the Cape Colony has been definitely adopted'. In 1927 only Cameron, on behalf of Tanganyika, and Strachey expressed doubts as to the desirability of the general move towards the creation of a new settler-dominated state in east and central Africa. Whether or not this new State would eventually be a part of the Union of South Africa remained to be seen. Time would tell, as Stanley put it in familiar terms, but this time with a larger geographical reference, '... whether it should enter the Union as a British leaven, or remain outside as a British counterpoise. In either event the measure of its strength and solidarity will be the determining factor in its efficacy and its security from submersion.' Northern Rhodesia and Nyasaland, he said, should be amalgamated at an early date under a single Governor, thus sharing labour resources and the benefits of mineral development. And he expressed the hope that Northern Rhodesia would not be joined to its southern neighbour, as this would '... take Northern Rhodesia definitely out of the Central and Eastern group and remove the only bridge over which Southern Rhodesia might conceivably at some future date think of entering that group'. Thus in 1927, as an extreme Hertzogism appeared to be rampant in the Union, British thinking about the future of her east and central African territories was on an unusually large scale, tending to link both east and central Africa in an anti-Union counterpoise. As Rudyard Kipling put it as late as 1929, '... we have to begin again the old Northern blockade—but this time—with a federated Uganda, etc, bloc.'[9] The apparent taming of Hertzog, the conclusions of the Hilton Young commission and the return of a Labour government to office in 1929 all put an end to counterpoise plans on this scale. By the end of the decade the era of Ameryism, with its vision of a white Dominion from the Limpopo to the Nile, appeared to be over.

2 Britain and South Africa

Towards the end of 1927 Amery visited southern Africa. He reported that since the 1926 imperial conference and the Balfour formula, which had explicitly acknowledged the equality of status of the Dominions and the United Kingdom, Hertzog and most of his party '. . . are now prepared not only to drop the demand for secession and accept the Empire but to look upon proposals for Imperial co-operation with goodwill instead of suspicion.' Though, he commented, the 1924 election had brought to power '. . . men who had never forgotten the bitterness of the South African War . . .' he was optimistic about the future. The greater the trade between Britain and South Africa, he argued, the tighter would be her links with the empire, and, the greater her economic development, the lesser would be English–Afrikaner political tensions. The expected economic development of South Africa and her increased integration into the imperial economic world would, in other words, lead to the disappearance of the Union's embarrassing politics.[10] In Southern Rhodesia he found in the new colony 'a spirit of fervent loyalty to the Crown'. There was a determination not to enter the Union '. . . except on terms that will enable Rhodesia not only to maintain its own British character but also to be sure of the generally Imperial character of South African policy . . .' If this aspiration was seen to be unrealisable then, Amery reported, Rhodesians would want to build '. . . an independent Central South African Dominion to check and counterbalance the parochial South African Union'.[11]

The attitude of British governments towards South Africa continued to be determined more by South African attitudes towards the empire than by South African racial policies. Britain's position as a colonial power was well put by Amery during his visit to South Africa: he was, as he told Hertzog in a public speech, '. . . a friend, a good South African and a fellow Paramount Chief'.[12] Some other British advisers were less optimistic about developments in the Union. Clifford reported in 1928 that there was a distinct '. . . pro-German and pro-foreign—not to say anti-British—policy in respect of trade and industries'. From this he drew the conclusion that before anything like a 'great British South Africa' could be achieved the territories outside the Union would need strengthening so that if they were to throw in their lot with the Union they would be able '. . . to maintain Empire solidarity and to redress the foreign inclinations which seem to inspire Union policy today'.[13] Hertzog had already put forward his demands for the transfer of the High Commission territories, and although there were other reasons for stalling on the Union's claims this, as far as Bechuanaland was concerned, became linked to the question of northern counterpoise. The time had come, Clifford suggested, when it might be advisable to regard Bechuanaland's future as being linked to Rhodesia rather than to the Union, and he put forward the proposal that the Governor of Southern Rhodesia might be made a High Commissioner for a group of territories which included Northern Rhodesia, Bechuanaland and Nyasaland. Amery wrote, 'I should like to see Bechuanaland, or the northern part of it, go into Southern Rhodesia.'[14]

By the end of the 1920s Southern Rhodesian aspirations towards southward expansion were back in the picture. Rhodesian settlers found Amery's approach as refreshing as he had found theirs. The Devonshire declaration had shocked the settler community in the Rhodesias, but, as Sir John Chancellor wrote, Amery's attitude that trusteeship could be shared with the settler community in the Kenyan context had completely altered the situation '. . . and weakens arguments that might have been used in the policies announced in the Duke of Devonshire's White Paper of 1923 against the amalgamation of areas occupied by natives with European areas'.[15] By 1934 this had frozen into official Dominions Office policy. It was no longer inevitable, it was felt, that the protectorate would join the Union, and in the event of the formation of a larger unit in central Africa north of the Union the claims of Southern Rhodesia to the reversion of 'at least' the northern half would have to be considered. Throughout the 1930s the Southern Rhodesian government re-stated its claim to the northern half of Bechuanaland, though realising, as Huggins, the Prime Minister, put it in 1937, that nothing could be done '. . . with the Dutch asking for the Protectorates'.[16]

In 1929 Tshekedi Khama tried again to have the company's concessions cancelled. This time the British government, though it was doubtful of the legal validity of the concessions, did its best to stop his efforts. Tshekedi went to Cape Town, where he armed himself with the advice of King's Counsel and the London Missionary Society. His lawyer, D. Buchanan, K.C., was of the opinion that the concessions could be legally terminated with a year's notice, as were the imperial legal advisors. But Athlone persuaded Buchanan to withhold this opinion from his client. He advised the Secretary of State that in the light of Northern Rhodesian experience it was clear that mineral development by reputable companies was beneficial to African interests and that the weight of public opinion in South Africa would be against any policy designed to prevent the exploitation of the mineral resources of the protectorate. Athlone took an active role on behalf of the British government in negotiating with both the British South Africa Company and Sir Ernest Oppenheimer for new concessions, and in getting these and a new minerals ordinance accepted by both London and Tshekedi Khama. His aim was to give a firmer legal base to the Chartered Company's concessions so that they could not be repudiated by the chiefs in future. A *terra clausa* policy. Athlone argued, would add weight to Union demands for a hand-over, whereas opening the territory up would strengthen against ultimate absorption, 'when ...' they may be able to hold their own'. Tshekedi, Athlone wrote, and his people 'are definitely opposed to all progress in their Reserves'. But Tshekedi hammered home the point that the British government had changed its mind. Before it had discouraged mining, but now it favoured it. He was also clearly able to distinguish the difference between economic development which the Nwgato controlled and that which would control them. In August 1929 Tshekedi confronted Athlone in Cape Town with his objections. 'We object because we know that when mining takes place in a country it won't be a nation. We know we can uplift ourselves by means of cattle, not by means of mining. Could the Government tell him of a people who when the Europeans came into a country did not scatter?' But Athlone faced him down with the threats that non-development of the minerals would lead to agitation in the Union for transfer, and Tshekedi was, as Athlone put it, '... shrewd enough to realise that however objectionable mining may be to his people its consequences fade into insignificance when compared to the disaster which he feels sure would overtake his people if the Bechuanaland Protectorate were transferred to the Union'.[17] After a long time out in the cold it seemed that the Chartered Company was back in business in the protectorate. Anglo-American, de Beers and other South African mining corporations also took part in the new offensive. Sir Ernest Oppenheimer held out the bribe that there was no reason why some of the capital going to Northern Rhodesia should not be invested in the protectorate.[18] Chartered arranged for the diamond rights to be controlled by de Beers. The British government produced a new minerals ordinance providing for the systematic payment of royalties in place of a fixed rental.

It seemed possible that the protectorate could be the scene of mineral developments along the lines of those taking place in Northern Rhodesia. With this in view, old protectionist objections to development faded into the background. Furthermore it might make more feasible the building of the external counterpoise. The imperial government should, Clifford wrote, increase its freedom of action so that if the protectorate developed there could be a 'severance of the fetters' which bound it to the south and a consideration of a northern destiny. Tshekedi himself seemed to favour this too. He feared that the Union was taking over the administration of the Caprivi Strip in an enveloping movement and felt that if he could not remain under British protection he would prefer to be transferred to the government of Southern Rhodesia. This, Athlone felt, could be used to prepare public opinion for a change in policy.[19]

In October 1929, after the 'black menace' election in the Union, which returned to power a Nationalist government with a majority no longer dependent upon the support of the British-oriented South African Labour Party, the imperial position in southern Africa had once again to be reassessed. Though the 'black menace' was primarily internal, Smuts's pronouncements on Africa north of the Limpopo had been a prominent election issue. When Smuts called for '. . . a British confederation of African States . . . a great African Dominion stretching unbroken through Africa' he was accused by the Nationalist Party of being '. . . the apostle of a black Kaffir State . . . extending from the Cape to Egypt in which white South Africa would vanish'.[20] The Nationalists, when in opposition in 1923 and while electioneering in 1929, were vocally anti-expansionist regarding the north. Nevertheless Hertzog in power was of necessity acutely aware of the effects of developments in the north upon the Union, and in the 1920s and 1930s his governments aimed at a measure of co-operation with the north, pressed hard for the transfer of the High Commission territories, vigorously opposed the Italian conquest of Ethiopia, and refused to consider the return of South West Africa to the Germans. But while it is inaccurate to regard South African governments during this period as being 'little South African', there still remained a difference between Smuts's approach and that of the Nationalists which reflected a real difference as to what the South African State should be and to whose benefit its resources should be devoted. The interests of Afrikaner workers did not lie in the absorption of countries without a colour bar, and the farmers continued to oppose free entry of cattle and produce from surrounding territories. On the other hand it was logical for a Nationalist government to press for the

o

protectorates, the absorption of which could not only help solve the 'native problem' but could also obliterate the possible threat which the territories posed, as long as they were under Colonial Office rule, to the South African conception of how that problem should be solved. Smuts's aspirations towards the north, on the other hand, reflected the interests of the English-speaking townsmen, of the mining industry, with its desire for an uninterrupted flow of foreign labour and its ambitions to extend its financial empire northwards, and of manufacturing industry, searching, as it grew, for a stronger position in neighbouring markets.

From the imperial point of view Clifford reported after the 1929 election in terms which linked not only the High Commission territories but also the Rhodesias to the context of the British position *vis-à-vis* the Union. He commented once again on the friendly attitude of Hertzog towards the British connection but warned that the Prime Minister, having come to power by 'sinister spirits that have been conjured from the vasty veld', ran the risk of being driven into the wilderness by his own extremists. This became the common form of imperial analysis of both South African and Rhodesian settler politics: the men in power might appear unpalatable to British tastes but ought to be propitiated, for lurking still further to the right there were always worse to come. With this in mind Clifford reiterated the importance of maintaining and strengthening the points that remained under direct British control in southern Africa.

In the High Commission and the Territories we have a practical interest in this country of considerable importance. To the North we have in two Rhodesias and Bechuanaland the possibility of building up a strong pro-British community which may influence the Union's progress along right lines. The integrity of the above position must, I feel, be maintained.[21]

This analysis was supported by Stanley when he took office as High Commissioner in South Africa. The British connection, he wrote, 'hangs on a slender thread'. This being the case, the British government should not 'throw away the few trump cards which it still holds, but should play its hand as to give them their greatest value. I have in mind the British Central African States—the Rhodesias and Nyasaland—and the High Commission Territories, most particularly the Bechuanaland Protectorate.' These could, he advised, if strengthened by a form of closer union, be 'a very potent factor in the preservation of British interests'.[22]

The analysis which the African leadership in the Union made of their situation did not stand still during the 1920s, and though they still tended to support the British position there were signs that the gap which Africans perceived between British and Afrikaner responsibility for the situation was closing. Loyal appeals to the king for intervention and the invocation of the spirit of nineteenth-century British liberalism, though they kept some tactical importance, were replaced by different understandings and tactics. In 1921 the Reverend Mahabane of the Cape African National Congress, surveying the international scene, spoke precisely in the terms of which Lloyd George had been warning. He referred to the anti-imperialist struggles in India; to Egyptian demands for self-rule; to the 'martyrdom in a great cause' of Mr Macswiney, the Lord Mayor of Cork, whom he held up as a lesson to the Bantu people on the precious nature of liberty; and to the clamour of British West Africans for political representation.[23] Clearly Afrikanerdom was not the only enemy and the African struggle was not an isolated one. Clements Kadalie, who created the Industrial and Commercial Workers' Union, pointed out in 1924 when Africans were divided as to whether to support Smuts or Hertzog that the British too played the 'game' of exploiting Africans. In 1927 the ICU sent Kadalie to Geneva to the conference of the International Labour Organisation to 'expose for all time the colour prejudice of the Union government'. He found interest on the left in both Europe and England, where, he wrote of a visit to Parliament, 'All the Labour members were anxious to get first-hand information on the situation in South Africa'. An exaggeration, perhaps, as the official wing of British Labour was not particularly welcoming of Kadalie (he was denied fraternal delegate status at a conference of the Trade Union Congress), but he made contacts on the left, and men like Lord Olivier made known their readiness to help make public what was happening both in Southern Rhodesia and in the Union [24]. The perception that imperialism and capitalism rather than the Afrikaner were the enemy also took hold on the left of the African National Congress, culminating in the Communist-inspired call for the adoption of the goal of the South African Native Republic. When making this call to Congress in 1930 its president, J. T. Gumede, also surveyed the risings of oppressed peoples around the world and the revolutionary struggles in Asia against British imperialism, and he called for a revolutionary struggle, in alliance with the revolutionary masses outside South Africa, for freedom 'from all foreign and local domination'.[25]

But Gumede's call was defeated, and this kind of analysis represented a minority strand in inter-war African thinking on international strategy. The old guard of the African leadership was still ready to appeal to British liberalism, though with a more realistic purpose than before. First, they allied themselves firmly with the campaign to prevent a South African take-over of the High Commission territories, and secondly they aimed generally at educating public opinion, in Britain and at the League of Nations, about conditions inside South Africa. Throughout the period of the Nationalist/Labour Ministries African opinion in South Africa made clear its opposition to the series of Bills which made up the government's segregation package. While a general and coherent critique of the South African government's practices did emerge, the vocal opposition was focused on the campaign of the enfranchised elite to defend the old Cape franchise. There was much scope here for appeals to British principles, for it was with Britain that the Cape Policy was identified. This identification, and the background threat of republicanism, provided an excuse for affirmations of African loyalty and for calling on the imperial factor to remain an operative part of South African politics. Even Kadalie in 1931, in a role different from that of labour leader, moved a resolution at the non-European conference calling for the maintenance of existing constitutional relations between Britain and South Africa, and for the British government to refuse to allow South African secession from the empire without a referendum of all her inhabitants. The old-guard leadership supported him, amid much general approbation of Britain's conduct of 'native policy'. The British government, said Walter Rubusana, was 'the most humane he had ever known': under British policy, said Selope-Thema, 'there is room for growth'. Though this was not quite so realistic an overall picture of the British position as the analysis which made it the imperial guarantor of the South African system, it was a clear preference between two immediate evils, with immediate practical aims.[26]

African leadership responded directly to white moves abroad. In 1929 Smuts gave his Rhodes lectures calling for an extension and consolidation of the white man's sphere in Africa[27] and in September 1930 Hertzog, speaking in London, urged the harmonisation of British policy in her colonies with South African policies. In January 1931 the non-European conference met to consider their response and resolved on an old tactic, though with a new purpose, the sending of a delegation abroad, not to plead for intervention but to educate public opinion. Of the proposed delegation only D. D. T. Jabavu eventually went abroad, and he wrote for propaganda purposes a pamphlet called *Native Disabilities in South Africa*.[28] It made it clear that Africans in the Union no longer asked Britain to intervene in South African affairs but that Hertzog had himself overstepped the mark by asking for a harmonisation of policies. The Union government's policy, wrote

Jabavu, was 'based on a foundation of repression', and 'the effect of a liberal British policy in other African colonies is exactly what is needed . . .' The pamphlet contained a comprehensive and detailed denunciation of Union legislation and practices, and ended with support for the British position in southern Africa. The Cape franchise, said Jabavu, had been 'responsible for developing an unchanging loyalty to Britain . . .' Africans in the Union wanted to urge

> that Great Britain should adopt the policy of keeping her direct hold on the Protectorates contiguous to the Union . . . your power of protection over these and the other British possessions in north-eastern Africa should be greatly tightened rather than relaxed.
> Do not be in haste in conferring self government in any of your colonies. We Blacks much prefer direct rule under the Imperial Government . . .

Black South African opinion on this had clarity and continuity. As Mahabane said in 1933:

> The Native view of this question of the proposed incorporation of the Native Territories into the union was correctly given expression to by Mr M. S. M. Makgatho of Pretoria in his Presidential Address to the Native Congress delivered some fifteen years ago, when he quoted the pathetic words of the Rich Man in Hell when he pleaded with Father Abraham that he would send Lazarus to his father's house, for, said he, 'I have five brethren, that he may testify unto them, lest they also come into this place of torment.'[29]

Thus for the imperial government counterpoise politics could, if need be, be matched with humanitarianism, and the Union's African leadership remained on the whole a part of the imperial constituency. But they appealed no longer to a missionary public alone. Their campaigns aroused considerable interest on the British left, where a critique of southern African conditions began to develop. Books like Leonard Barnes's *Caliban in Africa* and *The New Boer War* and Olivier's *Anatomy of African Misery* helped to build up the body of public opinion which acted as a brake on how far Britain could go in co-operation with the Union.[30]

Olivier's *Anatomy of African Misery* was provoked by the introduction of the industrial colour bar and by Hertzog's attack on the African franchise. It was a comprehensive damnation of the doings of the Union, and drew a clear distinction between South African and British policies. He attacked the South African land Act of 1913 but praised Southern Rhodesia for attempting, while it could still be done, a 'peaceful and equitable' division of land between black and white, which would provide as much land for Africans as they could or were likely to want to use. South African principles, he urged, should be confined within that country's own borders. The High Commission territories must 'obviously' be kept outside the Union. Unless Britain wanted to be associated with the dangers to civilisation and world peace represented by South Africa it should not 'concede a further inch of administrative authority to that government'. Southern Rhodesia, on the other hand, had, he felt, a government 'liberally inspired', and Britain should resolutely maintain the repudiation of the Union's principles which had already grown up in Rhodesia.[31] Barnes also denounced the Union, suggesting that the country should no longer be a part of the empire or that there should be a 'solemn protest' by the British government in association with the governments of the other Dominions. He forecast that in time the economic importance of South Africa in relation to the rest of the continent would dwindle but that in the meantime, to prevent the spread of its influence, there should be 'a kind of moral *cordon sanitaire*' drawn along the line of the Limpopo. This had to some extent been achieved by Rhodesia's aloofness, and the colony had been 'a buffer between the worst forms of colour mania and the rest of the continent'. But, he warned, there were loopholes, particularly in the development of the Northern Rhodesian copper fields, where, he predicted, 'the decisive battle between Afrikanerism and humanitarianism will be fought and won'.[32]

In *The New Boer War* Barnes again set out to urge that Britain could do something positive about oppression in South Africa. He argued that she could undermine the Afrikaner position by adopting and securing different policies in her own neighbouring territories and by making them less dependent on the Union. If there was a great difference in well-being between British-ruled and Union-ruled Africans, he thought, this would 'impart an upward tendency to native economic life in South Africa generally'. Barnes bitterly attacked the Union's tariff policies, which were designed to foster internal industrial growth. The Union's farmers received huge subsidies by way of compensation, but those in the High Commission territories did not. Rhodesia had safeguarded her freedom of fiscal action and her British preference and had cut down on the expense of helping to protect the Union's industries. The High Commission territories, on the other hand, had had to accept the Union's tariffs and to subsidise the growth of industry inside the Union, while at the same time their chief product, livestock, was embargoed. Barnes wrote, 'The system might have been especially designed to secure the economic stagnation of the Protectorates.' But, he concluded,

Britain held the Union in 'pathetic awe' and placed a very high premium on continued Afrikaner membership of the empire. The cost of 'Boer loyalty' had only slightly been met by British magnanimity. '. . . the big drain has been on the material and spiritual pockets of the natives. Britain has, in effect, fumbled about with her small change, and then, jerking her head towards the native, remarked, "My friend will pay." '[33] But the radical critique was far from the British government's interpretation of the situation. As the Secretary of State, J. S. Thomas, said in 1934, anything that would '. . . widen the breach in South Africa, when so much has been done to heal it, would be bad statemanship'.[34] Controversy over the High Commission territories must not be allowed to embitter relationships with the Union.

During the 1930s Africans in the Union still directed complaints to Britain. They protested against the Status of the Union Act,[35] and there was a good deal of gloom about what was felt to be the final end of British protection inside South Africa. They countered the developing South African argument, put forward as part of the offensive for the High Commisssion territories, that segregation was only a form of trusteeship. But there was also a tendency to widen the appeal and to look northwards for political allies and comfort. In January 1930 T. D. Mweli Skota called upon the African National Congress to summon a 'monster Conclave' of Africa, with delegates from Egypt, Ethiopia, west Africa, Kenya, Nyasaland, the Rhodesias and the High Commission territories. The speeches of Smuts and Hertzog abroad had, he said, been '. . . an eye-opener . . . to the negro throughout the whole world. Our friends in the North see in them a serious danger looming over the sky of the black or negro race.'[36] In this he was right, for the Colonial Office was increasingly to find that open co-operation with South Africa would have been 'embarrassing' to it in the rest of Africa.[37] Identification with Africa and a disillusionment with Britain was sharpened by the Ethiopian war. All Africans, said Jabavu, were 'staggered' by the destruction of the last indigenous African State; the European 'veneer' had been scratched and the 'White savage' hidden beneath had been revealed. James Calata told the Cape African Congress in July 1938 that Africans realised that in bargaining with Italy Britain had let Ethiopia down and that '. . . the position has its parallel in South Africa. Great Britain is about to let go of the Protectorates.' Jabavu defined the role of the African leadership in South Africa as being the defence of African interests outside the Union as well, in particular '. . . to prevent Africans in the Protectorates from being forced into the Union'.[38]

3 Defending white Africa

The threat of Hertzog in power without a coalition partner had produced a most gloomy imperial view of the future of the Union of South Africa. During the 1930s British doubts about the Union's 'native policy', combined with hostility to Afrikaner nationalism, did lead to the checking of South African ambitions, particularly with regard to the High Commission territories. But by 1933 there was far less reason for gloom about British interests in South Africa, the prospect of a direct clash of economic interests faded, and a Union government, reconciled to empire, moved towards the development of joint defence plans with Britain. After Britain went off gold in 1931 South Africa, in a deepening recession and faced with an outflow of capital, tried to maintain the gold parity of its currency. Hertzog attacked those who wished to follow the British example as wanting '. . . to undermine South Africa's national independence and freedom . . . Their purpose is to bind South Africa economically to Britain . . . they are trying to deprive us of the freedom we won politically.'[39] But Hertzog failed in his attempt to demonstrate economic independence, and his political power collapsed under the impact of recession and the flight of capital from the Union to Britain. In December 1932 South Africa abandoned the gold standard, Hertzog accusing 'the organised power of money' of bringing about the national humiliation of the Afrikaner. In the ensuing political crisis Hertzog and Smuts created out of their National and South African parties a United Party 'fusion' government. By so doing they had apparently recreated a government of the centre, which won a huge election victory in 1934, leaving two rump nationalist parties, one British and one Afrikaner, outside. It was a coalition much to British tastes. For one thing it appeared that the republican extremists had been isolated from power, and though the 'fusion' compromise was based upon legislation which made explicit the Union's sovereign status the new government saw itself as a co-operating member of the Commonwealth.

The coalition was also based upon a broad economic compromise. During the 1920s gold-mining wealth had been believed to be a wasting asset, but the new higher gold price of the 1930s led to a mining boom. Between 1910 and 1932 some £26 million had been invested from abroad in the South African gold mines, and this figure was equalled in the years 1933–6. Nationalist economic policies, which were to divert the profits of the foreign-owned mining industry to build up indigenous industry and agriculture,[40] could now be pursued in an entirely different context. The Hertzog–Smuts coalition produced the excess profits tax in 1933, which enormously increased the State's revenue from the mining industry and which provided the basis of a redistribution favourable to Hertzog's rural supporters without the necessity of a direct confrontation with overseas economic interests or an alteration in the fundamental relationship between the State and the mining industry, which had been presaged by Afrikaner radicals. A conservative government in the Union with a huge income had little need for the support of white economic radicalism. The Afrikaner revolution was diverted, and the respectability of the Union, dependent on the inflow of capital from abroad, seemed assured. Indeed, the Union government went out of its way to demonstrate its financial respectability and its wish to co-operate with Britain. The Union had taken no advantage of the Hoover moratorium and had been the only member of the Commonwealth to continue interest payments on its £16¼ million war debt to Britain, much to the disgust of nationalist political opinion inside South Africa. In August 1934, sealing its international probity, the Union entirely repaid its war debt.[41]

There was co-operation in other areas also. The development of defence plans during the 1930s illustrates the Union's conception of its role in the north, the degree to which the British government wanted to co-operate, and the underlying basis of the situation, which was that the Union was the strongest power on the sub-continent, and that it and Britain shared a common interest in resisting any challenge to the imperial and colonial *status quo*. The new Union government was apparently aware of the value of its imperial shield. In 1934 Sir William Hankey, the Secretary to the British Cabinet, visited South Africa to discuss defence plans, and reported that '. . . all the leading men realise that the Royal Navy is a shield and protection of the Empire in general and S. Africa in particular'.[42] There appeared also to be an awareness of the Union's dependence upon the British trading connection. The High Commissioner reported that South Africa feared the consequences of the current developments in the international situation, as '. . . both mining and agriculture know . . . that if war means the loss of the United Kingdom market, they are finished'.[43] During the 1930s other South African anxieties developed. As early as 1934 Smuts began to exhibit fear of Japan, claiming that '. . . there were signs of Japan wanting to establish a footing in Mozambique and Abyssinia. If Singapore went, South Africa would come into the front line.'[44] His fears of the possibility of Japanese agression, especially against Mozambique, were shared by the Union's Defence Minister, Oswald Pirow.

These views had wide currency inside the Union. Reflecting them,

Hedley Chilvers published in 1933 a book called *The yellow man looks on* in which he warned of Japanese designs. In his foreword the mining magnate Sir Abe Bailey summed up the argument. South Africa was 'one of the treasure-houses of the world', with huge gold, diamond and other mineral resources and with 'a lower population pressure than that of any other mineralised country on the globe'. The Yellow Peril was 'one of the best arguments for the maintenance of the Union's connection with the British Commonwealth', for only in this way 'will they continue to enjoy the protection of the British Navy'.[45]

Finally, there was the Union's most important defence 'frontier'—the north. The revival of German colonial claims and the Italian conquest of Ethiopia altered the framework of the Union's policies by threatening the continuation of the comforting *pax Britannica* to the north which had existed since 1918. And in this sphere the Union was in a position to offer defence co-operation. In 1933 Pirow told a meeting of the Committee for Imperial Defence that while the Union's forces would not serve outside Africa they would be willing '... to assist in the protection of territories in other parts of Africa, as this in effect would be protecting whites against natives', and he asked the CID to consider defence co-ordination between the Union's borders and Uganda.[46] The strength of Pirow's anxiety in making this offer can be measured against the background of protest and suspicion which any defence entanglements with the British government aroused among nationalist Afrikaners in general and the Nationalist opposition led by D. F. Malan in particular, and the latter consistently attacked the 'fusion' government of Hertzog and Smuts on the grounds that it was committing the Union to an imperialist war on the side of the British empire as Botha was alleged to have done in 1911. The Union government's position was a complex one. Inside South Africa, particularly on the ideological right wing of the Nationalist Party, and among the German population of South West Africa, there was considerable sympathy with the new Germany, as well as a body of support for the view that Germany might be more reliable in the preservation of white supremacy in Africa than France, with its policy of arming Africans.

But the Union was bound to resist the return of the former German colonies; not only South West Africa, in which it had a direct interest, but also Tanganyika, for fear of the effect this might have on the likelihood of 'native unrest'. The fear that German and Italian activities would disturb not only the *pax Britannica* but the *pax Europeana* as a whole also explains the violence of the Union's opposition to the conquest of Ethiopia and the Union government's rather lonely attempts to maintain League of Nations resistance. As the Union delegate put it, the conquest was a '... danger to the black peoples of Africa and [a] menace to our own white civilisation'.[47] While Hertzog, Pirow and Smuts were all 'appeasers' and anxious to press Britain to avoid a European conflict into which the Union might be drawn, the logic of the Union's position on the African continent drove it towards the development of defence policies in collaboration with Britain, and Britain's position as a colonial power, with forces which could be inadequate to meet a real threat on the African continent meant that it, in the last resort, would rely upon the Union.

Though from the British point of view an expression of South African willingness to involve itself, however tenuously, in imperial defence schemes was welcome, it posed certain problems related to the aims of Union policy. What role was the Union seeking in the north? How would this affect the British settlers in central and east Africa? And what would be the effect upon Africans of a defence alliance based upon the south? Hankey advised that though the Union's keenness should not be dampened it must be made clear that Britain had '... absolutely no apprehension of danger from the natives,'[48] and he stressed African quiescence over the past twenty-five years except for outbreaks of 'religious fanaticism'. Yet there was, he wrote, a possibility with the spread of education and the increased demand for labour, that 'tribal' discipline would be relaxed, and this could lead to co-operation between different tribes in times of unrest. If this happened, he thought, co-operation in the use of air power and troop-carrying aircraft could be invaluable. In a 'major emergency', he concluded, 'It could be a comfort for us to know that ... the Union of South Africa had a plan for sending air forces if we found it necessary to ask for them.'[49] Thus the Union could, if the need arose, be an auxiliary arm of British rule in south, central and east Africa, and to this extent British thinking overlapped with the Union's. As Pirow put it after the Italian conquest, it seemed clear that South Africa should be '"the elder brother" to the rest of British Africa".'[50]

The 'elder brother' defence policy naturally had implications for the Rhodesias. The Southern Rhodesian government was anxious to review its defence arrangements in the light of the Abyssinian war and, nearer home, the disturbances on the Copperbelt in 1935, and was worried about the extent to which the British government would involve the central African territories in a defence system dominated and controlled by the Union.[51] Pirow did not appear to have been interested in the political arrangements with the northern territories, and he envisaged the creation, to the north of the Union, of two federations, one in central and one in east Africa.[52] Yet while he indicated that the amalgamation of Southern Rhodesia and the Union would 'tend to upset the political balance in South Africa', he was reported in 1936 as being in favour of making '... Pretoria a centre for the organisation of African defence'.[53] Both Southern Rhodesia and the Union were concerned at the defencelessness of the Portuguese ports of Beira and Lourenço Marques. In addition both countries opposed the training of African troops. The Union government had always objected to the creation of black armies in Africa, and Pirow in particular in the 1930s criticised the French and Italian governments for so doing.[54] In Southern Rhodesia's case this was a reason for pressing for early amalgamation with the north. As Huggins wrote in 1936, there was allowed in the north something which '... is foreign to our policy and foreign to the policy of the Union, and that is the training of native troops'.[53]

The possible defence advantages of a closer union between Southern Rhodesia and its northern neighbours were also considered. The Southern Rhodesian internal security situation was considered to be adequate, and it was supposed that the colony had nothing to gain in this field from closer union, as it would never permit the employment within its borders of black African troops from the north. On the other hand, when the CID considered the problem in 1938 it felt that racial tension on the Copperbelt between white and African workers made inter-racial violence there a possibility. African forces, it thought, could not be employed in a disturbance in which they might have to act against whites, and the only solution would be to ask for the assistance of Southern Rhodesia. It was also felt that in the event of closer union between the Rhodesias plans could be made for an interlocking defence system, and the CID recorded in 1938, '... interchange of troops between Southern Rhodesia and other colonies contemplated in the event of war or a native rising'.[56] Yet the CID was ambivalent as to the defence implications of closer union. On the one hand, it was feared that if Southern Rhodesia controlled the defence policy of the central African region it could weaken imperial defence there because of the colony's opposition to the use of African troops, while, on the other, advantage was seen in the use of Southern Rhodesia as a white nucleus of force. The defence dilemma was the one which constantly faced the white rulers of south, central and east Africa: how to create African forces for use against an external challenge to white colonial rule without creating the conditions in which local colonial or settler control would be threatened. In 1938 a memorandum of the Overseas Defence Committee approved the policy of relying on Southern Rhodesia, remarking that the experience of the 1935 Copperbelt disturbances showed that adequate numbers of white settlers were likely to volunteer their services when needed. While the memorandum strongly approved the policy of not giving military training to Africans in central Africa it remarked that '. . . if other nations are going to build up large forces of Africans, or the world situation is such that we must prepare in Central Africa for aggression by other powers employing Native forces, there will be no option but for us to follow suit.'[57]

In his evidence to the Bledisloe commission General Gifford, while stressing the importance of maintaining the African units in Northern Rhodesia and Nyasaland, felt that Britain must be in a position to count upon the Union in case of trouble. The former commander of the Southern Rhodesian forces, Major General Edwardes, expressed the view that internal security could not be maintained in Northern Rhodesia by the settlers alone, and would have to rely on Southern Rhodesia and possibly the Union in the case of a 'native rising'.[58] Over all of central Africa the Copperbelt was felt to be the area about which there was most cause for anxiety. For the rest, in spite of 'subversive propaganda' from an 'external source', it was felt that Africans did not possess the powers of organisation to translate discontent into serious revolt. The Overseas Defence Committee also stressed the need for the training of settlers in Northern Rhodesia because an African regiment 'may possibly not be completely reliable' in the case of internal disturbances. The general conclusion of the defence debate was that the three territories relied in essence upon Southern Rhodesia for internal security and upon the Union in the case of a general war. The internal defence of British central Africa would be built upon the whites of Southern Rhodesia, while the base upon which external defence would be built was to be the Union.[59]

In November 1938 the Chiefs of Staff Sub-committee of the CID reviewed the position. As they saw it the basic situation was that the Rome–Berlin axis and the revival of German colonial claims posed problems not only for the Commonwealth as a whole but for the Union in particular, and they summarised the situation as follows. 'British influence in Africa combined with control of sea communications is the main guarantee of South African integrity. It is therefore in the ultimate interest of South Africa herself to help us maintain our present predominant position in Africa and the Middle East.'[60] There was some anxiety that peacetime arrangements with South Africa '. . . might lead the Union to feel that they had a right to have a say in questions concerning our African colonies', and Colonial Office representatives warned that it could be 'disastrous' to give the impression that east and central Africa relied upon the Union to help crush African revolt. Such arrangements would not only be criticised in the United Kingdom, they said, but also by Africans, who would get to know of them '... by the usual infiltration of information, which is continually at work in Africa'.[61] On the other hand arrangements had already been made to co-ordinate security in central Africa through the use of Southern Rhodesian troops, and it was perceived that South Africa might ask why it was possible to co-operate with Southern Rhodesia and not with the Union. On the whole, by the end of 1938 it was felt that with the possibility of impending war, co-ordinated but conditional defence arrangements need not lead to any political difficulties. In February 1939 the British High Commissioner in South Africa reported that while Smuts had the 'warmest admiration' for Chamberlain's policies, he now felt that war was inevitable and that the dictators had to be destroyed, and in May Malcolm Macdonald, the Secretary of State for the Dominions, suggested approaching the Union with a view to drawing up joint wartime plans for the east African theatre.[62] Yet British uncertainty regarding South Africa's reliability remained. Hertzog and Pirow continued to make determined efforts to avoid war, and with regard to Africa north of the Union suggested the satisfaction of German colonial claims at the expense of Portugal and Belgium. As Pirow explained to Hitler in November 1938, east Africa up to Ethiopia was the territory of the 'European Africans' and was '... integrated as a result of its internal relations to the great stretch of territory of the whites in Africa, which extended in a chain from Abyssinia to the Cape. This was a community of a white master race as opposed to the Negroes.' Though it was recognised that Germans too would defend the white position, they would '... always be Germans first and Africans second—whereas the Africans had a feeling of independence'.[63] Yet, even though throughout Pirow's unsuccessful efforts at mediation he remained inflexible regarding the Union's support for the maintenance of the British position in Africa, the political crisis of September 1939, when the 'fusion' government of the Union split on the issue of entry into the War, was to show that British anxiety had been well founded. It was not until the Union had actually entered the war with Smuts as Prime Minister that it became, after five years of tentative negotiation, a partner once more in imperial defence in Africa.

Notes

1 Cab. 27/349, June 1927.
2 'The new problem of Africa', *Round Table*, XVII, p. 447.
3 J. C. Smuts *Africa and Some World Problems*, Oxford, 1930, No. 1, 'African settlement'.
4 L. S. Amery, *My Political Life*, London, 1953, p. 406. As Lord Gladstone had been, Amery was also eager to promote the development of the Bechuanaland protectorate. When Birchenough and Malcolm approached him with proposals to make effective the company's mineral rights the Secretary of State, Malcolm, reported, '. . . said that it was not his idea that large countries should be kept as preserves for a few native tribes to wander about in doing nothing in particular just as there are areas in Canada for the preservation of the few remaining herds of buffaloes. (This was his expression.)' (Ch. 8/2/2/11, Malcolm to Chaplin, 22 January 1925. Amery himself wrote that the Protectorates were 'human Whipsnades'. (*Political Life*, p. 415.)
5 L. S. Amery, *The Forward View*, London, 1935, chapter 4.
6 A. S. Cripps, *An Africa for Africans*, London, 1927.
7 Lord Olivier, *White Capital and Coloured Labour*, London, 1929, p. 230, and chapter 24.
8 Cab. 27/349, 8 June 1927, meeting on federation in east and central Africa between Amery, Ormsby-Gore, Sir S. Wilson, Grigg, Cameron, Stanley, Strachey and others.
9 Ch. 8/2/1, Kipling to Chaplin, 1 August 1929.
10 D.O. 117/75, D 10866, secret, Memo for Cabinet, 5 October 1927.
11 D.O. 117/75, 5 October 1927.
12 L. S. Amery, *The Empire and the New Era*, 'Collected speeches', London, 1928.
13 D.O. 117/20, D 11424, secret, 17 October 1928.
14 See R. Hyam, *Failure*, chapter 5, and D.O. 117/120, 3 February 1929, Amery minute.
15 Ch. 8/2/1, Chancellor to Chaplin, 6 October 1927.
16 D.O. 116/6, Memo, October 1934, and D.O. 116/7, No. 123, Huggins to Macdonald, 24 March 1937.
17 D.O. 116/3, Athlone to Secretary of State, 18 March 1929, and Athlone to Secretary of State, 3 September 1929.
18 D.O. 117/149, secret, Clifford to Harding, 15 April 1929.
19 D.O. 116/3, High Commissioner to Secretary of State, 23 August 1929.
20 See G. H. L. Le May, *Black and White in South Africa*, London, 1971, p. 53.
21 D.O. 117/172, D 13436, Clifford to Davis, 15 October and 16 October 1929.
22 D.O. 121/101, Stanley to Thomas, 11 October 1932. This was considered a most important despatch, and was circulated to other members of the government, and to the king.
23 Quoted in *From Protest to Challenge*, ed. T. Karis and G. Carter, I, Stanford, 1972, pp. 290 ff.
24 C. Kadalie, *My Life and the I.C.U.*, London, 1970, pp. 60, 103, 115–16, 128, 137. Kadalie saw not the guns with which African chiefs on their official visits had been intimidated but the East End of London, which led him to conclude

that the '. . . poverty-stricken streets, stunted and pathetic human beings . . . were the bedrock and reality on which Western civilisation was built'.
25   Karis and Carter, I, pp. 308–9.
26   *Ibid.*, pp. 274 ff.
27   See below.
28   The pamphlet is printed in Karis and Carter, I, pp. 281 ff.
29   Karis and Carter, I, p. 252.
30   Barnes's books were published in London in 1930 and 1932, and Olivier's in 1927. They drew attention to the issues involved in the transfer of the protectorates before the Curtis–Perham controversy of 1933, as Hyam maintains in *Failure*, pp. 140 ff.
31   Olivier, *Anatomy*, pp. 93, 101, 126, 227–9. What Africans in South Africa had been saying about their situation clearly made an impact on Olivier's account.
32   L. Barnes, *Caliban in Africa*, chapters 9 and 10.
33   L. Barnes, *The New Boer War*, pp. 16–17, 161–2 and 228.
34   Quoted in Hyam, *Failure*, pp. 130–1.
35   The Act gave South Africa legal equality of status with Britain. The protests were remarked upon by Margery Perham in her article in the *Times* of 6 July 1934; see M. Perham, *Colonial Sequence*, London, 1967, p. 127.
36   Quoted in Karis and Carter, I, pp. 307–8.
37   See the objection by the Colonial Office, noted on PRE 1/174, 1933, Memo.
38   Quoted in Karis and Carter, II, Stanford, 1943, pp. 42, 48 and 137.
39   See C. M. v.d. Heever, *General J. B. M. Hertzog*, Johannesburg, 1946, pp. 206–7 and 231–8.
40   See generally L. Katzen, *Gold and the South African Economy*, Cape Town, 1964.
41   T. 160/499, F. 56/3.
42   Cab. 63/69, Hankey to Stanley, 5 July 1934.
43   Cab. 63/69, P. Lieshing to Harding, 18 July 1934.
44   Cab. 63/69, Hankey to Baldwin, 7 September 1934.
45   See Cab. 21/883, 18 November 1938, Minute, and also H. Chilvers, *The Yellow Man Looks On*, London, 1933, pp. viii–ix.
46   Cab. 63/69, 24 July 1933.
47   See P. N. S. Mansergh, *Survey of British Commonwealth Affairs: Problems of External Policy*, London, 1952, p. 231.
48   Cab. 63/69, 5 July 1934.
49   Cab. 63/68.
50   Cab. 21/47, quoting the *Volksblad*, 14 August 1936.
51   Cab. 21/642, 4 and 27 August 1936.
52   He suggested that the highlands of Kenya be demarcated as a white area just as the Union had designated the Transkei as an African one, though he disclaimed any interest in Kenyan policies.
53   Cab. 21/427 and Cab. 21/642, 28 August 1936.
54   Cab. 21/427 and Cab/814.
55   Cab. 24/269, 7 May 1936.
56   Cab 21/465, 21 and 29 March 1938.
57   Cab. 21/466, O.D.C. paper, No. 607, secret, 17 October 1938.
58   Cab. 21/466, 21 April 1938.

59 Cab. 21/466, 17 October 1938.
60 Cab. 21/883, 14 November 1938.
61 Cab. 21/883, Harding to Clark, Draft, December 1938, and other comments.
62 Cab. 21/883, Clark to Harding, 20 February 1939, and Macdonald to Inskipp, 17 May 1939.
63 Report of the Pirow–Hitler conversations, quoted in A. Vandenbosch, *South Africa and the World*, Kentucky, 1970, and Mansergh, *Problems*, pp. 262–3. Mussolini commented, after Pirow had explained this to him, that the Union's Defence Minister was '. . . an outstanding example of the rapidity with which a race living in another latitude could deteriorate . . . Pirow was quite right when he always described himself as an African.' Pirow was far more highly thought of by British politicians. Amery reported that he had made a very good impression in London, and Sir W. Clark expected him to be the Union's next Prime Minister. See pp. 246 ff for the Union's opposition to the return of Tanganyika to Germany and for the British proposals to Germany for a new colonial regime in central Africa. See also D. C. Watt, 'South African attempts to mediate between Britain and Germany, 1935–38', in K. Bourne and D. C. Watt, *Studies in International History*, London, 1969. The impression that Pirow was 'very pro-German' (p. 404) is derived from the German records and appears to be irrelevant to the goals which the Union government actually pursued during the period.

CHAPTER 11
Towards a second failure
1930–39

1 Closer union of the Rhodesias

By the end of the 1920s the policy tangle in east Africa and the rapidity of developments on the Copperbelt had the effect of reopening the debate on the desirability of partitioning Northern Rhodesia, and this stimulated the ambitions of the settlers in both Rhodesias in the direction of closer union of the two territories. The Copperbelt was of particular importance also to South African mining interests, which interested themselves in the policies the British government was formulating for the north. The general range of options as they saw them was summed up by Chaplin in his evidence to the Hilton Young commission. If things went 'reasonably well in the union politically', and if the Copperbelt developed quickly, then their political future lay in an overall southern union. He felt that things in the Union had got over the worst, from the British point of view, and that '. . . civilisation in its ordinary progress will come from the Union'. If development in Northern Rhodesia was slow, 'then the interests of the native will come more to the front'. If development was rapid but things went the wrong way in the Union, then it might be an answer to build up a bloc of Northern States but this could have the effect of driving the non-British element in the Union back on itself and intensifying anti-British feeling.[1] Chaplin's view that the wealth of the Union should be used to develop the northern territories was shared by others. Clifford reported that Sir Ernest Oppenheimer believed that Northern Rhodesia would become far richer than her southern neighbour, and that there was considerable Rand enthusiasm to invest in it. Control of the Copperbelt was a vital imperial interest. Both Smuts and Oppenheimer urged the importance of not allowing the new mines to fall under the control of American capital. Smuts told Hankey in 1930 that American efforts to take over the copper fields were 'very serious'. The empire, he pointed out, already paid the United States a vast war tribute and import bills for cotton, petrol and copper, and could materially reduce this if Northern Rhodesian copper was secured for imperial refineries. If, he wrote, imperial resources were not used to secure '. . . our financial and industrial position in the world, I foresee very grave difficulties from the burdens which our peoples are called upon to bear'.[2] Sir Auckland Geddes recalled that in 1930 'those in high places' thought that it was both a European and a British interest that powerful imperial firms should take a hand in the development of the new field.[3] Development of the north by London-linked South African finance capital was clearly more preferable to imperial interests than reliance upon American money, regardless of differences with the Union over 'native policy'.

Against this background the Hilton Young commission was unable to make any conclusive recommendations regarding the future of Northern Rhodesia. The Governor of Nyasaland, Sir Charles Bowring, put forward a new version of the old threefold division: Barotseland under the High Commissioner for South Africa; the centre to Southern Rhodesia, and the association as soon as possible of North Eastern Rhodesia and Nyasaland with the east African colonies.[4] The majority of the commission came to the conclusion that the railway belt could go in with the south, while the chairman's minority report recommended the creation of a single High Commissionership for the 'Central territories'—comprising both Rhodesias, Nyasaland and the Bechuanaland protectorate. The Southern Rhodesian government disagreed with all these suggestions. Northern Rhodesia, it said, should aim at uniformity in 'native policy' with Southern Rhodesia, and not with east Africa, and no action should be taken that would prejudice a future union between the two territories. It was particularly unfortunate, the government observed, that the future of Northern Rhodesia had been discussed in relation to Nyasaland, as it was clear that this had both influenced and prejudiced the views given regarding the north's relationship with the south.[5]

In 1930 the Labour government in Britain, in an effort to reverse the trend away from the Devonshire declaration which marked Amery's term of office, published a White Paper reaffirming the policy of African paramountcy set out in 1923.[6] This aroused threats of settler rebellion in Northern Rhodesia, and though for a time it appeared to put an end to speculation about the absorption of the north into a white Dominion with Southern Rhodesia it did, in the longer run, by increasing the political awareness of the central African settlers, bring the north and south closer together. Many felt, in any case, like Lord Buxton, who had no doubt that '... the paramountcy affair was intended for Kenya and Co., not for Rhodesians'. Smuts, summing up the white southern view, called it, 'the stupid White Paper on paramountcy'.[7] Nevertheless Labour in office was decidedly cool towards Southern Rhodesian aspirations for early consideration of amalgamation with the north. Amalgamation of the two territories was not rejected in principle but was declared to be premature. And it was not only unwillingness to hand northern Africans over to the southern settlers which accounted for the British government's caution. The Cabinet was told that it was '... impossible for HMG to consider, in present circumstances, any diminution of their direct responsibilities in relation to the mining areas of Northern Rhodesia'. In any case, a decision had not yet been taken as to what Northern Rhodesia was: partition was still a possibility and the Cabinet was advised that the Southern Rhodesian government be informed that any future amalgamation would not necessarily be with a territory with boundaries coterminous with those of the existing Northern Rhodesia.[8]

The settlers in both north and south grew in confidence and revived their amalgamation demands during the 1930s in spite of the Labour government's stance during its brief term of office. In 1933 came renewed demands from the northern settlers, which were met not only with missionary criticism but with hesitancy from the 'large capitalist interests', which hoped for a long period of Crown colony government, as they were fearful both of the possible tax policies of a settler government and of the growth of white trade unionism, which could not be checked by a government dependent upon white votes.[9] The settler government in the south pressed confidently forward during the 1930s with its plans for an extension of its responsibilities to the north. Development of these plans necessitated the formation of a 'native policy'. In 1934 the new Rhodesian Prime Minister, Huggins, together with Carbutt, the Chief Native Commissioner, came up with a scheme for the division of British central Africa into white and African territories. It was the old railway belt scheme with a difference. In the south and in the railway belt, Carbutt wrote, white interests would be paramount and '... white development in Southern Rhodesia would be freed of the embarrassing necessity to consider native interests . . .' Africans, Carbutt thought, were prone to migration, and the 'native problem' of both Southern Rhodesia and even the Union could be solved if they were to migrate to a great black State in British central Africa which would include Tanganyika. Less far-fetched and of more significance was that the scheme was part of a plan to change the basis of the Rhodesian political system, which still rested on the premises of the old Cape system of equal rights for all civilised men. As Carbutt put it, 'To say that the white man will never submit to political domination by the black man, is in Southern Rhodesia an undeniable truism. It follows that no matter what heights of civilisation the native obtains the white man will not admit him to political equality.' Following upon this line of analysis, Huggins suggested, precisely as Hertzog had been doing since 1905, that the Rhodes system was logically unworkable and politically impossible, and that an alternative form of political representation for Africans would have to be found. As Hertzog had eventually done, he turned to the idea of nominated white representatives to represent African interests and a development of the council system, though he did hold out the possibility that eventually the councils would elect representatives. Stanley's reaction was significantly similar to the way in which Athlone had greeted Hertzog's proposals. While Stanley disapproved in theory, he was sure that '. . . the franchise of the Colony cannot indefinitely be left capable of producing a state of affairs in which Europeans might become a hopeless minority of the electorate.' And, as in South Africa, there was the veiled warning from Huggins that while whites should take '. . . a sympathetic and helpful view of native development . . . it is not likely to happen if there is in any way a fear of political power being exercised by the natives'.[10]

In 1935 the customs union between Southern Rhodesia and South Africa disappeared. Southern Rhodesia's future now involved the building of her own industrial sector, and the most obvious market, with the south sealed off behind new tariffs, was the north. In May 1936 the Southern Rhodesian Legislative Assembly passed a resolution asking for the early amalgamation of the two Rhodesias under a constitution conferring the right of self-government. At the beginning of 1937 the Southern Rhodesian government produced plans for a 'native policy'. Councils would be advanced, as Tredgold put it, '. . . by means of an Act . . . on the broad lines of Act No. 23 of 1920 of the Union of South Africa', and the admission of more African voters to the voters roll would be stopped—an approximation to the Hertzog policy.[11] The British response to the new Rhodesian proposals had to take into account not only the position of the imperial government as 'trustee' but also the policies of the Union, and imperial strategy in general, which involved the British position not only *vis-à-vis* southern Africa but also towards the rest of the continent. Over a long period British advisors in southern Africa had been far less suspicious of Rhodesian 'native policy' than of the Union's, the tone having been set by Amery in 1927 when he reported that the conduct of policy in Rhodesia was 'much more liberal' than in the Union. In 1929 permission to go ahead with the Land Apportionment Act had been given partly in response to the argument that experience in the Union was 'a striking example of having delayed too long'.[12] In the light of Southern Rhodesia's comparatively favourable image the British government's reaction to Huggins's proposals was not wholly negative. Stanley warned that as increasing numbers of Africans became landowners in the Native Purchase Areas there would be an increase in the number of African voters which would make the common roll system inoperable, and that there would be an 'anti-native' panic. In any case, he argued, an increased number of Africans on the voters' roll would not solve the problem of providing for representation of the political interests of those in the reserves, and he concluded:

Obviously the interests of the Natives in the Reserves, who have, under our present laws, no practical possibility of qualifying for a vote or even of being properly represented by voters of their own colour, will be far better served if the fear of the European of being dominated by a handful of 'educated' Natives is removed

The admission of an elite to political equality, it seemed, would have to be sacrificed in order to secure a less hostile white approach to the problems of the African majority. In London in July 1937 Malcolm Macdonald told Huggins that the existing system of franchise could not be abolished 'unless an effective substitute could be provided, and that appeared to depend largely upon how the system of Native Councils developed, and upon the practicality of establishing in due course a general Native Council for the whole territory.'[13] Though it was without positive enthusiasm, the possibility of allowing Southern Rhodesia to switch to the Hertzog policy was envisaged by the British authorities.

The British government's reaction to the amalgamation plan as put forward by the Southern Rhodesians was not favourable. Initially Huggins was told that it would be politically impossible from the parliamentary point of view, but it was agreed that there should be an enquiry into closer co-operation between the two Rhodesias and Nyasaland, on the strict understanding that the British government would not relinquish the control it had over the 'native policies' of the northern territories nor its reserve powers in the south. With the revival of German colonial claims the time was felt to be 'inopportune' for Britain to be seen to be relinquishing any measure of 'trusteeship'.[14] Huggins was at first disposed not to accept the enquiry, but in October

1937 he extracted a concession, blackmailing Macdonald with the warning that if amalgamation was entirely ruled out there was a risk of '... premature entrance into the Union, which would be a disaster for Southern Rhodesia and for British Africa as a whole'.[15] He agreed to accept the enquiry, provided it was not to be tied down by instructions not to report on the advisability or otherwise of amalgamation of the Rhodesias, and the British government consented, though Macdonald and Ormsby-Gore told the Cabinet that there could not be an amalgamation leading to an enlarged territory with the same constitutional status at present accorded to Southern Rhodesia.[16]

In 1936 the Governor of Southern Rhodesia had seen fit to warn the British government of what he considered to be the unmistakably anti-British trend of Union politics and to urge that it was important to imperial interests '... to secure the preservation of a distinctively British element beyond the Limpopo, strong enough to function as a counterpoise to nationalistic Afrikanerdom from outside ... or as an internal leaven...'[17] Stanley went on to argue that to leave the northern territories weak and isolated would be to risk their 'engulfment', one by one, on the Union's terms. As a further inducement he offered the hope that the association of Southern Rhodesia with two northern territories '... might be expected to divert the development of native policy in Southern Rhodesia from the risk of approximation towards the less liberal policy of the Union'. His priorities were clear—the old imperial interest in a counterpoise first, a liberal 'native policy' second. In view of the obvious element of counterpoise strategy involved in any closer association of the territories of British central Africa, Union government opinion might have been expected to be wary of the Southern Rhodesian moves. Yet this did not appear to be the case, as the Union was concerned not with its own northward expansion (though it did have territorial aspirations *vis-à-vis* the High Commission territories) but with the security of white political dominance in Africa. Pirow, as Hankey reported in 1934, opposed the extension of the Union's territory northward and envisaged three entities, the Union, the Rhodesias, and an east African group, which would work together closely, '... particularly in economic and native policy and defence, which was connected with native policy'.[18] The aim of this approach was to reinforce and derive the advantages from a compliant British presence to the north without courting the dangers of admitting a political Trojan horse into the Union.

In April 1937 the British High Commissioner in South Africa reported that Pirow attached much importance to the 'solidarity' of policies among States and colonies south of the Sahara. 'He insisted on the conception that the interests of white civilisation must be considered first at all times and under all circumstances.' Though the High Commissioner felt that Pirow ought to realise that this was opposed to the British attitude towards 'subject races' in Kenya and elsewhere, from the point of view of the Union (as from that of the central African settlers) the development of regional arrangements to the north could only strengthen the white paramountcy of which Pirow talked.[19] Smuts too was understood to favour the development of regional arrangements to the north of the Union, and indeed in his view closer association between Southern Rhodesia and territories to the north would not preclude eventual closer association with the Union, though he envisaged 'something of a Federal character' rather than the type of union he had worked for in 1923.[20]

2 Britain and South African segregation

The gold-mining boom and the expansion of the South African economy during the 1930s had important implications for the extension of the economic involvement of South Africa with the territories to the north. In September 1936 Duncan, the South African Minister of Mines, met the Governors of Northern Rhodesia and Nyasaland, along with Huggins and Stanley, in Johannesburg in order to inform them that it was the intention of the Union government, in the next parliamentary session, to lift the ban on the recruitment of labour by the mines north of latitude 22° south.[21] The northern territories were conscious that, if they resisted the Union's labour demands, they were not in a position to stop the voluntary flow of labour southwards, where pay was higher, without the co-operation of the Union government. This co-operation, they felt, they would only get if they agreed to the Union's recruiting officially the 'ascertained surplus' of labour in the north. At first the northern territories asked for a formal agreement along the lines of the Union–Mozambique convention, but Duncan declined, offering instead a chance to approve a plan put forward by the Chamber of Mines, which felt that it would get as much labour without an agreement. The north then suggested that it could agree to recruitment only if the local social structure was not damaged and the needs of the northern territories employers were met. At the beginning of 1937 the South African government urged the British government to react favourably to its new needs. Duncan, then the Governor General designate, called on

Ormsby-Gore to press the Union's case. His government's arguments were that the Chamber of Mines was suffering from a severe labour shortage, which 'deeply concerned' the Union; the prosperity of South Africa closely depended on the mining industry, and they were therefore 'most anxious' that the British be sympathetic to an increase in northern recruitment. The existing situation was that South Africa depended on illegal migration, while Southern Rhodesia had preferential access to the labour surplus of the northern territories. 'The importance to Great Britain of the South African market and the dependence of the Union on the continued prosperity and expansion of the gold mining industry require no emphasis,' the Union urged. 'It is therefore obvious that it is to the advantage of Great Britain that the governments of Nyasaland and Northern Rhodesia adopt a sympathetic attitude towards the establishment of a regulated flow of labour...'[22] The British attitude on the negotiations which followed was to hold out for the principle that the northern territories would have first call upon their own labour, that recruiting would be limited to what 'the tribal life will stand', and that arrangements be made for transport and remittances; but it is clear that Britain could not and would not stand in the way of a new increase in the flow of labour southwards. By 1939 the new pattern was emerging. The Witwatersrand Native Labour Association, which recruited for the Rand mines, wanted its Nyasland quota raised from 8,500, the first agreed figure, to 15,000, and its Northern Rhodesian quota from 1,500 to 5,000.

While the new labour demands enmeshed the north firmly within a southern African system, they helped to set the formation of the political pattern in the opposite direction. The Southern Rhodesian government was distinctly churlish about the new competition for labour which it believed to be rightly its own. In April 1939 also, after negotiations in Cape Town, a new trade agreement between Southern Rhodesia and South Africa came into effect.[23] The Union, clearly putting the interests of its farmers and their protection ahead of those of its manufacturers and the expansion of their market, refused to relax restrictions on the entry of Southern Rhodesian tobacco and cattle. Stanley, the Southern Rhodesian Governor, reported, '... the general effect of the Cape Town negotiations on the minds of my ministers has been to render any policy of closer political union with the South even less attractive to them than it was before.'

Both high 'politics' and trade were thus developing in a direction different from that implied in the new labour situation. The vital labour question which affected the nature of life in the northern territories never reached the higher strata of British policy making. From London the southern African system appeared as a unity: there would be no impeding of its economic working but there was also concern about the ultimate political control of the whole. This determined the way in which the game for control of the north was played. The labour demands made the separate political strength of the north, if it were not to be sucked under and lose its role as counterpoise, more important, and not only to the government in London but also to the settler government in Rhodesia if its interests were not always to be placed second.

The Dominions and Colonial Offices jointly summed up the issues for the British Cabinet. First, it was said, there were the aspirations of the settlers in both Rhodesias, a group which was 'very loyal' to the British connection. It was felt among white Rhodesians, especially in the south, that the Copperbelt could prove to be for a united Rhodesia what the Rand had been to South Africa. (Though Rhodes had failed to find the second Rand to be the economic base of an effective anti-Afrikaner polity, Huggins had not forgotten the control of mineral wealth which had been the basis of the Transvaal's power.) On the question of 'native policy' the memorandum reminded the Cabinet that His Majesty's government 'regards itself as a trustee'. In white-settled areas it pursued 'the dual policy of complementary and parallel development.' In Southern Rhodesia, however, the general tendency, while 'not unsatisfactory', was more towards the Union's views, and policy favoured 'segregation of natives in their own areas and the limitation of their opportunities to compete with Europeans'. The view of the northern settlers was that white interests should similarly be given predominance on the railway and copper belts. Such a division of Northern Rhodesia, the Cabinet was told, would imply a 'great restriction' upon African development, as although the mines employed white workers and depended upon white capital '. . . they are no more dependent upon white agricultural settlement than the mines in Ashanti and Nigeria'. Amalgamation of the Rhodesias would mean the end of British control over 'native policy', and, it was percipiently noted, even a loose form of association could endanger British influence in this field if it came into conflict with strong southern pressures. Thirdly there was the question of control of the mines. In 1931 it had been felt that 'as a matter of Empire policy' the mining areas should remain directly under the British government. By 1937 the matter was even more crucial. The memorandum stated: 'These mines may before long be the governing factor in the copper markets of the world, and their output will become essential to national defence in the event of war, and of primary importance to the Empire's trade and manufacture in peacetime.'

The memorandum also considered the possible union of Northern Rhodesia and Nyasaland and the effect that closer association of the two Rhodesias would have upon this. Two major obstacles were seen in the way of joining together the northern territories The first was that the whole of Nyasaland was in the conventional basin of the Congo and that existing treaties made a customs union between it and Northern Rhodesia impossible, and the second was that Nyasaland's public debt and its liabilities under bridge and railway schemes meant that its budget was under Treasury control while that of Northern Rhodesia was not. In any case it was felt that in the event of a northern amalgamation Barotseland would have to be constituted as a separate area. It was noted, however, that 'educated natives' in both Northern Rhodesia and Nyasaland were strongly opposed to closer association with the south, but not to an association of their two territories, and the memorandum reproduced for the Cabinet as an example the resolution of the Ndola Welfare Association passed in 1933, which read:

While this Association would welcome amalgamation with Nyasaland, where laws and conditions are similar to those in this country, it humbly asks that the Government will not agree to the amalgamation of Southern Rhodesia and Northern Rhodesia, such a step would . . . be greatly to the detriment of the interests and the legitimate aspirations of the native population of this country. . .

Finally the two Secretaries of State considered the concept of 'British central Africa', which embodied the argument that while the Union was becoming un-British and east Africa was predominantly African, between the two could be created a bloc in which '. . . British ideas and British civilisation would predominate'. On the one hand, they commented, giving increasing responsibility to the settlers could prevent them from developing an 'anti-Whitehall complex' and a British counterbalance could be useful; on the other hand it might not prove possible for years to produce a territory which really could be a counterbalance to the Union; the white population of central Africa was still small, and an enlargement of their sphere could result in a weaker counterbalance. The Cabinet agreed to the appointment of a commission under the chairmanship of Lord Bledisloe.[24]

In 1934, when reporting on his political impressions of the situation in South Africa, Hankey had remarked that the 'native problem' was essentially the same from Kenya to the Cape: throughout the question was, as he put it, 'Could Africans be kept in tutelage for ever?' Hankey wrote, 'Before I left England I tried to discover what was the difference between the Dutch and British treatment of the Natives, and I have been trying to find out ever since . . . I doubt if it can be said with truth that there is a distinctively British or distinctively South African treatment of natives.'[25] Hankey was not, as he himself pointed out, an expert on African affairs, and perhaps because of this, while the experts concentrated upon differences in approach, he had grasped the essential point that, by indirect or direct rule, paramountcy, parallelism or segregation, white men intended to retain power for the foreseeable future and to exercise it for their own benefit, local or imperial. As indirect rule spread in east and central Africa its advocates tended to dilate upon the differences between it and South African policies. Yet the indirect rulers saw themselves as working within a virtually endless time span and promoting a policy which lead to the build-up of '. . . bulwarks against political agitation and averting . . . social chaos . . .'[26] Malcolm Macdonald was aware of the fundamental conservatism of the policy when he remarked of the dispute between the Union and Britain over the protectorates that while the difficulties were caused by the differences in 'native policy' between Britain and the Union, this was '. . . probably not so serious as it was sometimes represented to be'.[27]

Some of the nicer points of the discussion about trusteeship and incompatibility of the Union's policies must also be considered in the light of the readiness of sections of the British government to appease Nazi Germany in Africa and the plans to involve her in the administration of central Africa. The British plans for an area of joint administration included Portuguese territories, and the Committee for Imperial Defence in its comments pointed out that it was 'equally evident' that if there was not to be a marked salient northwards into the area of the new regime they would have to consider the inclusion of Northern Rhodesia and Nyasaland. They could see no 'positive disadvantages'.[28]

Yet as the 1930s progressed so too did critical analysis of the Union's policies. In 1938 the High Commissioner, Sir William Clark, reported that there were three possibilities for the Union: 'Identity', 'Differentiation' and *'laissez-faire'*. The last, he felt, was no longer possible. 'Identity', which he saw as being derived from the Cape, was the 'principle of civil and political equality' and was, he remarked, a policy of 'principle rather than practice'. He went on, 'It seems difficult to dispute the proposition that the policy of identity, however effective as an ideal, was bound to end in a blind alley. If carried to its logical conclusion, the result would be disastrous for both the white and ultimately for the black.' Thus Clark was firmly within the tradition, imperial, South African and Rhodesian, which rejected the possibility of an African participation in a single political system with whites, as this could lead to the eventual meaningful exercise of political power by Africans. The remaining alternative, 'differentiation', he described, correctly, as 'fathered on Sir Theophilus Shepstone' and upon the 'Rhodes-Hofmeyr organisation of the Transkei and Ciskei'—a British South African rather than an Afrikaner tradition. The Union's present policy, he wrote, was based upon this tradition; the Hertzog government's policy of segregation had two main points—the provision of the 'necessary' land and the creation of separate representative institutions. He commented favourably on the creation of the Natives' Representative Council, and pointed out that the land which it was envisaged would be provided under the 1936 Act would amount to one-third of the productive areas of the Union.[29] Yet there was, he felt, a 'fundamental hollowness' about the segregation policy.[30] Taxation of Africans was severe in relation to their resources; health and education services were poor, the land available did not allow the existence of a self-sufficient African peasantry, and the theory of the policy gave no satisfactory account of the role of educated Africans or how the demand for labour was to be met in a properly segregated society.

In general during the 1920s imperial critiques of the Union's approach to the 'native problem' had looked upon the Glen Gray tradition and the councils system embodied in the Act of 1920 as signs of the Union's willingness to move towards a 'liberal' solution. Against the background of the spread of indirect rule, however, Clark differentiated between two ways of creating separate African political mechanisms outside the white system. The Rhodes council system, embodied in the Act of 1920, he saw essentially as an attempt to break down the power of the traditional leadership, and he contrasted this with the British policy of maintaining and using tribal organisation as in the High Commission territories.[31] The nub of his criticism of the Union's policy was not to defend the 'identity' strand of the old Cape tradition but to attack the Union for abandoning the chieftancy as an instrument of African government. He wrote, 'There is a general feeling in the Union, frequently expressed to me by General Smuts, that native chiefs are no good and never will be any good; and I doubt whether any real endeavour is being made to work a system of indirect rule, seeking gradually to improve the chiefs.'[32] Even in tribal areas, he wrote, no effort was being made to learn from the 'experience amassed in British colonies' and the tendency was towards direct rule. Thus Clark rejected the claim that the Union's policy was comparable to the British idea of trusteeship,[33] but the rejection was on new grounds: that the Union's policy did not approximate to indirect rule, and that segregation was a sham on welfare grounds. This basis of criticism of the Union's policy presaged the emergence of a new attitude towards the policy of Southern Rhodesia. Here the 'identity' policy could be abandoned too, as it was no longer the essential criterion by which a good 'native policy' was to be judged in imperial eyes. A more practical approach began to emerge, a judgement based upon what the government spent for the benefit of the African population. In addition there was a new ideological emphasis— which judged southern systems according to their approximation to the now entrenched orthodoxy of indirect rule.

Notes

1 Ch. 8/2/1, Hilton Young Commission evidence, April 1928.
2 D.O. 117/120, 17 October 1928, and S.P., vii, Smuts to Hankey, 21 March 1930, p. 455.
3 See O. Lyttelton, Viscount Chandos, *Memoirs of Lord Chandos*, London, 1962, p. 128, where he discusses the formation of the British Metal Corporation, the overall strategic concept of which was, for defence reasons, to make the empire self-supporting in non-ferrous metals. See also T. Gregory, *Ernest Oppenheimer and the Economic Development of South Africa*, Cape Town, 1962, p. 395.
4 Minutes of evidence taken before the Joint Select Committee on East Africa, Reports, 1930–1, vii.
5 D.O. 114, Conf. Print Dominions, No. 117, No. 1 Rodwell to Secretary of State, 18 March 1929.
6 Cmd. 3574, 1930.
7 B.P., Buxton to Chaplin, 2 January 1931, and S.P., v, Smuts to M. C. Gillett, 25 November 1930, p. 465.
8 Thomas and Passfield suggested in their joint memorandum that the only possible addition to Southern Rhodesian territory in the near future would be the white farming area around Livingstone. See Cab. 23/66, 15 April 1931, and Cab. 23/67, 1 July 1931, C.P., Nos. 84/31 and 162/31.
9 Cab. 24/269, 137 (37).
10 D.O. 116/6, Nos. 198 and 206, 24 September 1934 and 10 July 1934.
11 D.O. 116/7, No. 110, 26 January 1937.
12 D.O. 117/75, D 10866, 5 October 1927, and D.O. 114, Conf. Print., Moffat memo, 1 March 1929.
13 D.O. 116/7, No. 112, 5 July 1937, and *ibid.*, Machtig to Stanley.
14 Cab. 24/269 and Cab. 23/89, 21 July 1937.
15 Cab. 24/271, Huggins to Macdonald, 23 August 1937.
16 Cab. 23/89, 13 October 1937, and Cab. 24/271, September 1937.
17 Cab. 24/269, 137 (37).
18 Cab. 21/383.

19 Cab 24/269, No. 121, 23 April 1937.
20 Southern Rhodesia National Archives, Smuts to T. Fletcher, 16 February 1937, and Cab. 23/88, 26 May 1937. It was felt that because of the Union's interest in Northern Rhodesia and Nyasaland as labour recruiting fields their amalgamation with Southern Rhodesia could lead to a demand from South Africa for a labour supply guarantee, and also for the incorporation of the High Commission territories. (Cab. 26/269.) It is of interest that this Cabinet paper, prepared in 1937, referred specifically back to the South Africa Act of 1909, and criticised the paper prepared in 1931 (C.P. 84/31) which stated that the Union had no claim to any part of Northern Rhodesia, commenting that it 'seems to have gone too far', thus appearing still, in 1937, to be acknowledging a residual Union claim.
21 D.O. 116/6, Stanley to Harding, 21 September 1936.
22 D.O. 116/7, High Commission for South Africa to Dominions Office, 12 January 1937, and D.O. to H.C.S.A., 23 January 1937, and M. Macdonald to te Water, 8 January 1937.
23 D.O. 116/6, Stanley to D.O., 22 February 1939.
24 Cab. 24/269, 137 (37). The other members of the commission were three members of Parliament representing the Conservative, Labour and Liberal parties, I. Orr-Ewing, W. H. Mainwaring and E. Evans; a former colonial civil servant, T. Fitzgerald; and a businessman, P. A. Cooper. On the commission's work see R. Gray, *The Two Nations*, London, 1960, part 1, chapter 5.
25 Cab. 63/69, Hankey to Batterbee, 14 September 1934.
26 Sir Donald Cameron, the Governor of Tanganyika, quoted in H. F. Morris and J. S. Read, *Indirect Rule and the Search for Justice*, London, 1972, p. 3.
27 Cab. 23/86, 1937; cf. Hyam, *Failure*, p. 154. In Macdonald's view the government of the Transkei did not compare unfavourably with much of Britain's colonial administration.
28 See PRE 1/247, C.I.D. memo 1236-B, and W. W. Schmokel, 'The hard death of imperialism: British and German colonial attitudes, 1919–39', in *Britain and Germany in Africa*, ed. P. Gifford and W. M. Louis, New Haven, Conn., and London, 1967.
29 The 1936 Representation of Natives Act removed African voters in the Cape from the common roll, substituting white representatives elected on a separate roll, and the Natives Trust and Land Act provided for the addition of land to the African areas as a *quid pro quo* and a redemption of the promise made by the Land Act of 1913. These Acts were a fundamental part of the Smuts–Hertzog coalition agreement.
30 In March 1940 he put it even more severely: segregation was not a policy but '... a device for making more workable the policy that the white man is to be dominant in every aspect of political, economic and social life'. (D.O. 114/99, No. 92.)
31 Though he commented that in the 1927 Native Administration Act there was a strand of the tendency, favoured by the British, to make use of traditional authorities. The stout opposition put up by the chiefs in the High Commission territories against transfer to the Union was not free of the perception that the Union's policies would, in the first place, damage their own position.

32 D.O. 114/91, Dominions, No. 183, 8 April 1938.
33 A claim which was frequently made by the Union government; see, for example, the address of Heaton Nicholls, the Union's High Commissioner in London, to the Empire Parliamentary Association in 1938, where he claimed, in the face of fierce attack from Clement Attlee, that the Hertzog policy afforded '. . . full opportunity for the development of native autonomy . . . It fits in with the British concept of government.' (D.O. 35/903, Y6–315, 16 November 1938.)

CHAPTER 12

The counterpoise outside
1939-45

1 The Bledisloe commission and closer union

The non-committal approach towards closer union of the Rhodesias which was favoured by both the Dominions and Colonial Offices was to some extent compromised by the Bledisloe commission's conclusions. The commissioners warned against what they saw as the danger of overemphasising the conflict of interest between white and black in central Africa. 'We are,' they wrote, 'impressed, as a result of our visit to Central Africa, by the opportunities provided for the social and economic progress of the natives by successful European enterprise, in contrast with the absence of such opportunity in those areas where European development is lacking.' They were of the opinion that, as long as expression was given to the African point of view, there were no grounds for assuming that an extension of settler constitutional responsibility would prejudice African interests. The report was not, in general, critical of Southern Rhodesian policies, though it suggested that the pass laws, to which it largely attributed the unanimity of opposition among northern Africans to closer association with the south, might be modified. It advocated the nomination of whites to represent African interests in the Legislative Assemblies of each territory, commenting that the Southern Rhodesian common roll was ineffective as a means of representation. With regard to Nyasaland it noted that it had really only been since the Governor's conference of 1935 that any considerable body of opinion had favoured its inclusion in an amalgamation scheme and commented that 'The idea . . . received some encouragement from the growing dependence of the industries of these territories (especially Southern Rhodesia) upon the supply of native labour from Nyasaland'.[1] After taking note of suggestions that Northern Rhodesia and Nyasaland be retained as separate entities, but with the boundary adjusted to lie along the valley of the river Luangwa, the commissioners felt that this, though it would better reflect divisions between peoples than the existing boundary, would delay the even distribution of economic progress in central Africa, as it would exclude the eastern territories from the expected benefits of Copperbelt development. They advised instead the fusion of the two administrations into one for a single territory, an arrangement which they felt would not preclude, and could well precede, co-operation with the south.

They concluded that the three territories faced fundamentally similar problems and that British policy from the 'broad Imperial standpoint' was to enable the different races to work together to promote economic stability and expansion; to make them able to maintain their security under the British flag, and to contribute to the defence of British Africa and the empire as a whole. All three, it was felt, would benefit if their future were to be planned as part of a single bloc of British territory from the Limpopo to Tanganyika, and the community of interests which they had discovered would 'lead them sooner or later to political unity'. The British government should, they thought, accept this principle. Nevertheless both federation and amalgamation between the territories as an immediate proposition were ruled out. The 'native policies' of the three were, it was remarked, still in the early stages of experiment. Though Southern Rhodesia had progressed most in social and development services, its policy, they observed, had a 'restrictive tendency' which would limit the opportunities open to Africans. As Southern Rhodesia would have predominant power in an amalgamated territory, the commission thought that there should be greater certainty as to its policy and that some modifications might be necessary. The commissioners not only advised that the settler population should be better prepared by being afforded greater opportunity for participation in government, but also doubted the 'practical wisdom' of amalgamation before African fears had been 'substantially removed'. Thus ammunition was provided for both sides: the settlers could push for acceptance of the principle and consequent action upon amalgamation, while the doubters could clutch at the excuses for further delay.

The Bledisloe report was a greater embarrassment to the British government than it was to Huggins and the settlers. In the House of Lords debate which followed its publication only Lugard took a firm stand on trusteeship and rejected closer union between north and south. Bledisloe himself urged that the question was not which race should be paramount, as the races could be partners. Others saw the question in the light of German ambitions, and Elibank, for example, urged the 'solidifying of the British race and traditions' as a step towards a federal South Africa stretching from the Cape to Tanganyika. The Dominions and Colonial Offices found themselves on the defensive, and they gradually developed a policy of evading a commitment on the principle of amalgamation while conducting further enquiry into the differences in 'native policy' in the three territories. In July of 1939 Huggins met MacDonald and Inskipp in London, and the two Secretaries of State tried to extract from him a statement on Southern Rhodesian 'native policy'. Sooner or later, as Inskipp put it, Africans in all three territories '. . . would be in a position to compete with the Europeans and administer their own territories'. Was there to be a policy of retarding their advance towards this goal? MacDonald admitted that in practice there was little difference between the policies north and south of the Zambesi but claimed 'some difference in ultimate objectives', and he told Huggins that in return for a British commitment to closer union they would need a statement as to the ultimate objectives of Southern Rhodesian policies.[2]

Bledisloe continued to press his point of view on Ministers. He urged Antony Eden, the new Secretary of State for the Dominions, who was himself inclined to treat the matter as one requiring action, that there were two reasons for going ahead. First, if the British government did not accept the amalgamation principle differences in policy between the south and the north would widen with the course of time, and secondly, while some variations in Southern Rhodesian policies were urgent, changes had to be made in the north as well in order to avoid severe labour disturbances on the Copperbelt. Bledisloe also pulled out the counterpoise card: the need to form '. . . a co-ordinated 'bloc' of British territories north of the Limpopo has . . . become more insistent since the outbreak of the war, especially in view of the state of political opinion in the Union of South Africa.'[3] To this Stanley added his voice, emphasising the danger of delaying amalgamation. Only Smuts, he felt, had halted the rise of anti-British sentiment in the south, and he was already seventy years old. The three northern territories, if consolidated, could '. . . well become a factor of great moment in high politics'.[4]

The degree of apparent success which the amalgamation movement was having brought the Anti-slavery Society back into the field. In March 1940 Eden and MacDonald met a deputation which included Harris, Wedgwood, Charles Roberts, Noel Buxton and Arthur Creech-Jones. On behalf of the society the latter expressed fears of an amalgamation taking place during the war and '... apprehension about the way in which native discrimination and the practice of the colour bar is percolating northward from South Africa'. In reply both MacDonald and Eden expressed confidence in the reasonableness of the Southern Rhodesian leadership—the former claiming that Huggins and Tredgold were becoming increasingly liberal, and Eden, 'speaking as a non-expert', putting forward the view that there was no ground for regarding the rulers of Southern Rhodesia as '... violently reactionary or anything approaching it'.[5]

While the Dominions and Colonial Offices wanted a further enquiry into 'native policies' in central Africa, it was felt that political conditions ruled out a formal enquiry, and the decision was taken to send Lord Hailey, who was already visiting east and west Africa to report upon colonial policies, to conduct a one-man enquiry in central Africa. Hailey found little difference in land policies between Northern and Southern Rhodesia, and indeed remarked that the south had made far greater progress towards the introduction of individual tenure for Africans. He commented that in the south there was a lack of faith in the traditional authorities, which had led to the creation of councils upon South African lines rather than the indirect rule of the north.[6] Yet, more realistically than most 'native experts', the central point which Hailey made concerned the problem of the industrial colour bar, discussion of which was in any case coming to the fore in official analyses of the difficulty of harmonising policy between north and south. The most important divergence in policy which Hailey could find, he wrote, was not in the extent of government provision for the betterment of the material and social conditions of Africans but in '... the limits which Southern Rhodesia imposes upon the employment of Africans in industry and in the administrative services, and which it would propose to apply to their association in the political institutions of the country'.[7] The primary aim of the politically dominant whites in an amalgamated State would, he felt, be to introduce the industrial colour bar to the north. This could lead both to trouble with African labour and, he warned, a feeling of anxiety on the part of capital, which might well prefer an area in which European labour was less influential. While he noted the existence of African opposition in both northern territories to closer association with the south, this, he thought, need not be a 'decisive consideration'.

The Bledisloe commission's report had recommended the amalgamation of the administrations of the two northern territories. In Whitehall the immediate reaction had been that this would involve an extensive reorganisation of the administrative services and would impede the implementation of Northern Rhodesia's new copper-financed development programme. And as it was thought that obstacles to the amalgamation of the northern territories with the south were 'not necessarily of an enduring character', such reorganisation should be deferred until the question of amalgamation with Southern Rhodesia had been resolved.[8] Hailey also felt that an amalgamation of Northern Rhodesia and Nyasaland would be comparatively simple, that it would reunite divided peoples and give a strengthened administration the opportunity to develop a united policy on the supply of labour. Yet it could not be brought about as long as fusion of the two Rhodesias was an open issue. Thus both Hailey and Bledisloe had favoured the juncture of Northern Rhodesia and Nyasaland, but practical consideration of this was thwarted by the demands made by the settlers in the two Rhodesias for amalgamation.

Hailey pointed to a crucial difference in the political forces behind the formulation of policy in Northern and Southern Rhodesia. In the north it was the British government which was dominant, though the Copperbelt whites were gaining in power; in the south it was a responsible legislature against which the British government could not initiate action. Yet though he felt that there was little likelihood of Southern Rhodesian policies being modified by views expressed in Britain, or brought into line with British practices in the north, he did not entirely dismiss association of the two Rhodesias. Considered historically, he wrote, differing views on 'native policy' had been a long-standing cause of difference between Britain and large sections of South African opinion, and, he continued,

The growing desire shown by many responsible figures in the Union for the extension of its influence in other parts of Africa is based on the conviction that South Africa must eventually be the champion of the cause of white civilisation in other territories, where it is deemed to be prejudiced by some aspects of the policy favoured by Great Britain in regard to native affairs . . .'

This alienation between Britain and African whites could, he thought, be avoided in the case of Southern Rhodesia, where the 'native question' was not quite so central to politics as it was in the Union and where he found a growing willingness to regard Africans as an integral part of the colony. 'Parallelism', he commented, though it might restrict the political role of Africans, could be the means of bringing about an improvement in the immediate well-being of the population in the reserves and in the welfare services provided in urban areas, and

'Whatever may be the political or social aspirations of Africans for the future, matters such as these must be of great immediate concern to them.' In the long run, Hailey forecast, relations between Southern Rhodesia and South Africa were more important than the amalgamation of the Rhodesias, and it was more likely that Southern Rhodesia would go south if offered a satisfactory arrangement. And he warned, 'The Native question divided South Africa and ourselves: we did not want it to be a cause of estrangement with Southern Rhodesia.' In January 1940 he advised that it might be possible to link the two Rhodesias, even retaining different native policies, 'by a piece of constitutional carpentry', a line of thought which had been taking hold in Whitehall as well. Thus while it was felt that 'native policies' might not be reconcilable between north and south, it was seen as preferable to link the two rather than force Southern Rhodesia into adopting a 'South African' option. Though it underestimated both the confidence of the Southern Rhodesian settlers and their dislike of Afrikanerdom, this type of thinking, especially if 'constitutional carpentry' that would allow local variations in policy were possible, was the most likely to move a reluctant British government more towards sympathy with settler aspirations for closer union between the Rhodesias.

2 Britain, South Africa and the war

British feelings about trends in the Union remained pessimistic even after Smuts had brought the country into the war. In March 1940 in a review of developments Clark pointed out that Britain had a closer concern with the course of internal affairs in the Union than with those of any other Dominion, because of the existence of the High Commission territories, the effect which the Union's policies had upon India and '... most of all ... with policies and developments which may effect the relations of British and Dutch' because of the implications these had for the growth of Afrikaner republicanism. The years since 1936, Clark noted, had been the time of the 'Decline and Fall of Fusion' during which there had been not only a hardening of opinion on the 'native question' but an increase in the pull of Afrikaner unity, which had been worsened by the Union's entry into the war. He remarked perceptively upon the close parallel between the end of fusion and the situation in the first few years of the Union—which had also seen the breakdown of political coalition and the polarisation of politics, worsened by the country's entrance into an 'imperial' war. Against the background of Afrikaner nationalist sympathy for Nazi Germany, which was in some circles ideological and in others based upon the hope that a British defeat would provide the opportunity for the declaration of a South African republic, Clark predicted correctly that those Afrikaners who had followed Hertzog into fusion would now be swallowed by Malan's 'purified' Nationalists. As opposed to this, he warned, the British element in the State was weak.[9] Republicanism, secession, civil war and 'the possibility of intervention by the UK' were all part of his scenario for the future. Typically, too, he pointed out the dependence on the gold mines, which afforded the country low internal taxation and high agricultural subsidies, and warned of the apparent fragility of this dependence. Apprehension about what would happen when the gold ran out continued to be a backdrop to analyses of the Union's future.

Both the apparent weakness of the base upon which the British connection with the Union rested, and Smuts's ambitions regarding post-war Africa, were factors in British official thinking upon the Rhodesian problem. In 1939, on the outbreak of the war, Smuts had announced the Union's obligations to stand by the British colonies from Kenya to the south 'like an elder brother on the African continent' and had proclaimed that 'our interests, many of our future markets, are situated there'. In April 1940 he put forward the view that the true destiny of the Union, even within its own borders, could only be realised by keeping a clear view 'of the larger African point of view'. The Union, he said, should be the leader of Pan-African development, and he envisaged a mutual relationship between Africa to the north as a raw materials supplier and the Union's industries as exporters.[10] Though the war reawakened in Smuts far-ranging desires and dreams for the rearrangement of the African continent, these did not necessarily involve the actual incorporation of the Rhodesias, or hostility to their amalgamation. According to Bledisloe, Smuts even felt that '... the contemplated Union of the Rhodesias had better be the first step'.[11] Nevertheless certain Afrikaner politicians remained apprehensive that Rhodesia might be joined to the Union under cover of the war: Pirow warned of the possible electoral effects, and J. G. Strijdom, later to be Union Prime Minister detected 'British-Jewish influence' which planned for Smuts '... to proclaim a republic which will absorb the Rhodesias and possibly other British territories. In this way they hope to suppress us Afrikaners.'[12]

By August 1941, as South African thinking on post-war Africa developed, Lord Cranborne observed that Smuts '... had certain very large ideas re Africa ... He might take amalgamation very hard.'[13] In September the new British High Commissioner in South Africa, Lord Harlech, formerly David Ormsby-Gore, reported on talks he had held with Smuts, Denys Reitz, the Minister for Native Affairs, and the new South African Permanent Secretary for External Affairs. Smuts had expressed the view that Northern Rhodesia would have a far greater future than Southern Rhodesia, that the white population of the Copperbelt would increase, and that both capital and white labour would be drawn from and closely associated with the Witwatersrand. South Africa, Smuts felt, was not an agricultural country, and its future lay in the development of its metallurgical and secondary industries. This, he predicted, would lead to the growth of white urbanisation after the war, which would bring about the death of South African racism and nationalism. After the war, he said, he planned a great programme of industrial expansion, '... and the market was not only South Africa but the whole of Africa south of the Sahara', wise planning for which was being 'held up by too many small, introspective colonial administrations'. Harlech reported also that Hofmeyr, the Deputy Prime Minister, regarded the amalgamation of the Rhodesias as '... altogether premature and even ultimately indeterminate'. The talks, Harlech concluded, '... re-emphasised my feeling that the Union leaders are determined to have their say and influence on the whole future of the greater part of Africa'.[14]

Lord Harlech's reports built upon Smuts's analysis and contained the germ of the new diagnosis of South African affairs which emerged during the war. It seemed clear to him that the gold would run out, and that because South African agriculture was uncompetitive, the country's future would be industrial. (The Union government itself was planning on the assumption that gold production would have shrunk to one seventh of the existing size in twenty-five years' time.) British South Africans supported industrial growth and hoped that it would populate the cities. Harlech wrote, 'If indeed South Africa is to remain part of the British Commonwealth and the present movement for secession defeated, if even existing British interests—financial and economic—are to be preserved it can only be by industrial development and increasing the voting strength of the cities and industrial towns'.[15] The interests of British manufacturers in the South African market would, he wrote, 'have to be buttressed from within rather than from without', and he urged that British firms should follow the American example (in particular of the motor industry) of establishing branch factories in the Union. He noted that the wartime withdrawal of competitors for the

African market had left them open to the Union and that '... under the aegis of the Prime Minister there is developing a distinctive South African neo-imperialism'. But in peacetime, he felt, South African industry would not be really competitive and might not capture the African markets. The Union's policy of industrial protection was, he pointed out, in effect a policy of the protection of civilised labour. But industrialists were growing impatient about the barriers against the use of African labour, and this could be regarded as a hopeful sign. Thus the industrialisation of the Union could be a 'powerful liberalising force'. Thus British political and industrial interests appeared to merge with the requirements of a liberal 'native policy'. Harlech looked forward to an industrial rather than a mining South Africa, where the lead was taken by British subsidiary factories; the cities were filled with English-speaking voters; and politics were influenced by liberal industrialists (echoes of Milner's ideas, with industry replacing the mines). The interests of the British connection, of British industry and of British liberalism would be served by British support for South Africa's post-war economic development.

But for the short term there was much pessimism. The South African war effort depended on Smuts alone. English-speaking South Africans were politically very weak. There was the danger of an Afrikaner insurrection, the police were unreliable, and Smuts relied on the 3rd Division of the Union Defence Force, which had been organised as an internal security force to deal with Afrikaner insurrection. This possibility was more of a present danger to Harlech than African insurrection.[16] In the face of the bitter internal divisions the Randlords sought to revive the conservative coalition which had saved them in the 1930s, and tried hard to persuade Smuts to offer a senior ministerial post to Hertzog's former Minister of Finance, the leader of the rump of his supporters, Havenga.[17] Of native policy, like Clarke, Harlech was highly critical, on conventional liberal lines.

Into this context Harlech fitted his ideas on post-war policy for the Rhodesias. Here too are the outlines which were to become policy after the war. First, the Rhodesian settlers emerge with a relatively favourable image. The African peoples were generally backward and their former rulers 'cruel, treacherous and bloodthirsty'. The whites on the other hand, were 'emphatically British and emphatically not Afrikaner'; they were 'essentially permanent colonists', not 'planters'. They were, he wrote, not to be blamed for Rhodes's doings, and it would be unfortunate if their good relations with Britain 'were severely strained' because of 'alleged errors' in 'native policy'. 'Above all,' he wrote, appearing to extend the interpretation of the powers given to the settlers in 1923, 'it must be remembered that in 1923 the governmental administration of the natives of Southern Rhodesia was in fact handed over by the Imperial Government to the European Rhodesians for better or worse.' He then went on to develop what was later to come to be a major justification for permitting the formation of a federation in central Africa. He had talked to Huggins, he wrote and the latter had remarked on the way people in England believed it possible to have a single 'native policy' for all Africa. Yet, Harlech wrote, there could never even be the same policy for Uganda and Kenya, and Southern Rhodesian Africans were not suited to the kinds of policy that had succeeded in, say, the Bechuanaland Protectorate. 'It is quite conceivable,' he concluded, that 'British Central Africa could be a governmental unit for certain purposes with quite a variety of different native policies . . .' Southern Rhodesia, it seemed, could thus be excused from the orthodoxies of 'indirect rule', and the problems of conflicting 'native policies' in a federation could be circumvented by offering all things to all men.

Harlech clearly expected that the multiplicity of separate administrations in Africa would be in some way reorganised after the war. He urged greater continuity in the formation of policy for Africa, and he urged upon Attlee an end to the constant change of Ministers in the Colonial Office and the appointment of someone with knowledge and interest. But here he had exposed the weakness of the policy-making structure: such Ministers did not exist, and Africa hardly interested British politicians. As Attlee wrote, in terms reminiscent of Milner's, 'It is not too easy, in present conditions, to get down to the major problems such as the future of Africa . . .'[18] Once again this future was to be affected and arranged for by those whose real concerns lay elsewhere.

Smuts's imperialism, with his long-term view of the development of the South African economy, was based upon an imperialist economic relationship with an Africa that would be dominated by the Union and did not require the formal absorption of territories which could remain formally under the British umbrella. But his were not the only eyes in the Union looking at the future. Afrikaner nationalist opposition to a larger Union was not based only upon the isolationist tradition expressed ever since the escape from 'liberalism' made by the Great Trek, but upon a twentieth-century attempt to escape from 'cosmopolitan capitalism'. During the 1920s and 1930s Afrikaner nationalism was based not only upon the hopes of the renascence of republican independence but upon the fears of the white poor and white working class, and had become an essentially National Socialist nationalism. Liberal capitalism, especially when dominated by a foreign country and by huge mining companies, posed to white workers the threat of being submerged as capital sought cheap labour. A larger 'imperial' South African State seemed to express these needs: it would be a State which would cease to devote itself, as the existing South African State did, to the interests of Afrikaner workers and farmers. Thus there were very real differences within South Africa as to what the nature of the South African State ought to be and for whose benefit its power and resources ought to be used. Smuts's aim, South African expansion within the framework of a British Commonwealth, which would increase South African political and economic influence, was quite incompatible with the compromise, bitterly fought out between Hertzog and Malan, which was embodied in the programme of the Nationalist Party in December 1939, which stated the party's conviction that for reasons of history, geography and national and State development 'Suid Afrika *as witmansland* net een bestemming het—'n vrye onafhanklike Republiek, afgeskei van die Britse Kroon en Ryk'.[19] Any other kind of South Africa would compromise the purpose of its existence as a white man's country.

Also, during the war, the old question of State-assisted migration from Britain to South Africa was raised. The British government had come round to the view that there was no longer a surplus population in the United Kingdom, but still considered that after the war 'British stock' ought to be an important source of an increase in the Dominions, which they expected (along with the Australian government) would want to increase their populations for defence and economic development reasons.[20] In south Africa possible large-scale immigration from Britain became a violent political issue. While Smuts took the view that the Union needed a considerable increase in its white population and planned to recruit immigrants from both Britain and Europe, the Nationalist leadership was violently opposed to the government's immigration plans. These were seen as an act of 'sabotage and violence' (the words are D. F. Malan's) against Afrikanerdom, and as part of a plot with imperial interests to destroy it, strengthen the British element in the Union, and provide a work force for decentralised British industry in pursuit of a plan to link the Commonwealth more closely to Britain.[21] The British government's attitude was that Smuts should be supported in his plans to attract skilled immigrants, but the impression should not be given publicly that Britain was pressing migrants on to South Africa.[22]

By 1944 South African aspirations began to take clearer shape.

During the war a good deal of consideration had been given in London and by the Dominions to the types of regional bodies that might be created after the war. In 1944 the British Cabinet considered the kind of regional organisation which might be created for Africa and the interest the Union would have in it. Smuts had suggested that the British colonial empire be reorganised into larger units, each with its own development council, upon which the Dominion most closely associated with the area would sit.[23] He also envisaged an international regional body for the whole continent. There was considerable British reluctance to fall in with his views. In the first place, Stanley, the Secretary of State for the Colonies, told the Cabinet, Britain could not allow the extension of '... the influence of South Africa into areas where that country is regarded with the deepest suspicion and dislike. The inhabitants of West Africa would resent very deeply an association which would appear to bring them under the predominant influence of the Union.'[24] On the question of a regional development council for the southern part of the continent, Stanley opposed the inclusion of east Africa on a body dominated by the Union, on the grounds that this would '... undoubtedly increase the Union's political and economic penetration and from our point of view is most undesirable'. In April 1944 Stanley told the Cabinet that there were 'strong objections' to Smuts's proposals but that there could be an advantage in a 'Regional Commission covering Southern and Central Africa (with the Union of South Africa as an outside power) to include Northern Rhodesia, Nyasaland, Portuguese East and West Africa and the Belgian Congo. The inclusion of these foreign territories in British areas would lessen the danger of Union domination on the Commission.' Both he and Cranborne were agreed that to combine east Africa and South Africa within the ambit of the same regional council would be extremely difficult, even though the omission of so large an area of the empire as east Africa could cause misunderstandings with the United States.[25] Thus willingness to rely upon the Union, both before the war and during its early years, had been replaced by an awareness, as gloomy reports from the south piled up, that the policies pursued in the south, and African reaction to them, could be a threat to the continued stability of British Africa. Furthermore, even Smuts's South Africa could well pursue economic aims not entirely compatible with those of Britain, and there was no guarantee that the Union would remain in United Party hands for very long. British South African leaders—the mining and industrial magnates—were, as Lord Swinton reported gloomily in 1944, 'fatalistic ... after Smuts the political deluge'.[26]

It was not only Afrikaners in South Africa who were unenthusiastic about the new war. When war had come the attitude of Africans in the Union had been very different to their reaction in 1914. Instead of a pledge of loyalty to the Crown, the cessation of political activity and fervent support for the empire's war effort, the African National Congress passed a resolution in December 1939 'That unless and until the Government grants the African full democratic and citizenship rights, the African National Congress is not prepared to advise the Africans to participate in the present war, in any capacity'. In 1941 the congress's president, Dr Xuma, noted that west, east and central Africans had all taken part in the campaigns in Africa which had defeated fascist Italy but that when blacks in South Africa had volunteered they had been restricted by the government to the role of manual labour, and he called again on the government for civil rights in return for African aid in the war effort. In 1943 the congress set out its claims in a pamphlet[27] subtitled 'the Atlantic Charter from the African point of view.' In it they made clear to the world as a whole their opposition to the Union's policies. The charter, they wrote, must be applied to South Africa if fascism was to be rooted out. The High Commission territories should not be transferred. Specifically they attacked Smuts's plans for a regional regrouping in Africa designed to extend South African influence, hoping '... that the mistakes of the past whereby African peoples and their lands were treated as pawns in the political game of European nations will not be repeated'. Once again it was made clear that African opinion inside the Union opposed the extension of its influence.

British advisors also remained pessimistic about the Union's 'native policy'. In 1942 Smuts had made a pronouncement that had been regarded hopefully in some circles as heralding a change in the Union's approach. Segregation, he said, had been a failure, and this had 'sadly disappointed' the country. 'Isolation has gone and segregation has fallen on evil days too.' The Union had to look at its policies from a continental and not a purely South African standpoint. Trusteeship was the basis of policy, and while there was a temptation to emphasise the domination of the trustee, responsibility should be emphasised instead.[28] But like so many things said during the 'liberalisation' of Southern Africa under the ideological impact of the second world war these words were little more than the temporary adoption of a new style of rhetoric which was to be abandoned when hostilities were over. The British High Commissioner in South Africa from mid-1944 onwards, Sir Evelyn Baring, was well aware of this, and he continued to be generally hostile to the trends in the Union's policies, distinguishing between them and those of Southern Rhodesia. Towards the end of the war he noted the bitterness among English-speaking South Africans at Britain's failure to support the Union's aspirations in Africa, and their feeling that nothing had been done to strengthen the hand of the Smuts government against the Nationalists. With regret Baring concluded that it would be difficult to reconcile a '. . . proper native policy with one of keeping (through the support largely of English-speaking South Africans) the white rulers of a country situated at a strategical key point of increasing importance within the orbit of the British Empire'. Even so, he thought, African interests (in the High Commission territories) should not be sacrificed by the British government in order to remain friendly with a United Party government in Pretoria.[29]

Baring's approach was consistently 'liberal' and not wholly characteristic of the thinking which went into British policy formation. He made a point of meeting the leaders of the South African National Congress, R. V. Selope-Thema and Dr Xuma, and reported favourably upon their representations of the opposition of Union Africans to the incorporation of the High Commission territories in the Union. He answered Harlech's plan, put forward during the war, for a partition of the Bechuanaland Protectorate handing part to Southern Rhodesia, part to the Union, and preserving a rump protectorate, with the objection that there was 'a moral argument' against handing Africans over to the Union. Hailey and Harlech had worried about how to avoid a break with whites in Africa, but Baring had an inkling of the future question, which was how far British interests could be served by keeping in with the whites and breaking with the blacks. Yet while he counselled against giving in to Union pressure on a matter like who should govern the High Commission territories he was not fundamentally hostile to Smuts's plans for extending the Union's economic influence. In 1945 Smuts told the South African House of Assembly that while the Union had no desire to swallow territories to the north it wished to enlarge groupings in Africa and to promote a conference system which could discuss matters of mutual interest, excluding the 'native question'.[30] Baring, while not entirely prepared to accept Smuts's disclaimer regarding territorial expansion, noted that the Union mining houses, always searching for a 'hedge' against gold, had invested heavily in Northern Rhodesia, while enquiries were being made about possibilities of investment in other colonial territories. A system of conferences for Africa, provided the Union did not acquire an 'economic stranglehold', could, Baring thought, well be promoted.

In mid-1945 Baring again warned of the Union's ambitions with regard to Rhodesia. Smuts had recently met Sir Harold Howitt, who had discussed with him the possibility of a Union government loan to Rhodesia for the purpose of buying Rhodesian Railways. Smuts had been receptive, and indicated also that he favoured the creation of a single political entity made up of the Union and both Rhodesias. Smuts's musings on this occasion are not to be taken too seriously in view of his open disavowal, in the House of Assembly in March 1945, of the ambition to absorb territory and his preference for a system of friendly conferences. What is of interest is Baring's strong reaction to what he called Smuts's 'sensational' remarks.[31] Though it had been widely agreed that after the war there should be increased co-operation with the British African States and possibly the formation of some kind of loose confederation, the Union government had been cautious in its approach and had not indicated that it was opposed to the amalgamation of the Rhodesias and Nyasaland. A loose confederation, Baring wrote, should be encouraged, but the formation of one entity with the Union 'we must clearly oppose . . .' There was a significant shift in what he saw as the real obstacle. Whereas twenty years before Buxton had been 'loth to drag in the natives', Baring warned of the political disadvantages of bringing the South African conception of race relations to central Africa and the bitterness it would cause. 'If the Union's aim is a single entity,' he wrote, 'the obstacle will be African opinion.' The Union's leaders had so far been prepared to wait for the voluntary adherence of the northern States. But 'the awakening political sense of Africans throughout Southern Africa' might render their goal unattainable. Baring wrote, 'what the Northern Rhodesian African feels—and to my mind rightly feels—about the amalgamation with Southern Rhodesia applies *mutatis mutandis* to the Africans of the three High Commission Territories and his ideas concerning the transfer of those territories to the Union.' But while the British government appreciated that both central Africans and the population of the High Commission territories had objections to being transferred to local white control, it was prepared to sacrifice the former to the requirements of counterpoise politics and to continue to protect the latter for the same reason, while claiming benisons for trusteeship.

3 Britain and closer union

It was against the background of the Union's aspirations and the development of Britain's attitudes towards them that the discussions regarding closer union of the Rhodesias took place during the war. In 1939, in the face of Huggins's pressure, a 'formula' had been arrived at in which the British government admitted the possible advantages of a link-up but expressed reservations with regard to differences in 'native policy'. Hailey's report, which was in essence equivocal, had followed. In October 1941 Cranborne and Moyne put forward a joint memorandum on the Rhodesias to the Prime Minister for decision. They were critical of Huggins's continued pressure, and denounced '... the increased violence of his declarations'. Referring to the doubts entertained both by Bledisloe and Hailey on 'native policy' differences, they warned that there could be much parliamentary opposition to closer union, not only inspired by the Aborigines Protection Society but also because of the opposition of British trade unions to the extension of the South African policy of the industrial colour bar. A further difficulty, they added, '... is the undesirability of raising during the war any question of territorial readjustment in Africa, which would afford an opportunity for the Union Government to raise similar questions in which they are interested'. They recommended that the decision should be postponed until after the end of the war, and Churchill agreed.[32]

A decision had been taken, yet the matter did not rest. In 1943 Baring reported on Southern Rhodesia in terms which picked up the more optimistic strands in Hailey's review. Though he had felt, the High Commissioner wrote, that segregation was as much a part of Southern Rhodesian policy as it was of South African, he had recently been much encouraged by evidence of a changing outlook on 'native affairs' in Southern Rhodesia.[33] In 1944 he again reported a 'tide of better feeling' in Southern Rhodesia regarding Africans, and, he stressed, there was also a growing strength of Rhodesian nationalism among young white Rhodesians which '... might possibly ... with good fortune, be used to help maintain Southern Rhodesia as a buffer State between the Union and Colonial Office territories'.[34] In April 1944 the British Cabinet considered its attitude towards closer union. After the war Huggins was thought to be going to ask for the creation of a State comprising the two Rhodesias and Nyasaland, governed by a single Cabinet and legislature, and with the same constitutional status as that enjoyed by Southern Rhodesia alone. The joint views of the Dominions and Colonial Offices were put before the Cabinet by Cranborne and Stanley. There were, they stated, 'serious objections' to Huggins's plans. African opinion in the two northern territories and elsewhere would oppose it, and so would a large section of opinion in the United Kingdom. Though during the war years the Northern Rhodesian administration had accepted the white miners' demands for a colour bar, which existed in practice on the Northern Rhodesian mines and railways, Cranborne and Stanley attacked the Southern Rhodesian Industrial Conciliation Act on the grounds that it in effect imposed a colour bar, which had '... no place in the African policy of His Majesty's Government in the United Kingdom'. A single white-dominated, amalgamated government, they thought would '... not subscribe to the general policy of His Majesty's Government in regard to the development of the native population of tropical Africa'. In addition to this they felt that it was doubtful whether the white population of the new territory would be large enough to enable it to develop into the powerful self-supporting British Dominion which the advocates of amalgamation claimed was their object. The new State might find itself in dificulties, and could either become dependent upon the United Kingdom or '... probably, it would gravitate into the Union of South Africa, which would thus be extended to the borders of Tanganyika'. On the other hand, they warned, if amalgamation was rejected, Southern Rhodesia '... might feel obliged to turn to the Union if they thought their approach to the North was definitely barred'. This should not be encouraged, as it would involve Southern Rhodesia in the white racial strife of the Union; retard the development of its secondary industries and the flow of immigration; possibly endanger African land tenure, and lose for the United Kingdom control over important sources of raw materials. Finally, they concluded,

The spread of Union influence northward would also greatly strengthen those forces in Northern Rhodesia and also Nyasaland and the East African territories which are opposed to His Majesty's Government's policy of political, economic and social advancement for the African population in partnership with the immigrant communities.

The conclusion was that an effort had to be made to prevent Southern Rhodesia from having to make a straight choice between amalgamation with the north and incorporation into the south. British policy should be '(1) to encourage the maintenance of Southern Rhodesia as a State independent of the Union and (2) while ruling out amalgamation at this stage, to foster closer connection between it and its two Northern neighbours.' A refusal to consider sympathetically any of the local aspirations towards closer union would, it was felt, lead to a breakdown of co-operation with the local settler communities. It was thus recognised that the existence of the settler communities placed a limitation on British policy choices and, just as in the early 1920s, that a disaffected settler community could be of no use to the furtherance of British aims. The problem was seen as being one of reconciling and satisfying the settlers without departing from the general aims of British African policy. It was clear, the memorandum stated, that a federation in the ordinary sense of the word was 'not a practicable proposition' in the case of territories in entirely different stages of constitutional development. Some advance in the status of Southern Rhodesia, such as full admission to Empire discussions, might be a way of mollifying its government,[35] but it was clear at least that '... a purely negative attitude would be difficult to maintain'. The Cabinet gave its approval to the proposal that the British government take the initiative and propose the creation of an advisory standing council for the three territories and the placing of the temporary inter-territorial secretariat on a permanent basis.[36] When this decision was communicated to Huggins he was 'disappointed' but not, it was remarked, unduly surprised or upset.

The stage had been set for the post-war slide into federation. The hoped-for modifications in Southern Rhodesia's 'native policy' did not appear. Instead, in the Rhodesian election campaign of 1946 Huggins proposed the barring of further African voters from the voters' roll and the nomination of two Europeans to represent Africans. The general feeling in the Dominions Office that Huggins's views were in advance of those of the electorate and that to thwart him would bring more conservative men to power was reinforced by a warning from the Governor of Rhodesia that Huggins's opponents would like to follow the line that Malan was proposing in the south. In Whitehall H. N. Tait of the Colonial Office minuted that Huggins had told him that if unchecked the African vote would control the country in twenty years. 'We cannot expect the Southern Rhodesian Government to contemplate such a position ... Some arrangement as in the Union for having specially appointed representatives of native interests in the Assembly is probably unavoidable.'[37] Once the very contemplation of the possibility of African political power was ruled out, Huggins's proposals did not seem to be out of line with Colonial Office thinking on the question of representation. Defence of the Rhodes franchise as a political mechanism in east and central Africa had passed into different hands; to a certain extent it had become a 'left wing' solution, advocated by those suspicious of the conservative motives they saw behind indirect rule.[38] The officials, on the other hand, felt that Huggins, by proposing separate representation, was holding out the eventual possibility of African representatives being chosen through the council machinery—which they compared to the practice of the administration in Nyasaland of establishing a chain of representation between Africans and government without the resort to a direct 'civilisation franchise'. Also attention was really focused elsewhere. Between 1946 and 1948 Huggins was unable to command an automatic majority in the Rhodesian Legislative Assembly, and the spectre of his displacement by a reactionary white labour- and rural-based coalition was easy to invoke. The victory of Malan's Nationalists in the Union election fulfilled the most gloomy of imperial predictions, while Huggins's decisive electoral victory soon after seemed to underline the need to support 'moderation' in Southern Rhodesia by further appeasement of settler ambitions.

Notes

1 Cmd. 5949, 1939, paras. 283, 404 ff and 443.
2 D.O. 35/825, R 8/219, 24 July 1939.
3 D.O. 35/825 R/24, Bledisloe to Eden, 1 December 1939; minutes on 27 November 1939; D.O. 35/825, R 8/248, Bledisloe to Eden, 26 January 1940.
4 D.O. 35/825, R 8/239, Stanley to Machtig, 10 July 1940.
5 D.O. 35/825, R 8/239, 14 March 1940.
6 D.O. 35/825, R. 8/271.
7 D.O. 35/825, R 8/281. The Southern Rhodesian industrial conciliation legislation created an effective colour bar by fixing minimum wage rates rather than by an actual legal barrier, as was the case in the Union's mining industry.
8 D.O. 35/825, R 8/239.
9 D.O. 114/99, No. 192, 15 March 1940.
10 J. Smuts, *Plans for a Better World*, London, 1942, pp. 240–1, and *id.*, 'Greater South Africa', pp. 243 ff.
11 D.O. 35/825, Bledisloe to Eden, 3 March 1940.
12 M. Roberts and A. Trollip, *The South African Opposition*, London, 1949, p. 41; see pp. 201 ff for the alleged plot by Smuts and Hertzog to turn South Africa into a republic within the empire.
13 D.O. 35/825, R 8/2/70, 13 August 1941.
14 D.O. 35/826, R 8/289, Harlech to Cranborne; B. K. Long, an editor of the *Cape Argus*, member of the House of Assembly and one of Smuts's long-standing associates, wrote in his diary on 26 January 1943, 'We are a small people, but we expect to have a rather important say in the future of the African continent.' (B. K. Long, *In Smuts' Camp*, London, 1945.)
15 D.O. 116/8, High Commission to Secretary of State, 26 June 1942.
16 D.O. 116/8, 12 August 1941 and 16 April 1943.
17 *Ibid.*, 18 May 1942 and 29 August 1942.
18 For the Harlech–Attlee correspondence see D.O. 35/1141, R 370/2, January 1943.
19 My italics: '. . . South Africa, as a *"white man's country"*, only has one destiny, a free, independent republic, separated from the British Crown and

Empire'. (Quoted by Roberts and Trollip, *Opposition*, p. 32.)
20 D.O. 35/3320, M 822/24.
21 Smuts planned to take 25,000 for 1947: 10,000 from the UK, 10,000 from northern and southern Europe and 5,000 displaced persons. See the extracts from the South African press in D.O. 35/1, 320 M 822/24, and D.O. 35/1135, M 822/349.
22 D.O. 35/1325, M 822/65, secret minute by C. W. Dixon, 15 June 1944.
23 Mansergh, *Problems,* pp. 174–6, comments that Smuts's plans envisaged a '... discharge of regional responsibilities by the Dominions on a scale not contemplated before 1939'. See also W. K. Hancock, *Smuts and the Shift of World Power*, London, 1964, who sees Smuts' plans as being part of a vision to strengthen the British into a third great power in the post-war world and by grouping overseas dependencies into units large enough to manage without the Colonial Office to 'iron out the schizophrenic distinction between Commonwealth and Empire'.
24 Cab. 66/49, 18 April 1944.
25 Cranbourne; Cab. 65/42, 27 April 1944.
26 Swinton; D.O. 35/1122, Swinton to Cranbourne, 18 March 1944.
27 See Karis and Carter, II, where 'African claims in South Africa' is reprinted; see also pp. 181 ff.
28 J. Smuts, *The Basis of Trusteeship in African Native Policy*, issued as New Africa pamphlet No. 2, January 1942.
29 D.O. 35/1172, Y 706/7, Baring to Secretary of State, 6 April 1945.
30 *Ibid.,* and D.O. 35/1172, Y 701/1/7, and D.O. 35/1119, G 581/57, Report of the Union's House of Assembly debates, 22 March 1945.
31 D.O. 35/1274, G 581/1116, secret, Baring to Machtig, 28 August 1945, and D.O. 35/1275, G 581/59, Baring to Secretary of State, 6 April 1945.
32 D.O. 35/826, R 8/288, 23 October 1941.
33 D.O. 35/1162, 209/17, Baring to Emrys-Evans, 28 September 1943.
34 D.O. 35/1162, R 216/20, Baring to Machtig, 21 October 1944.
35 Cab. 66/48, 6 April 1944.
36 Cab. 65/42, 27 July 1944.
37 D.O. 35/1162, R 216/8.
38 See, for example, Cab. 27/400, Memo, 1930, by W.B. (Secretary of State for India) on the East African franchise question, and cf. J. C. Wedgwood, who recorded his opposition to indirect rule, which he saw as the use of chiefs as oppressors, and his preference for direct rule by the colonial service until it was possible '... to start some political franchise, however limited, for Europeans, for Indians, and for Africans on a common electoral role'. (*Memoirs of a Fighting Life*, London, 1941, p. 183.)

ARGUMENT

The South African War had been fought to preserve British supremacy in southern Africa, and maintaining what could be saved of that supremacy was Britain's overriding interest in southern Africa in the years that followed. It was this interest which dominated British policies towards the territories that bordered on South Africa. The controversies which were generated by the long natal process and rapid and spectacular demise of the Central African Federation have tended to distort the historical focus with regard to the Rhodesias. For the calculations of all parties regarding the Rhodesias have since 1900 fundamentally been calculations about South Africa. The new Dominion which was created in the south in 1910 was forged out of a major war and a highly contentious process of conciliation. As a result, two conflicting political heritages governed British attitudes to the post-war settlement. That of the Conservatives derived from Chamberlain and Milner and looked to the consolidation of British military victory, a strengthening of the British element in the new State (if necessary by the use of Rhodes's counterpoise) and the subsequent curbing of Afrikaner political power in southern Africa. The Liberal solution was based upon Afrikaner conciliation, the hope that the loyal co-operation of defeated Afrikanerdom could be secured by the extension of self-government and the harmonisation of British and Afrikaner interests. The Liberal election victory in 1905 marked the end of the ascendancy of the Milner regime and the close political alliance of the British government with British South African mining interests. The subsequent Liberal attempt to rest British influence upon a reconciled Afrikaner leadership raised bitter political controversy which continued to influence attitudes and policies well after the formation of the Union in 1910.

The English–Afrikaner division, though its importance should not be underestimated, was not the only line of division in white South African politics. To put matters simply, there grew up among Afrikaners in the post-war years a divergence of interests between an increasing class of 'poor whites' and those who were taking the opportunities to do well out of the peace. English-speaking South Africa was rather more self-consciously divided between capital and labour, and while labour rallied readily to imperial symbolism in time of war it otherwise became increasingly alienated. The logic of white South African politics in the first decade after Union lay in the development of class alliances which overrode national ones, until, in 1924, the Botha–Smuts section of the

Afrikaner leadership, now merged with the Randlord party, confronted, and was defeated by, a coalition of Afrikaner nationalism and English-speaking labour. In this situation the 'liberal solution' was soon undermined. The first years of Union seemed to have vindicated it: Botha and Smuts crushed the revolts of white labour against the mine owners on the Rand; took the Union actively into the war in 1914; and defeated a nationalist Afrikaner rebellion. Yet the Union government began to lose Afrikaner support, which meant that British influence depended upon the continuance in power of a government regarded by a growing number of Afrikaners as renegade and British-dominated.

Into this context must be fitted the Union's expected take-over of the Rhodesias. In the Milner period after 1902 Company and Kindergarten circles looked forward to the addition of Rhodesia to a British-dominated federation. This ambition aroused no little suspicion among men like Steyn and Merriman that the company was looking forward to palming off an unprofitable investment at huge expense to the South African public. But after 1905 the intense bitterness of Company circles against the 'liberal solution', and the company's adoption of an energetic campaign of development in Rhodesia, made them, by the time the Union was being formed, determined to hold Rhodesia as a last stronghold of British South Africa. Later, once Botha and Smuts had proved their imperialist credentials, Rhodesia became the necessary addition of English-speaking support to help replace the waning Afrikaner base of the Union government. The policy of Rhodes and Milner which had looked to Rhodesia as a counterweight to Afrikaner ascendancy had gradually merged with, and became a precondition for the success of, the Liberals' attempt to maintain in power a pliant Afrikaner leadership.

Before 1914, when the company's charter was due for review, the Liberal government began to prepare itself for eventualities by trying to sort out the company's claim to own the public land of Southern Rhodesia, and by making provision, against the background of the Union's 1913 land Act, for what it regarded as sufficient African lands, to prepare for the expected joinder with the south. The outbreak of war interrupted developments, but the years 1914 to 1918 weakened Company and English South African opposition to Rhodesian incorporation in the Union. Before the war the company's interests were seen as lying in the long-term commercial exploitation of the Rhodesian lands of which it claimed to be owner. Its defeat in the land case, and the increase of influence on the board of men who were more wholly commercially motivated and less under the sway of the

Rhodes–Jameson tradition of English South African politics, changed the direction of Company policy. Conveniently Botha and Smuts were now the idols of imperialist circles in both Britain and South Africa, and the political case for handing the company's responsibilities over to the Union was strong. Furthermore only from the Union government could the company hope to receive the level of capital compensation it sought for its assets. In the Union the war years deepened the division between Botha and Smuts and Hertzog's rapidly rising Nationalist Party, which persistently portrayed the Union government as the tool of British capitalism and imperialism. As the overtly republican challenge to the settlement of 1910 was sharpened so the British government firmed to the use of Rhodesia to strengthen imperialist forces inside the Union. But at the same time the aversion of the Southern Rhodesian settlers to the Union's politics increased.

Beyond these calculations about electoral power in South Africa there were seriously differing conceptions as to what power in the new Dominion should be used for. One matter at issue was the way in which white power over Africans was to be exercised. Among British hopes was that a moderate Afrikaner leadership, with the support of a united South African public opinion, would somehow provide a fair and just 'solution' to the 'native problem'. The difficulties of exercising imperial influence in this regard were familiar to British policy makers: too close an identification of the imperial factor with African interests could only be damaging to British influence throughout white southern Africa. The British government stood for some well-meaning principles, and it believed itself to have considerable 'influence' in southern Africa. Yet it also operated on the belief that any attempt to exercise 'influence' in *this* sphere would create an atmosphere of hostility in which 'influence' would no longer be there. Yet 'influence' apart, the British government did have levers of persuasion. It controlled the High Commission territories and the country to the north of the Union, South African aspirations to which had been conditionally acknowledged.

Imperial commitment to the Cape *evolué* policy was limited: in southern and central Africa as a whole the British government sought to promote a pattern of territorial segregation and institutional separation the principles of which had been laid down in the schedule to the Act of Union and to which it hoped Union policy would eventually approximate. In the High Commission territories, where African lands had been guaranteed in the schedule, the British authorities placed their emphasis on securing administrative separation combined with the functioning of some form of African assembly. In Rhodesia, where the immediate problem was to render African land holding secure, the major imperial intervention was to ensure that the reserves policy would not dissolve into theory before the Union took over. Where there were white settlers it was imagined that 'native questions' could best be dealt with by experts free from electoral pressure. Where old African institutions had been destroyed, territorial and administrative separation was to be combined with the creation of separate local councils. The Cape Policy was dead, and while the British government insisted where it could that its memory be honoured by preserving the traces it did not aim at promoting political integration in any part of southern Africa. The Union, it was hoped, would fit in with the British-conceived pattern, which offered no danger to white power and placed few obstacles in the way of the flow of African labour. In the early years of the Union the Liberal High Commissioners, Gladstone and Buxton, all too eager to believe that their party's trust in Afrikaner power had been justifiable, readily accepted anything offered by Botha and Smuts that looked as if the Union were going to adopt a reasonable 'native policy'. Not until Hertzog was in power did sour realism become uppermost in the official view of South African policies. Moral disapproval became the dominant note after 1924, even though there were those at times who failed to find any great differences between British and South African policies in southern Africa. And without reducing the element of moral concern one must add other considerations. There was some advantage to Britain in appearing to African opinion as the defender of African rights. African loyalty to the empire, in preference to local white dominion, had often been manifest, and the habit of looking to Britain for deliverance died hard and slowly. While it was not top of the list of priorities, no British government would without good reason wish to change the attitude embodied in the affirmation 'We Basutos are black Englishmen and not Boers'. As Bede Clifford wrote in 1926, Africans were '. . . one of our biggest allies in the country'.[1] In addition the early fears of an African rising combining tribalism and Ethiopianism, and later anxieties about the effects of urbanisation and economic pressures upon African acceptance of white rule, were a vital part of the background to the formation of policies, and fears of the possible cataclysmic effects of the Union's policies were also an ingredient of British disapprobation.

The development of a 'native policy' for the Rhodesias took place at first entirely within this southern context. Not until the inter-war years was it related to the secondary context of east Africa, and Africa as a whole. By then the new orthodoxies of African policy—'trusteeship' and 'indirect rule'—were of use only as moral measurements as regards Southern Rhodesia and only of marginal practical influence in Northern Rhodesia. It is hard to see trusteeship as a guiding influence before this time.[2] In 1922 the British government was prepared to hand over Rhodesia to guardians of proven improbity, and when this failed were content to repeat the policy of creating a settler State which it by now knew to have failed in 1910, and earlier. The trust in the 1923 letters patent was exercised more seriously on behalf of the British South Africa Company than on behalf of the Africans. Though the policy of African paramountcy eventually predominated in most of British Africa, in 1923 it was the Devonshire declaration and not the letters patent that was anomalous, and during the 1920s and 1930s the southward forays of the trustees continued to be broken on the lines of white settlement. While during the inter-war period there was an opening gap between Britain's perceptions of her own and South Africa's policies, the gap between Southern Rhodesia's and those of the territories to the north was seen to be closing. Instead of a white man's Africa which ended at the Zambesi, the basic notion developed of an area that crossed the Zambesi in which settlers were to be co-trustees. By 1951 even the minor differences which Hailey had found between the 'native policies' of Southern and Northern Rhodesia were being ironed out in the official mind. As the 1950 White Paper put it, the '. . . most striking conclusion . . . is the degree of similarity between the policy and practice' of the Southern Rhodesian, Northern Rhodesian and Nyasaland governments. Differences related largely to 'methods and timing' but the ultimate objective was the same, namely '. . . the economic, social and political advancement of Africans in partnership with Europeans.'[3] Ultimately too one cannot wholly separate the central policy of using British territories as a counterpoise in South African affairs and the marginal concern of trusteeship. As early as 1927 Amery linked these together when he observed that the '. . . future position of the Empire in South Africa is going to depend largely on the Protectorates and Rhodesia, both as regards native development, and on a smaller scale as regards British white developments'. Britain could, as he put it, '. . . give a lead to the whole of South Africa as well as help to keep the British uppermost'.[4]

The most notable feature of British plans for the Rhodesias is that they were never realised. In 1922 the settlers upset British calculations by refusing to be the internal counterpoise: in the 1950s settler intransigence and African power combined to make the external counterpoise unviable; and in the 1960s the settler Frankenstein monster created to serve imperial interests turned upon them. Yet from this one should not conclude that British designs were peripheral to the mainstream of south and central African history and that the only 'real' forces were local ones. If the twentieth-century 'imperial factor' is seen as a small chiding voice in Whitehall urging a more moral 'native policy' upon white southern Africa, then clearly it was of little account, though metropolitan disapproval can be damaging to the colonial psyche. But the influence of Britain on South Africa was more than this, and was not only external but part of South African internal politics. The Chartered Company, the Randlords, English South Africans and the Rhodesian settlers were all part of the 'imperial factor', politically speaking, and seen as forces which could help maximise British influence. Furthermore, before 1945, Britain was the guarantor of the small white State which controlled the world's largest goldfields, and this was realised by successive South African governments. Little attempt has been made in this account to describe Rhodesian settler interests or to recount the tale of settler politics: attention has been focused instead on the circumstances which led to so small a community being allowed to exercise so much control over its own destiny and those of others. The crucial question seems to be not why they made certain decisions but why they were allowed to make them. The answer in the first place is that the white Rhodesian community was a small but important part of the white South African political community. There was constant awareness, for example, of the dangers of Britain appearing to foster the African cause in the Rhodesias, less for fear of Rhodesian settler reaction than because of the damage it would do to British popularity among white South Africans as a whole. More important than this was the white Rhodesians' role as the imperial constituency. The small white community in Rhodesia after the first world war could clearly have been coerced into union, and even if a choice were to be offered the consequences of the wrong choice could have been made financially unacceptable. Yet the price to be paid for this would have nullified the purpose of Rhodesia's joining the Union. There could be, after all, no point in a Trojan horse filled with disaffected Greeks. It was part of the British experience that English South Africans did not lend themselves unconditionally to imperial purposes. If their aspirations had been sacrificed in the interests of a deal made to suit the British government, Smuts and the company, the Rhodesian settlers could well have taken seriously the anti-capitalist rhetoric in which much of their politicking was conducted and added their weight to the English-speaking labour elements in the Union which, in alliance with Hertzog, were soon to destroy the 'liberal solution'.

In Britain the convention that the finances of the Chartered Company were a matter outside politics had been preserved since 1897, when both Liberal and Conservative leaders resisted attempts to have them investigated by the Raid committee.[5] The Colonial Office peered fitfully at the company's finances through a miasma of suspicious ignorance, but officials did not consult the financial press, and their knowledge of the company's conduct of its primary function, that of maximising its profits for its shareholders, was minimal. The British government protected the company from the radical onslaughts on the legitimacy of its operations, and in Whitehall and Westminster there was a fundamental acceptance of the company's claims to have rendered an imperial service and to be entitled to profit from it. In the end it was the acuteness of the financial crisis rather than political reservations that inhibited the government from treating the company more generously.

The fact that the company was not spectacularly profitable has often been remarked upon as if this cast a more virtuous light upon its motivations. But its failure was certainly not for want of trying. Much investigation of the 'official mind' has been undertaken to illustrate the motives of imperialism, but the company had a 'mind' too, the operations of which were all too apparent to central Africans both black and white, whose world continued to be shaped and affected by the company long after 1924, and who were quite willing to drag its financial affairs into the political limelight. The British government's shield was of avail to the company in 1897, again at the time of the Cave commission, again between 1922 and 1924, when its rights were entrenched in the Southern and Northern Rhodesian settlements, and again during the 1930s when the Northern Rhodesian government showed signs of challenging Chartered's rights to mineral royalties. After the second world war a Labour government in London lowered the shield slightly and made it necessary for the company to come to terms with settler pressure for a share of its mineral royalties. Finally, in 1964, British willingness to offer protection was of no avail against African insistence on the elimination of the company's special position.[6]

For its part the company was consistently wary of the possibility of settler anti-capitalism, and this led it to co-operate with the venture of Southern Rhodesian responsible government, which it had earlier opposed (it found itself in a similar position twenty years later over federation), while on occasion it sought to protect itself by the implication that an attack on its interests could lead to the turning off of company investment and the reduction of the confidence of 'City' capitalists in general. This concern mirrored that of mining interests as a whole in southern Africa about the possibility that white economic radicalism could gain the upper hand and change the economic order by claiming that a larger share of the rewards of mineral exploitation should be directed to local uses. And though the Rhodesian settlers did not inspire really serious fears in this regard, the situation on the Rand, where a strike before the war had led to an extravagant government reaction against alleged syndicalists and where, after the war, organised white workers were increasing their power, was of crucial concern. Sir Lewis Michell, a South African member of the company's board, expressed the fears of the circles in which he moved when he warned Lyttelton Gell that 'Bolshevism is rampant on the Rand . . .' and that 'there is a collective madness about Labourites which will not be cured without bloodletting'.[7] In Southern Rhodesia, however, it was Company circles that were able to a large extent to set the social and political tone. Only in Northern Rhodesia did a serious challenge to the company's rights materialise, and there the white labour movement, as in the Union, was mollified by the concession of a colour bar. In general, settler politics were of quite a different character, for white Rhodesia was in a real sense a reactionary community: owing its existence to a reaction against the growth of Afrikaner power, it developed its political identity in a reaction against both British Liberalism and Afrikaner nationalism between 1910 and 1923. By the 1930s the gap between the Rhodesian settlers and the metropolitan world had widened, and this culminated in the post-war reaction to socialism, the modern world and decolonisation. These attitudes were generally shared by English South Africans. It was as early as 1922 that J. Molteno, a former Speaker of both the Union and Cape parliaments, wrote that he was '. . . convinced that just as the Dominions are on the upgrade so the people in Great Britain are on the down . . . the character of the British islands is changing . . . there seems to be a want of purpose and no destiny. There is no leadership, no statesmanship . . . and the only bright spot is the monarchy.'[8]

While British and British South African capitalists looked askance at the threat posed by white labour in southern Africa they were also uneasy about the political consequences of the so-called poor white problem. Their fear of a Nationalist government in South Africa not only arose from the fact that from the imperial point of view the overtly anti-imperial politics of Hertzog's Nationalists contributed to disintegrative forces within the empire (and, it was felt in Whitehall, set a bad example to the Irish) but also contained the anticipation that the solution of the poor white problem would involve an attack on established economic interests. If one viewed the poor white problem as arising out of land shortage there were two avenues of approach to a solution: either find more or take measures towards some redistribution of what there already was. Expansion was therefore the most conservative of answers, as it was a way to alleviate white distress without disturbing arrangements within the Union. Nationalist politicians, who had a far closer contact with poor white problems, also had a better appreciation of what was involved in the process of white social dislocation in the post-war period. Nationalist politics was interested in greater access to land, in white settlement schemes and the extension of easier State credit for farmers. Yet this was not all: the drift to the towns and the existence of white poverty within them also needed a political answer, and the clearest target was the concentration of wealth controlled by 'English' interests. Thus the prospect of Nationalist power in South Africa contained not only the threat of republicanism but also that of an offensive to change the functioning of capitalism in South Africa. Long before the formation of the Pact in 1922 there had been a good deal of conscious common ground between Labour and Nationalist elements in the Transvaal, though their flirtations had been interrupted by the claims of rival Nationalist loyalties during the first world war. The events of 1922 alerted British South Africa to the possible consequences in the field of economic policy of an alliance between the two parties. More seemed to be in the offing than just an attack on the employment policies of the mine owners: the Labour Party was asking for socialism, and the Nationalists were developing an attack upon British imperialism in South Africa which seemed to embrace an attack on the 'system' as one designed to exploit South Africa for the benefit of British interests. All the Latin American countries, wrote A. H. Moll in 1920, got more from their natural resources by means of nationalisation and taxation of exports than did South Africa. South African resources were being siphoned off to rescue England's waning credit. The country was, in short, being economically exploited by Britain.[9]

Yet the apprehended economic revolution never came. Hertzog, like other nationalist leaders, appeared dogmatic and irrational to British observers (and historians) and heroic to his followers. In fact, like other nationalist leaders, he dealt as much in continuities as in contrasts, particularly in his 'native' and 'imperial' policies. Though the Pact government legislated to protect the position of white labour against African competition, this was the limit, in spite of all its rhetoric, of its attack upon capitalist interests. The nationalisation of the mines, or at least a radical reorganisation of mining taxation; the prospect of a State banking system and a vast liberalisation of credit which had so alarmed the British-controlled banking interests in South Africa, both of which had been on the horizons of Labour and radical Nationalist politicians, failed to materialise. Labour, though it got its colour bar, became disillusioned, while radical Nationalists turned their political energies towards ensuring the Afrikaner character of the white trade unions and into the co-operative building of Afrikaner capitalism. General Hertzog and his Finance Minister, Havenga, pursued steady conservative economic policies with a tempered economic nationalism, and British and British South African capitalism, its wings only slightly clipped, settled down to live harmoniously with Nationalist political power. By the end of the 1920s the Nationalists had achieved a redefinition of South Africa's political status within the empire and a legislative form of protection for 'poor whites'; Hertzog in power had proved far less dangerous than expected. And then in the 1930s the economic transformation that followed the gold-mining boom secured the basis of the compromise between Anglo-South African and Afrikaner interests.

Yet within South Africa relations between English South Africans and Afrikaners remained bad, and this contributed to the survival of a jaundiced British view of the Hertzog governments. At first suspicion was particularly marked in the field of 'native policy'. Early apprehensions of what Hertzog's 'segregation' might mean were shared both by those who feared for African interests and by those who worried about the economic effects of the suggestions of its more extreme proponents. Yet soon it appeared not to be so much of a departure: true, Hertzog was determined to attack the Cape franchise, but then he came up with the offer of land, which the Botha–Smuts governments had not done, and a further development of the council system. From the British point of view two schools of opinion on South African policies began to evolve. For those with a close knowledge of South African and colonial affairs the more acute nature of the oppression in the Union was obvious, but for non-specialists who took the broader view there were clear and even encouraging similarities between South African and British policies in Africa, and this absolved the former from suspicion. Thus the Nationalist threat petered out on the humanitarian as well as the political and economic fronts, and especially once Smuts was in coalition with Hertzog the South African danger seemed to have gone.

In colonial Africa the inter-war years were for Britain a curious period of leisurely planning, and it was generally assumed that a major reorganisation of the colonies to the north of the Union would take place. Plans for the East African Federation (which would have had the advantage of enmeshing the mandated territory of Tanganyika more firmly in the imperial net) absorbed much of the attention of those concerned with African affairs, and expectations were that such a federation would include Nyasaland and at least a part of Northern Rhodesia. In central Africa there were two forces running opposed to this: there were those who were still playing counterpoise politics with the Union and those whose concern was to arrest any southward advance of the pernicious doctrine of African paramountcy which had been forced upon the Kenyan settlers. These two coalesced into a policy for the settlers of central Africa: a union of the two Rhodesias, especially once it appeared that the north had valuable copper deposits, would enable them to establish a viable British counterweight and at the same time create a settler State immune from African paramountcy. Before the second world war these ambitions did not advance very far. There was British hesitation about turning over both Copperbelt and Africans to settler control, but the vital point was that as anxiety about South Africa receded, and while anxiety about African political pressure had hardly appeared, Britain had no interest in creating a settler counterpoise. Not until the outbreak of war again polarised political forces in the Union did closer union of the Rhodesias become a serious prospect. When Botha and Smuts had taken the Union into the war in 1914 the British response, in spite of the outbreak of rebellion in the Union, had been gratitude and optimism, and policy afterwards aimed at strengthening the 'loyal' forces still further. But when Smuts took South Africa into war a second time the serious internal divisions in the Union produced a different British response. Though Smuts continued to expect an accretion in the Union's power in Africa, the attitude of the British was pessimistic. This time round, in the light of their new prognostications about South African politics, they aimed at strengthening the loyal forces outside.

Even before the Nationalist victory in the South African elections in 1948 the British government, looking southward, was moving towards agreeing to a partial satisfaction of the Rhodesian settlers' aims. After 1948 the matter became more urgent. The choice was seen, as James Griffiths, Labour's new Secretary of State for the Colonies, put it, between central Africa being a country '. . . maintaining our traditions and principles' or one in which '. . . other principles and other traditions might prevail. These are the traditions and ideas which come from the Union of South Africa.'[10] This apprehension was assiduously and successfully fed from Rhodesia, and became, when the Central African Federation was under fire for its obstruction of African liberation, one of the justications for its formation. As Lord Chandos, the Conservative Secretary of State, wrote, there was a deep penetration of Afrikaner elements into both Southern and Northern Rhodesia, and 'It was calculated that Afrikaners would certainly hold political power within a decade . . . [federation] had the effect of immediately diluting Afrikaner influence.'[11] A federation would also, it was expected by men as well informed as Lord Hailey, influence the development of Southern Rhodesian 'native policies' in a liberal direction.[12]

By the 1950s Afrikaner nationalism had a rival for the part of bogey man. The possibility of African political power now had to be taken into account. The fear of African revolution was not an entirely new ingredient in Britain's African policies, and had long been a part of her disapproval of South Africa, where oppression in the relatively advanced (for southern Africa) conditions of industrialisation was felt to be producing the ultimate threat to the entire structure—the 'Bolshevik native'. (Clements Kadalie wrote, 'Our destination was the ICU of Africa . . . Is it not a wonder that the exploiters of African labour saw the writing on the wall when they witnessed this new evolution of once downtrodden people on the march?'[13]) But by the 1950s British policy was coping with a more immediate threat and was looking for ways to accommodate and influence the development of African nationalism within her colonial empire. In the 1950s it was by no means clear how far and how quickly the white man would have to relinquish control of east and central Africa. Central African partnership seemed to promise useful compromise. In Chandos's words, '. . . Mau Mau terrorism and Malan's *apartheid* were the disastrous extremes to which any country might drift.'[14] Harold Macmillan, as Prime Minister, put federation in a northward context; he told Walter Monckton, whom he sent to investigate it, 'If we fail in Central Africa to devise something like a workable multi-racial State, then Kenya will go too . . . [and Africa will become] . . . a maelstrom of trouble into which all of us will be sucked.'[15] Lord Alport, the British High Commissioner in Salisbury, summarised her position. 'Success in Central Africa,' he wrote, 'would have a profound effect on the politics of the whole continent. It would help curb the excesses of both black man and white man.' A dissolution of the Federation, he predicted, would eliminate British influence in Africa south of the Sahara, would lead to a polarisation of African and European racialists and could cost Britain economic and strategic advantages. 'My mind went back to Milner,' recorded Alport, that misunderstood pro-consul, who had forecast the consequences for both black and white in South Africa of the premature withdrawal embarked upon in the interests of a liberal policy.[16] Thus federation was in a sense an anachronistic echo of the old Cape policy—an alliance of the British settler and the African *evolué* against the Afrikaner which would satisfy imperial predominance, the moral requirements of a liberal 'native policy', and provide the safety valve without which dangerous consequences might be expected from an oppressed African population.

Like the British government, the Nationalist government of South Africa had to formulate policies for the end of empire in Africa. South Africa found itself after 1945 in a position of unexpected isolation and exposure: 'dazed and amazed', as Smuts wrote, by the United Nations' refusal to sanction the incorporation of South West Africa and the international assault on the issue of internal policy towards Asians. In place of Smuts's mixture of ambition and political myopia the Nationalists soon developed a gloomy apprehension about the nature of the post-war world, an attitude well expressed by Eric Louw, the Union's Minister for External Affairs, when he lamented that '... one by one the lights of European colonial rule in Africa are going out.'[17] There was far more of regret and misgivings than perception of an opportunity to dominate. Afrikanerdom was on the defensive, even though the long-abominated imperial factor was on the retreat. In essence the policy it followed was like that of pre-war governments—the search for a protective shield: if the colonial empire would no longer serve, perhaps the Commonwealth would, and if not, South Africa could hide behind a general anti-Communist Cold War defensive alliance. While Smuts, as late as 1945, had been prepared to include the British settlers in the north within the same polity as the Union—as he put it, '... to knit together the parts of Southern Africa which belong to each other'[18]—the Nationalists after 1948, like Hertzog before, were more inclined towards an alliance of common interests, and in the 1950s welcomed the building of federation in spite of the obvious elements of anti-Afrikaner motivation and the implied condemnation of *apartheid*. During the 1950s the white communities in southern Africa were further apart than ever and there was no substance in the spectre of an expansionist Afrikanerdom which had been raised in Salisbury and in London. In the Union the Nationalist government, bent on the eradication of British influences and the banishing of blacks from the South African polity, showed little interest in Rhodesia. There the settlers were busy making the best of the brave new world of federation and felt aloofly superior about the lurid goings-on to the south. Yet the Federation and the Union both wished to stop the southward advance of African power, and thus while the Federation existed it served South Africa's purposes despite having been created partly with the intention of frustrating them. The disintegration of the federal shield posed new problems for South Africa, for its existence had made possible the pursuance of a relatively isolationist policy on the African continent. Once it was gone, the new South African republic began to create its own shield, a fortress State, and tentatively to seek political accommodation with black States. This latter policy was a continuation of that of the previous Nationalist governments of Hertzog, Malan and Strijdom, which had all sought to consolidate the external shield and had had few qualms about co-operating with British imperialism in its role as an authority on the African continent, however hostile they were to its power internally. It represented also the continuing flexibility of Afrikaner responses and the attempt to render South Africa respectable by marrying the old policy of segregation to the devices of decolonisation and showing willingness to behave as an ex-colonial power should.

Britain was less able to respond to the end of federation, which left Southern Rhodesia on its hands, because it had never really had a policy *for Rhodesia*. The supervision of the territory by the Colonial Office had been remote and irresponsible in the sense that officials were in no way accountable to the people whose lives they made decisions about. Officials scored points off the company's administration in confidential minutes but rarely acted, though there is little doubt that the existence of Whitehall supervision restrained the company. With a settler administration in Salisbury, the practice of uninvolved criticism (now slightly more sympathetic) continued. Where there was more than comment on what went on in Rhodesia it was aimed at promoting the country's association with surrounding territories. Before 1923 British policy had attempted to structure Rhodesia with a view to its entry into the Union; afterwards, where it had aimed at change, it had tried to make Southern Rhodesia's institutions compatible with association with her northern neighbours. Once both the internal and external counterpoise policies had collapsed there was no British policy for Southern Rhodesia itself because there never had been one. Coming to grips with settler power had not been on the British agenda because settler power had, from Whitehall's point of view, been seen as a plus factor in southern African politics.[19] By the 1960s this was out of date, since settler power was not only a negative factor in African politics, it even strengthened those forces in South Africa it had always been supposed to counter. The Rhodesian settlers could no longer be used to protect British 'influence' and interests in the south, and British power over Rhodesia had therefore become largely irrelevant, though there was anxiety lest toleration of the settler regime should damage British relations with black Africa or that a deteriorating situation should touch off a conflagration in South Africa in which British interests would suffer.

African political organisations in southern Africa had initially looked to the imperial factor for salvation from white oppression. Though during the first years of union and after the Great War they made known their hostility to any extension of the Union government's sphere of power, they were not anti-British. Yet within the Union the perception that British imperialism was also an enemy grew between the wars, especially as socialist influences made themselves felt among black leadership. The development of Pan-Africanist sentiment and the influence of Garveyism, with its emphasis on Africa for the Africans, also contributed to the growth of anti-imperialism.[20] By the time of the second world war the fervent loyalty to King and Empire which had been manifested in 1914 was changing into a feeling that this time the Union and British governments should live up to their expressions of idealism. With the war over, African organisations within the Union continued to address appeals to and to seek contact with the outside world, but it was to the United Nations that they appealed, and African politicians rather than British socialists and liberals with whom they sought contact. African political movements in the rest of southern Africa followed suit more slowly. Loyalty to the Crown remained the dominant form of external political expression until after the second world war. Tactically there was far more point in appealing for imperial protection in territories which were under British rule and in which the Crown stood between Africans and domination by either the Union or Rhodesian settlers. Yet the influence of the war years soon became apparent. With the war over, as Ndabaningi Sithole wrote, 'It was no longer "Down with Hitler"; it was "Down with British colonialism and imperialism".'[21] Furthermore the imposition of federation upon the Rhodesias and Nyasaland shook the faith which conservative African leadership had in Britain. The last of the constituencies upon which British influence rested waned away. By the time the Central African Federation collapsed English-speaking white South Africa in the republic and Rhodesia had been alienated from Britain, as had African nationalism. It was Afrikaner Nationalist government, offering stability in return for protection, that was left most favourably disposed to the 'imperial factor'.

Notes

1. Quoted in Hyam, *Failure*, p. 116.
2. See *contra*, Hyam, *Failure*, pp. 22 and 183.
3. Cmd. 8233, 1951.
4. Quoted in Hyam, *Failure*, pp. 119–21.
5. See J. Butler, *The Liberal Party and the Jameson Raid*, London, 1968, pp. 175 ff.
6. See P. Slinn, 'The role of the British South Africa Company in Northern Rhodesia, 1890–1964', *African Affairs*, LXX, 1971.
7. Gell papers, B.S.A. 3, Michell to Gell, 26 November 1918; 17 July 1920.
8. J. T. Molteno, *The Dominion of Afrikanerdom*, 1923, pp. 228–9.
9. A. H. Moll, *The Necessity for Independence*, Cape Town, 1920.
10. Quoted in N. Rhoodie, *Apartheid en Partnership*, Pretoria, 1966, pp. 250–1.
11. Lyttelton, *The Memoirs of Lord Chandos*, London, 1962, p. 387.
12. See T. Creighton, *Anatomy of Partnership*, London, 1960, p. 22.
13. C. Kadalie, *My Life*, p. 221.
14. Quoted in Rhoodie, *Apartheid*, pp. 250–1.
15. Birkenhead, *Walter Monckton*, London, 1969, pp. 340–1.
16. Alport, *Sudden Assignment*, London, 1965, pp. 20, 59–60 and 186.
17. E. Louw, *South Africa and the African Continent*, Stellenbosch, 1959.
18. Quoted in S. C. Nolutshungu, 'The Pan-African policy of the governments of South Africa, 1945–70: an introductory outline', *Collected Seminar Papers on the Societies of Southern Africa*, University of London Institute of Commonwealth Studies, 1971, II, p. 121.
19. It continued to be seen as such in some circles even as federation was disintegrating; see K. Kirkwood, *Britain and Africa*, London, 1965, pp. 106 and 109, where he talks of British observers seeing Southern Rhodesia as having a role to play in the promotion of a non-racial federation in all southern Africa and writes, '. . . it is especially unfortunate that Southern Rhodesia's potential role as a liberal lever in South Africa was dissipated by Federation.'
20. See P. Walshe, *Rise of African Nationalism*, chapter 8 and pp. 329–39, and Kadalie, *My Life*, p. 217.
21. N. Sithole, *African Nationalism*, second edition, London, 1968, p. 51.

APPENDIX I PERSONAE

Some biographical information on those most influential in the making of the policies discussed.

British Ministers for the colonies and Dominions since 1910

Harcourt, Lewis, Viscount, 1863–1922. Son of Sir William Harcourt. Liberal member of the House of Commons 1904–17. First Commissioner of Works 1905–10 and Secretary of State for the Colonies 1910–15.

Law, Andrew Bonar, 1858–1923. Canadian-born, Scottish-educated businessman. Unionist member of the House of Commons from 1900. Leader of the opposition to the Liberal government 1911–15. Secretary of State for the Colonies 1915–16; later Chancellor of the Exchequer; Prime Minister 1922–3.

Long, Walter Hume, 1854–1924, Baron Wraxall. Conservative member of the House of Commons 1880–1921. President of the Board of Agriculture; president of the Local Government Board; Chief Secretary for Ireland. Secretary of State for the Colonies 1916–1918 and afterwards First Lord of the Admiralty. Southern Africa was far from his central concern, though he had friends in the Chartered Company.

Milner, Alfred, First Viscount, 1854–1925. Governor of the Cape Colony and High Commissioner in South Africa 1897–1901 and Governor of the Transvaal and Orange River Colony 1901–05. Member of the War Cabinet 1916–1918 and Secretary of State for the Colonies 1919–1921. Helped to provoke the South African War, sustain Afrikaner nationalism and doom African hopes; guardian of the imperial position in South Africa and outside. Wrote brilliant official prose but from most other angles a *bete noire* of South African history.

Churchill, Sir Winston, 1874–1965. Churchill was a war correspondent in South Africa, Under-Secretary of State for the Colonies 1905–08, and Secretary of State for the Colonies 1921–22. Throughout he was a member of the Liberal Party and was bitterly resented by those around Milner for having slighted his record in South Africa, and was suspect both as a radical and as joint architect (with Lord Eglin) of the 'sell out' of the imperial position in South Africa between 1906 and 1908.

Devonshire, Ninth Duke of, 1868–1938. Eton and Trinity, Cambridge. Unionist member of the House of Commons 1891–1908. Governor General of Canada 1916–21. Secretary of State for the Colonies 1922–24.

Amery, Leopold, 1873–1955. Indian-born, Harrow- and Oxford-educated; editor of the *Times History of the South African War;* Assistant Secretary of the Imperial War Cabinet 1917–18; First Lord of the Admiralty 1922–24; Secretary of State for the Colonies and for the Dominions 1924–29. An aggressive, small man of the imperialist right.

Thomas, J. H., 1874–1949. General Secretary of the National Union of Railwaymen 1918–31 and Labour member of the House of Commons

1910–36. Secretary of State for the Colonies in 1924 and 1931–36, and for the Dominions 1930–35. Founded the tradition that Labour Colonial Secretaries also were not in office to preside over the dissolution of the empire.

Ormsby-Gore, William, Fourth Baron Harlech, 1885–1964. Eton and New College, Oxford, Conservative Member of the House of Commons from 1910. Under-Secretary of State for the Colonies 1922–24 and 1924–29. Postmaster General 1931; Minister of Public Works 1932–36 and Secretary of State for the Colonies 1936–38. High Commissioner in South Africa 1941–44. Close personal connections with Dougal Malcolm.

Webb, Sydney, Lord Passfield, 1859–1947. A founder of the London School of Economics, the Fabian Society and the *New Statesman*. Secretary of State for the Colonies 1929–31.

MacDonald, Malcolm, b. 1901. Son of Ramsay MacDonald, Labour member of the House of Commons 1929–45. Parliamentary Under-Secretary for the Dominions 1931–5; Secretary of State for the Dominions 1935–39 and for the Colonies 1935 and 1938–40.

Eden, Robert Anthony, Lord Avon, b. 1897. Eton and Christ Church, Oxford, Conservative Member of the House of Commons 1923–57. Secretary of State for Foreign Affairs 1935–38, 1940–45 and 1951–55. Prime Minister 1955–57. Secretary of State for the Dominions 1939–1940.

Cranbourne, Viscount, later Marquess of Salisbury, 1893–1972. Eton and Christ Church, Oxford. Conservative member of the House of Commons from 1929. Secretary of State for the Dominions 1940–42, 1943–45 and for the Colonies 1942–43.

Stanley, Oliver 1896–1951. Eton and Oxford. Conservative member of the House of Commons from 1924. Between 1933 and 1940 Minister of Transport and Labour; President of the Board of Trade and the Board of Education and Secretary of State for War. Secretary of State for the Colonies 1942–43.

High Commissioners and Governors

Selborne, W. W. Palmer, Second Earl, 1859–1942. Liberal-Unionist member of the House of Commons 1886–95. Under-Secretary of State for the Colonies 1895–1900. First Lord of the Admiralty 1900–05. Milner's successor as Governor of the Transvaal and Orange River Colony and High Commissioner in South Africa 1905–10.

Gladstone, Herbert John, First Viscount, 1854–1930. Youngest son of W. E. Gladstone. Liberal Chief Whip 1899–1905 and Secretary of State for Home Affairs 1905–09. First Governor General of the Union of South Africa 1910–14.

Buxton, Sydney, Earl, 1853–1934. Under-Secretary of State for the Colonies 1892–95; Post Master General 1905–10; President of the Board of Trade 1910–14. Governor General of the Union of South Africa and High Commissioner 1914–1920. The second Liberal Cabinet Minister to be sent to South Africa, Buxton disappointed those who had counted on the humanitarian associations of his name and continued Gladstone's policy of committing imperial influence to Botha and Smuts, with whom he sought to build a close personal association.

Prince Arthur of Connaught, 1883–1938. Eton, Sandhurst and the army. Governor General of South Africa 1920–23.

Athlone, First Earl, 1874–1937. Sandhurst, the Matabeleland campaign of 1896 and the South African War, 1899–1900. Governor General of South Africa 1923–31 and of Canada 1940–46.

Stanley, Sir Herbert, 1872–1955. Eton, Balliol and the civil service. Came to South Africa as Gladstone's private secretary, 1910–14. Stayed on in the Imperial Service as Resident Commissioner of Rhodesia 1914–18; Imperial Secretary in South Africa 1918–24; Governor of Northern Rhodesia 1924–27. In Ceylon as Governor 1927–31 and then back in southern Africa as High Commissioner in South Africa 1931–35 and Governor of Southern Rhodesia 1935–41. A major influence on the making of the British policies described herein.

Clarke, Sir William, 1876–1952. Eton, Trinity College, Cambridge, and the diplomatic service. Lloyd George's private secretary 1906–08; Indian 1910–16; Overseas Trade 1917–28. High Commissioner in Canada 1928–34 and High Commissioner in South Africa 1934–49.

Baring, Sir Evelyn 1903–73. Indian Civil Service 1926–34. Governor of Southern Rhodesia 1942–44. High Commissioner in South Africa 1944–51. Governor of Kenya 1952.

Clifford, Sir Bede, 1890–1969. Secretary to Prince Arthur of Connaught 1921–23; secretary to Lord Athlone 1924; Imperial Secretary in South Africa 1924–28; first representative of HMG to the Government of South Africa 1928–31.

Chancellor, Sir John, 1870–1952. Army background. Governor of Mauritius 1911–16 and Trinidad 1916–21. Governor of Southern Rhodesia 1923–28 and High Commissioner, Palestine, 1928–31. Was bored by his Rhodesian posting.

Colonial Office officials *et al.*

Anderson, Sir John, 1858–1918. Entered Colonial Office 1879; main experience of Borneo, Sarawak and the Straits. Permanent Under-Secretary of State 1911–16.

Just, Sir Hartman, 1854–1929. Entered Colonial Office 1878. Visited South Africa 1902–03. Assistant Under-Secretary of State 1907.

Fiddes, Sir George, 1858–1936. Secretary to Milner 1897–1900 and to the Transvaal administration 1900–02. Assistant Under-Secretary of State for the Colonies 1916–21 and Permanent Under-Secretary 1916–1921.

Lambert, Sir Henry, 1868–1935. Entered the Colonial Office 1892. A specialist in both emigration and southern African affairs. Assistant Under-Secretary of State 1916. Permanent Under-Secretary 1924–25. The unsung creator of the self-governing colony of Southern Rhodesia.

Davis, Sir Charles, 1873–1938. Entered Colonial Office 1897. Assistant Under-Secretary of State 1921–25. Permanent Under-Secretary of State for the Dominions 1925–30.

Masterton-Smith, Sir James, 1878–1938. Civil Servant. Private secretary to Churchill as First Lord of the Admiralty and after. Imported by Churchill from the Ministry of Labour into the Colonial Office as Permanent Under-Secretary 1921–24.

Kerr, Philip, Lord Lothian, 1882–1940. One of Milner's 'kindergarten'. Assistant Secretary to the Inter-colonial Council 1905–08; editor of *Round Table* 1910–1916; private secretary to Lloyd George 1916–21; secretary to the Rhodes Trust 1925–39.

Hankey, Sir Maurice, 1877–1963. Australian-born, married a South African. Secretary to the Cabinet 1916–38 and general *eminence grise*.

Hailey, William, First Baron, 1872–1969. Indian Civil Service 1895–1934. Director of the Africa Research Survey 1935–38. Member of the Permanent Mandates Commission of the League of Nations 1935–39.

British South Africa Company directors and servants

Rhodes, Cecil John, 1853–1902. Established the diamond monopoly of de Beers Consolidated and acquired large gold-mining interests, creating Consolidated Goldfields. Created the British South Africa Company in 1884. Prime Minister of the Cape Colony 1890–96. The archetypal capitalist–imperialist.

Jameson, Sir Leander Starr, 1853–1917. A doctor from Edinburgh who went to Kimberley, became a close associate of Rhodes's, assisted in the conquest of Rhodesia and was its first Administrator—1889–94—during which time he parcelled out land and laid seeds for rebellion. Used the BSAC's police in an attempt to invade the South African republic in 1895: imprisoned in Britain for six months. Resurfaced during the South African War as leader of the imperialists in the Cape Colony, of which he became Prime Minister 1904–08. Leader of the Unionist opposition in the South African House of Assembly from 1910–12. President of the British South Africa Company 1913–17 after lifelong unscrupulous pursuit of its aims.

Birchenough, Sir Henry, 1853–1937. One of the most politically active of the Chartered Company's board, of which he became a member in 1905 and president in 1925. A member of its executive committee for the Rhodesias. British Special Commissioner to investigate prospects of trade with South Africa after the south African War (wrote Cd. 1844 of 1904); served on numerous government trade and industrial commissions.

Malcolm, Sir Dougal, 1877–1955. Eton, New College, Oxford. Private secretary to Lord Selborne in South Africa 1905–10. Left the colonial service to join the Chartered Company, becoming a director in 1913 and its president in 1937. Member of the executive committee for the Rhodesias, and did much of the company's political business with the British and South African governments. Related by marriage to Ormsby-Gore.

Fox, Henry Wilson, 1863–1921. English lawyer who became editor of the *South African Mining Journal* 1892–94; Public Prosecutor in Rhodesia 1894–98; manager of the Chartered Company 1898; director in 1913. Member of the House of Commons 1917.

Gell, Philip Lyttelton, 1852–1926. Businessman with extensive interests. Director of Chartered Company 1899–1925. President in 1920. Close friend of Milner's.

Coryndon, Sir Robert, 1870–1925. South African-born member of the Pioneer Column to Rhodesia in 1890. Fought in Matabele war of 1893 and the rebellion of 1896. Private secretary to Rhodes, Administrator of North Western Rhodesia. Transferred to British government service, becoming Resident Commissioner in Swaziland; entrusted with Rhodesian Land Commission of 1915. Later Governor of Uganda and then Kenya.

Chaplin, Sir Francis Drummond, 1866–1933. Harrow and Oxford. *Times* correspondent in Johannesburg 1896–98. Manager of Rhodes's Consolidated Goldfields. Represented mining interests in Transvaal Legislative Assembly 1907–10 and Union House of Assembly 1910–14, when he became Administrator of Southern and later Northern Rhodesia, 1914–23. Re-elected to Union parliament 1924–29.

Newton, Sir Francis, 1857–1940. West Indian-born, Rugby and Oxford. Barrister. Acting Administrator of the Bechuanaland Protectorate at the time of the Jameson raid. Joined Chartered Company service as Treasurer of Rhodesia in 1903. Switched to support of responsible government at the right moment and became Rhodesian representative in London.

South African politicians

Botha, General Louis, 1862–1919. Commandant General of the South African republic's forces 1900–02. Leader of the Nationalist Party Het Volk and Prime Minister of the Transvaal 1907–10. Prime Minister of South Africa 1910–19. Bridge-playing landowner who fitted well into the world of English politicians into which he moved.

Smuts, Jan, Field Marshal, 1870–1950. Born Cape Colony; educated Stellenbosch, Cambridge. Advocate, Attorney General, South African republic, 1898. General, South African republic forces. Assisted Botha with foundation of Het Volk. Chief drafter of South Africa Act. Deputy to Botha in Union government 1910–19. Commander, British forces in east Africa, 1916. Member of Imperial War Cabinet 1917–18. Prime Minster of the Union 1919–24, 1939–48. Leader of the opposition 1924–33. Deputy Prime Minister to Hertzog 1933–39.

Hertzog, General J. B. M., 1866–1942. High Court judge in the Orange Free State 1895–9; General 1899. A founder of the Oranje-Unie, became leader of the Orange Free State in place of a reluctant ex-President Steyn. Minister of Justice 1910–12. Minister of Native Affairs 1912. Resigned, in protest against Botha's and Smuts's collaboration with Britain, to form the National Party. As its leader Prime Minster of the Union 1924–33; Prime Minster of the United Party government 1933–39. Bark proved bigger than bite.

Malan, Daniel, 1874–1959. Minister of the Dutch Reform Church. Helped Hertzog to found the National Party in the Cape and first editor of its newspaper, *Die Burger*. Member of the House of Assembly from 1917; holder of numerous ministerial portfolios in Hertzog's National Party governments. Leader of those Nationalists who refused to accept fusion with Smuts; leader of opposition 1933–48. Prime Minister 1948–54.

Strijdom, Johannes, 1893–1958. Advocate. National Party member of the House of Assembly 1929–58. Leader of the Transvaal Party and member of Malan's opposition to Fusion. Minister of Lands 1948–54. Prime Minister 1954–58.

Merriman, John, 1841–1926. Member of the Cape parliament 1896–1910 and of the Union parliament 1910–24. Prime Minister of the Cape 1908–10. Passed over by Gladstone in choice of first Union Prime Minister and refused to join Botha Cabinet. Strongly both anti-imperialist and in support of the Cape African franchise.

Fitzpatrick, Sir James Percy, 1862–1931. Cape-born, English-educated. Partner of Herbert Eckstein, the mining financier. Active in South African republic, where he was an opponent of the Kruger government. Member of the Legislative Council of the Transvaal Colony 1903–07 and of the Legislative Assembly 1907–10, and Unionist member of the House of Assembly 1911–30. Supporter of the mining interest and the imperial connection. Better remembered as the author of *Jock of the Bushveld*.

Pirow, Oswald, 1890–1959. National Party member of the House of Assembly 1924–29, 1933–43. Minister of Justice, Railways and Defence 1933–39. Founded National Socialist New Order 1941.

Oppenheimer, Sir Ernest, 1880–1957. German-born diamond dealer. Established Anglo-American Corporation 1917; chairman, De Beers Consolidated, 1929. Member of South African House of Assembly and supporter of Smuts 1924–38. Dominated southern African mining industry.

Duncan, Sir Patrick, 1870–1943. Private secretary to Lord Milner, a member of his kindergarten and Colonial Secretary of the Transvaal 1903–07. Unionist member of the House of Assembly and Minister in Smuts's Cabinet 1921–24. Minister of Mines in the Fusion Cabinet 1933–36. First South African to be Governor General of the Union, 1936–43, during which time, in September 1939, he exercised the royal prerogative of refusing Hertzog a dissolution in order to allow Smuts to form a pro-war ministry.

Coghlan, Sir Charles 1863–1927. Born and educated in the eastern Cape heartland of English South Africa. Served in the South African War on imperial side. Emigrated to Rhodesia, becoming attorney and local politician. First Prime Minister of Southern Rhodesia 1923–27.

Huggins, Godfrey, First Viscount Malvern, 1883–1971. English-born surgeon. Emigrated to Rhodesia in 1911. Prime Minister 1933–53; Prime Minister of the Central African Federation 1953–56.

The opposition

Khama, c. 1837–1923. Chief of Ngwato; accepted British protection 1886; led the opposition to transfer of the Bechuanaland Protectorate to the Chartered Company; visited England 1895.

Dube, John, 1871–1946. Zulu, educated United States and returned to Natal as teacher, missionary. Founder of newspaper *Ilanga Lase Natal*. First chairman of South African Native National Congress, 1912. Later member of Native Representative Council.

Plaatje, Solomon, 1875–1932. Tswana court interpreter. Interpreter for British during the siege of Mafeking 1899–1900. Published first Tswana newspaper; first Secretary of South African Native National Congress. On delegation against land Act to United Kingdom 1914–18 and to Versailles 1919; visited Canada and USA. Later member of both African Political Organisation and African National Congress. Prolific writer.

Khama, Tshekedi, 1905–59. Regent of Ngwato 1926–50. Educated in South Africa at Lovedale and Fort Hare College. Persistent opponent of spread of southern African influences in the protectorate.

Kadalie, Clements, 1896–1951. Malawi-born; emigrated to South Africa, where he founded the Industrial and Commercial Workers' Union, which was the first mass organisation of African opposition.

Harris, Sir John, 1874–1940. Missionary in the Congo Free State and active in the campaign for reform; secretary to the Anti-slavery and Aborigines Protection Society and prolific author on colonial questions; Liberal member of the House of Commons 1923–24.

Cripps, Arthur, 1869–1952. Charterhouse and Oxford. Went to Rhodesia in 1901 as a missionary for the Society for the Propagation of the Gospel and spent most of the rest of his life there.

Olivier, Sydney, First Baron, 1859–1943. Entered Colonial Office 1882; experience largely West Indian. Governor of Jamaica 1907–13; home civil service 1913–20. Secretary of State for India in the first Labour government 1924.

Wedgwood, Josiah, First Baron, 1872–1943. South African War service 1900–01; resident magistrate in the Transvaal 1902–04. Member of the House of Commons 1906–42. Chancellor of the Duchy of Lancaster 1924.

APPENDIX II DOCUMENTS

South Africa Act, 1909

Sec. 150. The King, with the advice of the Privy Council, may on addresses from the House of Parliament of the Union admit into the Union the territories administered by the British South Africa Company upon such terms and conditions as to representation and otherwise in each case as are expressed in the addresses and approved by the King, and the provisions of any Order in Council in their behalf shall have effect as if they had been enacted by the Parliament of the United Kingdom of Great Britain and Ireland.

Sec. 151. The King, with the advice of the Privy Council, may, on addresses from the Houses of Parliament of the Union transfer to the Union the government of any territories other than the territories administered by the British South Africa Company, belonging to or under the protection of His Majesty, and inhabited wholly or in part by natives, and upon such transfer the Governor-General in Council may undertake the government of such territory upon the terms and conditions embodied in the Schedule to this Act.

Schedule

1. After the transfer of the government of any territory belonging to or under the protection of His Majesty, the Governor-General in Council shall be the Legislative authority, and may by proclamation make laws for the peace, order, and good government of such territory: provided that all such laws shall be laid before both Houses of Parliament within seven days after the issue of the proclamation or, if Parliament be not then sitting, within seven days after the beginning of the next session and shall be effective unless and until both Houses of Parliament shall by resolutions passed in the same session request the Governor-General in Council to repeal the same, in which case they shall be repealed by proclamation.
2. The Prime Minister shall be charged with the administration of any territory thus transferred, and he shall be advised in the general conduct of such administration, by a commission consisting of not fewer than three members . . .
3. The members of the Commission shall be appointed by the Governor-General in Council, and shall be entitled to hold office for a period of ten years, but such period may be extended to successive further terms of five years. They shall be entitled to a fixed annual salary which shall not be reduced during the continuance of their term of office, and they shall not be removed from office except upon addresses from both Houses of Parliament passed in the same session praying for such removal. They shall not be qualified to become, or to be, members of either House of Parliament . . .
14. It shall not be lawful to alienate any land in Basutoland or any land forming part of the native reserves in the Bechuanaland Protectorate and Swaziland from the native tribes inhabiting these territories.
16. The custom, where it exists, of holding pitsos or other recognised forms of native assembly shall be maintained in the territories.

Charter of the British South Africa Company, 1889

Art. 33. And we do further will, ordain and declare that it shall be lawful for Us Our heirs and successors and We do hereby expressly reserve to ourselves Our heirs and successors the right and power by writing under the Great Seal of the United Kingdom at the end of twenty-five years from the date of this Our Charter and at the end of every succeeding period of ten years, to add to alter or repeal any of the provisions of this Our Charter or to enact other provisions in substitution for or in addition to any of its existing provisions. Provided that the right and power thus reserved shall be exercised only in relation to so much of this Our Charter as relates to administrative and public matters. And We do further expressly reserve to Ourselves Our heirs and successors the right to take over any buildings or works belonging to the Company and used exclusively or mainly for administrative and public purposes, on payment to the Company of such reasonable compensation as may be agreed, or as failing agreement may be settled by the Commissioners of our Treasury . . .

Supplemental charter, 1915 Art. 2. So much of Article 33 of the Principal Charter as provides that it shall be lawful for Us, Our Heirs and successors, at the end of twenty-five years from the date of the said Charter, and at the end of every succeeding period of ten years, to add to, alter, or repeal, any of the provisions of the said Charter, and at the end of every succeeding period of ten years, to add to, alter or repeal, any of the provisions of the said Charter relating to administrative and public matters, or to enact other provisions in substitution therefor or in addition thereto, shall be read and construed subject to the proviso that if at any time after the 29th day of October, 1914, the Legislative Council of Southern Rhodesia shall, by an absolute majority of the whole number of the Members of the Council as then constituted, pass a Resolution praying the Crown to establish in Southern Rhodesia the form of Government known as Responsible Government, and shall support such Resolution with evidence showing that the condition of the territory financially and in other respects is such as to justify the establishment of the form of Government aforesaid, it shall, be lawful for Us, Our heirs and successors, if We or They at any time think fit to accede to the prayer of such Resolution, to add to alter, or repeal, any of the provisions of the said Charter relating to administrative and public matters or to enact other provisions in substitution therefor or in addition thereto for the purpose of establishing Responsible Government.

The order in council of 1898

Sec. 81. The Company shall from time to time assign to the natives inhabiting Southern Rhodesia land sufficient for their occupation, whether as tribes or portions of tribes, and suitable for their agricultural or pastoral requirements, including in all cases a fair and equitable proportion of springs or permanent water.

83. A native may require, hold, encumber, and dispose of land on the same conditions as a person who is not a native . . .

84. The company shall retain the mineral rights in all land assigned to natives . . .
85. No natives shall be removed from any kraal or from any land assigned to them for occupation, except after a full enquiry by, and by order of the Administrator in Executive Council approved by the High Commissioner.

The Rhodesian letters patent of 1923

39. (1) There shall be a Native Department, the permanent head of which shall be appointed by the Governor-in-Council, with the approval of the High Commissioner, and all Chief Native Commissioners, Superintendents of Natives, Native Commissioners and Assistant Native Commissioners . . . shall be appointed in like manner and subject to the like approval . . .
2. The salaries of the officers mentioned in the preceding sub-section shall be fixed by the Governor-in-Council with the approval of the High Commissioner, and shall not be increased or diminished without his approval.
3. The officers mentioned in this section may at any time be removed from office by the Governor-in-Council, with the approval of the High Commissioner, but not otherwise.
40. (1) The Governor-in-Council may, and if requested so by the High Commissioner shall suspend any of the officers referred to in the last preceding section for misconduct . . .
44. The Governor shall furnish to the High Commissioner any information relating to native affairs which The High Commissioner may request.
47. (1) It shall be lawful for the Governor-in-Council, subject to the approval of the High Commissioner, at any time after the commencement of these Our Letters Patent, to establish by Proclamation in any Native Reserve or Reserves such Council or Councils of indigenous natives, representative of the local Chiefs and other native residents as may seem to him expedient, for the discussion from time to time of any matters upon which, as being of direct interest or concern to the native population generally or to any portion thereof, he may desire to ascertain or they to submit, their views.
(2) It shall also be lawful for the Governor in Council subject to the like approval, to make regulations conferring on any such Council such powers of management in connection with local matters affecting the indigenous natives as can in his opinion be safely and satisfactorily undertaken by them. . . .

BIBLIOGRAPHY

Unpublished

British Government records. Cabinet papers concerning defence, Rhodesia, South Africa, etc, series Cab., chiefly Cab. 21; Cab. 23, containing minutes to 1939; Cab. 65 and 66, minutes and memoranda. Colonial and Dominions Office records: C.O. 417, South African High Commission (including Rhodesia); C.O. 551, Union of South Africa to 1926; C.O. 525, Nyasaland; C.O. 767, Southern Rhodesia, 1924–5; C.O. 795, Northern Rhodesia after 1924; C.O. 537, supplementary (and secret); D.O. 1 and 2, Southern Rhodesia, 1926; D.O. 9, South Africa, 1926–39; D.O. 35, Dominions (including South Africa, Rhodesia, South African High Commission); D.O. 117, Dominions, supplementary. Confidential prints: C.O. 879, Confidential print, African; D.O. 114, Dominions Office, confidential print; D.O. 116, Confidential print, Dominions, South Africa.

Harcourt papers. Papers of Lewis, later Viscount Harcourt, relating to his period of office as Secretary of State for the Colonies. Held privately.

Milner papers. Papers of Viscount Milner relating to his period of office as Secretary of State for the Colonies. Bodleian Library, Oxford.

Gladstone papers. Papers of Viscount Gladstone relating to his period of office as Governor General and High Commissioner in South Africa. British Museum.

Buxton papers. Papers of Lord Buxton. Held privately.

The Anti-slavery and Aborigines Protection Society. Papers relating to South African and Rhodesian affairs. Rhodes House Library, Oxford.

Gell papers. Papers of P. L. Gell, relating to the British South Africa Company. Held privately

Chaplin papers. Papers of Drummond Chaplin relating to his period as Administrator of the Rhodesias. National Archives of Rhodesia.

Printed collections of papers

Smuts papers, vols. I–IV, ed. Hancock and v. d. Poel, publ. Cambridge, 1966, and vols. V–VII, Cambridge, 1974.

Milner papers, ed. C. Headlam, publ. 1931–33.

British Government Command Papers

1896

C. 8060. Instructions re armed forces in British South Africa Company territories.

C. 8130. Report of the Matabeleland Land Commission

1897
 C. 8547. Report by Sir R. E. R. Martin, K.C.M.G., on the native administration of the British South Africa Company.
1898
 C. 8732. Correspondence relating to proposed changes in the administration of the British South Africa Company.
 C. 8773. Charter of the British South Africa Company. Orders in council.
1903–4
 Cd. 1844. Present position and future prospects of British trade in South Africa. Report received from Mr Henry Birchenough.
1905
 Cd. 2399. Report of the South African Native Affairs Commission, 1903–05.
1906
 Cd. 2978. Report of the Departmental Committee on Agricultural Settlement in British Colonies.
 Cd. 2979. Evidence.
1907
 Cd. 3407. Emigration.
1908
 Cd. 3889. Report of the Natal Native Affairs Commission.
1914–16
 Cd. 7264. Correspondence relating to the constitution of Southern Rhodesia.
 Cd. 7508. Correspondence relating to the Native Land Act, 1913, including a copy of the Act.
 Cd. 7509. Correspondence re ownership of land in Southern Rhodesia.
 Cd. 7645. Correspondence relating to the continuance of the administrative provisions of the charter of the British South Africa Company (with copies of the charters of 1889 and 1900).
 Cd. 7648. Report of the Board of Trade for South Africa and Rhodesia.
 Cd. 7970. British South Africa Company. Supplemental charter.
1917–18
 Cd. 8462. Dominions Royal Commission report re empire settlement.
 Cd. 8672. Report re the empire settlement of ex-servicemen.
 Cd. 8674. Papers relating to the Southern Rhodesian Native Reserves Commission. Report, 1915.
1920
 Cmd. 347. Correspondence with the Anti-slavery and Aborigines Protection Society relating to the native reserves in Southern Rhodesia.
 Cmd. 1042. Despatch to the High Commissioner for South Africa transmitting the Order of His Majesty in Council of 9 November 1920.
1921
 Cmd. 1129. Cave Commission: correspondence and report.
 Cmd. 1273. First report of a committee appointed to consider certain questions relating to Rhodesia.
 Cmd. 1471. Second report.
1922
 Cmd. 1573. Despatch transmitting the draft letters patent for Southern Rhodesia.

1923
   Cmd. 1914. Correspondence re settlement of British South Africa Company's position in Southern and Northern Rhodesia.
   Cmd. 1984. Agreement between Secretary of State for the Colonies and the British South Africa Company for settlement of outstanding questions relating to Southern and Northern Rhodesia.
1924–25
   Cmd. 2387. Report of the East Africa Commission.
1928–9
   Cmd. 3234. Report of the Commission on Closer Union of the Dependencies in Eastern and Central Africa.
1929–30
   Cmd. 3574. Statement of the conclusions of His Majesty's Government in the United Kingdom as regards closer union in east Africa.
1930–31
   Cmd. 3731. Correspondence with regard to native policy in Northern Rhodesia.
   Report of the Joint Committee on Closer Union in East Africa, vol. I, Report, vol. II, Evidence, vol. III, Appendices, 1930–1.
1931–32
   Cmd. 4141. Correspondence arising from the report of the Joint Committee on Closer Union in East Africa.
1935
   Cmd. 4948. Aide-Mémoire handed to the Prime Minister of the Union of South Africa by the Secretary of State for Dominion Affairs on 5 May 1935.
1935–36
   Cmd. 7509. Despatch from the Governor of Southern Rhodesia relating to the proposed amendment of the Southern Rhodesia constitution.
1938–9
   Cmd. 5449. Report of the Royal Commission on Rhodesia–Nyasaland.
1952.
   Cmd. 8707. High Commission Territories: history of discussions with the Union.
Colonial No. 73. Report to the Governor of Northern Rhodesia by Mr Justice Maugham—North Charterland concession enquiry.

Southern Rhodesian government

Report of the Native Affairs Enquiry Committee, 1910–11.
Land Commission, 1925. C.S.R. 3, 1926.
NADA, Journal of the Southern Rhodesian Native Affairs Department.

Northern Rhodesian government

Report of the Native Reserves Commission. East Luangwa, 1924–25. NRC 1.
The British South Africa Company's claim to Mineral Royalties in Northern Rhodesia. Government Printer, Lusaka, 1964.

Government of the Union of South Africa

1923. White Paper. Correspondence re terms for inclusion of Southern Rhodesia in the Union.

British South Africa Company

Annual reports and Reports of extraordinary general meetings. Printed for the board:

H. Wilson Fox, Notes and information concerning land policy, 1912.
—Memorandum on land settlement, 1913.
H. Birchenough, Memorandum on Northern Rhodesia land policy and land settlement, 1913.

H. Wilson Fox (1915), *Journal of the Royal African Society*. 'Rhodesia and the war.'
—(1916), *Nineteenth Century*. 'A platform for an imperial party.'
—(1917), *ibid.* 'The empire and the new protection'.
—(1917), *ibid.* 'The development of the empire's resources'.
—(1918), *United Empire*. 'The payment of the war debt by development of empire resources.'
H. Birchenough (1915), *Journal of the Royal African Society*. 'The war and trade in Africa.'
'Africanus' (1917), *Journal of the Royal African Society*. 'A Central African Confederation.'

Unpublished theses

Duignan, P. J., 'The native administration of the British South Africa Company, 1890–1923.' Stanford Ph.D., 1961.
Fage, J. D., 'The achievement of self-government in Southern Rhodesia, 1898–1923.' Cambridge Ph.D., 1949.
Hyam, R., 'The African policy of the Liberal government, 1905–09.' Cambridge Ph.D., 1963.
Krishnamurthy, B. S., 'Land and labour in Nyasaland.' London University Ph.D., 1964.
MacGregor, R., 'Native segregation in Rhodesia.' London University Ph.D., 1940.

Newspapers and periodicals

The Times; African World; The Round Table; United Empire; Journal of the Royal African Society.

Published works and pamphlets

Alport, Lord, *Sudden Assignment*, London, 1965.
Amery, L. S., *The Empire and the New Era*, London, 1928.
—*The Forward View*, London, 1935.
—*My Political Life*, London, 1953.
Aston, G., *The Defence of United South Africa as part of the British Empire*, London, 1910.
Barnes, L., *Caliban in Africa*, London, 1930.
—*The New Boer War*, London, 1932.
Beaverbrook, Lord, *The Decline and Fall of Lloyd George*, London, 1963.
Beer, G. L., *African Questions at the Paris Peace Conference*, New York, 1923.
Beloff, M., *Imperial Sunset*, vol. I, London, 1969.
Bennett, G. (ed.), *The Concept of Empire*, London, 1953.
Birkenhead, Lord, *Walter Monckton*, London, 1964.
Blake, R., *The Unknown Prime Minister*, London, 1955.
Bourne, K., and Watt, D. C., *Studies in International History*, London, 1969.
Brookes, E. H., *A History of South African Native Policy*, Pretoria, 1924.
Buchan, J., *Prester John*, London, 1910.
Bunting, B., *The Rise of the South African Reich*, London, 1969.
Butler, J. R. M., *Lord Lothian*, London, 1960.
Butler, J., *The Liberal Party and the Jameson Raid*, London, 1968.
Buxton, Earl, *General Botha*, London, 1924.
Carrothers, W., *Emigration from the British Isles*, London, 1929.
Chandos, Lord, *Memoirs of Lord Chandos*, London, 1962.
Chilvers, H., *The Yellow Man Looks On*, London, 1933.
Creighton, T., *The Anatomy of Partnership*, London, 1960.
Cripps, A. S., *The Sabi Reserve: a Southern Rhodesian Native Problem*, Oxford, 1920.
—*An Africa for Africans*, London, 1927.
Curtis, L., *Letter to the People of India*, Bombay, Madras and Calcutta, 1917.
Davies, M., *Incorporation in the Union of South Africa or Self-government: Southern Rhodesia's Choice, 1922*, Pretoria, 1965.
Denoon, D., *A Grand Illusion*, London, 1973.
De Kiewiet, C. W., *A History of South Africa*, Oxford, 1957.
Evans, M. S., *Black and White in South Africa*, London, 1916.
Fitzroy, A. *Memoirs*, London, 1925.
Fyfe, H. H., *South Africa Today*, London, 1911.
Gann, L., *A History of Northern Rhodesia*, London, 1964.
—*A History of Southern Rhodesia*, London, 1965.
Gifford, P., and Louis, W. R. (eds.), *Britain and Germany in Africa*, New Haven, Conn., and London, 1967.
Gollin, A. M., *Milner*, London, 1964.
Goodfellow, C. F., *Great Britain and the South African Confederation 1870–1881*, Oxford, 1966.
Gouldsbury, C., and Sheane, H., *The Great Plateau of Northern Rhodesia*, London, 1911.
Gray, R., *The Two Nations*, London, 1960.
Gregory, T., *Ernest Oppenheimer and the Economic Development of Southern Africa*, Cape Town, 1962.

Guinn, P. *British Strategy and Politics, 1914–18*, Oxford, 1965.
Hailey, Lord, *The Republic of South Africa and the High Commission Territories*, Oxford, 1963.
Haggard, R., *King Solomon's Mines*, London, 1887.
Hancock, W. K., *Survey of British Commonwealth Affairs*, vol. II, London, 1937.
—*Smuts*, vols. I and II, Cambridge, 1962 and 1968.
—*Smuts and the Shift of World Power*, London, 1964.
—and v. d. Poel, J. (eds.), *The Smuts Papers*, vols. I–VII, Cambridge, 1966–73.
Harris, J. *The Chartered Millions*, London, 1920.
Headlam, C. W. (ed.), *The Milner papers*, London, 1933.
Hobson, J. A., *Imperialism: a Study*, London, 1902.
Huttenbach, R. A., *Ghandi in South Africa: British Imperialism and the Indian Question, 1890–1914*, Ithaca, N.Y., 1971.
Hyam, R., *Elgin and Churchill at the Colonial Office*, London, 1968.
—*The Failure of South African Expansion*, London, 1972.
Kadalie, C., *My Life and the ICU*, London, 1970.
Karis, T., and Carter, G., *From Protest to Challenge*, vols. I and II, Stanford, Cal., 1972–74.
Katzen, L., *Gold and the South African Economy*, Cape Town, 1964.
Keith, A. B., *Responsible Government in the Dominions*, Oxford, 1909, 1928 edition.
Kirkwood, K., *Britain and Africa*, London, 1965.
Le May, G. H. L., *British Supremacy in South Africa*, Oxford, 1965.
—*Black and White in South Africa*, London, 1971.
Lewsen, P. (ed.), *Selections from the Correspondence of John X. Merriman*, vols. I and II, Cape Town, 1960.
Long, B. K., *In Smuts' Camp*, London, 1945.
—*Drummond Chaplin*, London, 1952.
Louis, W. R., *Great Britain and Germany's Lost Colonies*, Oxford, 1967.
Louw, E., *South Africa and the African Continent*, Stellenbosch, 1959.
MacDonald, R., *Labour and the Empire*, London, 1907.
Macmillan, W. M., *Africa Emergent*, London, 1949.
Malcolm, D., *The British South Africa Company*, 1939.
Mallet, C. *Herbert Gladstone: a Memoir*, London, 1932.
Mansergh, P. N. S., *Survey of British Commonwealth Affairs: Problems of External Policy*, London, 1952.
—*South Africa, 1906–61: the Price of Magnanimity*, London, 1962.
Mason, P., *Birth of a Dilemma*, London, 1958.
Markham, V., *The South African Scene*, London, 1913.
Marais, J. S., *The Fall of Kruger's Republic*, Oxford, 1961.
Marks, S., *Reluctant Rebellion*, London, 1969.
Meintjies, J., *General Louis Botha*, London, 1970.
Moll A. H., *The Necessity for Independence*, Cape Town, 1920.
Molteno, J., *The Dominion of Afrikanerdom*, London, 1923.
Morris, H., and Read, J., *Indirect Rule and the Search for Justice*, London, 1972.
Mungeam, G. H., *British Rule in Kenya, 1895–1912*, Oxford, 1966.
Oldham, J. H., *White and Black in Africa*, London, 1930.
Olivier, Lord, *White Capital and Coloured Labour*, London, 1929.
—*Anatomy of African Misery*, London, 1927.

Pachai, B. (ed.), *An Early History of Malawi*, London, 1972.
Palley, C., *The Constitutional History and Law of Southern Rhodesia*, Oxford, 1966.
Palmer, R., *Aspects of Rhodesian Land Policy*, Salisbury, 1968.
Perham, M., *Colonial Sequence*, London, 1967.
Plaatje, S., *Native Life in South Africa*, London, 1916.
Ranger, T. O., *The African Voice in Southern Rhodesia*, London, 1970.
Rhoodie, N., *Apartheid and Partnership*, Pretoria, 1966.
Roberts, M., and Trollip, A., *The South African Opposition*, London, 1949.
Robinson, R., and Gallagher, J., *Africa and the Victorians*, London, 1963.
Rolin, H., *Les Lois et l'administration de la Rhodésie*, Brussels, 1913.
Sacks, B., *South Africa: an Imperial Dilemma*, Albuquerque, N.M., 1967.
Shepperson, G., and Price, T., *Independent Africa*, Edinburgh, 1958.
Sithole, N., *African Nationalism*, London, 1968.
Smuts, J., *Wartime Speeches*, London, 1917.
—*Africa and Some World Problems*, Oxford, 1930.
—*The Basis of Trusteeship in South African Native Policy*, 1942.
Stokes, E., and Brown, R. (eds.), *The Zambesian Past*, Manchester, 1965.
Tatz, C. M., *Shadow and Substance in South Africa*, Pietermaritzburg, 1964.
Thompson, L. M., *The Unification of South Africa*, Oxford, 1960.
Vanderbosch, A., *South Africa and the World*, Kentucky, 1970.
v. d. Heever, C. M., *Hertzog*, Johannesburg, 1946.
'Vindex', *The Political Life and Speeches of Cecil John Rhodes*, London, 1900.
Walker, E. A., *A History of Southern Africa*, London, 1957.
Wallis, J. P. R., *One Man's Hand*, London, 1950.
—*Fitz: the Story of Sir Percy Fitzpatrick*, London, 1955.
Walshe, P., *The Rise of African Nationalism in South Africa*, London, 1972.
Wedgwood, J. C., *Memoirs of a Fighting Life*, London, 1940.
Weinthal, L. (ed.), *The Story of the Cape to Cairo Railway and River Route*, London, 1922–24.
Windrich, E., *The Rhodesian Problem*, London, 1975.

Articles

'Africanus', 'A Central African Confederation', *Journal of the Royal African Society*, 1917.
—'Reconstruction in Central Africa', *ibid.*, 1919.
Hetherwick, A., 'Nyasaland today and tomorrow', *ibid.*, 1917.
Nolutshungu, S. C., 'The Pan-African policy of the governments of South Africa, 1945–70: an introductory outline', *Collected Seminar Papers on the Societies of Southern Africa*, University of London Institute of Commonwealth Studies, 1971.
Ranger, T. O., 'Revolt in Portuguese East Africa: the Makombe rising of 1917', Kirkwood, K. (ed.), *African Affairs, No. 2*, St Anthony's Papers, No. 15.
Slinn, P., 'The role of the British South Africa Company in Northern Rhodesia, 1890–1964', *African Affairs*, vol. 70, 1971.
Wallace, L. A., 'Native policy in Northern Rhodesia', *Journal of the Royal African Society*, 1922.

Wills, H. A., 'Problems of constitutional reform in Jamaica, Mauritius and Trinidad, 1890–95', *English Historical Review*, October 1966.
Wilson, N. H., 'The future of the native races in Southern Rhodesia', *South African Journal of Science*, 1921.

INDEX

African National Congress (South Africa) (South African Native National Congress), 199, 203
  first world war, 23
  Land, South Africa, 84/5, 131–4
  Rhodesia, 96, 137
  second world war, 241/2
Afrikaners
  anti-capitalism, 35, 143, 238/9
  first world war, 39/43
  in Rhodesia, 24, 40, 52, 55, 67, 109, 137, 152, 159, 260
  nationalism, 4, 11, 256, 263
  revolt, 22, 24, 37, 54, 108, 114/5, 237
  second world war, 234 ff, 257/8
Africans, 3, 11, 12
African Political Organisation, 139
African troops, recruitment of, 23, 132, 206–9
British policies in southern Africa for, 6, 30, 61, 145 *passim*
Federation, 260
franchise, Rhodesia, 30, 55, 157 ff 217/8, 229
franchise, South Africa, 25 *passim*, 31, 137, 201
opinion, in South Africa, 31, 198 ff, 241
Rhodesias, policies for, 6, 26, 90, 121, 133
and Rhodesian responsible government, 154 ff
South African Native Convention, 31
South African policies, 26 *passim*, 124/5, 132 *passim*
Amery, L., 126/7, 132, 143–5, 148–50, 153/4, 166, 178 *passim*, 189 *passim*, 211 n, 265
Anderson, Sir J., 60–3, 68, 71/2, 79, 82, 96, 102, 109/10, 267
Anti-slavery and Aborigines Protection Society, 64, 125 *passim*, 142
African franchise, Rhodesia, 157 ff
African lands, 96 ff, 127
BSAC lands claim, 69
federation, 231
League of Empire Resources, 102
Rhodesia, responsible government in, 157 ff
South African policies, 98
Asians, 4, 38 n, 84, 261
Atherstone, W. J., 92/3
Athlone, Lord, 173–5, 178/9, 196/7, 267
Attlee, C., 228, 238

Baring, Sir E., 241–4, 267
Barnes, L., 201–3
Barotseland, 117, 166–9, 215, 223
Beaumont commission, 124/5, 173
Bechuanaland Protectorate, 75 ff, 82, 115 *passim*, 177 ff, 195, 198
Beira, 24, 113/4, 160, 208
Birchenough, Sir H., 16, 100, 171, 187, 268
Bledisloe, Lord: commission, 209, 223, 228 ff
Botha, General L., 4, 19, 22/3, 36, 53, 70, 108, 114, 269
  and Africans, 30/1, 83 ff, 92, 124/5, 135
  Asians, 84
  Bechuanaland Protectorate, 80
  Caprivi Strip, 118
  hereeniging, 143
  Hertzog, 36/7
  Labour, 35
  Mozambique, 113/4
  Rhodesia, 49–53, 66/7
Botswana, *see* Bechuanaland Protectorate

British South Africa Company (the Chartered Company), 6, 10–13, 46 ff, 57, 255/6
  Bechuanaland Protectorate, 75 ff, 177 ff, 195 passim
  Cave commission, 129
  charter, 274
  formation of Union, 48
  land in Southern Rhodesia, 65–9, 97, 126
  Liberal government, 52
  mineral rights, Northern Rhodesia, 170, 182–5
  Northern Rhodesia settlement, 165 ff
  Southern Rhodesia, government of, 43 ff, 64 ff, 128, 142, 171 ff
  supplemental charter, 70–2, 274
Buxton, S., 6, 108 passim, 114–17, 216, 266
  Northern Rhodesia, 166/7
  Rhodesian Africans, 154 ff
  South African policies, 124/5, 129, 135/6, 145
  Southern Rhodesian responsible government, 150 ff

Campbell–Bannerman, Sir H., 52
Cape Liberalism, 13, 25/6, 30, 200, 217, 251/2
Caprivi Strip, 115–18, 197
Carter, Sir M., 173 ff
Cave commission, 129, 145 ff, 168/9
Chancellor, Sir J., 172 ff, 195, 267
Chandos, Viscount (O. Lyttelton), 226, 260
Chaplin, Sir D., 6, 24, 53/4, 113 passim, 125, 151, 214, 269
Churchill, Sir W. S., 14, 30, 244, 265
  Northern Rhodesia, 166/7
  South Africa and Rhodesia, 149 ff
  Southern Rhodesia responsible government, 149 ff, 172
Clark, Sir W., 224, 234 passim, 267
Clifford, Sir B., 194 passim, 252, 267

Coghlan, Sir C., 51, 70, 151–3, 156/7, 170, 188, 270
Congo reform campaign, 97–100
Commonwealth, 4, 133, 204
Copper, Northern Rhodesia, 180–2, 191, 202, 207–9, 214 passim, 222, 230/1, 236
Coryndon, R. T., 96, 123, 269
Cranbourne, Lord (Lord Salisbury), 235/6, 240, 244, 266
Creech-Jones, A., 231
Cripps, A. S., 129, 139, 173, 175, 192, 271
Curtis, L., 154

Development, 76, 100/1, 190–4, 196, 211, 222
Devonshire, Duke of, 160, 168/9, 265
  declaration, 177, 179, 187, 189, 195, 215, 253
Dube, J. L., 96/7, 270
Duncan, Sir P., 220/1

East Africa, 177 ff, 208, 258/9
East African Commission, 183/4
  and Northern Rhodesia, 111 passim, 166, 169, 179 ff
Eden, Sir A., 231/2, 266
Elgin, Lord, 29
Empire Resources Development Committee, 100–2
Ethiopia, Italian conquest of, 197, 203, 206–8

Federation of Rhodesia and Nyasaland, 1, 208, 238 ff, 243 passim, 249, 259 ff
Fitzpatrick, Sir P., 32, 37, 270
Fox, H. W., 15, 17, 92, 100/1, 152, 268

Garvey, M., 133
Germany, 13, 22, 218, 231
  BSAC, 142
  East Africa, 115/6, 132
  Mittel Afrika, 24

Nazi, 4, 224, 235
   South Africa, 194, 197, 206–10
   South West Africa, 22/3, 115–18, 132
Gell, P. L., 6, 17/18, 128, 139, 142, 147, 268
Gladstone, H., 16, 21/2, 52–4, 266
   Bechuanaland Protectorate, 78 ff
   Northern Rhodesia, 62/3
   South African policies, 63, 83/4
   Southern Rhodesia land, 68, 95/6
Gold
   Southern Rhodesia, 12
   South Africa, 12, 186, 204/5, 220/1, 235/6, 242, 254, 257/8
Gumede, J. T., 199/200

Hailey, Lord, 232–4, 260
Hankey, Sir W., 205, 207, 219, 223/4, 268
Harcourt, L., 6, 94, 97, 265
   Bechuanaland Protectorate, 78–80
   BSAC, 66, 69, 141
   Northern Rhodesia, 62/3
   South Africa, expansion, 32; policies, 84/5
   Southern Rhodesia, 71/2
Harris, J., 97 ff, 125–8, 157 ff, 170, 231, 271
Havenga, N., 237, 258
Hertzog, General B. M., 4, 35, 53–5, 114, 143, 200, 217, 256–9, 269
   and Africans, 28, 81, 83, 137, 173
   Bechuanaland Protectorate, 177 *passim*
   Britain, 193/4, 198
   dismissal by Botha, 36/7, 53
   East Africa, 177
   fusion, 204, 234/5
   Southern Rhodesia, 177
Hilton Young commission, 214 ff
Hitler, A., 210
Hobson, J. A., 34, 103
Huggins, Sir G., 195, 208, 216 ff, 231, 244

Industrial and Commercial Workers' Union (ICU), 176, 199
Immigration, British to southern Africa, 14–17, 239
Imperial Cold Storage Company, 178/9
Industrial colour bar, 201, 232, 244/5, 247, 256, 258

Jabavu, D. D. T., 200/1, 203
Jabavu, J. T., 31
Jameson, L. S., 13, 36/7, 53, 70, 79/80, 91, 100, 268
   Raid, 20/1, 75
Japan, 205/6
Just, Sir H., 63/4, 82, 94, 109, 267

Kadalie, C., 199/200, 260, 271
Kerr, P. (Lord Lothian), 134, 268
Khama, 79
Khama, Segkoma, 178/9
Khama, Tshekedi, 195–7, 271
Kenya, 192/3

Labour
   African, 14/15: in Northern Rhodesia, 90; Mozambique, 112/3; South Africa, mines, 33, 220–2, 252
   white: on Copperbelt, 217, 256; in South Africa, 35, 160, 198, 250
   See Industrial colour bar
Labour Party, England, 52, 128–30, 133, 138, 157/8, 178, 193, 199, 215/6, 255, 261
Lagden, Sir G., 27
Lambert, Sir H., 14–16, 45, 60, 71/2, 92–5, 110, 117, 122, 145, 152, 180, 267
Land Act, South Africa, 30/1, 33, 83, 91, 124/5, 134/5
Land
   division of in South Africa, 124/5, 224/5, 227

288 Index

division of in Southern Rhodesia, 13, 90 ff, 125 ff, 137 ff, 218
Law, A. Bonar, 97, 109
Lewanika, 90, 117
Liberal Party, England, 35, 52, 102, 249/50
Liebig's Extract of Meat Co., 94
Lloyd-George, D., 22, 126–8, 133, 162
Long, W., 37, 114, 117, 126, 265
Lourenço Marques, 112/3, 208
Louw, E., 261
Lozi, 26, 90, 117/8, 170
Lugard, Lord, 230

MacDonald, M., 210, 218/9, 224, 227, 231/2, 266
MacDonald, R., 29
Macmillan, H., 260
MacNeill, J. G. S., 94
Maguire, R., 64/5, 178
Mahabane, Rev., 199, 201
Malan, D. F., 4, 35, 55, 206, 235, 239, 246, 262, 269
Malawi, *see* Nyasaland
Malcolm, D., 95, 109, 151, 153, 166, 168, 171, 268
Merriman, J. X., 28, 30, 33, 48, 52, 92, 101, 112, 250, 270
Milner, A., 6/7, 14–18, 20, 28, 33, 36, 53, 62, 126/7, 143–49, 265
Morel, E. D., 98, 139
Msimang, R. W., 132, 139
Mussolini, B., 213

Namibia, *see* South West Africa
National Party, South Africa, 143, 159, 251, 261
and Africa, 197 *passim*, 239
Ndebele, 13, 20, 88/9, 123, 131, 141, 174
Ngcayiya, Rev. H., 131
Njube, 88/9
Northern Rhodesia, 45, 72, 88–90, 179 ff
amalgamation with Southern Rhodesia, 223 *passim*, 243
division of, 115–17, 165 *passim*, 214
labour in, 90, 220/1
Nyasaland, 166, 193, 223, 232/3
reserves, 180 ff
settlers, 166, 182, 216 *passim*
South Africa, 62 ff, 109–12, 145
Nyamanda, 131
Nyasaland, 23, 108 *passim*, 115, 117, 169/70, 180–2, 185, 224
Hilton Young commission, 215
labour for South Africa, 220/1
Northern Rhodesia, 166, 193, 223, 232/3

Olivier, S., 175, 192, 199, 201, 271
Oppenheimer, Sir E., 196, 214, 270
Ormsby-Gore, D. (Lord Harlech), 18, 126, 158, 169/70, 219, 236/7, 266

Pirow, O., 205 ff, 270
Plaatje, S., 99, 137, 270
Poor whites, 16, 49–51
Portuguese Africa, 112 *passim*, 188/9, 210, 224
Privy Council, reference of BSAC's land claim to, 68/9, 96 ff, 126 *passim*, 141

Reserves
Southern Rhodesia, 90 ff, 121 ff, 129, 136, 172 ff, 252
Northern Rhodesia, 180 ff
Responsible government
Transvaal, 19
Southern Rhodesia, 59–61, 70–2, 145 ff
Southern Rhodesia, letters patent, 275
Rhodes, C., 12, 14, 18, 32
Rhodesias, amalgamation of North and South, 109 ff, 191 ff, 198, 208/9, 215 ff, 229 ff, 244 ff
Rubusana, W., 99, 200

Segregation, 26–8, 83, 129, 175, 224/5, 251
Selborne, Lord, 15/16, 18, 28, 32, 53, 76, 89/90, 117, 266
memorandum, 48/9
Selope-Thema, R. V., 133, 139 n, 200, 242
Shona, 13
Sithole, Rev. N., 263
Smuts, J. C., 4, 7, 19–21, 35–7, 108, 118, 269
Africa, 112/3, 179 passim, 191, 197/8, 200, 240, 261
Africans, 134, 136, 156/7
copper, 214/5
Federation of Rhodesias, 220
first world war, 23
hereeniging and fusion, 143/4, 148, 204
immigration, 239
Japan, 205
Northern Rhodesia, 167/8
second world war, 210, 234 ff, 240 passim, 261
segregation, 83, 241
South African War, 34/5
Southern Rhodesia, 49/50, 144, 147, 150 ff, 168
Sotho, 89, 252
South African War, 1, 19, 34/5, 249
South Africa Act
schedule, 29/30, 48, 62, 124, 273
draft, 31
colour bar, 30/1
Southern Rhodesia settlers, 59, 108, 233, 244, 253/4
amalgamation of Rhodesias, 117, 184, 222 passim, 237 passim
East Africa, 189 passim
responsible government, 147 passim
South Africa, 50/1, 69/70, 145, 194, 221

South West Africa, 108/9, 115, 206, 261
Stanley, Sir H., 116, 123, 125, 154/5, 180 passim, 192, 198, 217–20, 231, 267
Stanley, O., 240, 266
Steel-Maitland, A., 99, 110/11
Steyn, President F., 35/6, 49, 250
Strijdom, J. G., 235, 262, 269
Swaziland, 80, 115, 136

Tanganyika, 111, 149, 189, 206, 216, 231, 259
Tati
Company, 82
district, 179
Thomas, J. S., 203, 226, 265/6
Trusteeship, British, 13, 26, 77, 83, 102, 127, 143, 147/8, 180/1, 190–2, 195, 218 passim, 243, 252
Tuli
block, 179
concession, 75

United States of America, 132, 134, 240
Beer, G. L., opinions re Africa, 111/12
copper, 234/5
South Africa, 236

Wedgwood, J., 94, 121, 130, 158, 170, 175, 231, 248, 271

Xuma, Dr, 241/2

Yeta, 118, 178

Zambesi, 62, 108, 110 passim, 127, 130, 253
Zambia, see Northern Rhodesia
Zulu, 19, 21, 28, 132